Emma Darwin

Also by Edna Healey

Lady Unknown: The Life of Angela Burdett-Coutts
Wives of Fame
Coutts & Co: The Portrait of a Private Bank
The Queen's House: A Social History of Buckingham Palace

EMMA DARWIN

The Inspirational Wife of a Genius

Edna Healey

HEADLINE

First published in 2001
by HEADLINE BOOK PUBLISHING

Extracts from the diaries of Fanny Wedgwood and Emma Darwin are
reproduced by courtesy of the Trustees of the Wedgwood Museum,
Barlaston, Stoke-on-Trent, Staffordshire, England

10 9 8 7 6 5 4 3 2 1

British Library Cataloguing in Publication Data

Healey, Edna
Emma Darwin: the inspirational wife of a genius
1. Darwin, Emma 2. Darwin, Charles, 1809–1882 –
Marriage 3. Author's spouses – Great Britain – Biography
I. Title
941'.081092

ISBN 0 7472 7579 3

Edited by Gillian Bromley

Designed by Ben Cracknell

Typeset by Avon Dataset Ltd, Bidford-on-Avon, Warks

Printed and bound in Great Britain by
Clays Ltd, St Ives plc

HEADLINE BOOK PUBLISHING
A division of Hodder Headline
338 Euston Road
London NW1 3BH

www.headline.co.uk
www.hodderheadline.com

To Denis and my family, with love and gratitude for all their
help and encouragement

Picture Credits

Contents

Acknowledgements

I am most grateful to Professor Richard Keynes for permission to see and use Darwin papers deposited in the Cambridge University Library, and the family papers in his possession. I have been particularly grateful for the sight of Emma's diaries. Professor and Mrs Keynes have given me every help and encouragement and I greatly value the friendship and assistance of their son, Randal Keynes, whose own biography, *Annie's Box*, has been an inspiration. He has given me access to many documents, in particular to those relating to the Darwins' visits to the Lake District.

I wish to thank most warmly the librarian at the Cambridge University Library and the archivist at the Darwin project there for all their expert help. I wish to thank the Wedgwood Museum Trust, Barlaston, Stoke-on-Trent, Staffordshire, England, for graciously allowing me to study and use the Wedgwood papers in Keele University Library. Much of Chapter 4 is based on their documents. The curator of the Wedgwood Museum, Miss Gaye Blake Roberts, and her colleagues have given me most kind assistance. The librarian at Keele University guided me most expertly through my research.

Conversations with Sir Martin Wedgwood, and in the past with the late Dame Veronica Wedgwood, have helped me understand the Wedgwood dynasty.

Mr and Mrs Harrison-Allen welcomed me at Cresselly and have allowed me to use family documents. I am grateful for their warm encouragement. Miss Valerie Allen was a most kind guide to the relevant areas of Tenby and district.

The dedication and enthusiasm of the curators and their colleagues at Down House make research there a delight and an inspiration. I have learned much from Nick Biddle's expert and loving recreation of the garden at Down House. I am most grateful to English Heritage for permission to publish extracts from documents in their possession.

I wish especially to thank Ursula Mommens, daughter of Bernard Darwin, and Ursula Vaughan Williams, widow of Ralph Vaughan Williams, who have kindly allowed me to use family documents. Their lively reminiscences have brought to life some of the Darwins of the past. I also remember with gratitude a useful visit to the late Nora Barlow.

I also owe thanks to local librarians at Stoke-on-Trent Archive Service and Staffordshire Records Office, Haverfordwest, Torquay, Ilkley and Shrewsbury, at the Shropshire County Archives, the Pembrokeshire County Record Office and the National Library of Wales. Ms Jo Barber at the Tenby Public Library was particularly helpful.

My thanks go also to the Librarian of Eton College for permission to reproduce extracts from the publication of Emma's letter to Anne Thackeray Ritchie, and to the curator of the Huntington Library, San Francisco, who has supplied the copy of the letter from Emma to Miss Cobbe. Both letters were brought to my attention by Randal Keynes.

I have relied most heavily on the following published works: Henrietta Litchfield, *A Century of Family Letters*; Eliza Meteyard, *Life of Josiah Wedgwood I*; Desmond King-Hele, *Life of Erasmus Darwin*; Robin Reilly, *Josiah Wedgwood I*; Barbara Wedgwood and Hensleigh Wedgwood, *The Wedgwood Circle*; Adrian Desmond and James Moore, *Darwin*; Randal Keynes, *Annie's Box*.

I am deeply grateful to Professor James Moore and Adrian Desmond for their truly great biography of Charles Darwin. I have learned much from conversations with them and with Dr Ralph Colp, whose studies of Darwin's illness have been of the greatest interest. I owe much to the work and friendship of Lord Briggs, who has kindly read through the rough draft of this book.

My publishers Heather Holden-Brown and Celia Kent have shown monumental patience and have given me the kindest encouragement; Gillian Bromley has most sensitively and skilfully edited the book. My warmest thanks to all three.

I could not have finished the book without my competent secretary, Cheryl Lutring, for whose constant and kind help I am deeply grateful.

Denis has borne manfully my Darwin obsession and has been my greatest support. To him, and to my family, I offer my love and gratitude.

Because this book is written for the general reader, it has not been thought necessary to add detailed notes and sources. However, they are available on the Internet at http://authorpages.hoddersystems.com/EdnaHealey

The Darwin Family

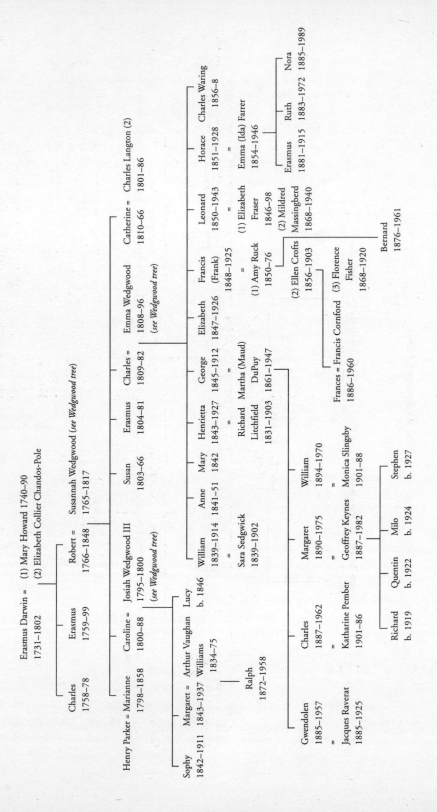

Erasmus Darwin = (1) Mary Howard 1740–90
1731–1802   (2) Elizabeth Collier Chandos-Pole

Charles   Erasmus   Robert = Susannah Wedgwood (*see Wedgwood tree*)
1758–78   1759–99   1766–1848   1765–1817

Henry Parker = Marianne   Caroline = Josiah Wedgwood III   Susan   Erasmus   Charles = Emma Wedgwood   Catherine = Charles Langton (2)
1798–1858   1800–88   1795–1800   1803–66   1804–81   1809–82   1808–96   1810–66   1801–86
(*see Wedgwood tree*)   (*see Wedgwood tree*)

Sophy   Margaret = Arthur Vaughan   Lucy   William   Anne   Mary   Henrietta   George   Elizabeth   Francis   Leonard   Horace   Charles Waring
1842–1911   1843–1937   Williams   b. 1846   1839–1914   1841–51   1842   1843–1927   1845–1912   1847–1926   (Frank)   1850–1943   1851–1928   1856–8
            1834–75   =   1848–1925
        Ralph   Sara Sedgwick   Richard   Martha (Maud)   =   (1) Elizabeth   Emma (Ida) Farrer
        1872–1958   1839–1902   Litchfield   DuPuy   (1) Amy Ruck   Fraser   1854–1946
                    1831–1903   1861–1947   1850–76   1846–98
                                (2) Ellen Crofts   (2) Mildred   Erasmus   Ruth   Nora
                                1856–1903   Massingberd   1881–1915   1883–1972   1885–1989
                                            1868–1940
                    Frances = Francis Cornford   (3) Florence
                    1886–1960   Fisher
                            1868–1920
                                Bernard
                                1876–1961

Gwendolen   Charles   Margaret   William
1885–1957   1887–1962   1890–1975   1894–1970
=   =   =
Jacques Raverat   Katharine Pember   Geoffrey Keynes   Monica Slingsby
1885–1925   1901–86   1887–1982   1901–88

Richard   Quentin   Milo   Stephen
b. 1919   b. 1922   b. 1924   b. 1927

The Wedgwood Family

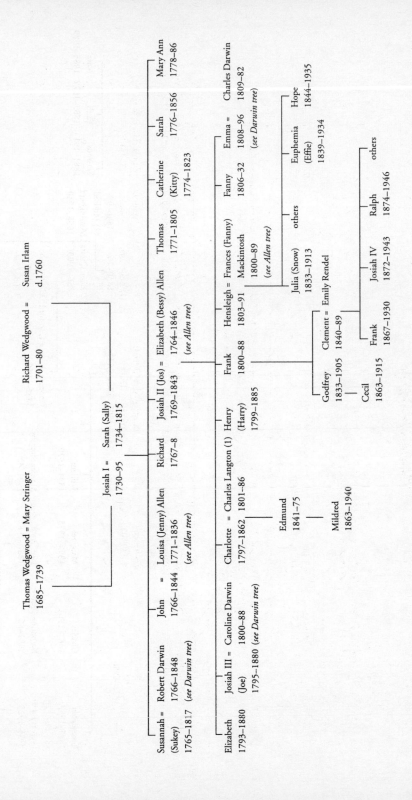

The Allen Family

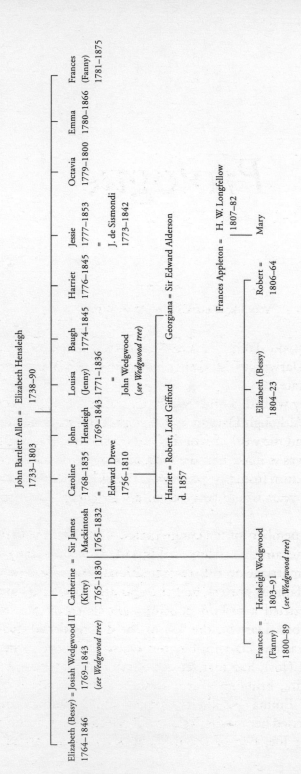

John Bartlett Allen = Elizabeth Hensleigh
1733–1803   1738–90

Elizabeth (Bessy) = Josiah Wedgwood II
1764–1846   1769–1843
(see Wedgwood tree)

Catherine = Sir James Mackintosh
(Kitty)   1765–1832
1765–1830

Caroline   John Hensleigh   Louisa (Jenny)   Baugh   Harriet   Jessie   Octavia   Emma   Frances (Fanny)
1768–1835   1769–1843   1771–1836   1774–1845 1776–1845   1777–1853 1779–1800   1780–1866 1781–1875
=   =
Edward Drewe   John Wedgwood   =
1756–1810   (see Wedgwood tree)   J. de Sismondi
                                                                                    1773–1842

Harriet = Robert, Lord Gifford   Georgiana = Sir Edward Alderson
d. 1857

                                        Frances Appleton = H. W. Longfellow
                                                           1807–82

Frances (Fanny) =   Elizabeth (Bessy)   Robert =   Mary
1800–89   1804–23   1806–64
Hensleigh Wedgwood
1803–91
(see Wedgwood tree)

Prologue

'Very like a marriage of Miss Austen's.'

ON 20 JANUARY 1839, EMMA WEDGWOOD MARRIED HER COUSIN Charles Darwin in St Peter's Church at Maer on her father's Staffordshire estate.

It was, as they wished, a quiet wedding, and made not a ripple in the outside world. Although Darwin and Wedgwood were famous names in the Midlands and the world beyond, Charles was only just beginning on the career that was to make him the most famous of them all. It was three years since his return from his epic voyage around the world in the *Beagle*; another twenty years would pass before his *Origin of Species* rocked the scientific world.

Most of the members of the congregation who filled the little church had known one another from childhood, linked as they were by friendship and marriage over three generations. Josiah Wedgwood I, the founder of the famous pottery, and the grandfather Charles and Emma shared, had married a distant cousin; their daughter Susannah had married Dr Robert Darwin, the son of the distinguished doctor, poet and scientist Erasmus Darwin. Charles Darwin was their son. Emma's father, Josiah II (Jos), had married Elizabeth (Bessy) Allen of Cresselly in Pembrokeshire, bringing a new strand to the already complicated family pattern. Emma was their youngest child. Emma's uncle John Wedgwood married her mother's sister; Charles's sister Caroline married Emma's brother Joe; two of her other brothers had married cousins.

Even Allen Wedgwood, the clergyman who married Charles and Emma, was another cousin. This very closely linked family had been, and would continue to be, the important background to their lives.

On this day, present or absent, all were delighted – especially Jos Wedgwood and Robert Darwin, who had been close friends since childhood. All three families were beginning to fear that at thirty-one, the much-admired Emma was doomed to spinsterhood. As for Charles, waiting nervously for his bride, his brother Erasmus beside him, he could not believe his good luck. Tall and slim, with a pleasant, good-humoured face, he had nevertheless always thought himself plain. Now, as he greeted the serene, charming young woman in the grey-green silk gown and flowery bonnet whom he had known, yet not known, all his life, he knew how right his father had been: he had 'drawn a prize'.

The wedding breakfast was brief – 'not very festive', Emma later remembered – for there was sadness mixed with joy that day. Emma's mother, the beautiful and brilliant Bessy Allen of the past, who would so have enjoyed this wedding, lay upstairs as she had for many years, crippled and in a clouded world. She had taken an interest in the preparations for the breakfast and wedding cake, and had been awake when Emma and her father had left for the church. She had admired Emma's gown and bonnet, glad that, for once, she had taken pains, then slipped away into the mist; she was asleep when Emma and Charles finally left.

The day had been also shadowed by the anguish of Charles's sister and brother-in-law, Caroline and Joe, who knew that their baby was dying. Their sorrow clouded the day for Charles's other two sisters, Susan and Catherine, and for their father, Dr Robert Darwin, in whose care the baby had been.

For Elizabeth, Emma's eldest sister, too, this was a day of mixed pleasure and pain. Though intelligent and sweet-natured, she was crookbacked and never married. She had taken her mother's place in the household and had come to think of Emma as her own child. In recent years she and Emma had taken care of their ageing parents, running the rambling old Maer Hall and tending the flower gardens. Now, though she would never complain, she must bear the burden alone. 'The ceremony was got through very stout heartedly,' she later remembered, and then there was not much more time but for Emma to change her clothes and pack her wedding bonnet and sit a little by the dining room fire with Charlotte and me before she set off, and I did not much mind anything but just the last. It is no small happiness to have had such a companion of my life for so long; since the time she could speak, I have never had one moment's pain for her, and a share of daily pleasure such as few people have it in their power to shed around them. Her sunny face would leave a vacancy.

The carriage drove off through the wintry garden on its way to Birmingham and the new railroad to London. As they waved goodbye, Emma's friends, the clever Tollet sisters, knew how much they would miss her. 'She was the only girl of our own age in the country worth caring much for.' They would remember the day as 'very like a marriage of Miss Austen's'.

CHAPTER ONE

The Triple Inheritance

CHARLES AND EMMA BROUGHT TO THEIR MARRIAGE A TRIPLE INHERITANCE bequeathed by three remarkable families: Darwin, Wedgwood and Allen. Financially they would always be secure: Josiah Wedgwood, the grandfather they shared, had created from nothing a fortune that in modern terms would have made him a multi-millionaire; Charles's father and grandfather were highly successful doctors and the Allens were wealthy country gentry. But they inherited much more than money: there were exceptionally talented men and women among their ancestors, and the union of Emma and Charles would produce a dynasty of unusually gifted descendants. To understand them it is necessary to look to the past; for their characters were partly formed before their births.

Charles and Emma were to some extent aware of their Darwin and Allen inheritance, but until several years after their marriage had little knowledge of their debt to Josiah Wedgwood I or of the magnitude of his genius. This is partly explained by the disappearance for decades after old Josiah's death of much of the Wedgwood archives, which bring the potter so vividly to life. After the death of Emma's father Josiah II in 1843, her brother Frank took over the direction of the Wedgwood pottery and inherited Etruria Hall, where he had been living since his marriage in 1832. Finding the cellars there filled with a dusty heap of old papers, with undiscriminating energy he cleared them out and sold tons of documents to a Birmingham scrap merchant. Josiah I's biographer, Miss Eliza Meteyard, tells the extraordinary tale of their discovery – one of the most astonishing stories in the history of archives.

'In 1848,' she wrote,

Mr Mayer, a native of Newcastle-under-Lyme, and already the earliest and greatest collector of Wedgwood's beautiful productions, on his way to the Continent had occasion to be in Birmingham for a few hours. As he was passing from one part of the town to another, a heavy storm broke over; and looking around for shelter, he saw he was on Snow-hill, the scene of Matthew Boulton's early labours, but at that date a neglected part of Birmingham. The nearest place was a waste and scrap-shop, and through its open door [he] entered. The outside was old, grimy, and dilapidated enough; the inside was worse. Piles of scrap-iron, copper, and brass, and old waste of every kind littered the floor. The battered oaken counter was grimy too; and as he passed up and down between it and the door – for the sleet-rain descended in a heavy shower – Mr Mayer observed on one part of the counter a pile of ledger-like looking books, their backs still thick as when filled with leaves, their outer edge collapsed – because empty. Opening one of these, in which a few leaves still remained, he saw to his great surprise that the writing thereon related to the wages of workmen in Etruria. Looking through other volumes equally collapsed, he found they were all business ledgers of this renowned manufactory.

'Why, my man,' he said to the grimy-looking master of the shop, 'these old ledgers all concern Wedgwood's business.'

'Ay, sir,' was the reply, 'they was thrown out of 'Trury a bit ago, after the death of the master – the son of old Josiah – and I wish I'd more of 'em, for the leaves be a useful size, and folks fancy their bits o' butter and bacon all the better if wrapped in clean writin'. The shops about here will take any amount of this sort o' thing. They likes big sheets – it's more convenient.'

'Had he more?' Mayer asked.

'Hundred-weights,' replied the man and called for a lad to show the gentleman up the ladder.

And there they were sure enough, piled up in mounds, filthy with the accumulated dust of years, and with gaps in their ranks as they stood, which only showed too well the inroads which had been made upon them, even whilst they stood there.

'Finding the richness of the prize,' continued Mr Mayer, 'on which I had thus unexpectedly laid my hand, I determined, if possible, not to lose it. I quickly descended the ricketty ladder, and under the before-mentioned plea of my interest in old writings and papers, I enquired of the owner if he would part with them.'

'Right gladly, sir, they're bits o' things, and not much use to me, or to anybody I suspect.'

On this being said no further time was lost. The great mass was weighed and sold at so much a hundred-weight. A number of large second-hand deal boxes were readily procured in the neighbourhood, and when they were packed and their contents paid for, they were carted to the Railway-station, nor did Mr Mayer lose sight of them till they were safe on their way to Liverpool.

As they originally stood in the old rooms of Etruria, they must have contained such materials for the history of a great industry as were perhaps never before collected together.

'Still,' wrote Miss Meteyard, 'we must be thankful for what are left. For many years Mr Mayer devoted all the leisure hours of his busy life to the selection and arrangement of these papers. The results of this labour are now cleaned and tastefully mounted; and of these, some thousands in number, I have made a general, as also a chronological, index.' Mr Mayer, knowing Miss Meteyard's interest in Josiah, allowed her to use these archives as the basis of her thorough two-volume biography, published in 1865. Sometimes criticized as hagiography, it is an indispensable, detailed account of the potter's life and times: it is certainly impossible to read it without admiration for a man whose letters show such breadth of intelligence, such energy and humour.

————————

Josiah Wedgwood I, the grandfather that Charles and Emma shared, came from a family of some substance in the little town of Burslem near

Stoke-on-Trent in Staffordshire. His great-grandfather had been a potter since 1680, producing plain black and mottled ware in a small pottery near the church, known as the Churchyard Works. Josiah's father, Thomas, inherited the pottery and a small dwelling where Josiah I, the last child of a large family, was born in July 1730.

Josiah's education was limited, taking place first at a dame school in Burslem, then, when he was seven, at an elementary school in Newcastle, a three-mile walk away across the fields. When he was nine his father died, and he left school to work in the pottery, owned now by his brother Thomas. Three years later smallpox nearly killed him and left him with a permanently damaged right knee. Having recovered, on 11 November 1744 he was officially apprenticed to his brother – pledging that 'cards dice or any unlawful games he shall not play'. During the five years of his apprenticeship he learned from Thomas the skill of throwing on the wheel. He continued to work for his brother for three more years, then left the Churchyard Works and became the partner of Thomas Whieldon, the best potter in the town. Here he learned the technical skill and managerial ability which were later to be the foundations of his success.

In due course Josiah set up as a master potter in his own premises in Burslem with a dwelling, Ivy House, rented for £10 a year from his well-to-do distant cousins, Thomas and John. Their brother, Richard, was equally prosperous as a cheesemonger, ten miles away in Congleton, Cheshire, and was a frequent visitor at Burslem. Often he brought with him his daughter Sarah, a tall, striking figure with a mass of tawny hair, riding pillion behind her father – and Josiah fell in love.

A competent young woman who had run her father's house since the death of her mother, Sarah was also better educated than most girls of her period. The Wedgwoods were Unitarians, dissenting from the Anglican creed. Champions of religious liberty, they also believed in the importance of women's education. Richard Wedgwood made sure that Sally, as she was called, could write and spell well. Moreover, 'she had a keen and accurate judgement; and there is that in her countenance as preserved to us in the cameos, which indicates, a great natural sense of beauty and form . . . she was one who could rise equal to superior fortune if it come and yet lose sight of no utility necessary to its beginning. She was an admirable housewife, could make wine and confections and spin flax': so wrote Eliza Meteyard.

Perhaps, then, it is not surprising that her father, reluctant to lose her, insisted that Sally should not marry Josiah until her suitor had made his fortune. The two young lovers, both determined characters, were prepared to wait the long years while Josiah gradually made his reputation as a successful potter. But in 1762, while riding to Liverpool, he had an accident which damaged the leg already weakened by smallpox. For months he remained at Liverpool, disabled, his career in doubt and his marriage yet further delayed. Yet this period was to be the turning point of his life. Josiah used the time to read widely, not only technical books concerning pottery, but literature, poetry, philosophy. In this he was encouraged by his brother-in-law the Reverend William Willett, a scholarly Unitarian preacher, with whom Josiah stayed while recovering from his injury, and to whose extensive library he had constant access. Even more important was a new friend, introduced by his doctor, who would change his life. For eighteen years the Liverpool businessman Thomas Bentley was to be his 'dearest friend' and partner, to whom he wrote hundreds of vivid, intelligent and humorous letters. One day perhaps Bentley's replies may be found to complete one of the most illuminating human correspondences of the century.

Bentley, the son of a gentleman farmer, was socially Wedgwood's superior, but, kindly and courteous, he never made Wedgwood feel the difference. Classically educated, as William Willett had been, at the Hinden Presbyterian Academy, he had subsequently been apprenticed to a cotton manufacturer for some years, then lived in France and Italy, where he became a good linguist. According to his friend, the theologian and scientist Joseph Priestley, he was 'a man of excellent taste' – just the man Josiah needed to deal with his aristocratic customers and also to provide a link to his pottery outlet in Liverpool. But his importance in Josiah's life reached well beyond the practical and social to the moral and intellectual levels. One of the founders of the Octagon, an unorthodox chapel in Liverpool, Bentley held strong nonconformist, rationalist religious beliefs that coloured his whole way of life. He wrote and spoke out courageously against slavery in Liverpool, a city many of whose businessmen made their fortunes out of the slave trade, and against the British war in America. His pamphlet on female education chimed with Josiah's own belief in the importance of this. Bentley introduced his friend to the works of the French philosopher Jean Jacques Rousseau, whose ideas would profoundly affect Josiah's upbringing of his own children. (It was strange that Rousseau, whose liberal and progressive theories would change educational attitudes for generations, was in practice neither liberal nor progressive: he sent his natural children to a foundling home.)

Through Bentley, Josiah was drawn into the circle of some of the most inventive and creative minds of the century; men of the Midlands whose energy and ability fuelled the Industrial Revolution. They met in each other's houses when the full moon made travel easier, and so called themselves the 'Lunar Society'. Josiah joined them when he was able. Other distinguished men came as their guests, among them the great American, Benjamin Franklin. It was in this circle that Josiah was to meet Dr Erasmus Darwin of Lichfield and so begin a lifelong friendship and a dynasty.

Returning to Burslem after his recovery, Josiah took up his career again with renewed skill and energy. Notwithstanding his success, however, Richard Wedgwood was still reluctant to release his prized daughter – Josiah had to serve the biblical seven years before Richard gave his permission – and even at the end haggled over the marriage settlement. Finally, as Josiah wrote to Bentley, 'all things amicably settled betwixt my Pappa elect and myself, I prevailed upon my dear girl to name the day, the blissfull day when she will reward all my faithfull services and take me to her arms to pleasures which I am yet ignorant of.' Sally and Josiah were married at Astbury near Congleton on 25 January 1764 – after which Richard, hitherto so domineering, became a fond father-in-law: 'my daddy', as Josiah affectionately called him. The following year, after the birth of his first child, Josiah wrote to Bentley: 'Accept the best respects of two married lovers who are as happy as the world can make them.'

Josiah was thirty-four and Sally thirty, an intelligent, capable woman who from the beginning of their marriage was treated as a respected partner. Better educated than her husband, she was able to act as his secretary on occasions and even to help with his experiments. Always wary of industrial espionage, Josiah kept his records of new glazes in secret code, which he taught Sally. 'I have just begun a course of experiments for a white body and glaze which promiseth well hitherto. Sally is my chief helpmate in this as well as other things, and that she may not be hurried by having too many *Irons in the Fire*, as the phrase is, I have ordered the spinning wheel into the Lumber room. She hath learnt my characters at least to write them [his code], but can scarcely read them at present.' He trusted her taste as well as her practical good sense: 'I speak from experience in Female taste,' he wrote to Bentley when experimenting with pyramid flower pots, 'without which I should have made a poor figure amongst my Potts: not one of which of any consequence is finished without the approbation of my Sally.' She advised him on the design of flower vases and of 'bough pots for the hearth'; and if Josiah Wedgwood's teapots were famous for 'lids that fitted and spouts that poured', it was Sally who made sure that they did.

Their first home was Brick House, a small two-storey house in Burslem with kilns at the back, leased from his cousins. Here, the year after the marriage, their first child was born: Sukey, Sally told her brother-in-law, 'was worth travelling 150 miles to see'. This infant prodigy was to become the mother of Charles Darwin; her brother Josiah, born four years later, was to be Emma's father. These two and John (1766–1844) were later followed by Thomas (1771–1805), Catherine or Kitty (1774–1823) and Sarah (1776–1856), who was to be Emma's devoted Aunt Sarah; two other children died in childhood.

By 1765 Josiah was highly successful. At his little pottery he had experimented with 'white body and glaze' and produced the strong, simple ware which established his reputation. He exported an 'amazing quantity of white stoneware and some of the finer kinds to the Continent, and much to the islands of N. America'. There were many reasons for his success. He was a highly skilled potter with great manual dexterity – even with a damaged leg that made the treadle work difficult, he could still throw a perfect pot. Some of his later descendants believed they had inherited his 'clever hands'. He was also a perfectionist and demanded the same high standards from his workmen, refusing to pass imperfect goods. 'This will not do for Josiah Wedgwood,' he is reported to have said as he raised his stick to smash an offending vessel. He brought order, discipline and strict timekeeping into the factory, though this was hard going. 'I am teazed out of my life,' he wrote in 1765, 'with dilatory, drunken, idle worthless workmen.' Drunkenness was an occupational disease in the Potteries. He also introduced division of labour, 'indispensable for specialised skill'. Tolerant and good-humoured by nature, he was amused to hear that his name struck terror into his workmen. In fact he was a good master, paid well and encouraged talent wherever he saw it, particularly among his artists. He sent a clever woman painter to his workshop in London, and he would like to have set up a training school for artistic boys and girls.

He was ahead of his time in sales promotion. His famous showplaces in London, first in Newport Street and then in Greek Street, were deliberately planned to encourage distinguished ladies and gentlemen to wander round and admire elegant pottery beautifully displayed, with the exhibits regularly changed. Shrewdly, he realized that if he attracted the 'great folk', as he called them, the 'middling folk' would follow.

His first real triumph came in that same year of 1765, when Queen Charlotte ordered a 'complete set of tea things, with a gold ground and raised flowers upon it in green'. He sent his brother John, who handled his London business, to the Court at St James's, saying, 'pray put on the best suit of clothes you ever had in your life,' to discover from Miss Chetwynd, the Staffordshire Semptress to the Queen, exactly what was required. Though such gilding was unfamiliar to him, the result was so successful that he could henceforth call himself the Queen's Potter, and his cream ware became famous as 'Queen's Ware'. When Josiah himself went to Court he was not in the least overawed. The master craftsman now knew his value. As a result of royal patronage, in two years he could write, 'It is really amazing how rapidly the use of it [i.e. Queen's Ware] has spread almost over the whole globe and how universally it is liked.'

Josiah was not only a great potter; he was one of the prime promoters of the canal-building campaign. In the summer of 1765 he dined with the local 'great folk', such as the Duke of Bridgewater and Earl Gower, who welcomed his advice concerning the plans for a canal that would link the rivers Trent and Mersey and provide a waterway across England. In the long negotiations that preceded the necessary Act of Parliament, Josiah, with Bentley's advice, played a key role, presenting a persuasive report to a committee of the House of Commons. Neither here nor in any of his meetings with distinguished men did Josiah feel inferior: the class barrier was bridged by mutual respect. The canal would be of immense value to him in providing safer transport, for until 1765 his crates of precious pottery had to be bumped along rutted country lanes to Birmingham, Liverpool or London. On 14 May 1766 Royal Assent was given to the bill providing for the opening of the Trent and Mersey Canal; work on its construction began on 26 July the same year, when Josiah cut the first sod at Burslem, and was completed in 1790.

Shrewdly, in 1766 Josiah bought the tract of land through which the proposed canal would run. Here, on the Ridgehouse Estate, he was to build a great factory with a village of workers' houses and a handsome house for himself. For by 1766 Josiah was world-famous. New archaeological discoveries in Italy, where excavations had revealed remains of Etruscan civilization and art, had aroused great enthusiasm for all things classical, and Josiah's vases had become all the rage. Fine ladies crowded his London showroom, blocking the streets with their carriages. The success of the pottery, at home and abroad, meant that Josiah needed larger premises and a house that reflected his growing importance. It was to be called 'Etruria Hall' after the Italian excavations which had opened his eyes to the glory of classical art, and inspired so much of his neo-classical work.

However, he decided that before he moved to new premises his leg, now hopelessly damaged, would have to be amputated. The operation was carried out at Burslem on 28 May 1768, 'the patient witnessing it', we are told; 'seated in his chair, [he] bore the unavoidable pain without a shrink or a groan.' If Josiah took the amputation with customary sangfroid, his clerk, Peter Swift, reported the event with equal lack of fuss. At the end of an invoice sent to the London office for 'piggins cream pots and salts' he added as an afterthought, 'Mr Wedgwood has this day had his leg taken of [*sic*] and is as well as can be expected after such an execution.' Sally may have been present; if not, she would not have been far away. She certainly dressed the wound in the following days, as Josiah told an admiring Bentley. By June he had taken 'two airings in a chaise and had left off the laudanum'; and before long, now with a wooden leg, he was cheerfully stumping around planning the 'new Etruria'. Sally's stoicism was equally admirable: their little ten-month-old son Dicky suddenly died at this time. 'Mrs Wedgwood', wrote Swift, 'has had severe trials of late but the great hopes of Mr Wedgwood's perfect recovery seems to keep her spirits up.'

Josiah planned a handsome, three-storey house for himself, but first he built a small house for Bentley where he hoped his friend would live. In fact it was more convenient for Bentley to live in London to supervise the decoration and display of the ornamental part of the pottery, and he never lived in it. Josiah decided to move into Bentley's house while his own was being built, and Sally skilfully contrived to surprise him with the completion of this operation on his return from London. When he reached Etruria, he was

> rewarded for all the risque and pains I had undergone in a tedious long and dirty journey. I found my Sally and family at Etruria! Just come there to take possession of the Etruscan plains and sleep upon them for the first night. Was not this very clever now of my own dear girl's contriving. She expected her Jos on the very evening he arrived; had got the disagreeable business of removing all over and I need not have been another night from home for the Indies. Tonight we are to sup 120 of our workmen in the Town Hall and shall take up our lodgings here at Burslem.

This feast, too, would have been of Sally's organizing.

It was during the negotiations for the Trent and Mersey Canal that Josiah's friendship with Dr Erasmus Darwin was established – though at first he and Bentley referred to their 'fat friend' with disrespectful amusement, and with slight annoyance at Darwin's pompous corrections of their pamphlet on the proposed canal.

Erasmus Darwin also had reasons for supporting the campaign. A huge man, he spent uncomfortable days wedged into the carriage he had invented, travelling to his patients along rutted country lanes; to glide along smooth canals would be a great improvement. Besides, he had a great interest in all advances in the mechanics of transport, and was himself experimenting in wind and steam power. However, his assistance to the canal project had to be anonymous; as a doctor he dared not offend important patients whose interests might be affected.

When Josiah Wedgwood met Erasmus Darwin both men were on the foothills of fame, but they had come by different routes and brought with them different traditions. Josiah, self-educated, a master craftsman, was steeped in Unitarianism and nonconformity; Erasmus, the well-educated professional man, was a rationalist, a sceptic and agnostic. As far as he was concerned, Unitarianism was a 'feather bed to catch a falling Christian'. He had been brought up in a well-to-do family, described as 'middling gentry', in a substantial mansion, Elston Hall, near Chesterfield. Educated at Chesterfield Grammar School and St John's College, Cambridge, he studied medicine at Edinburgh and in 1756 settled as a doctor in Lichfield. Here he rapidly established a reputation not only as a skilful doctor but as an accomplished poet. Well over six feet tall – a characteristic inherited by his son, Robert, and grandson, Charles – he was a man of boundless energy, with an enormous appetite for food and life, producing three children by his first wife, Mary Howard, two by his mistress, Mary Parker, and seven by his second wife, Elizabeth Chandos-Pole. Indeed, in spite of his great weight and a pronounced stammer, he seems to have had great success with the ladies.

His fame as a doctor spread to London: King George III would have liked Darwin as his personal physician – an honour Darwin declined – and the famous royal banker, Thomas Coutts, sent his neurotic daughter to him for the electric treatment with which he was experimenting. He also prescribed for her a large dose of opium, enough to get her intoxicated. He was a friend of Benjamin Franklin and, like Franklin, an inventive man of many talents. He designed a knitting loom, a weighing machine, a flying bird, a lightning conductor for Lichfield Cathedral, and sprung wheels for the carriage of his own design in which he travelled thousands of miles. In every sense he was larger than life. He spoke his own mind to rich and poor alike; according to his friend and neighbour, the poet Anna Seward, he was capable of 'jocose but wounding irony', but 'diligently . . . attended to the health of the poor'. He was also adept at attracting the wealth of the rich, as the Reverend William Bagshaw Stevens observed during the frequent visits of Darwin to the Derbyshire home of his patient, Sir Robert Burdett, father of the radical Sir Francis Burdett. Even so, it was some years after his establishment at Lichfield before he reached the peak of his fame; and then it was as a poet that he gained national prestige. After the publication of 'The Botanic Garden', Horace Walpole wrote to Hannah More, 'the author is a great poet . . ., the verses which describe the creation of the universe out of chaos are in my opinion the most sublime passage of any author.' Although Charles Darwin was to deny that his grandfather influenced him in his work on the *Origin of Species*, Erasmus undoubtedly helped to produce the free-thinking climate in which his grandson formed his theories of evolution.

As for Charles's grandmother, Mary Howard is one of the forgotten women who helped shape his life. The daughter of a lawyer and proctor at the Ecclesiastical Court at Lichfield Cathedral, she was a neighbour of Darwin in the Cathedral Close. Polly, as she was called, was seventeen when she married Erasmus, and bore him three sons, the first, perhaps significantly, after an eight-month pregnancy. According to Anna Seward, another resident in the Close, Polly was 'a blooming and lovely young lady' with a mind of 'native strength; an awakened taste for the works of imagination; ingenuous sweetness; delicacy animated by sprightliness, and sustained by fortitude! These qualities made her a capable as well as fascinating companion, even to a man of talents so illustrious.' Sadly, she became painfully ill in the last years of her life and eased the pain with a combination of spirits and the laudanum to which she became addicted. Because she was left alone a great deal – Erasmus was often away for days at a time – she managed to hide her addiction until it was too late. Polly, like many other doctors' wives, found that the physician failed to see that his own wife needed healing. Much was expected of her in her husband's long absences; and when he was at home, she was expected to entertain his scientific friends and receive his medical students, for their home had been enlarged to include a small hospital with an operating theatre where he could demonstrate to students.

Erasmus later described the course of Polly's illness to his son Robert, who was considering marriage and wanted to know about his mother's death because he was worried that he might inherit a tendency to alcoholism. Polly's brother, Charles, had been a drunkard, 'both in public and in private', Erasmus told his son, 'and when he went to London he became connected with a woman and lived in a deba[u]ched life in respect to drink, hence he had always the gout of which he died but without any of the least symptom of either insanity or epilepsy, but from debility of digestion and Gout as other drunkards die'. Their friend Richard Edgeworth described how, when he called on Polly one evening, Erasmus arrived with an apparently lifeless man in his carriage. He had found him lying on the road and brought him home, only to discover to his horror that it was Polly's brother, Charles, dead drunk.

To his son, Erasmus wrote with painful honesty,

in respect to your mother, the following is the true history, which I shall neither aggravate nor diminish anything. Her mind was truly amiable and her person handsome, which you may perhaps in some measure remember. She was seized with pain on the left side about the lower edge of the liver, this pain was followed in about an hour by violent convulsions, and these sometimes relieved by great doses of opium, and some wine, which induced intoxication. At other times a temporary delirium, or what by some might be termed insanity, came on for half an hour, and then she became herself again, and the paroxysm was terminated. This disease is called hysteria by some people, I think it allied to epilepsy. This kind of disease had several returns in the course of 4 or 6 years and she then took to drinking spirit and water to relieve the pain, and I found (when it was too late) that she had done this in great quantity, the liver became swelled, and she gradually sunk, a few days before her death, she bled at the mouth, and whenever she had a scratch, as some hepatic patients do.

In the same letter Erasmus told his son, 'When your mother fainted away in these hysteric fits (which she often did) she told me you, who was not then 2 or 2½ years old, ran into the kitchen to call the maid servant to her assistance.' The experience must have had a searing effect on a young child.

As for the anxiety that had prompted Robert to ask for information, Erasmus reassured his son that although 'all the drunken diseases are hereditary and epilepsy and insanity were originally produced by drinking', he considered 'one sober generation could cure this which one drunken one had created.' Erasmus himself afterwards became abstemious, taking only water with his meals, until late in life when he added two glasses of home-made wine. Robert never forgot his father's counsel, drank very little himself, encouraged his sons to do likewise and even fiercely advised his aristocratic patients to curtail excessive drinking. His son Charles positively disliked wine and drank little; only at the end of his life would he take a little brandy.

There is no doubt of the depth of Erasmus's love for his young wife. Soon after her death he wrote in anguish in a long letter to a friend,

> Many hundred Nights I have watched to console and assist her, and was seldom for an Hour together in my Absence from Home free from Tears on her Account – Yet her Life was valuable to Her for She loved her Family most tenderly! and to me, as her Approbation stampt the Pleasures on all the Conveniences and Amusements of my Situation! the shady walk in my Garden, the Harbour, and the wild Woodbine and Primroses, that she planted and admired seem to have lost their Beauty and their Odour!

Polly, in her turn, remained to the end devoted to her husband. 'Dr Darwin', she told Anna Seward, 'combated and assuaged my disease from time to time, his indulgence to my wishes, his active desire to see me amused and happy proved incessant . . . Married to any other man I do not suppose I could have lived a third part of those years which I have passed with Dr Darwin: he has prolonged my days and he has blessed them.'

However, while Polly's death clearly caused Erasmus deep and genuine distress, he did not remain celibate long. The new housekeeper he hired to manage his establishment and care for his children, Mary Parker, became his mistress and bore him two daughters who were brought up in their home. Erasmus not only acknowledged and looked after them, he set them up as teachers in their own little school and even wrote a charming book for them on female education.

It is perhaps not surprising, then, that in later years Dr Robert Darwin was noted for a moodiness that sometimes clouded his habitual kindness. There had been terror and grief in his earliest childhood; and though his Aunt Susannah had come to care for her brother and his children after Polly's death, the advent of Mary Parker would have been a considerable disturbance. Then, when Robert was eleven, his brilliant brother Charles died. A medical student at Edinburgh and his father's pride and joy, Charles had become infected after cutting his finger dissecting the brain of a dead child. It was yet another twist of the black thread that ran through Robert's early life.

Further disturbance for the young Robert came with his father's marriage to a wealthy and beautiful window, Elizabeth Chandos-Pole. Erasmus had courted her passionately while she was still married, and on her husband's death had successfully wooed her. At her insistence they left Lichfield and moved to her mansion, Radbourne Hall, and then to Breadsall Priory near Derby. Robert was now one of a mixed brood along with his full brother Erasmus, his two half-sisters (the daughters of Mary Parker), and Elizabeth's children from her first marriage. The family would eventually be augmented by the seven children of Erasmus and Elizabeth. (One of these, Violetta, married Tertius Galton; their son, Francis, would play a role in Charles's life.)

Later there was yet more tragedy in the family. In 1799 Robert's elder brother Erasmus, by now an eccentric lawyer, with constant financial problems, 'fell into the water at the bottom of his garden and drowned'. Or so his father wrote. In fact it became generally accepted that Erasmus Junior had committed suicide. The elder Erasmus was heartbroken; henceforward, all his hopes of seeing one of his sons succeed him as a doctor were concentrated on Robert.

It is not hard to understand why the young Robert delighted in escaping to the stability and freedom of Etruria Hall. In the spring of 1774 he wrote to Josiah, 'I think every day of the happyness [*sic*] I enjoyed at Etruria.' Decades later his son, Charles, would likewise find happiness and relief from the constraints of his Darwin background at another Wedgwood home, Maer Hall.

In June 1769 the new works at Etruria were opened. Josiah himself threw the first pot while Bentley turned the wheel. His first six vases were perfectly turned, and were later painted with the figures of Hercules and his companions in the Garden of the Hesperides, with the inscription *Artes Etruriae Renascuntur*. 'Etruria' became the Wedgwood mark.

In July, Josiah and Sally and their children, Sukey, John and the new baby Josiah, moved into Etruria Hall. It was a handsome but unpretentious three-storey brick house, built on rising ground. Green lawns swept down to the canal and, as Meteyard wrote, the landscape gardener gathered 'the moorland springs into a lake breaking the levels here and there with knolls'. In 1794 the *Gentleman's Magazine* described the house and village as 'a colony newly raised in a desert where clay-built man subsists on clay'. Inside, it was elegant: ceilings, chimney pieces and door frames were decorated with Wedgwood plaques and embellishments. Josiah's great-granddaughter Julia Wedgwood recalled it from her childhood in the mid-nineteenth century.

> I well remember its green sweeps of lawn and tall trees, some seventy years ago as a delightful sojourn for children, perhaps all the more delightful because even at that date it was mainly a record of the past. The old drawing room, too large for the needs and income of its predecessor at that date, denuded of furniture and thus empty of breakable or spoilable material afforded a capital playground for a party of little cousins . . . At that date the rooks still nestled in green boughs above grass-bordered paths where now all is cinders and oven refuse. But we looked down on the canal . . . as a sort of spirit of the quiet green landscape . . . for Etruria would not have existed without it.

The landscape may well have been planned by Capability Brown; certainly he was an acquaintance of Josiah, who knew exactly how much he charged. But it was Bentley who was called in to help design house and garden, and Sally would certainly have had a hand in the choice of flowers, trees and shrubs. On their visits to London they chose rare shrubs and plants for Etruria, and in time the treeless waste they had bought was transformed into the charming landscape which Stubbs later painted. They grew the flowers that decorated Josiah's pottery, and handed on to their children and grandchildren their own delight in gardening. As they grew up the children would write to each other of planting and grafting, and even when separated by marriage they continued to exchange cuttings and advice. John, Josiah's eldest son, went on to found the Royal Horticultural Society.

The house itself was planned, like the factory, for practical use. The three storeys above ground were augmented by extensive cellars; two wings were added towards the end of Josiah's life. A long schoolroom and nurseries were on the top floor; Josiah's and Sally's suite, with a small kitchen, was on the first floor. Here too was Josiah's panelled study, looking across the lawns to the canal and beyond, over the flat Staffordshire landscape stretching to the horizon. His library was unusually well stocked, with books on art and architecture, poetry and history as well as on technical and scientific subjects. 'My wife says', he wrote to Bentley, 'I must buy no more books till I build another house, and advises me to first read some of those I have already. What nonsense she sometimes talks.' Dining room and drawing room on the ground floor were decorated with Wedgwood plaques and vases; there were classical fireplace surrounds and display cases for cameos and jewellery.

Etruria Hall, however, was not only a showplace reflecting its owner's new prestige; it was also his workplace, where he studied and experimented with new techniques. In the capacious basement he worked on his most secret processes. Constantly aware of the dangers of industrial espionage, he kept certain rooms padlocked; into those only Sally, and later their sons, were allowed to enter. Access was closely guarded: a flight of narrow brick steps led down from Josiah's study to an outside rear door, while a long secret passage connected the cellars to the factory.

There was plenty of room for company, and Josiah and Sally entertained distinguished visitors, serving them excellent meals on Wedgwood pottery – a different design each day. Earl Gower and his guests frequently visited them, and if Josiah was absent Sally would do the honours and show them round the pottery. Though it was a great transition to Etruria from the little Brick House in Burslem, neither of them was the least fazed by the 'great folk'. 'The Duke of Bridgewater very courteously invited me to dine with him and after dinner condescended to show me all his works', wrote Josiah to Bentley. He dined with Earl Gower at Trentham Hall and at the family mansion at Runcorn, and later 'spent a jovial evening at Trentham Hall with Lord Gower and the Duke', not as a tradesman, placed below the salt, but as a respected expert on many subjects, secure in the knowledge that he was a great craftsman, whose opinion was sought not only about pottery but about canals and transport, and in Parliament about industrial relations and even international affairs.

Soon Josiah Wedgwood was famous not only in Britain and Europe, but much further afield, his pottery sought by distinguished customers in Russia, China and North America. For he was not only a great potter, but also a shrewd salesman, aware that if he paid attention to the 'great folk' they would set a fashion which the world would follow. He increased his sales abroad by impressing ambassadors and their wives with the beauty of his wares. His most useful contact in this, as in much else, was his friend Sir William Hamilton, the British Ambassador at Naples, who had published four important folios containing engravings of the exciting discoveries of ancient artefacts made during excavations at Herculaneum and elsewhere. Sir William became a valued adviser to Josiah for many years. His sister, Lady Cathcart, also became his friend, and when her husband became the British Ambassador to St Petersburg, they acted almost as agents for Wedgwood's wares, wearing his cameos, displaying his vases on the Embassy mantelpiece and serving their dinners on his most splendid services. It was the subtlest and most effective of advertisements, attracting the attention of the Empress of Russia herself, Catherine the Great, who was particularly impressed by dinner services decorated with lovely countryside views.

From this outstandingly successful promotion came the greatest coup of Josiah's life: in March 1773 the Empress ordered a huge dinner service, each piece to be decorated with English scenery; destined for use at her country palace, La Grenouillière, it was to be suitably marked with a green frog on every plate. It was an immense challenge to provide nearly 1,300 paintings of English scenery with dwellings ranging from, as the catalogue described, 'rural cottages and farms to the most superb palaces, and from the huts of the Hebrides to the masterpieces of the best known London architects'. No servile flatterer, Josiah refrained from using royal palaces. One plate showed a view of Etruria Hall, just as Julia Wedgwood later remembered it in 'those faint indelible images of childish memory . . . The canal occupies the foreground and a barge is passing; but quiet fields surround the house on all sides and two ladies and a gentleman are stopping on the other side to look at it.'

In June 1774 the service was finished – the speed was astonishing, its beauty breathtaking. All fashionable London, including the Queen, flocked to see an exhibition of part of the service in the Greek Street showrooms; 'three rooms below and two above are filled with it, laid out on tables', wrote an admiring Mrs Delaney. The Empress, apparently, was 'highly satisfied with the execution of this work'. So she should have been. 'It must have cost about £3000 and there is some doubt as to the margin of profit.'

In the decade after the move to Etruria, Sally bore four more children: Tom in 1771; Catherine in 1774; Sarah in 1776; and Mary Ann in 1778. Having married at the age of thirty, between 1765 and 1778 she had, with the minimum of fuss, produced eight children, the last when she was forty-four. On that occasion Josiah proudly announced to Bentley,

> Mrs Wedgwood yesterday morning presented me with another fine girl and with as little trouble to herself and family as could be expected. She sent for the midwife whilst we were bowling (after making tea for us as usual in the afternoon) without so much as acquainting me with the matter, slipt upstairs just before supper, and we had not risen from the table before the joyfull tiding of a safe delivery and all well was brought to us.

It was not always so easy for Sally. There was at least one dangerous miscarriage when Dr Erasmus Darwin was called in and saved her life.

Indeed, stalwart though Sally was, the strain of these years was beginning to tell. She had been Josiah's nurse during the amputation crisis, his secretary during his illness convalescence and his adviser on the planning of the new houses and gardens, and he had consulted her on all his major projects at the factory. The moves from Brick House in Burslem to Little Etruria and then to the big house, Etruria Hall, with its large staff, had been entirely her responsibility. In Little Etruria, the house prepared for Bentley, where they spent some months, and in Etruria Hall, the plaster had scarcely dried when they moved in, and in the still damp rooms Sally developed the rheumatism that crippled her for the rest of her life. The deaths of two children added further stress: Richard had died aged ten months in 1768 and Mary Ann, always backward, died in her eighth year. Dr Erasmus had attempted a cure, but his drastic treatment – opium and electric shocks in a bath of cold water – had, not surprisingly, failed.

As the children grew up, Etruria Hall became not only their home but also their school. Like most Unitarians, Josiah gave much thought to the education of not only his sons but also his daughters. Barred from official positions in Parliament and the universities, Unitarians founded their own schools and academies where intelligent masters broke away from hide-bound attitudes and the rigidities of many old traditions, teaching new subjects like chemistry. Josiah himself gave lectures at Warrington Academy, one of the best in the country.

At first he sent his sons, John, Jos and Tom, to a boarding school in Bolton run by Philip Holland, a distant relative and a good Unitarian headmaster, and his daughter, Sukey, to a dame school in Lancashire. But their health suffered, and he decided that they should be taught at home where he could oversee their education himself. He and Bentley discussed the matter at length with Erasmus Darwin. Were his children to become craftsmen, or gentlemen? If the latter, then they must study the classics; but if the former, then modern languages and accounts would be of more use. The syllabus he designed for them covered most options, and also made time for fresh air and exercise.

My boys [he tells Bentley in 1779] are quite stout & well & we have formed a pretty regular school, which I have at present some notion of improving & continuing instead of sending them from home again, unless by way of finish for some particular parts of their education. Before breakfast we read English together in the newspaper, or any book we happen to have in the course of reading. We are now reading Ferber's Travels with the globes & maps before us. After breakfast they go & write an hour with Mr Swift [his clerk] & with his small portion of time & writing their French exercises, & entering some experiments which they make along with me, all which I insist upon being written in a plain legible hand, they have improved more in writing these few weeks than they did in the last twelve months at Bolton – After writing if the weather permits, they ride or drive their hoop, or jump a cord, or use any exercise they please for an hour & the remainder of the day is filled up with the French lessons & Mr Swift attends them here an hour in the evening for accounts in which their sister (Sukey) joins with them; & we have agreed to add four Latin lessons a week to the above business for which Mr Byerley & Mr Lomas have kindly offered their assistance. This last is only introduced to prevent their losing what they have already learnt, till I have decided upon this part of their learning.

As time went by, the curriculum broadened further. Joseph Wright and Stubbs gave them lessons in painting; John, Jos and Robert Darwin, who frequently studied with them, especially enjoyed the lessons on chemistry given by a distinguished scientist, Alexander Chisholm, brought by Josiah to give a series of lectures in Stoke.

The girls could join their brothers when they wished, but also had their own governesses, among them Everina, the sister of the bluestocking Mary Wollstonecraft. She must have made her mark, because later in life Robert Darwin wrote that Kitty Wedgwood had the most independent mind of any woman he knew. The lessons in accounting were not wasted on the girls, who in later life managed their great fortunes with admirable efficiency.

Josiah gave particular care to the education of his eldest daughter, Sukey. The Liverpool dame school he sent her to first was unsatisfactory – she became unwell and came out in 'pukes and boils' – so they sent her to stay with Bentley and his new wife in London, where she attended a Chelsea school, Blacklands. It was a great sacrifice, for Josiah adored Sukey, a lively and intelligent girl; but no one was better qualified to direct her studies than his friend Bentley, who had written pamphlets on women's education. He had no children, had lately remarried and loved Sukey as though she were his own daughter. He introduced her to the cultural life of London, taking her to plays, concerts and art galleries. She would also have been taken on Sundays to the Unitarian church in London which Bentley financed with some help from Josiah, and kept her Unitarian faith for some years after her marriage to Robert Darwin. Charles Darwin's mother had a privileged education.

When Sukey was back at Etruria Hall she shared her brothers' French lessons, given by a young émigré, M. Potet, whom Dr Darwin had discovered and employed to teach his son Robert and the Wedgwood boys at Lichfield. M. Potet was a success, so Josiah took him on for a year as tutor to his family, and Robert came to Etruria in his turn to join their lessons. The arrival of the lively Sukey could not have made life easier for poor M. Potet, who had been obliged to 'thrash the boys' until Josiah strictly forbade it. However, their French improved: 'we have begun that language at table,' Josiah had reported, 'and shall introduce it in a few days at school. We already market in French.' Sukey became sufficiently proficient to be able later to act as Josiah's 'French clerk'.

As the boys grew up, Robert Darwin became a part of the Wedgwood family. The same age as John, he would later keep him out of many a financial difficulty; and Jos became a close friend. When in later years Robert called Jos 'the wisest man I ever knew', it was a judgement based on a lifelong friendship.

In spite of all his other concerns, Josiah spent time with the children and made sure that learning and pleasure went hand in hand. There was fun at Etruria. In 1775 Bentley sent up from London 'a large play house which spread out upon the lawn was their unfailing rendezvous'. Robert Darwin came over from Lichfield to join the merriment. In 1772 Josiah searched in London for a barrel-organ to amuse the children; finally he hired one, and in March wrote to Bentley: 'The organ arrived safe and a most joyful opening of it we have had. About twenty young sprigs were made as happy as mortals can be and danced and lilted away.' No doubt Josiah too, wooden leg and all, stomped around with enthusiasm.

Sukey had been ill towards the end of her time in London and had returned to join her brothers at the Etruria school, where fresh air and exercise soon cured her. 'Sukey is now very well, & is pretty strong which I attribute very much to rideing on horseback,' Josiah told Bentley.

> We sally forth half a dozen of us by 6 or 7 o'clock in a morning, & return to breakfast with appetites scarcely to be satisfied. Then we are very busy in our hay & have just made a new garden. Sometimes we try experiments, then read, & draw a little, that altogether we are very busy folks, & the holidays will be over much sooner than we could wish them to be. Poor Sukey is quite out of patience with her old spinet & often asks me when her new one will come . . . my girl is quite tired out with her present miserable hum strum, & it takes half her masters time to put it into tune.

Sukey was an excellent musician, and her indulgent father took pleasure in obliging her in her impatient demands for a new instrument. He listened with fond pride as she accompanied her sister Kitty, the music drifting down through open windows to the canal on summer evenings. Later on, Sukey was able to give the great Erasmus Darwin piano lessons, though it would seem that, like his grandson Charles, he had no ear for music. Sarah too would become an accomplished pianist, drawing praise from no less a personage than Coleridge, who would later report that she played 'divinely'. The love of music and skill in performance were to be Emma's most cherished legacies from her Wedgwood forebears.

In 1779 Josiah decided to commission a family portrait. He had first considered his friend Joseph Wright of Derby, but then decided to give the work to Stubbs. He had originally wanted two paintings of the children, one, as he told Bentley, with 'Sukey playing upon her harpsicord, with Kitty singing to her as she often does, and Sally and Mary Ann upon the carpet in some employment suitable to their ages', the other to show 'Jack standing at a table making fixable air with the glass apparatus etc., and his two brothers accompanying him, Tom jumping up and clapping his hands with joy and surprised at seeing the stream of bubbles rise up just as Jack has put a little chalk into the acid. Jos with the chemical dictionary before him in a thoughtful mood; which actions will be exactly descriptive of their respective characters.' Josiah should have used Wright. One can imagine how he would have caught the expressive little faces in the candlelight. As it was, Stubbs was more interested in horses than humans, and neither Sally nor the children were well done. But it is significant that Stubbs chose to paint the Wedgwoods in the open air. He must have seen the family returning like this from their morning ride; unfortunately their vitality is lost.

The painting shows the extensive, still rural grounds of Etruria, though in the background a plume of smoke rises from the potteries. The infant in the cart was poor little backward Mary Ann, who died at the age of eight, in spite of, or perhaps because of, the drastic electric treatment given by Dr Erasmus Darwin. Beside her, the sturdy little Sarah would outlive them all, devoted to the last to her niece, Emma. Kitty, here in control of the cart, developed an unusually clear, masculine mind and would become the manager of the household. Although Josiah complained that Stubbs had not caught likenesses, there is something indicative of character in the body language of his eldest daughter and her three brothers. The stylish fifteen-year-old Sukey sits atop her horse with ease and self-confidence. Did Charles Darwin ever look with curiosity and regret at this portrait of the mother he only remembered in her black velvet dress? Jos turns to the artist his intelligent, enquiring face; John has already something of the sense of self-importance of the man who would turn his back on the pottery; and Tom sits upright, thoughtful as he would always be. As for their parents, Sally's maternal love reaches out in her outstretched arms; Josiah sits with the ease of a successful man of substance, at his elbow – improbable in that setting – one of his much-admired classical vases. Stubbs had stayed long enough at Etruria Hall to get the measure of the family. He had taught the children to paint and given them lessons on perspective. But they were all 'heartily tired' of the sittings for the portraits. 'Methinks', wrote Josiah to Bentley, 'I would not be a portrait painter upon any condition whatever.' The sittings had been an intolerable waste of his valuable time.

At the end of 1780 the Wedgwoods were stricken by the sudden death of their beloved friend Thomas Bentley. He had been unwell for some time, but his death at the early age of fifty had been unexpected. Josiah rushed to his bedside, but arrived too late. It was the end of an exceptionally close and fruitful friendship. For Josiah it was like the loss of his right arm; although he was to live another fifteen years, he never completely recovered from his grief. Bentley had been not only a friend and business partner but a critic and adviser, who stimulated his imagination and was a sounding board for his new ideas, not only on technique and design at the pottery but on the education of his children. He had certainly helped to shape the character of Josiah's beloved Sukey. Perhaps it was his voice we hear in one of her letters, thanking Josiah for his birthday greetings and hoping 'to make a return for it in my improvements as I know that is the best way & now is the only time for if I do not do it while I am young, I am sensible I never shall when I am old'. After a year with Bentley, she spent a holiday with the educational expert Richard Edgeworth, who wrote that Sukey possessed 'an extremely good solid understanding and is capable of anything we may please to teach her . . . her obliging behaviour and good disposition give much pleasure to himself and Mrs Edgeworth.'

As the years went by, Etruria Hall emptied. John left to study at the Unitarian Academy in Warrington, then took a course at Edinburgh University and finally travelled through France and Italy, making the Grand Tour in the style of the gentleman he expected to be. Jos and Tom also studied at Edinburgh University, later returning to help their father at the pottery.

Robert Darwin, too, was now away. At seventeen he went to study medicine at Edinburgh, afterwards in 1784 spending two terms at the famous medical college at Leyden in Holland, where he received his doctor's degree on 2 February 1785. His dissertation on 'Ocular Spectra' would later be published in the *Philosophical Transactions of the Royal Society*, earning him his fellowship. He also spent some months in Paris, where he was kindly received by his father's old friend Benjamin Franklin. By the summer of 1786 Robert was established as a doctor in Shrewsbury, where he rapidly became so successful that by the time he was twenty-two 'his income was £520, equivalent to about £40,000 today. Soon he was earning more than his father and in 1813 he received £3610 in fees.'

Sukey would certainly have watched with interest the progress of her neighbour and schoolfellow from a lonely, awkward little boy to the young man who returned from his continental studies, according to Anna Seward, 'grown to an uncommon height, gay and blooming as a morn of summer'. Anna was generally only too ready to swoon over handsome young men, but certainly he was six feet two in height and, in his father's opinion, had 'grown too thin'. That would not last. The successful Shrewsbury doctor rapidly became as stout as his father and was, his son Charles observed, 'the largest man whom I ever saw'. For her part, Sukey at this time was often in Derby, enjoying such social life as the little town offered, for there was little at the Potteries to amuse a young lady used to London life. When Erasmus Darwin and his new wife Elizabeth moved to Derby, Sukey was a frequent and welcome, though somewhat unwilling, guest at their home. 'Mrs Darwin is often very indifferent, seldom gets up till ten or 11 o'clock and sometimes goes to bed between eight or nine . . . as I am not used to these hours it would be very unpleasant to me, so I got myself excused in as genteel a manner as I was able.' Doubtless Robert Darwin came home for the town's great annual event – the visit of the judges to the Assizes – and saw his cousin at her brightest and best. Erasmus and Josiah watched their growing attachment, and hoped.

London had its season; for country towns, the Assizes provided the focus for balls and card parties, banquets and receptions, beginning with a ceremonial procession of dignitaries through the streets. 'You would not at any time expect either a studied or well digested letter from me,' Sukey wrote to her father, 'but more particularly now, when I tell you I am surrounded by gauze Ribbon &cc: which naturally lead young ladies to think of balls, dancing &cc – which are very flighty things & as uninteresting to you, as canals, & improvements upon the River Trent are to me.' Though we do not have Josiah's letters to her at this time, we can assume that he wrote in the same affectionate bantering tone as she did. Sukey now was taking the place of Bentley as her father's correspondent – and not only in frivolous vein. She could write intelligently to Josiah of the paintings of his old friend Joseph Wright of Derby. She managed to persuade Wright's guarding servant to let her in to see his latest works in his studio, and wrote about them with discernment to her father. She was also a guest at one of the meetings of the Derby Philosophical Society, founded by Dr Erasmus on the model of the Birmingham Lunar Society. (At this time, and for many years to come, scientists were called 'philosophers'.) 'The Philosophical Club goes on with great spirit, all the ingenious gentlemen in the town belong to it, they meet every Saturday night at each others houses. The last meeting was at Mr Streets. Miss S—s keep their brothers house, & consequently were obliged to make tea & preside at the supper table, they did not like this at all, but Doctor D. with his usual politeness made it very agreeable to them by shewing several entertaining experiments adapted to the capacities of young women, one was roasting a tube, which turned round itself.' Sukey might well feel superior; she had watched many such experiments with her brothers at Etruria Hall. She was an informed reporter on scientific affairs, describing the progress Erasmus Darwin was making with his pump for powering a windmill: 'he knows it is possible to raise water 30 feet high without a valve.' In another letter she explained why the pedometer she had sent to her father did not work. 'The little gold chain', she told him, 'ought to be part of the way out when the pedometer rests at the bottom of your pocket, and then every motion of your leg must make it tick.'

In these years, too, Sukey acted as her father's translator and secretary. 'Business is at a very low ebb,' she informed him in 1786, 'and your french clerk has very little to do, so that instead of having her salary increased as you mention she has only to petition it may not be taken away and she discarded.' She must have been well paid, for when, in 1794, he asked how her finances were, she replied, 'I am much obliged by your enquiries after my finances which are very good insomuch that I hope to be able to treat myself with a grand pianoforte as nothing else is now played upon & peoples ears are become so refined that I could not think of shocking them by the jarring sounds of a harpsichord.'

She was not afraid to report to Josiah the attacks made on him. In 1787 her London hostess Lady Clive complained that Josiah's 'religious principles cannot be right or you would not be acquainted with such a man as – as Dr Darwin – as for Her Ladyship, she would rather die than have his advice if there was not another physician in the world.' This was Sukey's gentle warning to her father of the growing political hysteria in London, a mood that could hold dangers for him. Josiah had always been a moderate Whig – or Liberal, as he would now be called – advocating peaceful change, favouring the reform of Parliament and supporting humanitarian causes. Now, in the disturbed last years of the century, he became more actively involved in politics. Both he and Erasmus were on the side of the American colonists in the War of Independence, and had long been friends and admirers of Benjamin Franklin – that 'evil genius', as King George III called him. Since 1788 Josiah had been prominent in Wilberforce's campaign for the abolition of the slave trade, which made him unpopular with those, like many of the businessmen of Liverpool, who were dependent on it for their wealth. His factory produced the cameo depicting, in the words of Erasmus:

> *The poor fetter'd slave on bended knee*
> *From Britain's sons imploring to be free.*

His support for the abolitionist campaign was taken up with enthusiasm by his children and grandchildren long after his death.

Most dangerous of all was Josiah's enthusiasm for the French Revolution, which earned him grave suspicion in governing circles. His open backing for his good friend Joseph Priestley, the scientist and Unitarian minister, now put him among the ranks of the dangerous radicals. In 1791 Priestley's house was ransacked and burned by a drunken mob because of his support for the celebration of the second anniversary of the fall of the Bastille. Having advised him to tone down the appeal which Priestley addressed to the government, Josiah now offered him a home; and neither he nor his eldest children, Jos and Sukey, hid their support for their friend. While staying with her brother John in London, Sukey saw Priestley and his wife just before they emigrated to America, and reported to her father that they were in good heart.

After the execution of the French king in February 1793 and the consequent war with France, Josiah and Erasmus and many of their friends were in danger of arrest, and worse; some, indeed, were transported to Botany Bay. Erasmus had become more radical and was a secret member of the Derby Society for Political Reformation, whose manifesto had been deemed a seditious libel by the government. The case came to court but Darwin escaped arrest, though he and Wedgwood were watched by some of the hundreds of government spies active at this time. In 1795 Erasmus wrote: 'I have a profess'd spy shoulders on the right, and another on the opposite side of the street, both attornies, and every name supposed to think differently from the minister is put in Mr Reeve's Doomsday book and if the French should land these recorded gentlemen are all to be imprison'd . . . Poor Wedgwood told me he heard his name stood high on the list.' But by this time 'poor Wedgwood' was beyond the reach of the King's spies.

———————

Emma may not have realized how much she had absorbed of Wedgwood attitudes and beliefs, but she certainly knew how much she owed to her Allen relations. From earliest childhood her aunts, especially the three youngest – Jessie, Emma and Fanny – lavished on their favourite niece an all-embracing love.

Emma's mother, Bessy Allen, was the eldest child of eleven, two boys – John, the heir, and Baugh – and nine girls. Brought up in a remote country house in Wales, Cresselly, near Tenby in Pembrokeshire, this remarkable family had a long, if not entirely uncontested, history. The Cresselly Allens were a branch of a line that claimed descent from the Cecils. Some asserted that the Allen family had come from Ireland in the fifteenth century; others that they came from Cornwall 'long before the Conquest', with the motto 'I scorn envie'. Certainly the ancestor of John Allen of Goodhooke,

Emma's great-grandfather, was said to have been of 'the first gentry that did join Henry VII, and venture his throat to put the crown on the right head'. In recompense Henry VII gave to his family 'ye place of constable of the Castle of Haverford West in Pembrokeshire'. John Allen himself first acquired the Cresselly estate through marriage to Joan Bartlett, the sole heiress of a yeoman family. She brought with her a comparatively simple house near Cresselly quay and a headland beneath which ran rich seams of anthracite. Their collier boats sailed laden from the quay – and the black gold made a handsome fortune.

John Allen of Goodhooke was remembered as a 'truly honest, sincere and religious man, affectionate and kind'. Like old Josiah Wedgwood, he was unassuming, always remaining close to his works; like him, his energy and attention to detail brought him wealth; like him, he was a straightforward practical man. However, in the complicated social rating of the day, he was 'gentry' and ranked higher than Josiah, who was always stamped as a man of trade or business. With his wife Joan, John Allen lived, as he wrote, 'till her death, Sunday ye 16th 1728/9 without one minute's penitence . . . she was sweet and beautiful, but above all a most prudent discreete sensible virtuous religious and good woman'. Was it from Joan Allen that Bessy Allen inherited her charm? Certainly this might well have been her epitaph too.

John and Joan had eleven children, of whom two concern us: John, the heir, Emma's grandfather, and his youngest brother, Roger, whose family was to play a minor role in Emma's upbringing. The eldest daughter, Margaret (Peggy), also deserves some notice as one of the many examples in Emma's family of the role senior daughters often played. Bessy herself, and Caroline Darwin, and Elizabeth Wedgwood, all took on great responsibility for the education and upbringing of their families, when death or illness removed the mother. Bessy remembered her Aunt Margaret as a formidable lady. John Allen relied on her a great deal after Joan's death. He sent her on a long journey from Wales to King's Lynn and London, and back through Bath, Bristol and across the Severn to Cresselly. She rode part of the way on horseback, part by post chaise, guided every step of the way by her father's instructions. He told her what clothes to buy, to leave good turn-up 'to last seven years', how to behave to relations and how to reward servants. At the end of his life, when he was travelling to Lewes in search of a cure, it was to 'my dear Peggy' that he wrote concerning his business affairs.

John Bartlett Allen, the heir, was trained for a higher calling, sent to Westminster School in London while for four years Peggy, it would seem, minded the colliery and the business. After school John Bartlett Allen joined the army, spent a year in Germany and fought in the Seven Years War. He has gone down in family history as a bullying disciplinarian – but his father had loved him dearly and was broken-hearted when his 'dear dear John' left home. After his father's death, John retired from the army as a captain on half pay. Like his father, he married an heiress: Elizabeth Hensleigh, the only daughter of John Hensleigh of Panteague, a successful attorney and burgess of Carmarthen. Like his father, he was to have eleven children, of whom the first three – Elizabeth (Bessy, 1764–1846), Catherine (Kitty, 1765–1830) and Caroline (1768–1835) – were born at their mother's family home, Panteague. Their Aunt Peggy remained at Cresselly Quay, presumably to take care of the business, until her marriage to Abraham Leach. Captain Allen was now a man of considerable wealth and wanted a dwelling to reflect his position. He built himself a handsome house

> on a very elevated spot, and though in the midst of a colliery, yet is so judicially skreened by plantations from the sight of those dingy volcanoes . . . that the front in which are the principal sitting rooms takes in nothing that can remind you of them, but looks down Cresswell River . . . a prospect, even when the tide is out, is not disagreeable . . . but when full in exhibiting a scene remarkably pleasing and lively from the small craft . . .
>
> Within the mansion you find a most desirable change of apartments and every accommodation that the most polished hospitality can supply, nor are there wanting in those pleasure grounds, good gardens, hot houses, or any of the fashionable appendages of modern society.

Cresselly was, and is, a plain, solid, grey stone house, undistinguished outside, but with surprisingly elegant, well-proportioned rooms. The delicate plasterwork of the baroque drawing-room ceiling suggests John Nash – who, as it happens, was working in Tenby at this time. Certainly he knew the Allens; many years later, in June 1816, Bessy's sister Kitty Allen wrote to him reminding him of their 'old acquaintance' in Tenby. The library, hung with paintings and well stocked with books, was warm and comfortable. The Captain was now established as a country gentleman; and here at Cresselly he and Elizabeth raised their two sons and nine daughters. After the three girls came John (1769–1843), then Louisa Jane (Jenny, 1771–1836), Baugh (1774–1845), Harriet (1776–1847), Jessie (1777–1853), Octavia (1776–1800), Emma (1780–1866) and Frances (Fanny, 1781–1873). Bessy's exceptional charm was universally acknowledged; Kitty, dark-eyed and serious, had something of her father's moodiness; Jenny was the beauty of the family; little Harriet the shy one; Jessie lively, warm and affectionate; Octavia sadly died young; 'good little Emma' was the only plain girl; Fanny had the sharpest mind of all the sisters.

The sons, John and Baugh, were sent to Westminster, their father's old school, and were later trained as barristers. Baugh, who grew up a jolly man and a passionate sailor, eventually became Master of Dulwich College, thanks to an eccentric legacy from its founder, the Elizabethan actor Edward Alleyn, insisting that its high master must always be an Allen. Bessy and her sisters were educated most probably at home, or possibly in a dame school in the village. Certainly someone taught them well, for they all wrote vividly and fluently and were obviously well read; perhaps it is Bessy herself who can take some of the credit for her cultured and articulate sisters. But there were other influences at work too. The girls may have inherited their good looks from their father, whose portrait by Sir Thomas Lawrence shows him as handsome, but their charm certainly did not come from him. His daughters remembered him to the end of their days with sharp fear. According to Emma Darwin's daughter Etty, 'he had a peculiarly odious disposition – jealous, ill-tempered and narrow.' He ruled the family with rough military discipline, demanding intelligent conversation and, if he did not get it, roaring and thumping the table. So, the family said, 'the brilliant conversation for which they were reputed' was ascribed to 'paternal castigations administered when they failed to shine in company'.

The Captain's wife, Elizabeth Hensleigh Allen, Emma's grandmother, died in 1790, aged fifty-two. As so often happens in history, the mother of this remarkable family disappears into the mists and is rarely mentioned in the extensive family correspondence. This may possibly be because great grief had kept them dumb. Charles Darwin's mother disappeared in the same way. Yet Bessy was twenty-six when her mother died and must have known her well, while even Fanny, the youngest, was nine and could not have completely forgotten her mother's death. Captain Allen did refer to 'my dear Elizabeth' when he left a bequest to her 'woman' in his will. Did Elizabeth have a hand in the design of the new house and the pretty ceiling in the drawing room? We do not know. Her story is a blank. Only once is her voice heard: her second daughter, Kitty, refused to marry on a Monday because her mother had told her it was bad luck; her own wedding, she said, had been on a Monday. Maybe it was not only the table that had been thumped.

After Elizabeth's death it was Bessy who ran the household and brought up her seven young sisters and was adored by them until the day she died. The historian James Mackintosh, a man of discrimination, wrote to her sister Kitty, who became his wife, that he 'sometimes suspected that you had all exaggerated the excellencies of your eldest sister . . . but I now adopt your worship . . . I never saw any other person whose acts of civility or friendship were so constantly refreshed from the well head of kindness.' Bessy's demanding role as eldest daughter was made more difficult by her father's shattering decision to marry again only two years after Elizabeth's death. The daughter of a coal miner, 'that woman' was heartily disliked by the family, who insisted that their father promise never to bring her to Cresselly. For once the domineering Captain agreed and, to his credit, built for his new wife a charming cottage on his land at Cresselly Quay. The couple had three daughters: two died young and, after their mother's early death, the third was brought to Cresselly where she was well cared for and much loved by her father. He was heartbroken when she too died young. From now on he became increasingly bitter, crippled by gout and an old wound; though in his favour it must be said that he showed great concern for his daughter Kitty's health when she was expecting her babies. Kitty Mackintosh was the child most like him, and he seems to have had a special affection for her. He left her a bequest of £800 – a considerable sum in those days.

In spite of their father's moods and marriage, however, the young Allens were a happy family, close and exceptionally affectionate; they would remember the beauty of the Welsh countryside all their lives. For Bessy there would never be a beach to compare with the great golden sweep of Tenby's shore, or a scene to rival the magic of the long line of Caldey Island over a phosphorescent sea. Scarborough, she later wrote, was very inferior. The balls she later attended there and at York were dull and funereal compared with those merry assemblies at Haverfordwest when they danced four nights in succession. They had so few amusements, as Fanny remembered, that they relished them all the more: Fanny's own passion was for the horse races on Tenby beach, and Jessie would never forget Penally and Tenby – her 'paradiso'.

In 1792, the Allen family began to disperse. Bessy, their 'sunshine', was the first to leave – as the wife of Jos Wedgwood. In August of that year he took his sister, Sukey, on a journey through Wales to Tenby. The French Revolution had discouraged travellers from making the European Grand Tour, and many were choosing instead to discover the beauty of Wales and Scotland. Visitors to Pembrokeshire could take the voyage by paddle steamer from Bristol to Tenby – in rough weather it could take fifteen hours – or go by ferry across the Wye to Chepstow and into Wales by coach. Or they could travel over appalling Welsh roads on the inland route. It was probably Sukey who, having always enjoyed the fun at the Derby Assizes, persuaded Jos to take her on a tour of Wales which was to include a visit to the festivities at Haverfordwest when the judges came on circuit. For Jos, the trip was a well-earned break from a period of great stress. Since leaving Edinburgh University he had – albeit latterly with the assistance of Josiah's nephew Tom Byerley – been his father's right hand at the pottery. John, the elder brother, had been sent on the Grand Tour and had become too much of a fine gentleman to see his future as a potter at Etruria; Tom, the younger, had developed a mysterious illness. Now old Josiah himself was under pressure and his health was failing; increasingly, responsibility for the works fell to Jos, at a time when the war with France was strangling trade and threatening to ruin the pottery.

Ironically, the decline in Josiah's health can be attributed in part to one of his greatest successes. In the spring of 1790 Josiah put in place the last and brightest jewel in his potter's crown – his copy of the Portland Vase.

Otherwise known as the Barberini Vase, this urn, said to contain the ashes of the Roman Emperor Alexander Severus and his mother Mammaea, had been excavated some time between 1623 and 1644 on the orders of Pope Urban VIII (Maffeo Barberini). Severus was murdered in AD 235 and his ashes were probably taken to Rome and there placed in the urn, which may already have been two or three hundred years old. Made of glass of a 'rich transparent dark amethystine colour' and decorated with figures carved on a layer of white glass fused to the darker glass when it was white hot, the urn had been somewhat damaged and repaired but was still a miracle of craftsmanship. Bought by Josiah's friend Sir William Hamilton, it was brought to England and sold to the Dowager Duchess of Portland, who kept it concealed in her museum. After her death on 17 July 1785, Hamilton's son bought it at the sale by auction for £1,029, having refused Wedgwood's offer. However, he agreed to lend it to Josiah to copy. 'After full and repeated examinations of the original work,' Josiah wrote to Hamilton, 'my crest is much fallen.' This 'exquisite vase' would be difficult to copy. He proposed modelling it in pottery 'much harder than glass . . . nearly as hard as agate'. He would reproduce the colour, but the engraving of the white figures demanded a highly skilled and expensive artist. Hamilton gave him advice, but the work was slow and difficult. Throughout Josiah was helped by his sons, Jos and Tom, both now qualified potters. Finally, in October 1787, he sent a good copy to Erasmus Darwin, who celebrated it and Josiah's other works in his florid 'Loves of the Plants'.

> Whether, o Friend of Art! the gem you mould
> Rich with new taste, with ancient virtue bold
> Form the poor fettered slave on bended knee,
> From Britain's sons imploring to be free
> . . . or bid mortality rejoice and mourn
> O'er the fine forms on Portland's mystic urn.

In a later poem, 'The Botanic Garden', Darwin further enthused:

> Whether, O Friend of Art! your gems derive
> Fine forms from Greece, and fabled Gods revive

> . . . Buoyant shall sail, with fame's historic page
> Each fair medallion, O'er the wrecks of age;
> Nor time shall mar, nor steel, nor fire, nor rust
> Touch the hard polish of the immortal bust.

It is a pity to record that work achieved with such craftsmanship and patience should in the future be dismissed as 'dead clay' by his grandson, Charles Darwin.

Though Josiah, like Erasmus, was ecstatic with delight at the results of his labours, the work had made him ill; 'age and infirmities overtake me', he wrote to Darwin. Consequently, it was to Jos that he turned when he wanted to promote sales of copies of the vase, now universally admired, in Europe. So, instead of making the Grand Tour as a gentleman, in June 1791 Jos travelled Europe as a salesman.

Throughout the continent at this time there were rigid social distinctions which separated gentlemen from 'men of business'. As one of the latter Jos distinguished himself in Holland, Berlin and Frankfurt, earning congratulations from the British Ambassador at The Hague, Lord Auckland, and the Royal Family, to whom he had been presented. 'Your son', wrote Auckland to old Josiah, 'is a very fine young man, with every appearance of having profitted [*sic*] fully by the excellent education you have given him and I have no doubt he will prove a source of great happiness and credit to you.' Yet for all this praise, Jos never forgot the class distinction which separated him from his brother.

To this serious, socially sensitive young man from the grimy Potteries, the family at Cresselly were doubly attractive – for they were undoubtedly 'gentry'. In the clear, bright Welsh air, among congenial company, Jos relaxed. Tenby at this time was still as Defoe had seen it, 'the most agreeable little town in England – considered another Naples'. It was romantically foreign: peasants in tall hats and red cloaks, buying and selling in Tenby market, chattered in their lilting language. John and Baugh Allen may have met Jos during schooldays in London; John and Jos were exactly of an age. Now Jos had the chance to meet their nine enchanting sisters and was dazzled, especially by the beautiful Bessy. Sukey Wedgwood, for her part, enchanted the old curmudgeon Captain Allen; later, he would remember that her sister Sarah was almost as charming. The Wedgwoods were not only delightful guests, they were very wealthy, and as such were welcome suitors.

'I have not been at Cresselly since,' Jos wrote to his father after his first visit to the Allens, 'but as I left them all very well I hope to find them so tomorrow. The family at Cresselly is altogether the most charming one I have ever been introduced to, and their society makes no small addition to the pleasure I have received from this excursion. I am very happy to perceive that their spirits are not much affected by their father's marriage. Our pleasures here are very simple, riding, walking, bathing, with a little dance twice a week.' Did Jos join the gentlemen bathing in the nude on Tenby's beautiful beach? It is difficult to imagine; but the enterprising Allen girls would have braved the cold sea, screened by the bath huts under the direction of Tenby's famous bathing women.

Jos was so enjoying himself that he hoped his father 'would have no objection to me staying a while longer as much on my sister's account as my own, for I am afraid she has little chance of bringing Miss Allen back with her'. This was the beginning of a lifelong friendship between the Wedgwoods and the Allen sisters, who for generations to come would be united in love and marriage. For Jos, it was the beginning of a love affair that lasted all his life: in December 1792 Jos and Bessy were married at Cresselly.

Old Josiah gave them Little Etruria, the house next to Etruria Hall that had been so carefully built for his partner, Bentley. His wife Sally, who did not usually show her feelings, gave her 'dear Bessy' a gold watch and welcomed visits from her new daughter-in-law through the 'little green gate' as Bessy always remembered. It was a deeply happy marriage, though Bessy always stood a little in awe of her grave and serious husband. Like his mother, Jos rarely revealed his emotions, but after the wedding he wrote a sincere, if somewhat stilted, love letter to his bride. Like his father, Jos had been impressed by Rousseau's theories on education, but he would have no truck with his belief in 'universal concubinage'. 'Who', he wrote, 'that has left . . . the tranquil but penetrating calm of an intimate and long continued union . . ., who would truck it for the wandering gratifications of ferocious contests of brutes . . . I am and will be your affectionate husband and we are and will be tender parents to our dear children. I have no pleasures that I can compare with those I derive from you and from them. Your idea fills me and I clasp you as the heroes of poetry clasp the shades of the departed.' Coming from Jos, these are strong words indeed, for whenever he was deeply moved he turned to classical imagery, and to the idealized Etruscan landscape of his father's pottery. It was a promise faithfully kept to the end of their lives.

Bessy's escape from the Captain's household encouraged her other sisters to take the marriage road to freedom. In 1793 Caroline married Edward Drewe, a Devonshire parson. He died in 1810 and three of their children also died young. Nevertheless, in later years Bessy could still describe her as 'so delightfully fresh in her hilarity and she is so willing and able to contribute her share to enrich society, that I think her very nearly the most agreeable woman I know'. Bessy and Emma were to visit her frequently at her houses in Roehampton and Edinburgh. Her daughters, Harriet and Georgina, became Lady Gifford and Lady Alderson, and Georgina's daughter was to marry the Marquess of Salisbury, Victoria's Prime Minister. They were to introduce Emma to the unaccustomed delights of high society. Also in 1793 Harriet, desperate to leave her bullying father, married Matthew Surtees, a clergyman of a 'peculiarly odious disposition'. It was an unfortunate choice: jealous, ill-tempered and narrow, he kept her as a slave all her life.

In 1794 Jos's elder brother John captured Bessy's sister Jenny Allen, the beauty of the family, whose charm is caught in Lawrence's portrait of her. 'With Jenny', so Bessy wrote, 'the sun always shines, and she seems to trip rather than slide down the hill of life'. Her 'incomparable cheerfulness' stood her in good stead, for there were to be more downs than ups on Jenny's hill of life; but she began her marriage comfortably enough as the wife of a wealthy banker whom Josiah had set up in a house in Devonshire Place in the fashionable heart of London.

For Josiah and Sally, the pleasure of seeing their two elder sons married and their first three grandchildren born were welcome distractions from anxiety and ill-health. Sally was crippled with arthritis; Josiah had pains in his 'no leg' and his sight was failing. His old friend Erasmus Darwin could offer no help: 'You know how unwilling we all are to grow old. I advise you to leave off the bark and take no medicine at present.' In the autumn of 1794 they travelled to Blackpool and Buxton in search of health, but by December it was obvious that a swelling in Josiah's jaw which he thought was toothache was cancer. Erasmus rushed over from Derby but could do nothing except provide large doses of laudanum. Strong and patient as always, Josiah bore the end with courage, as he had endured so long ago when his leg was amputated. Sally and her daughters nursed him with devoted care, and so that they might not be disturbed by his passing, he bade goodnight to Sally and Sukey and told them not to disturb him. Erasmus had left him a generous supply of laudanum, and, locking his bedroom door, he took his last dose. In the morning the carpenter, Greaves, unable to wake him, climbed up to his window and found him dead in bed.

At the end of his life, the great potter might well have reflected that men and women were more difficult to mould than clay. He had clearly seen the problem many years before, and had accepted that none of his sons would have his passion for his pottery, and that their education would fit them for lives different from his. Yet though his sons did not turn out as he hoped, both they and his daughters were a credit to their upbringing.

Josiah had set a pattern not only of dedication to his work, but also of idealism and high moral standards.

In politics a middle-of-the-road Whig, disliking the disturbing clamour of the Radicals, he was a humanitarian and an idealist. A champion of liberty, he was a supporter of the early stages of the French Revolution but, like many Whigs, became disillusioned with its later course. He would have made a good MP: during the negotiations for the Trent–Mersey Canal he was an excellent committee member, treating opposition with good humour and skilfully guiding the argument to the conclusion he wanted. He is remembered as a great craftsman, patient and dogged in the pursuit of excellence, technically skilled, an innovator; far-seeing and imaginative, he did much to awaken and the revival of interest in the glories of ancient Greece and Rome. Enjoying fame when it arrived, he appreciated it less for its own sake than for the recognition of his craftsmanship that it betokened.

His children and grandchildren, including Emma, would carry on his fight for humanitarian causes, in particular for the abolition of slavery; they all inherited the Unitarian beliefs, traditions and attitudes that would sustain Emma through the most difficult periods of her life. Jos, so admired by the Allen sisters for his moral probity, took up the campaign for parliamentary reform. If Jos became 'the wisest man' his relations had ever known, much was due to the Wedgwood inheritance. Josiah's love of wife and family, and their affection for one another, likewise set a pattern and standard for his descendants. Few great men of the period played with their children as Josiah had done. Like him, his grandson Charles Darwin would also be 'called to the dance' of the young. Again and again in the coming years, his voice, his easy charm and humour can be heard in the letters of his descendant. Charles Darwin believed that his passion for collecting must have been innate, since his siblings did not have it; though he did not know it, Josiah had taken the same delight in his own collection and careful arrangement of shells.

Though his career was tragically cut short, Tom did become, in the words of Humphry Davy, 'the father of photography', and he and Jos used their inherited wealth wisely, subsidizing poets, artists and scientists. Even John, who was so hopeless with money, made his contribution to history by founding the Royal Horticultural Society, passing on Josiah's love of gardening to his nephews and nieces, sowing seeds that would bloom in the gardens of Maer and Down. Educated far beyond the usual standard of women's education, Josiah's clear-minded daughters, Sarah and Kitty, as Bessy once said, proved that a woman could administer a great fortune as ably as a man. As for Sukey, she was a credit to the belief in women's ability that Josiah and Bentley had espoused so long before. He would have been delighted by her marriage to his old friend's son, Robert Darwin: he had equipped her to be a more than competent wife for a distinguished doctor. It is probably Sukey who encouraged Charles to look carefully at flowers. One of his few early memories was of his mother showing him the stamens of a flower. Through her Charles would inherit some of the qualities of old Josiah, his affectionate nature and love of his children, his generosity and tolerance and above all his persistence in pursuing, with infinite patience, his own original ideas.

CHAPTER TWO

The Second Generation

JOSIAH WEDGWOOD DIED ON 3 JANUARY 1795, SUKEY'S BIRTHDAY. SHE WAS desolate: throughout the last years of his life, she had written to him with easy affection when she was away, shared his delight in flowers, accompanied him as he pottered in his greenhouse, advised him on the floral decoration of his vases and acted as his secretary, his 'French clerk'. In his last illness he had helped her mother nurse him with skill and devotion as Erasmus saw. He welcomed her marriage to Robert in April 1796. She was 'a lady with distinct understanding and an excellent heart'. They built a house in Shrewsbury where Sukey helped to plan lovely gardens.

At least the grieving family was free from financial anxiety, for even though he had given substantial sums to his children during his lifetime, Josiah Wedgwood left a vast fortune. Sally was left Etruria Hall, part of the land and all her husband's personal papers and household goods; in addition, £10,000 was entrusted to the executors for her benefit. Jos inherited the Wedgwood factory and all the models and equipment. John and Tom received £30,000 and £29,100 respectively, and in addition Tom was left shares in the Monmouth Canal. Each of the three daughters received £25,000. While his father lived, Jos could never admit how much he disliked his work at the pottery, and none of Josiah's sons wished to remain in sight of the source of their wealth. Now, in modern terms millionaires, they could look further afield for new estates where they could live like the country gentlemen they wanted to be.

Finally, in the autumn of 1799, Jos bought Gunville House at Tarrant

Gunville, five miles from Blandford in Hampshire, where Charlotte, Harry, Frank, Hensleigh and Fanny were born. His cousin, Tom Byerley, was left to manage the pottery at Etruria, which Jos hoped to oversee by visiting for three months a year. A year later Tom Wedgwood bought the neighbouring Eastbury House, the remaining wing of a magnificent mansion built by Vanbrugh and now demolished. Here he settled with his mother, Sally, and his sisters Sarah and Kitty. In later years Elizabeth would remember Uncle Tom's frequent visits to their nursery while he was working out his theories on education. Tom was not insane at this time, Elizabeth later told Emma – only very 'restless'. Restless he certainly was, but also increasingly neurotic and suicidal. In February 1800 he sailed for the West Indies. Here he moved from Martinique to Nevis; but, as he wrote to Jos, in spite of the exquisite beauty of the scenery, and 'birds singing on all sides of me – oranges by thousands', he was 'plagued by headaches and indigestion and crippled and cramped in every energy of mind and body'. He was homesick. His letters arrived on 4 June, but by 24 June he was back in England on his way to his brother John's home at Cote House, near Bristol – then back to Jos at Gunville and finally for some months to London, where he worked on his theory of 'Time, Space and Motion', giving James Mackintosh a grant to write it up for him. He was not merely 'restless' at this time; he was also seriously addicted to opium, a condition that was made worse by his friendship with Coleridge in the winter of 1802.

For the next five years Jos and Bessy made Gunville the Wedgwood family headquarters. Jos was now what he had always wanted to be, a country squire, and did his best to establish himself as a gentleman, planting hundreds of trees, farming, hunting and shooting. He continued to leave the running of the pottery in Tom Byerley's hands, hoping that by making regular visits to Etruria he could keep control of the business from Dorset. He seemed to be fulfilling his ambition when in 1803 he was made Sheriff of Dorset, and, as his friend Tom Poole said, travelled 'en prince' in a handsome coach-and-four with outriders in scarlet uniforms – much to the delight of Bessy, who revelled in the travel she had been denied in Wales. But Jos was never totally accepted by the old country families. He was always Mr Wedgwood, the potter's son. As his brother-in-law James Mackintosh once said, 'A Wedgwood living out of Staffordshire must lose something of his proper importance.' For a man of liberal principles Jos was surprisingly rank-conscious. When Tom Poole, a good friend and a man of outstanding intelligence, asked if he could hope to marry Jos's sister, Kitty, he was abruptly rejected. Cultured though he was, Poole was a farmer with a rough Devon accent and, as he himself quietly accepted, of 'the middle rank' of their class, whereas Jos was at the top. When before his marriage his father had wanted him to take over the showroom in London, Jos agreed unwillingly to do so, but only temporarily. 'I have always been accustomed', he wrote, 'to consider myself as good as the next man.' The arrogance of the aristocratic customers offended him. Jos could never quite accept that although he was as good as the next man, the next man was not necessarily as good as him. Something of this attitude was to be inherited by Emma.

Josiah's eldest son John was as keen to leave London as Tom and Jos were to leave the Midlands, and invested his inheritance in Cote House, a magnificent mansion near Bristol. He did not regret Josiah's decision to leave Etruria, the village and the estate to Jos; John had never liked the grimy pottery and since his Grand Tour of Europe had developed a taste for gracious living. Unfortunately, neither he nor Jenny was good with money. Perhaps it was to give him an understanding of finance that old Josiah had set him up as a partner in the London bank Davison & Co.; if so, there was some irony in the fact that in 1816, caught up in the banking crisis of that year and the failure of Davison's, John would be saved from bankruptcy only by the financial support of his family and Dr Robert Darwin. From then onwards, recognizing his elder brother's financial incompetence, Jos took over the management of his inheritance. In the end, Cote House was sold, and John and Jenny moved to a small house lent by neighbours in Staffordshire at a peppercorn rent. But wherever they went, as Emma remembered, 'Aunt Jenny's warmth and gracious welcome was something quite unique in charm.' Emma grew up with their children, and enduring relationships among the cousins were established: John and Jenny's daughter Eliza often helped take care of Jos and Bessy in their old age, and when Emma married Charles Darwin it was their son, the Revd Allen Wedgwood, who officiated.

John inherited another legacy that would give him more lasting pleasure than money: a passion for horticulture that gave him an opportunity to make his mark in an area dear to his heart. Old Josiah and Sally had transformed the bare fields of the Etruria site, imported rare shrubs from a London nursery and created a lake, gardens and lawns; and they had transmitted their love of gardening to their children, who even when young discussed pruning and planting in their letters, and all their lives exchanged advice and cuttings from their gardens. At Cote House, John built extensive glasshouses where he grew grapes, peaches and pineapples. Becoming aware that it was difficult to find information on the practice of horticulture, on 29 June 1801 he wrote from Etruria to William Forsyth, gardener to King George III, suggesting the 'formation of a Horticultural Society' and sending him a plan for how this might be achieved. As John pointed out, there was a society for the encouragement of the arts and another for agriculture, but none for horticulture. His aim was 'to collect every information respecting the culture and treatment of all plants and trees as well culinary as ornamental'. His father and mother would have approved the linking of the useful with the beautiful, a connection central to all that Josiah had done at the pottery. Forsyth passed the letter to Sir Joseph Banks, president of the Royal Society, who wholeheartedly approved the scheme. Eventually, on 7 March 1804 the inaugural meeting of the Royal Horticultural Society took place at Mr Hatchard's, the bookseller's house in Piccadilly, with thirty-eight-year-old John in the chair. Thereafter, for some years he took an active role in the work of the Society. Today his portrait hangs in their headquarters, and his *Garden Book* is one of the treasures of the Society's Lindley Library.

John's younger sisters, Kitty and Susan, managed their inheritance more ably than their brother did his, having profited by the lessons in accounting at the Etruscan school. Kitty in particular had a brilliantly clear mind and, Dr Robert thought, a more independent judgement than any woman he had ever met. Both she and Susan gave large sums to charities, to poor hill farmers in Wales, and to animal welfare and temperance societies. Above all, both supported with energy and money the campaign for the abolition of slavery, and, like all the Wedgwoods, considered their inheritance a trust to be used for the good of humanity.

Tom and Jos, too, may have set themselves up in handsome estates, but they also gave generously, not only to charities but also through a trust fund they established to finance worthy causes and people. By this means they donated large sums for medical research like that conducted at Dr Beddoe's Institute in Bristol, where experiments in the inhalation of gases were conducted and early discoveries made in anaesthesia; they also funded poets like Wordsworth, artists like Wright of Derby, scientists like Joseph Priestley. Perhaps their most famous grant was to the poet Samuel Taylor Coleridge, who in 1798 was considering accepting a post as a Unitarian minister in Shrewsbury. Persuaded by their friends that this would be a tragic waste of a great genius, Tom and Jos offered him a grant of £150 a year. Jos explained their proposal in a typically stilted letter of 10 January 1798:

> My brother and myself are possessed of a considerable super-fluity of fortune; squandering and hoarding are equally distant from our inclinations. But we are earnestly desirous to convert this superfluity into a fund of beneficence, and we have now been accustomed for some time, to regard ourselves rather as Trustees than Proprietors. We have canvassed your past life, your present situation and prospects, your character and abilities. As far as certainty is compatible with delicacy of the estimate, we have no hesitation in declaring that your claim upon the fund appears to come under more of the conditions we have pre-scribed for its disposal, and to be every way more unobjectionable, than we could possibly have expected.
>
> . . .
>
> After what my brother Thomas has written, I have only to state the proposal we wish to make to you. It is that you shall accept an annuity for life of £150, to be regularly paid by us, no condition whatsoever being annexed to it. Thus your liberty will remain entire, you will be under the influence of no professional bias, and will be in possession of a '*permanent income not inconsistent with your religious and political creeds*', so necessary to your health and activity.

Coleridge accepted with some astonishment and used the grant to finance his tour through Germany with Wordsworth. He became a close friend of Tom, sharing his obsession with ill-health and encouraging his use of the opium that ruined him.

The poet had been brought to the attention of Tom and Jos by James Mackintosh, at this time a brilliant writer and lecturer and an eloquent barrister with a growing reputation in Whig circles in Westminster. He was probably introduced at Cote House by Bessy's brother, John Allen, a fellow barrister and Whig, who followed Mackintosh's career with great admiration. An affectionate and caring brother, John Allen was delighted when his hero fell in love with his sister Kitty, who at thirty-five had seemed doomed to spinsterhood. Dark-haired and handsome, Kitty was the most serious and intellectual of the family: she also seems to have inherited something of her father's moodiness. Mackintosh at this time was also thirty-five, a widower with three children. The son of an army captain who, like Captain Allen, had fought in the Seven Years War, he was brought up by a doting mother and aunts and was always to be comfortable in the company of older women. An infant prodigy, he was brilliant at his boarding school and at fifteen entered Aberdeen University. Here he was 'distinguished for his general courtesy and easy flow of elocution and the width and depth of his learning'. He founded a discussion group, the predecessor of the famous King of Clubs that he would later establish in London. At Edinburgh University he was remembered for the paper he delivered to the Royal Physical Society as a twenty-year-old medical student proving 'the existence in brutes of memory, imagination and reason'. Although he graduated as a doctor in 1787 and began practising in London, his real interest was in the debating societies of the capital. When his father died in 1788, he inherited a small family estate and married Catherine Stuart. More interested in politics than medicine, he and his wife travelled to Brussels, acquiring 'an uncommon facility in French'; on his return he wrote newspaper articles on international affairs. He now left medicine to become a barrister and was called to the Bar in 1795.

At first he had welcomed revolutions in America and France, but later rapidly became distinguished as a moderate progressive, noted for his balance and tolerance. At the outbreak of the French Revolution he was inspired to reply to Edmund Burke's condemnation in an article defending the French, which impressed the leading Whigs; as one said, 'He is argumentative without sophistry and sublime without extravagance.' Praised by Fox, he nevertheless earned the respect of his opponent, Burke, and visited the old man in his retirement.

In April 1797 Mackintosh's first wife died, leaving him with three children; Mary, his eldest daughter, was to become part of Emma's story under her married name, Mary Rich. Still deeply distressed at the loss of a wife who had shared his poverty and encouraged his career, he was nevertheless impressed by the quiet, serious Kitty Allen, who had seemed to him so wasted in the wilds of Wales when they first met at a country house party near Abergavenny. Kitty, for her part, thought Sir James the cleverest man she had ever known. They met again in Bath, where they declared their love; and again in 1797 at Cote House, where, in the ease and comfort of her sister's home, Kitty blossomed. They were married on 10 April 1798.

Captain John was at first nervous of his brilliant son-in-law. But Mackintosh was not only a dazzling talker; he could listen, and had a particular gift for drawing out the most difficult people. He quickly established common ground. Like Captain John, his father had fought in the Seven Years War and had also been wounded in action. Then, as a historian he must have been fascinated to hear about the recent French invasion of Wales. No doubt he also heard all about the scandal of the marriage of the Captain's niece, his brother Roger's daughter, to a M. Collos, a French prisoner of war who on his return to France had become a fishmonger in Paris. Mme Collos will appear again in Emma's life.

It was as well that Josiah did not live to see the tragic end of the one genius among his children. Tom was twenty-four when his father died and had been causing concern for some years. The nine-year-old who had shown such promise that he was sent with his older brothers to the Revd Holland's school at Bolton, and afterwards joined them at their lessons at the Etruscan school. A gifted chemistry student, he received special tuition from their distinguished tutor, Alexander Chisholm. Although only fifteen he was sent to Edinburgh University with Jos before taking up work at the pottery. As both a trained potter and a brilliant chemist, he joined Josiah in his experiments in the glazing and decoration of pottery – but in the laboratory in the basement of Etruria Hall he worked himself into a nervous collapse, with blinding headaches so severe that he rolled on the ground screaming in agony. Erasmus Darwin and other doctors diagnosed various causes: semi-paralysis of the colon, chronic dysentery, even worms. Coleridge, who became a close friend, later described his complaint as 'suppressed gout'. For five years from 1787 to 1792 he battled against pain, easing it with ever-increasing doses of opium and other drugs. In April 1792, however, a complete nervous breakdown forced him to give up his experimental work on his 'sun pictures' – early efforts at photography – and also to retire from his partnership in the pottery. Later, during a brief remission of his illness, he continued his research in London with his friend Humphry Davy, who, in a lecture to the Royal Society, referred to the discoveries of Thomas Wedgwood, 'the first photographer'. Tom had indeed discovered the process which led to photography, though he never found the way to fix his 'sun pictures'. Now he became passionately interested in the theory of education, studying in their nursery the development of Bessy's older children. Emma's elder sister Elizabeth would remember Uncle Tom and his visits to their nursery with great affection, though Bessy, who loved him dearly, would often find her patience sorely tried.

The rest of his short life was spent in a desperate search for health. It seems likely that at least part of Tom's problem was his sexual orientation, at a time when homosexuality was the crime that 'dare not speak its name'. More than one doctor – including Erasmus Darwin – suggested he should take a wife, but he had little interest in women; the only one he spoke of with enthusiasm was Mme de Staël. Sensitive, he found it difficult to make male or female friends, retreating to the arms of his mother and sisters and most of all to his brother Jos, on whom he was increasingly emotionally dependent. Dr Baillie, who as he wrote on 3 April 1802 'had seen Tom three times', noted that 'he has a disrelish for the common amusements of society and takes little interest in his earlier pursuits; his attention almost entirely absorbed in watching his health'. He noted that 'his bowels were torpid,' his food 'doesn't nourish the body' and 'he has in some measure lost the usual propensity towards the other sex.' His colon was 'contracted – possibly thickened – enlarged glands near the colon'. He diagnosed 'Hypochondriasis', which he worried was apt to last long. He recommended that Tom should amuse his mind with foreign travel, and prevent his bowels from becoming costive. This judgement is of particular interest since, as will be seen, his nephew Charles Darwin's obscure medical condition bears some similarity – except that Charles never lost the 'usual propensity'. A year later, Dr Baillie recommended that Tom be examined by 'various anatomists', but still no one could identify the cause of his illness. In the last years of his life he became increasingly addicted to opium, and was fatally encouraged in its use by Coleridge.

It may not have been Coleridge who introduced Tom to opium. His father's friend Dr Erasmus Darwin may well have been to blame, since he frequently prescribed heavy doses of the drug to his patients; if so, it was a tragic irony that the doctor who would have wished to save him should have prescribed the poison that would kill him. Erasmus seems to have been unaware of the dangers of opium addiction, since he frequently prescribed it to be taken 'in very large doses for conditions such as sleep-walking and Tetanus trismus; a grain every half-hour for painful epilepsy; a grain before bedtime for impotency and half a grain twice a day for anorexia'. For the daughter of Thomas Coutts, the royal banker, he recommended 'a very large dose so as to make the patient inebriate'. As for Tom, he urged him to 'find out something to teaze you a little, a wife or a law suit or some such thing'.

In 1802 Tom accompanied his sister Sarah to Pembrokeshire to visit the Allens at Cresselly, and persuaded Coleridge to join them. It is more than likely that his concerned sisters hoped Tom might find a wife among Bessy's three unmarried sisters, Jessie, Emma and Fanny (Octavia had died in 1800). Jessie was attractive, bubbling with vitality; Emma was good-natured but plain; and Fanny was the cleverest of the family. The two men stayed at an inn at St Clear, which the anthracite fires kept agreeably warm, day and night, while Sarah went on to Cresselly. Coleridge and Tom later joined the sisters at Cresselly where Coleridge basked in the interest of three such charming women; but Tom, restless as ever, took a cottage near by and resumed his own sport. There were to be no wedding bells.

Tom had been attracted to Wales not by the thought of capturing a wife but by the prospect of shooting partridge. He had sent ahead six dogs and two men, and was happier staying in a warm inn or cottage where he could relax quietly after a day in the woods. Just as in years to come his nephew, Charles Darwin, would surprisingly combine a passion for hunting and shooting with concentrated scientific research, Tom at this time was 'deep in time, space and motion', pushing his mind to the boundaries of thought. He was also taking opium, which he would have found difficult in the Allen household. So he stayed there for short periods only, returning in between times to the cottage. Meanwhile Coleridge remained at Cresselly, where, Tom told his brother, 'Col was a great favourite.' Certainly Sarah Wedgwood was at this time mesmerized by the dazzling poet – whose wife, he claimed, did not understand him – and would later remember how she and Jos championed him against his critics.

Coleridge at his best was difficult to resist, though his 'Kubla Khan' should have warned her:

> Beware, beware his flashing eyes and floating hair
> Weave a circle round him thrice
> And close your eyes with holy dread
> For he on honeydew has fed
> And drank the milk of Paradise.

But it would be some time before Sarah ceased to be his fervent admirer, and, under his spell, Tom would be led to death three years later.

Coleridge vividly described the Allen household at Cresselly in letters to his long-suffering wife, who was at home expecting another baby.

> Over frightful roads we at last arrived at Crescelly [*sic*] about 3 o'clock [he wrote], found a Captain and Mrs Tyler there (a stupid Brace), Jessica, Emma, and Frances Allen – All simple, good, kind-hearted lasses, and Jessie the eldest uncommonly so. We dined at half past 4 – just after dinner down came old Allen – O Christ! Old Nightmair! An ancient Incubus! Every face was saddened, every mouth pursed up! Most solemnly civil, like the Lord of a stately castle 500 years ago! Doleful and plaintive eke for I believe that the Devil *is* twitching him home. After tea he left us, and went again to bed, and the whole party recovered their spirits. I drank nothing but I ate sweet meats, and cream and some fruit and talked a great deal and sate up till 12, and did not go to sleep till near 2. In consequence of which I rose sickish.

At Cresselly, enjoying warm rooms, excellent food and plenty of his favourite clotted cream, Coleridge was in his element. There were lovely ladies to listen while he read his poetry and to accompany him on long walks, and Sarah to enchant him with her music.

> I am very comfortable here. Sally [Sarah] Wedgwood is really the most perfectly good woman, I ever knew, and the three Allens are

sweet, cheerful, and most innocent girls. I cannot help being idle among them. What sweeter and more tranquillizing pleasure is there than to feel one's self completely innocent among completely innocent young women! Save when I think of home my mind is calm and soundless. Sally Wedgwood plays on the Piano Forte divinely! Warm room, warm bedrooms, music, pleasant talking, and extreme temperance – all this agrees with me.

Writing to his friend Poole, he was even more enthusiastic: 'Miss S Wedgwood is a truly excellent woman; her whole soul is clear, pure and deep as an Italian sky.'

Sarah, never a beauty, blossomed under the spell of the poet. Who could resist those flashing eyes glowing with admiration? She not only played divinely but even melted the hard heart of Captain Allen. 'My father', wrote Fanny, 'is wonderfully pleased with her, and is nearly, if not quite, as great a favourite as Mrs Darwin with him.' Obviously Sukey had made a great impression on the old curmudgeon when she had visited Cresselly with Jos. Sarah's sister, however, the shrewd, clear-sighted Kitty Wedgwood, remembered Coleridge at Cote House and disliked him, finding his 'accent and exterior disagreeable' and his behaviour to his wife intolerable. But at this time, as Sarah later remembered, she and Tom were fighting Coleridge's 'despisers and hates'.

In old age Fanny Allen described Tom's visit and his charm to her niece, Emma's sister Elizabeth Wedgwood, praising 'his gracious and elegant manner' and the 'sympathy and great sensibility' which even subdued Captain Allen. She never forgot how, when 'they were all set down to dinner before Mr Allen, who was a great invalid, came in Tom rose and took Mr Allen's hand with so much respect and feeling. Mr Allen said afterwards he had never seen so fine a manner.' She also told Elizabeth how she disgraced herself one evening, when Coleridge, who 'was fond of reading . . . poems of Wordsworth', sat by her on the sofa and began to read 'The Leech Gatherer'. Elizabeth later recalled Fanny's account. 'When he came to the passage, now I believe omitted, about his skin being so old and dry that the leeches wouldn't stick, it set Fanny a thinking. That frightened her and she got into a convulsive fit of laughter that shook Coleridge who was sitting close to her, looking very angry. Perhaps to a person "who had not genius" Coleridge said, "the poem might seem absurd".' (Fanny's giggles might have been partly caused by the association of leeches with her formidable Allen aunt Margaret – now Mrs Leach.)

After this visit, restlessly searching for he knew not what, Tom travelled up to the Lake District with Coleridge, hoping to spend some time at Patterdale at the home of his friend Colonel Luff, who was 'mad after field sports' and with whom he hoped to 'run wild', hunting and shooting. On Christmas Eve 1802 they called on Wordsworth at Grasmere. The poet later described, in a letter to Jos written after Tom's death, how 'heart stricken' he was by Tom's appearance on this occasion, 'all skin and bone . . . deplorably changed which was painful to see, but his calm and dignified manner, united with his tall person and beautiful face, produced in me an impression of sublimity beyond what I ever experienced from the appearance of any other human being.' Tom had stayed with Wordsworth for five days in September 1797, when he was deep in abstruse meditations on time and space. Those five days, he noted, had 'gone like lightning'. During that visit Tom had tried to persuade Wordsworth to join him in a bizarre experiment in children's education – a research project which, he hoped, would be his own lasting legacy to humanity. He believed that the child should be shut away in a grey nursery 'with only a couple of vivid coloured objects to excite its senses of sight and touch'. Wordsworth had argued fiercely against such sacrilege as cutting the child away from Nature, the supreme source of good. He may have been thinking of Tom when he wrote,

> The country people pray for God's good grace
> And tremble at his deep experiments
> How this is hollow – 'tis a life of lies
> From the beginning and in lies must end
> Forth bring him to the air of common sense.

At the time of his earlier visit, Tom, under the influence of William Godwin, hoped to fund research into his theories with Wordsworth as an adviser. He would have given the poet a grant, as he was to give one to Coleridge. Wordsworth, however, would have nothing to do with such madness. And now, in 1802, he saw in Tom's worn face the result of such insane theorizing. At the end it was Tom himself shut away in a soundproof room, desperately seeking to break through the bounds of knowledge or life itself.

On Christmas Day 1802 Tom wrote a suicidal letter to Jos declaring that if his future plans failed, 'I will neither distress myself nor my friends by continuing a vain struggle against Nature, but in complete resignation yield to her an existence which she will not allow to be anything but a burden to myself and a perpetual source of anxiety to all around me.' He had tried in vain to give up opium; now, should all efforts fail, he would 'relieve myself from all further efforts and to minister such stimuli as shall diminish the tediousness and misery of my life to a bearable degree and take my chance for the consequences'.

He found some peace in the new year, staying in a cottage on the banks of Ullswater, Glen Ridding, belonging to Colonel Luff and his wife. But by April 1803 he was travelling once again, this time with a companion to Geneva; when war with France broke out, he escaped just in time to evade arrest under Napoleon's order to detain all English travellers. Back in London he tried for a while the experiment of cooking and house-keeping for himself and a male companion. In the autumn of 1803, fears of a French invasion roused him and in a new burst of energy he arranged for the removal of his mother and sisters for safety to Cote House – much to old Sally's annoyance: 'she was not in the lest alarmed,' Kitty told Tom. His mind was clearly not at this time affected, since with Colonel Luff he raised a company of eighty 'Wedgwood Volunteers' and also bought gold for himself and Jos. But by January 1804 he had sunk back into despair, writing from Cote to John: 'I have endured pangs and torments such as none can conceive . . . As far as the coldest prudence can procure me peace, I will have it. I am now endeavouring to habituate myself to my near exit without repugnance . . . I feel very certain that at the age of fifteen I held out more promise, and united a great variety of talent, a more ardent longing after all that is beautiful and good in morals, things and art.' He deeply regretted that 'all this should come to nothing'; but he was now almost at the end of hope.

Still he persevered, comforted by the love of Jos and Bessy and his sister Sarah's 'angelic kindness'. Sarah had assured him of her love; her 'taciturn-ity', she explained, 'has really been partly owing to the family infirmity' –

that is, the Wedgwood reticence. Tom never met Coleridge again, though the poet wrote urging him not to give up hope. 'Have you ever thought of trying large doses of opium in a hot climate, with a diet of grapes and the fruits of the climate,' he helpfully suggested; 'by drinking freely you might at last produce Gout and . . . a violent pain and inflammation in the extremities might produce new trains of motion and feeling in your stomach and organs connected with the stomach.' Eight weeks later Coleridge left for Malta, and passed out of Tom's life.

During the rest of 1804, Tom was taking increased doses of opium but was still capable of discussing helpfully John's permanently desperate financial situation. In October he once again he found some respite with the Luffs at Ullswater, and even tried unsuccessfully to buy a farm there, looking across at Glen Ridding and the crests of Helvellyn. But now his case was hopeless. In the summer of 1805 he planned to revisit the West Indies, but just before he was due to embark he fell ill and at last ceased to struggle against the mysterious malady that was destroying him. 'Three times', he told Jos, he 'tried in vain to give up the opium that had become his only refuge.' His sight was going and there was nothing left, as he told Jos, but to keep to his room, take a large dose and wait for death. A heartbroken Bessy broke the tragic news to her sister, Emma Allen.

> On Monday I think he got a little chilled, which brought on much internal pain. On Tuesday at midnight he rang his bell and told his servant to give him something, for he was very weak, but not ill. He told him to come in two hours time to see how he was and to call Jos at five. The servant did so and found him sleeping as he thought. When Jos came he also thought him sleeping and sat down an hour and a half beside him before he discovered that he was not; when he did he became alarmed and sent for Dr Crawford who immediately said that he was dying. Jos watched by him till seven in the evening when he expired.

Only Jos knew the depth of Tom's despair, but he locked up the tragic story in his heart and never spoke of it.

Bessy had never realized the extent of Tom's opium addiction – in her eyes he was 'really too good for this world . . . all his past kindnesses to me and mine . . . I feel myself quite unfit to make his panegyric, but I trust my children will ever remember him with veneration as an honour to the family to which he belonged.' And so they did. Tom was a saint in the eyes of Emma and her family, and Elizabeth and Joe remembered him as he had seemed to them, the kindest of uncles, often visiting them in their nursery and passionately interested in their education.

After Tom's death Dorset was too full of sad memories: 'his forsaken windows', wrote Bessy, 'remind me continually of himself and I can hardly forebear expecting to see him walking out in his way, throwing out one foot before the other as if he did not care whether the other ever followed.' As for Jos, he was stricken by the death of the brother he had loved so deeply. Now he turned back to his Midlands roots. He had bought the lease of Maer Hall and its 1,000-acre estate in 1802 as a base from which he could manage the pottery at Etruria, nine miles away. Below the rambling Elizabethan manor house a small lake stretched, shaped at the end with what Bessy called a fish's tail. Capability Brown was said to have had a hand in its design. Jos's brother, John, certainly helped plan and plant it. It had taken some years to prepare Maer Hall, planning the grounds with the same care that his father had given Etruria. Etruria Hall was now stripped of the beautiful Wedgwood embellishments to doors and windows, its books and pictures were removed and the house left to Jos's cousin, Tom Byerley, and his family. In 1807 Jos and Bessy and their seven children moved into Maer Hall, which became their beloved home for the next thirty years. It was here that their eighth child, Emma, was born.

Robert and Sukey Darwin were delighted to have them so near – just thirty miles from Shrewsbury. Sukey had created a comfortable and elegant home. She took her nonconformist faith to her marriage, supporting the Unitarian chapel in Shrewsbury: certainly her first child, Marianne, was baptized there – as Erasmus teasingly wrote, making the child 'a little Methodist'. It is not clear at what time the family became – officially, at least – conventional Anglicans, but certainly Charles Darwin was baptized according to the rites of the Church of England. It was perhaps necessary for Dr Robert to conform because of his distinguished patients; nonconformity was not popular in the years after the French Revolution. But Sukey was always very much her own mistress and, had she wanted, would have kept to her Unitarian faith, as her brother Jos did. Sukey's three younger daughters, Caroline, Susan and Catherine, were all deeply religious, although their grandfather Erasmus, their father Robert and his son the younger Erasmus were sceptics or agnostics. As for Charles, his mother probably took the younger boy to her nonconformist chapel on Sundays; certainly in his early adulthood Charles accepted with equanimity the prospect of becoming a country parson, encouraged by his sisters.

Sukey also passed on to her daughters the competence in household management which her own mother, the redoubtable Sally, had taught her. In this they would always be different from the Wedgwoods at Maer Hall, who had a decided dislike of what they called 'scrattling' – that is, doing housework. The doctor's house at Shrewsbury was always beautifully run, and even the maids were impeccably dressed. Each year Sukey organized 'two great feasts' for the doctors and medical officials at Shrewsbury. In 1807 she invited her brother to 'pop upon us' to meet her distinguished guest, 'Lady F'. These social occasions would have been no problem for Sukey, who had often helped her mother entertain elevated company at Etruria Hall. Like old Sally, she displayed with pride her father's best Wedgwood services.

Sukey was a discriminating customer at the Wedgwood factory – and always insisted on paying for her pottery. 'We are much obliged by your kind offer of furnishing us with earthenware, but cannot think of accepting it, as there is no reason for it, and also it would quite preclude our ordering anything in the future,' she wrote to John. In 1815 she and Robert were buying 'tea ware, broad green stained border, and gold inside . . . to be particularly well painted'. Charles Darwin must have grown up in a house filled with the best products of Etruria, including the first clay copy of the famous Portland Vase. But it seems to have made no impression on him.

Sukey writes to Jos with affectionate banter as she had done with her father.

My dear Jos., I am very glad to find I have a chance of seeing you at Maer, but from the expression in your letter I fear you mean to fob me off with a dinner, whereas I had intended passing a week with you. We are very much obliged by your kind intention respecting the dinner service, which we are in no kind of haste for, as it is not the custom of this town to give dinners in summer. I am therefore well inclined to follow your advice and wait for the very handsome pattern. My love to B., and tell her we have a couple of Doves for her; but as we do not yet know which are pairs, I shall not bring them with me, but you may prepare a cage. Our pair have not produced any young ones yet.

The beautiful doves Sukey bred at Shrewsbury were famous. It is extraordinary that her son Charles, in later life, as he sat smoking with the old pigeon breeders, does not seem to have remembered this.

The gardens, too, were mainly Sukey's responsibility, for Robert was excessively busy. 'The doctor is not in very good feather just at present; he is so much engaged that it harasses him a good deal. Surely warmer weather must come soon, and that, I hope, will give him more liberty.' Sukey had learned her love of gardening, one of the most important Wedgwood legacies, at Etruria Hall, and it figures largely in her letters to Jos and John. To Jos she wrote: 'The Dr sends you by to-morrow's Coach some suckers of the white Poplar, and, as they have good roots, he has no doubt of their growing. If you want more say so, and they shall be sent. It is the common white Poplar. It is become so fashionable a tree that Lady Bromley has sent for some cuttings for Baroness Howe, to decorate Pope's Villa at Twickenham, as all his favourite trees have been cut down.'

As for Robert, the slender lad she had once known gradually put on immense weight, his light piping voice seeming oddly incongruous with his bulk. He had his father's huge appetite – according to Miss Meteyard, he could 'eat a goose for a dinner as other men do a partridge'. When he reached 300 pounds he stopped weighing himself. He travelled long distances, his 'great bulk wedged in his famous yellow chaise', his heavy coachman often preceding him into the houses of the poor to see if the floorboards would bear his weight. Through deep snow and driving rain, in early morning or late at night, he drove to visit not only his rich patients, but also the poor, who regarded the immense doctor with respect and a certain amount of awe.

It seems to have been a deeply happy marriage. Sukey always wrote affectionately of 'the doctor', and he would take time off from his busy professional life to take her on jaunts to London or to Bath for the sake of her health. In 1805 Sukey had been deeply concerned about the mental and physical health of her brother Tom, and invited him to Shrewsbury to consult her husband. Robert recognized the hopelessness of his case, but still Sukey did not give up hope. In April 1805 she had persuaded a Mr Dugard, a Shrewsbury surgeon with some experience in such cases, to go to Dorset to look after Tom. This aroused the wrath of his Shrewsbury patients. 'There was', Sukey wrote with equanimity, 'medical commotion . . . a thundering letter from Mrs Evans and today Mrs Suton has favoured my husband with an epistle. I have not yet any thought of taking up my pen.' Nevertheless, Sukey was accustomed to getting what she wanted and Mr Dugard obtained leave of absence from his practice. However, he too saw that nothing could be done for Tom.

After Tom's death, Robert wrote to Jos: 'There were three modes of termination to be expected from your poor brother's state of health and that which has occurred was by far the least deplorable, as it was without pain. The moment the paralysis took place all sensation would cease . . . action and phrenzy were the other two.'

The first years of the new century saw the break-up of the old order. At Cresselly only the three youngest Allen daughters remained at home to bear the brunt of their father's bad temper. Jessie escaped to spend almost a year at her sister's homes; Bessy reluctantly returned for the summer of 1800 and was bullied into staying longer than she wished. Her father, now crippled, persuaded her that he was dying. In November Mackintosh wrote to Jos Wedgwood, now his brother-in-law:

> We left the 'two maidens all forlorn at the house that Jack built' in tolerable good spirits considering the gloomy solitude to which they are condemned. We have heard from good little Emma [Allen] (she really is the best girl in the world) and are happy to hear that the Squire has been pleased to be infinitely more cordial and gracious to his two poor prisoners than he ever was before, so that . . . an absolute want of amusement and a perpetual constraint in conversation, they may be pretty comfortable.

In 1803 the old Captain finally 'twitched his way to the devil' and John Allen became master of Cresselly. For the next nine years his three unmarried sisters, Jessie, Emma and Fanny, lived with him in perfect harmony. John remained unmarried, having fallen desperately in love with a married neighbour, Mrs Waddington. She and her daughter appear frequently in the family letters and deserve some notice, for, like minor actors in a stage play, they appear repeatedly in different disguises.

Mrs Waddington had once been the lovely Miss Port, mentioned in Fanny Burney's diary as the great-niece of the enchanting Mrs Delaney, 'a sort of miracle in her day'. Miss Port lived with her great-aunt in the grace-and-favour house at Windsor given her by George III, where the King and Queen often called informally. This royal society, and that of great ladies like Lady Louisa Stuart, daughter of the Earl of Bute, 'gave her a tone of sentimental exaggeration that she has never since been able to shake off'. So Lady Louisa wrote years later after a visit to her in Wales. 'Mrs Delaney lived at Windsor the last three years, visited by the King every day without fail . . . Do you wonder that Mrs Waddington should retain a hankering after everything elevated in every way . . . literature and "les beaux arts"?' Jilted by the King's aide-de-camp, Colonel Goldsworthy, and homeless after the death of Mrs Delaney, Miss Port married the elderly, wealthy Mr Waddington and lived in some style at Abergavenny, near Cresselly. Their daughter (yet another Fanny), who had been something of an infant prodigy and became a talented artist, often accompanied her mother on visits to Cresselly and sketched the house many times from the garden. Presumably John and Mrs Waddington welcomed her absence outside.

Taken on the Grand Tour by her mother, in Rome Fanny met a young German, Christian Bunsen, who wooed her in the Capitol by moonlight; he married her and they settled in Rome, where he became the Hanoverian minister at the Papal Court. Here they entertained lavishly. Fanny, now Mrs – later Baroness – Bunsen, had none of her mother's affectation, and although, as Emma once said, 'she does go on and on,' she was a useful guide and hostess when Emma and her sisters were in Rome, and in years to come received them in London, where from 1841 to 1854 Bunsen was the German Ambassador to the Court of St James's.

At Cresselly, the Allen sisters seem to have taken their brother's love affair in their stride, though later in Italy when Mrs Waddington tried to patronize them they responded very coldly.

In 1804 James and Kitty Mackintosh left England for India with their expanding family. Kitty already had two young children, Bessy and Fanny, and Robert – later his father's biographer – was born in 1806. With five children to consider, James had decided he must make his fortune and accepted the position of Recorder of Bombay. Before they left London, he was knighted and Kitty was presented to Queen Charlotte at Court. Bessy asked Fanny for news of this great occasion; she 'assumed that she would be in the presence chamber – a parcel of shabby plebeians looking on at the honours that had fallen on the family'. The fashionable dressmaker, Miss Stuart, had dressed Kitty 'uncommonly well and prettily', Fanny reported, 'and she cut an exceedingly good figure'. The Queen talked very graciously to her, and she met with great civility a great many people. The day cheered Kitty: 'there is nothing like a little vanity to buoy up the spirits.' The knighthood would also give a lift to the family's prestige, so Bessy reflected guiltily.

However, Mackintosh's Indian interlude proved a mistake. He made no fortune, and lost many Whig friends who criticized him for accepting office from the Tories. The venture lost him his place on the political ladder, and he never afterwards achieved the Cabinet post he merited.

The departure of James and Kitty left twenty-three-year-old Fanny Allen desolate: her brother-in-law had brought light and learning into her dull country life, and though she would have many suitors there would never be one to match this, her secret love. After his death she wrote a 'Notice of Sir James Mackintosh 1833': 'While M lived I did not suspect that I could have valued his society more than I then did . . . and till the tree fell I had no idea how widespread over me were its branches and how they filled up every space about me . . . like Milton's Raphael he was so sociably mild and so indulgent that never was a teacher of wisdom more approachable.' On the blank leaf of his copy of his *Discourses* she wrote: 'It is with deep and humble gratitude for the love he honoured me with, that I now enter this record of his affection which made the pride and much of the joy of my life for thirty-two years. December 29, 1836.' The influence of Mackintosh was indeed widespread over the whole of the Allen family, and both directly and indirectly helped to shape Emma's life.

CHAPTER THREE

Childhood

The happiest being that was ever looked on.
Emma Allen to Bessy Wedgwood

EMMA WEDGWOOD WAS BORN ON 2 MAY 1808 AT MAER HALL, IN A Staffordshire still rural. The youngest of eight children, she had a special place in the family. Fanny, two years older, was her close companion; they were 'the Dovelies', or 'Miss Pepper and Salt'. 'I always think of you as one person,' their elder sister Charlotte wrote. Fanny, plain and freckled, was orderly – Miss Memorandum; Emma, pretty and lively – 'Little Miss Slip-Slop'. As for Elizabeth, the eldest sister, she lavished on Emma all the frustrated love of an affectionate spinster. Emma was her child. 'Since from the time she could speak,' she later told Charles Darwin, 'I have never had one moment's pain from her and a share of daily pleasures such as few people have it in their power to shed around.' From earliest childhood Emma was described by her Wedgwood and Allen aunts alike in similar terms of extravagant praise. But her four brothers, Joe (Josiah), Harry, Frank and Hensleigh, kept her feet on the ground.

This childhood, spent lapped in love, gave Emma a stability and tranquillity that marked her all her life. For Emma, no flowers would ever bloom, no birds ever sing, more beautifully than they did at Maer. After morning lessons with her mother or Elizabeth she was free. She could rattle away on the old piano, or sit on the curving steps that swept down from the porch to the terrace and look out upon a landscape that bore the hallmarks of Capability Brown. Below the stone balustrade the still lake stretched, to a child's eye as wide as the sea, to its marshy end. Beyond, sheep grazed the steep, green meadows between wooded slopes. From the stone boathouse below the terrace Fanny and Emma and their brothers rowed to the world's end at the far shore, or ran the mile-long sandy path around the lake. Emma never forgot that sandy walk, and took the idea with her to Down many years later. And she always remembered the picnics at the Roman fort on the hills above Maer, and the pony rides across the heath.

In 1813, however, this age of paradise drew to a close – at least for five years. Jos had been overstretched financially for some time. The war with France had seriously damaged the pottery business. Orders from abroad had been cancelled, crates of pottery had gone astray, bills had not been paid. At home there was industrial unrest, and the hated recruitment officers were forcing unwilling recruits into the depleted army: Bessy wrote to her husband a heartbreaking account of villagers dragged from their homes. In these difficult circumstances costly repairs to Maer Hall had been the last straw, and it seemed that it must be either sold or let. Dr Robert Darwin persuaded Jos not to sell the much-loved old house, but instead to let it and move back to Etruria Hall – which still belonged to Jos. (Tom Byerley had moved to London during the last years of his life, and died there in 1810.)

However, the move was delayed because the Allen family too was facing a crisis. By 1812 John Allen's hopeless love affair with the imperious Mrs Waddington had come to an end, and he married the moody Gertrude Seymour, whose family shared his Whig politics. His three unmarried sisters were now homeless, for Gertrude was not an easy sister-in-law. For the next three years they moved from one married sister to another, staying with Bessy and Jos at Maer in 1812–13, then moving to the Mackintosh home in Westminster before eventually taking lodgings in Dulwich in 1815 to be near their brother Baugh, Master of Dulwich College. Finally, in that year they made the brave decision to spend three years on a Grand Tour of the continent: now that the war with France was over, like many of their countrymen and -women they sought the sun and culture of which they had been deprived since 1793. Jos had kept Maer Hall on to give his sisters-in-law their first refuge, but once they had moved to London he and Bessy could take their family to Etruria.

There was one more retrenchment Jos made at this time: in 1812 he discontinued his share of the grant to the poet Coleridge, which he had continued to pay after his brother Tom's death in 1805. It was a decision much criticized, both by contemporaries and by subsequent commentators, but one which Jos would never explain to his family. In theory Coleridge was no longer an opium addict; but in reality he was secretly obtaining the supplies he could not do without, and close friends who knew would certainly have informed Jos, who thus knew that his grant was helping to destroy a man he had once recognized as a genius. In fact he behaved in a perfectly honourable way: he could not discontinue Tom's share of the grant, and he did not withdraw his own until he had explained his situation to Coleridge and offered him the opportunity to insist that the contract be kept – in which event he would undoubtedly have continued to make the payments.

> When I joined with my brother Thomas some years ago, in giving you an annuity of one hundred and fifty pounds, it was not likely that I should ever find it inconvenient to continue the payment. My circumstances are now, however, so much changed that the payment of my share of that sum annually diminishes my capital, for my expenses have for some time exceeded my income. I mention this to you with perfect openness, and in the same spirit I add that my continuing the payment will depend on its appearing that I am bound in honor to do so. I hope you will write to me without reserve on this subject.

To his credit, Coleridge, equally honourably, accepted the loss with good grace.

By 1813, Jos and his family were established at Etruria Hall. It could not have been easy to go back. Stripped of its Wedgwood decorations and neglected for some years, his old home now seemed desolate, the potteries near by more smoky than they remembered. Jos worried that the move would upset the family, particularly Bessy. But his daughter Elizabeth reassured him: 'Mamma does not let the thoughts of leaving Maer harass her; she is in excellent spirits.' And, she said, 'You and mamma make us so happy that it does not matter where we are.' Typically, Bessy made the best of it, explaining to her sisters that the rides in the country around were better than she expected.

Nor were Emma and Fanny too upset by the move. For them Etruria Hall had its own excitements – large empty rooms where they could play without risk of breaking valuable pottery, secret tunnels and mysterious cellars (said to be haunted even today). Years later, Emma's niece, Julia, found it a perfect playground for children, with the canal, and tall trees to swing from. Nothing, however, concealed the 'grimy old pot shops', nor the disreputable old potters drunk outside the inns: heavy drinking remained an occupational hazard in the Potteries. Sometimes Bessy took the children on nostalgic visits to the gardens at Maer, sadly admiring the riot of roses.

One day not long after the move, the family visited a friend's house near Trentham Park for strawberries and cream. Did Jos tell them of the days when his father had dined at the great house there? The boys rode ponies while the girls were crammed into the wagon, and Emma and Fanny spent the day in 'silent enjoyment'. 'Very grave, and very demure all day, but they were happy while running about the Park,' Bessy wrote to her sister Jessie, who in reply sent 'a very tender kiss to the Dovelies, the tenderest to Emma, but do not tell her so. How much I should have liked to see her prim little face on the water.' Even at this early age, Emma was the favourite of all the Allen and Wedgwood aunts.

———————

Now that her fierce father was dead, Bessy took the children to Cresselly for summer holidays. Overland travel to Wales was extremely difficult, though, as always, Bessy made the rough journey fun – as Elizabeth's diary of 1812 shows. They set off from the Darwins' home in Shrewsbury in a chaise with post-horses, 'Mamma' in the dicky and Elizabeth and Charlotte kneeling or standing on the back seat. The country was beautiful but bridges were down, destroyed by storms; another chaise overtook them and got to the inn at the first stage before them, taking all the post-horses. One town where they stopped was crowded because the Assizes were in session and there was not a bed to be had; so they went on, with a 'brutal driver' who whipped the tired horses on and quite 'spoilt the scenery'. From Llandudno they had to walk up every hill, but the stages to Aberystwyth were 'most pleasant', and with four strong horses and an agreeable driver they made it to Plynlymmon. The children were fascinated by the little cottages with wicker instead of glass windows, and by the babble of Welsh tongues. Finally, they 'got to Cresselly to tea', to be smothered with kisses by innumerable voluble Welsh relations, so different from the sober Wedgwoods. Uncle John Allen was a kind host; Cresselly was anthracite warmed; there was good food and plenty of clotted cream. There were horse races at Tenby – Aunt Fanny Allen's favourite sport. There were little dances to which Charlotte was allowed to go, although she had not yet 'come out'. The old Welsh women with their tall hats and red cloaks made Tenby market as exotic as anything abroad. But Emma was not with the family on this 1812 journey; she and Fanny had been left in the care of Jos, his sister Sarah, and his mother old Sally Wedgwood. To Elizabeth's annoyance, the 'wretched Dovelies got measles' and the holiday was cut short.

Emma's favourite way to Wales was by sea from Bristol to Tenby. Then came the blessed sight of Uncle John Allen's carriage waiting at the top of the rocky steps, while a throng of shouting porters touted for custom. Later in life she would remember how clean and bright it all was to a child's eye: the wild flowers along the lanes, the Tenby urchins scrambling up the cliffs in search of birds' eggs, the donkeys on the beach and the alarming bathing women who took them into the sea in their quaint machines and ruthlessly dipped them in the icy water.

By 1818 it became possible for Jos to take his family back to Maer. First, however, perhaps as a reward for Bessy's patience, he took her and the four girls for a stay of seven months in Paris and Geneva. It was to be an educational tour for the girls and some social fun for Bessy. Many of her friends from Wales and Staffordshire had been among the crowds of English who rushed to the continent as soon as the war was over. Jos, too, needed a break. John's continuing financial troubles were a constant worry; and in 1817 his sister Sukey died probably of peritonitis. For some years she had been 'not quite ill and not quite well'; Robert had taken her to Bath for treatment, and his sisters Marianne and Caroline had nursed her with devotion. But to Jos she wrote sadly, 'everyone seems young but me'. Sukey's death deeply depressed Jos; they had been very close, especially in the last years.

Jos had always longed to travel, as his brother John had done, like a gentleman, not 'a man of business'. Mindful of his own social frustration, he was determined that there should be no doubt as to the status of his sons. They were to be gentlemen. He sent Joe and Harry to Eton, but Joe, slow and quiet, got little out of his classical education there, and Harry, though lively and intelligent, was too light-hearted to take work seriously. In later years he livened his barrister life by writing charming fairy stories. Considering Eton unnecessarily expensive, Jos despatched his younger sons, Frank and Hensleigh, to Rugby. Frank proved to be competent if unimaginative, and serious Hensleigh became the real scholar of the family.

Jos gave much thought to the education of his children, supplementing their schooling with good tutors. The renowned scientific writer Mary Somerville taught them mathematics, and in 1816 Harry had been sent to Geneva to be coached by a Swiss tutor, and this summer Frank and Hensleigh were to follow in his footsteps. Now it was the turn of the girls; for, like his father, Jos believed in the importance of women's education. Elizabeth and Charlotte had been educated at home by a carefully chosen governess, with additional tuition from a succession of excellent tutors; an opera singer gave them singing lessons at Dr Darwin's house, and Copley Fielding guided the talented Charlotte in painting. Now they were not only to be taught French, Italian and German and given dancing lessons, but also to be introduced 'into society'. Although Bessy always insisted that her girls should have the natural, easy manners for which the Allen girls were noted, nevertheless, as her sisters told her, the girls needed a little polish and their dress left much to be desired. 'My dear Elizabeth's clothes', Bessy once complained, 'are as near inadmissible as possible.' Charlotte at this time was in full bloom, with shining long fair hair (she reminded her aunts of the Countess G, one of Byron's loves), but she held herself badly. Later, at one Paris reception, the hostess called Charlotte over, 'whisked off her handkerchief, pulled down her shoulders, pinched her stays together and declared she held herself like a grandpapa'. As for Fanny and Emma, they would continue their lessons with tutors and, it was hoped, become fluent in French.

Sir James Mackintosh had given the travellers a sheaf of introductions to the famous, and made sure that they were entertained by interesting people. 'Yesterday was the grand procession of Longchamps we which made part of,' Charlotte told her brothers; 'it was the gayest sight I ever saw, the day was beautiful and there were such crowds of people that it appeared as if Paris must have emptied itself. They were all dressed in the gayest colours, and some of the equipages were most magnificent, particularly the Duke of Wellington's, which was the finest of all, the different ambassadors and some of the royal families. We got into the line of carriages and were more than two hours before we got home.'

There was also a more humble hostess anxious to help them – Mme Collos. It will be remembered that the daughter of Bessy's Uncle Roger had been wooed and won by a French prisoner of war, captured in the French landing in Wales in 1798. Bessy and her sisters had braved their father's disapproval by keeping in touch with Mme Collos when her husband was again imprisoned, and later when she went to live with him in Paris, where he kept a fish shop in La Truanderie. So, when the Paris trip was planned, Bessy asked her cousin to find them a good hotel; and on arriving at the Paris Barrier, they found a message from Mme Collos to say that she had booked them rooms at the Hôtel du Mont Blanc, rue de la Paix, 'a very gay situation', Charlotte reported.

> Yesterday we drank tea with Mdme Collos and after tea went to see the scholars of the dancing master. The girls were much amused by little Louis Collos who pressed me and the girls very much to dance, and when at last he prevailed on Fanny, he made her an elegant bow and kissed her hand with as good a grace as Sir Charles Grandison could, which had a very ridiculous effect, as the little gentleman is but seven years old and very little for his age; and when we got up to go to the dancing-school, he took out Emma, gave her his arm, and led her off.

Emma and Fanny made friends with Mme Collos's daughter, a little older than them, who spoke no English; the fluent idiomatic French for which Emma was later noted was absorbed in La Truanderie, together with the smell of fish. Her first letter, according to Etty, was unlike her later beautiful script. 'The words ran in a very tipsy fashion across the page and seem as if formed with much labour': 'My dear Frank, We have got such numbers of masters. Two belong to Charlotte and two to us. I like the Collos except the youngest Louis who bothers one very much. At the dancing school there is a little dance every Friday and we go and dance very often they are going this moment to put in the post-office. Yours Emma Wedgwood.'

For Bessy, too, Paris was an education. There was music, opera, balls and receptions; she met Mme Récamier and the Queen of Sweden. For the last three years Bessy had followed her sisters' continental travels with a passionate interest and understandable envy, reading their vivid letters describing meetings with the famous and notorious, visits to places she had seen only in her mind. She longed to be with them; she, the Mme de Sévigné of the family, would have enjoyed recording their tour. Now, in Paris, Bessy had the chance to meet the man who had been their kind escort during their three years abroad, Jean Charles Simon de Sismondi.

The Allen sisters' tour had been a triumph for three maiden ladies without much money, thanks largely to letters from James Mackintosh and his friend Mme de Staël, through whom they acquired useful cavaliers who in turn introduced them to fascinating people and places. The most important of these was a friend of Mackintosh whom they met at Geneva at the beginning of their tour. Sismondi was one of the many admirers who, like Mackintosh himself, gathered around the exotic Mme de Staël. Unconventional and flamboyant, with a taste for exotic turbans, de Staël dazzled many clever men with her intellectual brilliance. Mackintosh was mesmerized by her, and flattered that she treated him as 'the person she most delights to honour . . . I am generally ordered with her to dinner, as one orders beans and bacon.' A fierce opponent of Napoleon, she had been extradited from Paris during the war and had subsequently held captive distinguished audiences in London and Geneva, where her 'passionate harangues' silenced many a grand dinner party. 'In these harangues', as Jessie wrote to Bessy, 'there is such a burst of feeling, such eloquent language, and such deep thought, and so much action, that it is the most extraordinary and interesting thing . . . Her subjects were invective against Buonapart, praise of Bernadette, the state of Europe and above all the happiness of Englishment.'

Sismondi was one of the cleverest men in de Staël's entourage at this time. (Even Karl Marx was impressed by his understanding of the importance of the Industrial Revolution.) As a young man he had escorted de Staël on a tour of Italy with the German poet Schiller. His *History of the Italian Republics* had won him fame, and now he was engaged on a massive *History of the French*, which was to take him twenty-three years to complete. Kind and gentle, he was, however, odd in appearance, with a large head and little body; and there was something ridiculous in his hand-kissing and exaggerated bows. In 1816, in Geneva, he fell deeply and permanently in love with Jessie Allen.

Back at Etruria, reading aloud her sisters' letters at the fireside, Bessy had followed Jessie's courtship over three years' absence with great interest and some concern. Their youngest sister, impetuous Fanny Allen, had taken a strong initial dislike to Sismondi – could not bear to shake his hand – though later she changed her mind. Certainly during their tour he was to be the perfect *cavaliere servente*, giving them introductions to interesting people on their route. It was with some envy that Bessy, who loved dancing, heard that they were learning the daring new waltz. In Geneva at this time it was said that one must waltz one's way into society; in 1816 even plain Emma Allen took lessons, though her triumph was short-lived; she fell and hurt her leg and had to sit out with the chaperones and the 'non-dancing men'. Bessy and her daughters followed their progress on old Josiah's maps, and longed to follow.

The Allens wrote of their journey to Florence guided by the *voiturier* Populus, noted for his care of ladies. He arranged the journey, with food, lodging, coach and six horses, at a cost of £44, 'except at those towns where we chose to stop for our pleasure and there we were to pay him 15 francs a day'. They left Geneva on 26 February 1816, 'in a coach with six good horses', and headed on via Susa to Turin, Modena and Bologna, and on 19 March were writing to Bessy of their arrival in Florence. Sismondi was dissuaded from accompanying them – it was thought not proper – but he nevertheless made sure that they were received in Florence by Madame de Staël and her daughter, the Duchess of Broglie, who introduced them to a 'great number of foreign nobility as well as the English with which Florence is filled at this time'. Sismondi followed them to Florence and accompanied them to his mother's home in Pescia.

In 1817 their letters came from Rome, and Bessy learned with some disquiet that Sismondi continued his pursuit of Jessie. She refused him at first, but finally decided that if after a year's separation they found it impossible to do without each other she would agree to marry him. At the end of 1817 the three women decided to join their sister, Caroline Drewe, at Pisa, where she had brought her two dying daughters in the vain hope of a cure. When the Wedgwoods reached Paris in 1818, Jessie was still trying to make up her mind; Bessy welcomed the chance to meet Sismondi, who was there at that time, and relieved to find she approved of him. Charlotte was pleasantly surprised, finding him not nearly as ugly as he was said to be.

It was after she and her sisters had returned from Italy in the autumn of 1818 that Jessie finally agreed to marry Sismondi. The wedding took place at Cresselly in April 1819; Fanny, still hostile, refusing to attend the ceremony. It turned out to be a very happy marriage, Beauty and the Beast making a good match. Jessie, still pretty at forty-two, bubbling, vivacious and outgoing, was a perfect hostess for Sismondi in a Geneva notorious for its stiff attitude to foreigners. The couple were to play an important part in the education of Emma.

In 1819 the Wedgwoods left Etruria Hall and returned to Maer for good. While the house was being painted Bessy and the older children went to Cresselly, leaving Emma and Fanny in the care of Aunt Emma Allen. Second youngest of the Allen sisters, Emma was the plainest, well aware of what she called her 'half formed face'. But perhaps because she was often overlooked she had become a shrewd but kindly observer; her assessment of the two little girls, in a letter to Bessy of 15 November 1819, is a valuable record. Like her sisters and the Wedgwood aunts, she obviously adored pretty little Emma, though they all tried to conceal their preference from Fanny, who, like her Aunt Emma, was small and plain. Aunt Emma was thirty-nine at this time, and Fanny and Emma were thirteen and eleven. 'I marvel at the strength of the girls' spirits as much as I do at the perfection of their tempers, I feel now very sure that not only a cross word never passes between them, but that an irritable feeling never arises,' she reported.

> Fanny, to be sure, is calmness itself, but the vivacity of Emma's feelings, without perfectly knowing her, would make me expect that Fanny's reproofs, which she often gives with an elder sister air, would ruffle her a little; but I have never seen that expressive face take the shadow of an angry look, and I do think her love for Fanny is the prettiest thing I ever saw. But I am observing to

you what I am sure you have observed yourself a thousand times, but these little creatures have filled my mind more than any other subject lately, so I like to let a little of it out to you. I ascribe much of Emma's joyous nature to have been secured, if not caused, by Fanny's yielding disposition; had the other met with a cross or an opposing sister there was every chance that with her ardent feelings, her temper had become irritable. Now she is made the happiest being that ever was looked on, and so much affection in her nature as will secure her from selfishness; and I believe it is according to Sarah's theory that plant and weed do not grow together. I am almost afraid to tell you how active we are, for fear you should expect more fruits from it than we shall be able to produce. We get up all three of us now every day by candle light; to-day we were at breakfast at ½ after 7, and by 10 the Bible and the reading Italian was over with both girls, when I left them for Betley [eight miles off, where John Wedgwood and their friends the Tollets lived]. In general we find ample employment till 1, and then find an hour for music when we come in at 3 or half after. I believe I told you before that they declared their resolution of taking an additional half-hour to their music. I believe they have not missed doing so for one day since, between dinner and tea. The drawing has rather fallen, through mending stockings, talking nonsense, and playing with the kitten. I do not know what their father will say at such a show of cats, but 3 is now our number except at schooltime, and then kitten is expelled, for I found she made me idle as much as either of them; there is something very irresistible in the gambols of such a little crum of a thing. In spite of Joe and the cats, we contrive to keep the room very comfortable and tolerably tidy, it is what I labour most at. Their father's coming down tomorrow will, I hope, stimulate them to fresh exertions, as I assure them he approves of tidiness.

While Jos made sure that Emma and her sisters were given a good basic schooling and brought in excellent tutors and governesses for the family, Bessy had always been relaxed about formal education, having considerable sympathy with Jessie's theory that the less formality the better. The famous bluestocking Mrs Somerville (who gave her name to Somerville College, Oxford) had told Jessie that she believed in giving children only ten minutes' instruction at a time; anything longer was not absorbed. Nevertheless, in January 1822 the two youngest Wedgwood girls were sent for a year to Greville House, a boarding school in Paddington Green, at that time a village outside London. 'Fanny and Emma went very cheerfully,' Bessy wrote to Elizabeth, but 'shed a few tears at the parting, and Fanny was most affected, which I did not expect, but I think Emma always liked the scheme best.' Bessy and the elder girls had been similarly surprised in 1818, when Emma had been perfectly willing to be left in Paris while they went on to Geneva.

The school was 'a comfortable old house, run by Mrs Mayer, a good humoured motherly sort of woman, but not strikingly genteel'. Emma always claimed that she learned very little there. 'In French history they never got beyond Charlemagne, as with every new girl, the class began again at the beginning with Clovis.' But her talent for music was encouraged. She had always excelled as a pianist, and at Greville House she was produced as a star pupil to perform before Mrs Fitzherbert, George IV's morganatic wife. Emma had a crisp, fine touch, as her daughter Etty later remembered, and played with intelligence and clarity – though the slow movements tended to be 'too allegro', for even then Emma hated sentimentality in music, as in life.

One year at Greville House was enough; the girls were homesick, although they had the consolation of trips out on Sundays with their lively brother Harry, who was studying law in London. At the end of 1822 they returned to Maer Hall to be taught by Elizabeth and visiting masters and governesses.

Life at Maer was in itself a liberal education. Old Josiah Wedgwood had bequeathed a well-stocked library; having friends and business contacts all over the world, he had ordered books and illustrations from Italy, Russia, America and even China. All subjects were covered – art, science, politics, history and literature. Emma was famous in the family for having read the whole of *Paradise Lost* as a little girl, or so they claimed. The explorer Mungo Park caught her imagination, and years later she wrote to Charles Darwin, 'I remember being more interested in it when I was a child than in almost any book and admiring Mungo Park with all my heart.' Jane Austen was also a particular favourite; Emma and her friends often identified with Miss Austen's characters.

Some of the most distinguished men of the time enjoyed their visits to Maer. The novelist Anne Caldwell, a neighbour, recalled a visit by the Revd Sydney Smith:

It was his custom to stroll about the room in which we were sitting, and which was lined with books, taking down one lot after another, sometimes reading or quoting aloud, sometimes discussing any subject that arose. He took down a sort of record of those men who had lived to a great age. 'A record of little value,' said Mrs Wedgwood, 'as to live longer than other people can hardly be the desire of any one.' [In fact Allens, Wedgwoods and Darwins were on the whole remarkably long-lived.] 'It is not so much the longevity,' Sydney Smith explained, 'that is valued as the original build and constitution, that condition of health and habit of life which not only leads to longevity, but makes life enjoyable while it lasts, that renders the subject interesting and worth enquiry.' 'You must preach, Mr Smith,' said Mrs Wedgwood (it was Saturday). 'We must go and try the pulpit then,' said he, 'to see if it suits me.' So to the church we walked, and how he amused us by his droll way of 'trying the pulpit' as he called it.

As a girl Emma absorbed a knowledge of world affairs easily in their comfortable library at Maer Hall. As Anne Caldwell's sister Emma remembered,

I never saw anything pleasanter than the ways of going on of this family, and one reason is the freedom of speech upon every subject; there is no difference in politics or principles of any kind that makes it treason to speak one's mind openly, and they all do it. There is a simplicity of good sense about them, that no one ever dreams of not differing upon any subject where they feel inclined. As no things are said from party or prejudice, there is no bitterness in discussing opinions. I believe this could not be the case if there was a decided difference of party principle in the members of the family.

Old Josiah would have been delighted at this praise, and that his son, the solemn Jos, had passed on his ideal – that 'learning should be absorbed with pleasure'.

'The part of the intellectual character most improved by the Wedgwood education is good sense, which is indeed their pre-eminent quality,' Emma Caldwell wrote.

> It is one of the most important, and in the end will promote more of their own and others' happiness than any other quality. The moral quality most promoted by their education is benevolence, which combined with good sense, gives all that education can give. The two little girls are happy, gay, amiable, sensible, and though not particularly energetic in learning, yet will acquire all that is necessary by their steady perseverance. They have freedom in their actions in this house as well as in their principles. Doors and windows stand open, you are nowhere in confinement; you may do as you like; you are surrounded by books that all look most tempting to read; you will always find some pleasant topic of conversation, or may start one, as all things are talked of in the general family. All this sounds and is delightful.

In 1822, while Emma and Fanny were in London, Bessy had a fall from her horse and broke her arm. It was perhaps the result of the first of the epileptic fits which she was to suffer for the rest of her life. 'I think I shall not ride any more,' she wrote to Jessie, 'I am grown timid, and my arm continues weak. I don't think, however, it would hinder me if my spirit was better.' From now on she became increasingly restless, and found a relief in travel. So, just as old Josiah had made travelling part of Jos's education, in the summer of 1823 Jos encouraged Bessy to take the family, with Marianne and Susan Darwin, on a tour of Yorkshire that would be both pleasurable and educational. He realized that Bessy's health was failing and that the trip would be good for her. Since her fall she had lost confidence and, aware of her fading mental power, she needed, as she said, 'to refresh my oldness with a new scene'; travel always lifted her spirits.

Making Scarborough their centre, the party travelled to Bolton Abbey, which was a mixed pleasure: a long walk in the woods was, said Fanny, 'dull and a waste of time', but Charlotte discovered the delightful 'Valley of Desolation' which raised their spirits. They called at Rievaulx Abbey where Charlotte 'made a pretty drawing'. At Scarborough, Fanny and Emma were not much impressed. The town was 'a pleasant place, very pretty walking on the sands and on the cliffs each side of the bay,' Bessy wrote,

> but the beach very, very inferior to Tenby, and the whole place infinitely inferior. We went to the first ball, and the attendance was so thin that it quite discouraged the girls, and though I tried to persuade them to try again I could not succeed. The poor master of the ceremonies looked so melancholy that he excited my tenderest sympathy. I think public balls are getting quite out of fashion. At last York Race ball, which used to be a place where all the grandees of this very opulent county used to delight in shewing themselves, there were only seven couples. I think it is your stately quadrilles that have made the balls so dismal, because the English ladies now dance them as if they were at a funeral and dancing the dance of death. They used to hop them about in a very ungraceful manner, and finding that was *mauvais ton*, they now burlesque the French gentle movement.

At least in Scarborough they had the good fortune of a visit to an unusually good company of strolling players.

Eventually Bessy left Emma and Fanny, and Marianne and Susan Darwin, to make the best they could of the dull town and took her sister Fanny Allen, Elizabeth and Charlotte to stay with their old friend Sydney Smith, now a parson at Foston-le-Clay, eight miles from York, and were 'rewarded by four of the merriest days I ever spent'. Meanwhile Fanny and Emma whiled away the rainy days reading the letters of Lady Mary Wortley Montagu. Emma's own talent as a letter writer owes much to Bessy's love of reading aloud eighteenth-century letters, especially those of

Mme de Sévigné. Devout little Fanny worked away at William Paley's *Principles of Morals and Political Philosophy* – 'the sort of book I like very much', she wrote in her journal – and took herself to task because she had 'been idle, must improve, mustn't feel out of humour or jealous'.

They were back at Maer on 17 September after what Fanny called 'a very pleasant expedition'. Four days later, Aunt Kitty Wedgwood died at Shrewsbury, where she had been taken to be cared for by Dr Robert Darwin; Marianne and Caroline had nursed her with devotion. The passing of this competent, somewhat masculine lady was agreed to be a blessed release from a long and painful illness. Now only Aunt Sarah, Jos and Uncle John were left of the children of Josiah I.

The summer's holiday did little to improve Bessy's health; she gave up her galloping horse rides for good, and now divided her time between riding Peggy, her quiet donkey, over the wild heath and through the fields of Maer – excursions on which Emma often joined her, always remembering them with pleasure – and reading Sévigné by the fire.

On Christmas Day 1823, Fanny noted in her diary: 'Charles Darwin went.' It is remarkable that there are so few references to him in the family letters of this period, and that it is Fanny who records his coming and going. Did she perhaps even then have hope?

On the same day Fanny reflected that her character had not improved much. 'I must take Mamma for my model . . . In the course of years I may be as amiable and good as she is.' Amiable and good though Bessy undoubtedly was, she was not particularly religious. Churchgoing at Jeffreston Church in Wales had been a social rather than a religious occasion – a time for singing hymns and gossiping with neighbours, and for wearing Sunday best. In the summer of 1824, when Emma was sixteen, Bessy decided that perhaps it was time she was confirmed; but she did not consider it particularly important, and neither apparently did Emma – unlike Fanny, who presumably had been confirmed earlier and was now most devout. Bessy herself was away from home and left the arrangements – and the guidance – to Elizabeth. 'I hope she [Emma] will feel no objection,' she wrote. Emma might go with their friends, the Tollets, and Elizabeth and Fanny, and 'if your Aunt Sarah's horse and carriage are disengaged, I advise you to ask her to lend them to you, that you may make the most respectable appearance you can' – always a very important concern to the Allen sisters. As for the subject, 'do not let her be alarmed at that, it will be but little and the subject is simple.' Clearly she was not sure whether Emma would agree – 'if she were very averse to it, perhaps one ought not to press it any more than as an opinion that it is better done than omitted, as it is better to conform to the ceremonies of our Church than to omit them and one does not know that in omitting them we are not liable to sin.' Indeed, Emma, like her father and the Unitarian Wedgwoods, would never feel that such ceremonies were important. However, the entry in her diary for 17 September 1824 shows that she took the confirmation in her stride: 'Confirmed with Jessie', her Uncle John Wedgwood's daughter.

Two weeks later, Emma was leading the revels in a noisy family party. '30 Sept.,' her diary reads, 'Susan [Darwin], Catherine [Darwin] and Robert [Wedgwood, John's son] came: wicked times. 1st Oct Revels; 2nd Revels; 4th Revels; 5th Acted some of Merry Wives' 6th Oct, quiet evening!!!!!' That week Maer Hall, filled with young cousins and friends, rang with laughter from morning to night – overwhelming even the tolerant Bessy, who wrote to her sister Fanny: 'These young things have kept me in such a whirl of noise . . . I may say to you under the rose and without the smallest disrespect to the company that a little calm will be very agreeable . . . Susan and Catherine Darwin came here by the hack carriage . . . and the Tag Rag Company, led on by Harry, is again set up . . . he is épris au dernier point with Jessie Wedgwood . . . they have been dancing every night . . . she is looking very pretty, very merry sitting always by him.' She liked John Wedgwood's lively daughter and 'if they could afford to get married, I should desire no better.' But meanwhile, 'I don't like mounting guard every evening till it pleases them to go to bed, or watching them talking nonsense or playing Beggar My Neighbour or other such lover-like pastimes. Last night they performed some scenes in the Merry Wives of Windsor without Falstaff for Jos's and my amusement.' Emma, apparently, was 'very good' as Master Shallow, and Susan Darwin and Jessie Wedgwood as Mrs Page and Anne Page, 'both uncommonly pretty in long waists; Mrs Quickly, Elisabeth, excellently acted . . . If they had known their parts more perfect it would have gone off very well . . . After the play there was a ball. Elisabeth and Charlotte are too old for these revels.'

Susan and Catherine Darwin at this time were, according to their brother Charles, like Jane Austen's Lydia and Kitty, 'always running after anything in trousers'. Susan had hoped for a chance with Harry but 'she comes in second best'. It would be the story of Susan's life.

Emma was quite happy to be ridiculous as Master Shallow and to leave the flirting and pretty frocks to Susan and Jessie. Hers was a carefree, sunlit girlhood, which she would always remember with delight.

CHAPTER FOUR

The Grand Tour

I N FEBRUARY 1825 JOS, BESSY AND THEIR FOUR DAUGHTERS LEFT MAER ON a tour that would last until October. They planned to take a long break at Paris and Geneva, and then spend a month in each of the four great Italian cities, Florence, Rome, Naples and Venice. They had spent the winter evenings poring over guide books and travellers' journals, and the Maer library shelves still held Josiah Wedgwood's illustrated volumes on the classical discoveries at Pompeii and Herculaneum. His old friend, Wright of Derby, had painted a dramatic picture of the Vesuvius they hoped to climb. Now, primed with advice from those experienced travellers the Allen aunts, they loaded their lumbering travelling coaches for an absence of several months. Aunt Jessie in Geneva would provide their evening gowns and advise on suitable dress for the tour.

Bessy, at sixty-one, was frail, but she loved travel and was determined to make at least part of the journey. Elizabeth was thirty-two; Charlotte twenty-eight; Fanny nineteen; and Emma sixteen. For the next eight months each of the sisters kept a journal. Elizabeth's was brief and rather dull; Charlotte was more interested in painting views than describing them; Emma's was lively but often slapdash – dates were sometimes wrong (she recorded their arrival in Geneva as 26 February) – and there were gaps, usually because of illness. This did not worry Emma, for she knew she could always rely on Fanny to fill in the blanks. It was Fanny, little Miss Pedigree, who carefully recorded each stage of the journey. 'Left Maer February 7th, to London 9–14, crossed the channel – 3 hours by steam, Montreuil 16th, Paris 17th, Avallon 24th, Autun 25th, Pont d'Ain 27th – arrived Geneva January 28th.'

Thoughout their journey it is Fanny's level Staffordshire voice we mostly hear, always careful, shrewd and honest; and since in a few years that voice was to be forever silent, it is well to let her speak.

During their short stay at Paris, Bessy felt it her duty to give up an evening to spend with her cousin Mme Collos, in the humble surroundings of the fishmonger's house in La Truanderie – even though her daughters were being groomed for a much more elevated social life. Then it was on to Geneva, where an ecstatic Aunt Jessie greeted them. She adored Bessy, who had been in her youth a surrogate mother, and lavished on her sister's children all the affection of her warm, vivacious Welsh nature. They in turn responded with a love that lasted until her death – especially Emma, who established a particularly deep rapport with her aunt. Jessie at that time was forty-eight but still in full bloom – a great favourite with the men and, as her family noticed kindly, something of a coquette. In spite of her early reservations, her marriage to Sismondi had been a total success. Serious and scholarly and so different from her bullying father, he bestowed on her a gentle love and gave her security. He tolerantly accepted long visits from her family, retreating to his study and his interminable history. He was particularly impressed by Jos and charmed, as everyone was, by Bessy. Emma later confessed that she found him 'not very manly', and his elaborate courtesy and flourishing bows slightly ridiculous. She could not bear his hand-kissing and the way he called her 'ma petite Emma'. Her brother Harry had clearly felt something similar when he met Sismondi in England on his wedding to Jessie: 'We salute one another', he wrote, 'in the style of the frontispiece to "Les Précieuses Ridicules".' But he had been a great favourite in the intellectual circle of Mme de Staël, with many friends among the foremost literati of France, Switzerland and Italy; and he furnished the Wedgwoods with useful introductions to interesting people all along their route.

It was now obvious that Bessy would not be able to go further than Geneva, but she at least had the pleasure of watching her daughters waltzing at the 'very pleasant dance' Aunt Jessie gave for them at their apartment, and again at a ball where, as Emma reported, 'Fanny and Charlotte ventured on the Cotillon.' However, that weekend was 'melancholy' as they prepared for the journey which would take them onwards into Italy without Bessy. They consoled her with the prospect of meeting her at Milan on their return, and their hopes of finishing their Grand Tour with her at Venice.

Setting out with guides and couriers, they spent the first night out of Geneva at San Michele and breakfasted at Chambéry, preparing to cross the Alps from Sans le Bourg – according to Emma, a 'filthy place at the foot of Mount Cenis'. Even with six horses to each carriage, it took three hours to reach the top. It was so cold that 'the windows froze inside although they were all shut', wrote Fanny. And it was dangerous – 'Papa and Elizabeth narrowly escaped being overturned by the slipping of a horse.' The seven-mile descent was disappointing: 'clouds of drifting snow' made it impossible to see anything of their first entrance to Italy. Nor were they cheered up by the first villages: 'I never saw anything so wretched as the people and children at Susa.' At Turin there was even more poverty, though there was at last a fine view of the Alps.

Here they took a break. They were invited to dinner by an Italian acquaintance, where Emma 'met some pleasant men'. They dutifully did the rounds of the Turin galleries, but Emma did not 'care for any of them much', and Fanny did not admire the Michelangelo in a small private collection; indeed, both she and Emma took a dislike to the great artist from the beginning and said so, firmly. Emma in particular always refused to gush over famous pictures, however much they were praised in the guide books, and dismissed some galleries as a 'hum' – Wedgwood for humbug. On the other hand, at the Palace Museum in Turin she saw the van Dyck *Charles I with his Children* and 'liked it very much'.

This was to be the pattern for much of the tour – initial disappointment after long, uncomfortable journeys. From Turin to Genoa, as Emma wrote, 'it was ten hours without getting out of the carriage,' though presumably there were comfort stops. The Hôtel de la Ville in Genoa, she wrote, 'was handsome but it was bitter cold and odious to walk in the streets'. However, on the drive by the sea to Chiavari, Italy began to work its magic. 'The setting sun on distant rocks . . . I have never seen anything so beautiful before.' Emma would always respond more deeply to nature than to art. They slept at La Spezia and enjoyed 'fine sea views'. On the way to Pescia they called on friends of Sismondi whom the Allen aunts had met twelve years before. Observant Fanny noticed the round hats and costumes of the women of Tuscany, and all the girls sketched them.

Their first view of Florence, in the rain, was disappointing; the inn where they had a temporary booking was shabby. So on Wednesday 23 March they moved to lodge with a Mme Merveilleuse de Plantis, 'whose name', Emma thought, 'at least was encouraging'. But Florence, the city that Stendhal had praised as 'the cleanest city in the Universe, and undoubtedly to be numbered among the most elegant', was a disappointment. Stendhal's 'deliciously perfumed streets' were dirty, cold and wet. The visit to the much-praised Fiesole was dismissed briskly by Fanny: 'this day's work was all hum.' The celebrated views had disappeared in heavy mist, and they walked for four hours. They were desperately tired. Even the indefatigable Fanny was reduced to one line – 'too tired to enjoy the Royal Gallery' – though at the Tribune Emma thought Raphael's *St John the Baptist* 'the most beautiful in the world'. Early mornings, long drives and inadequate food in dirty inns had left them all exhausted. 'Even Papa', Charlotte wrote to her mother, 'is tired.'

It rained solidly for two days, so there were unremitting tours of unlit galleries where it was often too dark to see properly. Emma and Fanny decided they 'had not a proper taste for statues' and 'did not care for' old Etruscan bronzes. Their grandfather, old Josiah, must have turned in his grave. Michelangelo's *Day and Night* was 'very ugly', Fanny thought. Emma had stomach ache and Charlotte a bad cold, and the Sunday service at the English Church was a 'hum'. On a damp grey day they walked to the Boboli Gardens. 'Very pretty,' Emma admitted, 'but too much up and down.'

It was not only the galleries and gardens that were exhausting, for there were social engagements each evening. A singing master was engaged for the girls, and Elizabeth and Charlotte were expected to perform, accompanied on piano by Emma. One Sunday night an Abbé Panni called and 'we talked nothing but Italian – rather fatiguing,' Emma found, 'because of his Tuscan accent.' Nevertheless, Aunt Emma Allen had given her Italian lessons years earlier and Emma had a quick ear for languages, so at the end of the tour her Italian was fluent.

Altogether the Wedgwood sisters were not sorry to leave Florence – though back in England the Allen aunts could not believe they stayed so short a time in the city they themselves had found so magical. Jos was not happy either. There had been perilous moments on the descent from the Alps when he realized he was not young any more, and when the responsibility of organizing such a tour with four young women weighed heavily. Long journeys over rough roads had set off his lumbago. And he missed Bessy. They had been so seldom apart. She would have cheered them all. Although the girls kept their moans for their journals, he was concerned about their health – particularly Emma, who had suffered from migraines all her life. Their gruelling programme, the heat and peering up into the dark ceilings often brought on her headaches. So, as they prepared to leave Florence, Jos decided to travel the rest of the way under the guidance of a *vetturino*, who from now would be the equivalent of a modern package tour guide. They would pay a single price for transport, food and accommodation; the disadvantage was that they had to follow the rules of their *vetturino* – if they wanted a detour, they would have to pay extra. They 'take each carriage with three mules,' Fanny explained, 'and furnish us with everything. We set off every morning about 5 or 6, breakfast before we go, then go a long stage until 12,' when they took a long rest before continuing.

At 5 a.m. on 1 April they set out from Florence for Rome. Their road went through 'wild barren country', past the 'fine view' of Lake Balzano, 'through forests of oak trees' to Montefiascone, where 'the road was cleared at the sides because of robbers.' They stayed at 'poor mean little inns': one had no door to the sitting room and was so cold they could not sit down; another at Viterbo 'could not provide a looking glass, milk, butter, sugar, cups, teaspoons etc.' On 5 April they reached the Campagna, where they saw 'troops of horses and slate coloured cows with immense horns', and 'the road went up and down as if it had a convulsion.' At last, eighteen miles from Rome, they stood on a hill and saw the dome of St Peter's. On the same day they came into the city and found comfort in the Hôtel de la Grande Bretagne. Here they stayed for two days until they secured 'very nice lodgings in the Piazza Barberini with a pretty fountain'. They were to be in Rome for nearly a month. Now they could relax and enjoy the ever-changing spectacle of Easter in the Eternal City. For a time, as Charlotte wrote to her mother, 'Papa's temper improved' and he decided that 'Rome suited him very much.' The city glowed. Exotic characters posed on the Spanish Steps waiting for admiring artists; in the squares, pilgrims and white-robed penitents jostled with peasants from the country, their solemn chants mingled with the music of guitars and pipes – a vibrant accompaniment to the unceasing pageantry.

On their first day in Rome they walked to St Peter's; Emma 'admired the court and fountains very much but . . . did not care much for the inside'. Later they climbed up the cupola and 'Papa even went up into the ball.' 'It was a wonderful sight,' wrote Emma, 'looking down into the Sistine Chapel.' Nevertheless, Michelangelo once more received a sharp rebuke: 'I never saw anything so hideous as that last judgment of Michael Angelo. I quite dislike him for wasting his talents on anything so ugly.' On another occasion she considered: 'he makes his women so hideous.'

When later they attended a service in the Sistine Chapel, Emma enjoyed the music: 'I liked it very much, there was a fine soprano.' She was fascinated by the castrati – 'there were men', she reported, 'who sounded exactly like women' – unlike Stendhal, who heard 'the sacred capons of the Sistine Chapel' with violent disgust. 'Never did I in all my days', he had written, 'endure so daemonic a caterwauling.' To their nonconformist eyes the Catholic ritual was a constant source of fascination mixed with distaste. One day, as Fanny noted, they watched penitents in white woollen dresses with hoods over their faces and knotted ropes by their waists, followed by a cardinal with a priest holding his train and carrying a cushion. 'When someone clapped their hands they all knelt down. Another clap prostrated themselves, another got up on their knees – then spoilt the effect by spitting and blowing their noses.' There was much to annoy the sturdy Wedgwoods. Emma disliked the 'mummery at Vespers in St Peters'; nevertheless, they all rushed to see the splendid processions. Emma and Fanny went to see the Pope officiate at Santa Maria Novella. Stendhal had seen the Pope elevated before the altar like a god; Emma saw him 'a pale old man' walking to the church before his cardinals. When they visited the Pantheon – according to Fanny, 'the most perfect temple in Rome' – they heard that 'some wicked Popes took off the gilded dome and make a Baldeschino in St Peters. One does nothing but rage at the Popes at almost every step.'

Each day was spent visiting museums and Roman ruins. Here, as in Turin and Florence – and unlike many of the tourists who thronged Rome at this time, armed with Baedekers, and wrote gushingly in their journals – Emma refused to profess admiration she did not feel and vigorously maintained her own opinion. So she would do all her life. But for artists she liked – such as Guercino – she always had a word of praise. A single Doric column of grey marble in St Paul's Church was the 'most beautiful I ever saw'. All tourists to Rome were recommended to see the Coliseum by moonlight. The Wedgwoods had expected to be disappointed; in fact they were bowled over. Even Fanny allowed herself a burst of enthusiasm, admitting that she viewed it 'with some sentiment'.

The sisters took their cultural duties seriously, but there were times when they allowed themselves the frivolity of shopping. Fanny was quite interested in a mosaic shop, but 'never wished to see another'. And there were times when they rebelled. 'On April 20th we settled to go a round of churches but the first one gave us such a hating fit that we resolved to enjoy ourselves at a villa and walked up a hill among wild flowers to a grove of cypresses.' This would have been very pleasant for Emma, who had a lifelong love of wild flowers. Also, each evening there was some different entertainment. Jos had come armed with introductions to Roman ladies who held open house most evenings, where the Wedgwood girls shone musically if not conversationally, and were much praised: Elizabeth and Charlotte sang exceptionally well in English, French and Italian, and Emma was a talented accompanist.

Their most useful acquaintance in Rome was Mrs Bunsen, the former Fanny Waddington who, with her mother Mrs Waddington, would appear and reappear in Emma's life like minor characters in a stage drama. Mr Bunsen was the Hanoverian representative at the Vatican. When the Allen sisters were in Rome in 1817, Mrs Waddington had been there on a long visit to her daughter and, to the annoyance of the Allens, who remembered her as their brother John's *bien amie*, played the *grande dame* and had tried to patronize them. But Emma and her sisters liked Fanny Bunsen – whose evening parties were popular in Rome – and were grateful for her help; they were always welcome at Mrs Bunsen's receptions and often turned to her for advice on what clothes to wear or where to go. However, some evenings were a 'hum'. At one party at Mrs Bunsen's there were 'mostly Germans. German ladies must be a vulgar race judging by the specimens we saw,' Fanny wrote tartly. But Emma only remembered the gentleman who played the pianoforte so beautifully, and Jos was pleased to renew an old acquaintance he had met thirty-four years earlier, when he had toured the German courts with his father's superb copy of the Etruscan Portland Vase.

Two of the Wedgwoods' most bizarre evenings in Rome were spent at the receptions given by the society ladies of the city for poor pilgrims to Rome, which Elizabeth described vividly in a letter to her mother.

We went last night at 7 to see the pilgrims at supper. All pilgrims are fed and lodged for three days, and waited on at supper by a society of ladies and gentlemen, princesses and cardinals. We went very luckily without Papa, who would have been heartily tired as it turned out, but we had an amusing evening. We knocked at the door and were announced as four foreign ladies, and found ourselves in a great hall with tables with lamps and writing things, and a few men in red gowns laughing and talking and bustling backwards and forwards. There we stood helpless some time, not knowing where to go; till at last the old man in red who let us in, after a quantity of gabbling and gesticulating which we could make nothing of, fairly put us out into the street again and shut the door on us. By this time the carriage was gone, so there we staid in the dirt and the dark, till the door was opened again to let in some more ladies, and we pushed in after them and followed them thro' the hall and several more places, full of bustle and pilgrims and soldiers, till we got upstairs to where the women pilgrims were to sup. There we found two very long well lighted rooms with tables down each side and I should think some hundreds of ladies without their bonnets and most of them in white aprons to serve. There was a middle room besides, where there was a set of women with towels on their heads, listening to a sermon from a man in red. After this they went on their knees, and said such a number of Ave Marias that I was tired waiting to see the end, and they must have wanted their suppers terribly which they did not get till near ten o'clock. The Princess Doria was going about directing, and the Queen of Etruria's daughter and two other young Princesses Ruspoli, who looked as if they were carrying about the trays for fun. We were almost the only strangers there, as the Princess had given orders that none should be let in that night, as she was expecting the King and Queen of Naples.

On another night they saw the washing of the pilgrims' dusty feet. This the ladies did, as Emma said, 'in good earnest': they took off the dirty stockings, washed the feet and then, to the girls' amazement, kissed them.

Elizabeth, Charlotte, Fanny and Emma all wrote excited accounts of this event – but it was observant little Fanny who noticed that, after the washing of the feet, the ladies 'wash their own hands with lemon juice'.

Their most enlivening evening was that when the visit of the King and Queen of Naples was celebrated with the illumination of the dome of St Peter's and a firework display. Mrs Bunsen had advised them to go in full dress – but reminded them that they needed to be smart for the party given by a duke in the Sala de Teatro afterwards. 'So,' Elizabeth wrote, 'to prevent catching cold Charlotte and I put pink handkerchiefs on our heads, and our black satins, which are the most comfortable gowns in the world.' Emma merely noted: 'it quite answered my expectations.' Once again it was Fanny who carefully recorded the evening.

> At ½ past 6 they placed paper lanterns – at eight they lighted the torches which was a wonderful thing as they did it almost all at once and it looked like magic . . . to see them going about so fast. One man climbed to the top cross [which] showed the size of the building to great advantage, he looked so small. Then to the Teatro to see the fireworks – magnificent, a girandolo of 7,000 rockets, as it is said, was wonderful and they fired cannons which had a very good effect.

After that they went into 'the Salle de Teatre [*sic*] but everybody looked so stupid that we went away as soon as we had taken some ice – it was a very warm evening.'

Rome had been a complete success. All the girls were sad to leave the Eternal City – especially Fanny, who had made a very dear Italian friend in Giulietta Persiani, the daughter of a family they had come to know. Bessy had worried that Jos might not be enjoying himself, but Elizabeth reassured her: 'I think he enjoys what he sees here as much or more than any of us. He has not so much pleasure in the travelling itself but he liked that better when he had thrown all trouble and anxiety off his shoulders by going with a vetturino.' There had been one evening at the Bunsens' with some 'grand folk' when Jos had been ill at ease; as observant Fanny noted, 'such mingling will not do.' But even Jos was sorry to leave, as Charlotte reported to her mother.

We like Rome so much that all Jessie's scoldings cannot persuade us to be sorry we left Florence so soon. Now that we are within a week of the end of our month here, I grudge every day that passes. I scarcely know why I like it so much. I think it suits Papa too very well. All his time that is not occupied in seeing sights, he employs, as it appears very much to his satisfaction, in looking out of the window and watching the idle groups of common people that this square is constantly filled with. They are so picturesque, and I think handsome, that they afford constant amusement. We want nothing, my dear Mama, but that your strength would have permitted you to come with us; but when we are resting from our travels our life is much more fatiguing than on any journey, which would never have done for you; even Papa has sometimes been quite fatigued at the end of the day.

At 5 a.m. on 9 May their travelling coaches rumbled out of Rome and set off for Naples. They had been waiting since 3 a.m. for their *vetturino*, to the annoyance of the punctual Jos. They changed horses at Albano and drove through volcanic country to the Pontine marshes, where they saw their first buffaloes. It was not a comfortable journey. On Tuesday they had lunch at a 'horrid inn'; on Wednesday at Montecello 'begging children followed us down the hill like a pack of hounds.' No doubt they were encouraged by Elizabeth's sympathetic face; at Maer she was famous among beggars as a soft touch. But there were compensations: their road took them along a beautiful coast where, while the horses were fed and watered, they 'walked by the sea with a most agreeable cicerone', and for a while they drove through beautiful country 'very like England'. At Capua on the seventeenth they slept in another 'nasty inn', their chamber the hottest room they had ever been in. The last stages were 'unbearably hot and dusty' – but in the cool of the evening there were fireflies to guide them along the road to Naples.

Naples was an immediate success. It was very hot and Vesuvius was shrouded in mist, but the Hôtel des Îles Brittanique was 'deliciously cool', the rooms 'most exquisite, so large and clean'. And, as practical Fanny noticed, 'all the eating things were very clean.' The scene outside was gay, with bright-uniformed soldiers swaggering through the narrow streets, elegant ladies driving in decorated carriages. It was still as Goethe had described in his *Italian Journey* of 1789 – a work that Coleridge had introduced to Jos, who in turn would certainly have recommended it to his daughters to be read in their month's preparation. 'One of the greatest delights of Naples is the universal gaiety,' Goethe wrote.

> The many-coloured flowers and fruits in which Nature adorns herself seem to invite the people to decorate themselves and their belongings with silk scarves, ribbons and flowers in their hats. In the poorest homes the chairs and chests are painted with bright flowers on a gilt ground; even the one-horse carriages are painted a bright red, their carved woodwork gilded; and the horses decorated with artificial flowers, crimson tassels and tinsel. Some horses wear plumes on their heads, others little pennons which revolve as they trot. The scarlet skirts and bodices, trimmed with gold and silver braids, which the women of Nettuno wear, the painted boats, etc., everything seems to be competing for visual attention against the splendour of the sea and sky.

Jos had long wished to visit Naples, having since childhood been steeped in the glories of antiquity. When his father Josiah had sent him on the tour of Germany and Holland to promote Wedgwood ware, the young man had studied hard in preparation and was praised at the royal courts for his understanding and explanation of classical mythology. Although normally a man of few words, unwilling to show emotion, all his life when he felt profoundly he turned to the classical figures that had touched him so deeply for images to help him express himself. When saying farewell to his beloved brother Tom, he had written, 'I feel like Aeneas clasping the shade of Creusa . . . I call up your image, but it is not substantial.'

His daughters found much to interest and entertain them. The opera was a great joy, especially for Emma. One night they went to Il Fondo to see *The Barber of Seville*, with Lablache as Figaro and a delightful Rowena. Fanny was unimpressed, pronouncing 'the ballet wretched, dress indecent'; but Emma loved the music and found Lablache very amusing. They took expeditions to Baia along the 'delightful road by the sea' and to Paestum in 'a nasty little Caleche'. They dined at Salerno and slept that night at Eboli at a wild sort of inn. Paestum 'went far beyond my expectations', wrote Fanny. 'I enjoyed this expedition more than any other, the temple of Neptune was especially beautiful but was spoilt by pestering beggars and an impudent begging priest' – who, the waiter told them, was a 'santo'. Pompeii was disappointing – they were all too exhausted to enjoy it, though they watched frescoes being uncovered and admired the mosaic 'pavements, the stucco pillars painted red, the oil shops with large jars sunk in the counter'.

On 23 May they left by sea along the 'very pleasant coast' for a six-day break based at Sorrento. It was not a success. Emma was now running a high fever, the inn on the Piazza di Sorrento was 'not a pleasant place', wrote Fanny, whose diary records the next weeks. They were marooned, by a *vetturino* over-careful for their safety, in 'orchards of oranges behind high walls' in a stifling heat and locked in at night. They felt confined, and even outside the walls in the country they were surrounded by 'high hills that nothing but mules can go up'. On the first day Elizabeth, Charlotte and Fanny took a 'giro on mules and asses westward up a steep hill covered with myrtle, pink convolvulus, cistas, with fine views of the sea, to a convent at Carmaledi'; but Emma was now too ill to leave the inn. Jos stayed with her while her sisters rode up the mule track to the convent at St Agata. They returned 'hot and cross with Sorrento' and the orange groves that hemmed them in. Fanny 'couldn't think what the poor wretches do for two or three months'. There were no books; to the Wedgwoods, this was a serious blow.

The next day followed a similar pattern. Elizabeth, Charlotte and Fanny took a three-hour boat trip to Amalfi, 'not at all a beautiful situation'. They took lunch in a 'dirty inn', were plagued by beggars and Elizabeth had a severe headache. The day was 'a complete hum'. Meanwhile Emma sweltered in the inn still in a high fever, and Jos wrote a jaundiced letter to Bessy.

> All these boasted places only confirm my preference of England and of Maer. I am quite surprised at the attachment of your sisters to Rome, especially as I suppose they had not a carriage constantly, for the filthy habits of the people and the total neglect

of the police as to cleanliness, make the town very disagreeable even for a man to walk about it, and intolerable I should have supposed for English women. As one instance, towards evening you every now and then hear vessels emptied of water, or some less innocent contents, from the windows of the houses, without notice; and as far as I could ever perceive without the precaution of looking whether the street was clear . . . I believe I shall quit this country without any desire ever to return to it, but if possible with a deeper detestation of the principles which cause its degradation, and a more hearfelt approbation of the contrary ones which are in operation in our own happy country, and of the men who are supporting them. I don't know whether the Italians are subject to the same annoyance, or whether, if subject, they become insensible to it, but the mere importunity of the miserable beggars that you meet with at every step, and who ask for alms with loud cries and as much earnestness as if their existence depended on succeeding in each instance, makes a walk a scene of persecution. In short this country has so many odious or painful circumstances which move one's indignation, contempt, or compassion so powerfully that the charms of scenery and of climate cannot have their proper effect. In short I remain at least as good a John Bull as I came out . . . You must not think however that I have looked only at one side I have had much pleasure, and I have satisfied a wish almost as old as my memory, and I must not expect to escape the lot of human nature that there is disappointment in the gratification of all desires . . . I trust that this first long separation will be our last.

On Sunday with immense relief they returned to 'dear Naples' and the next night enjoyed 'two or three pretty things' in the opera at the Teatro Nuovo.

Emma was still not well enough to join them for the most exciting trip of their stay – the ascent of the crater of Vesuvius. At least Emma could be sure that her alter ego, the methodical Fanny, would write a faithful record.

Wednesday June 1st: At Resina we mounted the donkeys and rode for nearly 2 hours, the night was warm but the moon was covered with clouds. We passed several fields of lava all rough as if it had been ploughed. We walked up the steep part with the help of a man and a rope apiece. It was very steep and bad walking from the ashes being deep it took us an hour and a quarter, but I was very little tired. It was a very dull morning raining, and the sun would not rise, but the expedition was quite worth while. The crater looked much finer than I expected and there were several streams of steam coming out of it and in one place there was fire enough to boil an egg. The descent did not take us long but it took a rantipole party of girls and young men a much shorter time. There were a couple of hot places in our way down, one I could only just bear my hand on. After we had gone some distance from the cone it seemed wonderful how we could have got up it, it seemed so steep and so high, but while we were mounting we could not judge the distance at all; it looked a very little way, when we were half way up.

The next morning they left Naples for Rome.

Saturday 4th June 1825: Came to Rome from Naples little after 11. The road from Genzano to Albano is very pretty and English looking. We lighted at the Hotel de l'Europe and in the evening walked to the Borghese gardens. Heard from Mamma that she and Aunt Jessie will meet us at Milan: this will be delightful.

They paid a last visit to St Peter's, where, as Fanny recorded,

we saw the remains of some folly: the Pope has been making two or three (I forget which) new saints. Then we went to the Palazzo Castiglione where we saw several beautiful ceilings particularly one by Domenichino and another by Guercino. It was by Aunt Fanny's advice we went and it is quite worth while. We drove through the Jews Quarter which is locked up at 8 at night, to Mrs Bunsens and after our call there came home.

In Rome, Emma and Fanny renewed their friendship with the Persianis:

> After dinner we went to the Persianis: they had got us a
> permission to see the Ludovisi Villa. We took Giulietta with us
> and went to the Villa. We saw Guercino's Aurora which is
> beautiful though it was too dark to see it well, and some statues
> which seemed very beautiful particularly Arria and Petus, and a
> gladiator. I was very sorry not to have seen them by a good
> light though statues look something very fine by twilight . . .
> Altogether this day's journey about Rome has made me feel very
> fond of it and I leave it with some sentiment. We took leave of
> Giulietta and I shall be very sorry not to see her again.

The next day they left Rome – another 5 a.m. start – took the old Florence
road and then turned off to see the much-praised cascades at Terni. They

> arrived at Narni at 1 and after a couple of hours rest set off for the
> cascade 4 miles off. We were obliged to pay a great deal of money
> a head and they wanted to fob us off with one little carriage but
> we would not submit. We had to go up a long hill and we were
> bothered with beggars but the view was very fine, and so was the
> cascade, four miles off. I have not much pleasure in cascades. I
> think it would have been better not to have mounted the hill at
> all, but to have kept along the river till we got opposite the cascade.
> Most of the party except myself had headaches which is very apt
> to happen when there is something to be seen.

Fanny herself was indefatigable and, like her sisters, was a conscientious traveller not because Jos drove them to the sights but
because she herself was interested in them.

Although Jos was now impatient to get to Milan and Bessy, the tour he
had planned had to be followed according to the *vetturino*'s route. They
headed for the Appennines, and Emma, revived in the cooler air at Foligno,
saw 'troops of people going to reap in the Campagna with fiddle and
guitar at their head!' But the Adriatic was 'hideous' in comparison with

the Mediterranean. Ancona's Trajan arches were 'handsome', but Ancona was 'more stinking than any town we have ever seen'. Pesaro was at least 'flourishing', and there were smart ladies in Ravenna. 'For the first time' on the road to Faenza 'the Appenines look grand.' In Bologna they 'took a valet de place and went to a Goldoni play'. Emma was very much amazed, annoyed by 'the impertinence' of ladies and gentlemen who 'stared at us as though we were wild beasts'. Dutifully they toured the art collection at the Ducal Palace and then moved on to Piacenza ('a stupid town') and Lodi, where they slept. At 10 a.m. the next day they rattled triumphantly into Milan, and one hour later Aunt Jessie and Bessy arrived from Geneva. '*We talked all day,*' Emma wrote.

They had intended to spend the last weeks of their tour in Venice. But Bessy was obviously not well enough; and in any event, they were all sated with sights. Instead they decided to go back to Geneva and rest there with Jessie. She went ahead to prepare while they saw more museums (a head of Guercino was admired); that evening Emma enjoyed Rossini's *Cenerentola* at the opera. 'The music very pretty – but the audience chattered.' To music-loving Emma this was sacrilege.

The drive to Domodossola was through Emma's kind of country, past Isola Bella in 'a beautiful changing light', up the Simplon through bright green chestnuts and beeches, then into Simplon itself – 'a nice cheerful place with sloping green lawns and larch trees'. The Swiss side was 'more grand and immense'. After the dust and heat of the south, Emma revived in the mountain air.

At Chêne, Jessie greeted them with tears of joy. Here in her lovely cool villa they rested; Jos nursed his lumbago and Bessy recovered from the fatiguing drive from Milan. They stayed for some weeks, during which Jessie took her nieces on expeditions on the lake and in the mountains. They took a trip of ten days to Chamonix, where Emma, who had been ill again, was now sufficiently recovered to join the others for a muleback excursion, as Fanny recorded in her journal:

Friday: Emma joined us and we went up to La Flechière. It was a very fatiguing thing for the mules up a little zigzag path in a stony place where a winter torrent comes down. After mounting for a long time we came in a wood of immense larch trees and here it was magnificent. Almost over our heads we saw through the trees the rocky tops of the mountain we were climbing with patches of snow, and on the other side, the snowy points of Mont Blanc looking immensely high from the base of the mountain being hid from us by the wood we were going through. After two hours fatiguing climb we got to the top where somebody has built a house. We staid some time there to rest ourselves, and we watched the people going up Mont Blanc, we could just distinguish with the telescope 9 little black specks and it seemed impossible they got up to the top and half way down again that day. We were obliged to walk all the way down again for it was so steep; it took us nearly two hours, most part of the way exposed to the hot sun, with poles in our hands so that we could not use our parasols. We returned to the Inn and after resting a little, set off for St Martin. The evening was beautiful and we sat out till bedtime on the balcony there with a brilliant full moon.

Jos was now impatient to be back home. He pleaded a canal meeting in London and in September they set off with Emma's brother Hensleigh, who had been spending some months in Geneva at a professor's house learning Italian. He and his tutor rode outside the carriages, and they made all speed back, via Dijon, Reims and Calais, and home to Maer.

Jessie, heartbroken at the departure of her beloved sister and her family, was consoled by the promise that Emma and Fanny would return again the following year.

Not many Victorian fathers would have personally taken four daughters on such an exhausting tour; aristocratic families in the earlier period of the Grand Tour usually sent their sons, in the charge of a 'bearleader'. But Jos himself as a young man had longed to visit the Etruria of his imagination, and the enthusiastic accounts of Florence relayed by the Allen aunts had whetted his appetite. If three women with little money could happily wander around Italy for three years on their own, he certainly could shepherd his four sensible daughters. In this, as in all their education, he followed the precepts he had carefully thought out and written in his diary when his children were young. 'One can scarcely recollect with sufficient force that every act of interference and direction does harm, and nothing can excuse it but the necessity of preventing a greater injury to the child . . . Nothing well done, but by inclination,' he wrote. 'Art of education is leading inclination.' This was a Wedgwood tradition handed down from his father Josiah I and passed on to Emma and thence to her children. It is striking that throughout the tour the impetus that drove the young women on their punishing round of museums and churches, that impelled Emma to seek out music teachers and Fanny art teachers, came from within themselves. The combination of Jos Wedgwood's own quiet good sense with the freedom inspired by Rousseau ensured that Emma was unusually well educated for a girl of the period.

CHAPTER FIVE

Continental Pleasures and Country Pursuits

A FTER THE LONG JOURNEY FROM GENEVA, IT WAS A RELIEF TO EMMA TO relax with her Staffordshire friends, to ride over to neighbouring Betley Hall, up the long, tree-lined avenue to the comfortable Georgian house where the Tollet family greeted her with such warmth. Here, as at Maer, were extensive grounds and lakes. Here too was a good library, where she could enjoy easy conversation with her clever friends Ellen and Georgina. Their father, George Tollet, was described in his obituary in 1855 as 'a Whig of the Old School . . . kind and frank and highly esteemed by all who knew him'. He was also keenly interested in the new agricultural methods, and some years later Charles Darwin was to value his advice. In 1838 he plied the elder man with questions on the inheritance of characteristics such as timidity in cattle, and later still referred to George Tollet's experiments in cattle breeding in his *Variation of Animals and Plants under Domestication*. Ellen Tollet was highly intelligent and became a friend of Mrs Gaskell and Florence Nightingale, with whom in later years she was to work. Charles admired her judgement; in 1854 he asked his publisher, John Murray, to send the first pages of *The Origin of Species* to her so that she might advise on his style. Ellen remained, until her death in 1890, Emma's closest friend.

Once the initial pleasure at being home had passed, Emma found Maer dull after the excitement of their foreign travel. Uncle John's delicate son,

Allen Wedgwood, had become vicar of the little church on the estate, and too often occupied the most comfortable chair on the veranda, nursing his real and imaginary ailments, indulging his obsession with his food and his mealtimes; the family found him a bore. Joe, Emma's eldest brother, hardly ever uttered a word; the lively Harry – now enjoying London life as a barrister – mocked, 'the country is a very good place to see good company but is very blank in itself, and so I dare say Joe and Allen have found it by this time, what a flow of soul! I pity even Squib [the fox terrier] when I think of it.'

But before long there were most welcome guests. In June 1826 Jessie and Sismondi came to Maer Hall on a visit. Their evenings were 'entirely filled up with music' and Sismondi was enthralled. He wrote with rapture at the singing of Elizabeth and Charlotte. 'Je n'ai pas éprouvé un moment de plaisir égal a cela qui me donnait un palpito atroce ou "O Notte Suave".' Sismondi then let Jessie go alone to pay a last visit to Cresselly, while he went to Paris to continue research for his *History*.

Fanny and Emma eagerly agreed to return with them to Geneva for a six-month visit. Much as Emma loved Maer, she longed to be back in the mountains with her dear Aunt Jessie. They took with them their cousin Edward Drewe, the son of Bessy's sister Caroline; Jessie the matchmaker thought he would make a good husband for Emma, especially as he would inherit an estate from his father's family.

Bessy saw them off, surprised 'at my own tranquillity at the thought of losing them for so long a time'. Emma wrote from Calais on 25 November 1826 that Aunt Jessie could not 'have borne leaving England if we had not gone with her but now she does not mind', and that Edward, their young escort, 'is very happy running about looking at carriages and seeing about passports'. The journey had its own diversions: 'We came over,' wrote Emma, 'with half a dozen smugglers who teased us very much to wear some plaid cloaks for them.' They were in Geneva in time for a ball commemorating the freedom of the Swiss Republic on 1 January 1827. On 4 January, a day of 'disagreeable snow and wind', Emma wrote to Elizabeth:

This was a very democratic occasion. We were to dance with whoever asked us. The first man I danced with was very disagreeable and vulgar, which put me rather in despair for the rest of the ball; however, the rest of my partners were very tidy, so I liked it very well. I had the good luck to dance with one or two Englishmen. I was quite surprised to see the shopkeepers here look so much worse than any English shopkeepers. I had much rather dance even with Mr Timmis than with most of the people there. When I was afraid any particularly horrid-looking man was going to ask me to dance I began such a very earnest conversation with Fanny that they would not interrupt me. The room looked very gay from having a great many people in uniform, especially the Prince of Denmark and his three governors. Sismondi was very indignant with the behaviour of some English young ladies sitting by us, who, when anybody asked them to dance that they were not acquainted with, looked very glum and answered, 'Je ne danse pas.'

Dancing was Emma's greatest delight during their visit – especially since the waltz was now all the rage. Their brother Frank wrote in some envy to Fanny, 'I suppose you and Emma will be turning away all winter like teetotums,' and that he hoped 'to get a waltz at the Stowe Ball'.

There were grand balls to which they were invited. The Prince of Denmark at the Casino 'was a very pretty sight', Fanny told her mother – 'only in the middle of the ball they danced a cotillion which I should think lasted upwards of an hour, which cut a great many people off from dancing.' They were amused but, like Aunt Jessie, not shocked by the flirtation of the young Prince with a Mrs Lambton. Fanny thought it ridiculous that they were supposed to go to all the balls in white (the colour of mourning) for the death of the Duke of York, and was surprised to 'see all the old men come to the balls here . . . Sismondi looks very unhappy at them. I never saw such an anxious looking man as he is.' Jessie explained his anxiety to Bessy: 'If Emma and Fanny are not immediately taken out to dance he swears he can hardly stay in the room. If they dance he can look on unwearied and support all the ennui of a ballroom which he never could bear since he gave up dancing.' Her husband, she went on, 'thinks Edward all the fools on Earth not to be in love with Emma, he cannot see how it can be avoided.' Kindly Sismondi, however, always acted as if Fanny were the prettier.

Jessie must have enjoyed these evenings, remembering the Cresselly days when she and her sisters would dance all night at the Haverford Assizes. As for Emma, though she still thought dressing grandly a bore, she found it amusing to arrange extravagant hairstyles. 'I have made great progress in hair dressing,' she wrote, 'and I make both our heads look very dashing. We have only had the odious hairdresser once, and then we disliked him so much that I mean to have a fight.' It was easy to be happy with the ebullient and affectionate Aunt Jessie, who did her very best to add a little continental polish to the two fresh-faced country girls. However, the Thursday afternoons in the grand red-and-gold drawing room under the critical eye of Jessie's formal friends were heavy going. Still, even a dull evening party was revived for Emma when 'it finished with dancing, for I had the fidgets wanting to dance.'

Emma developed an affection for Sismondi, in spite of his ugliness and his gallantry, though she never quite got over the affectation of his manners: 'I am afraid he will never leave off kissing our hands.' Sismondi, who remembered the brilliant talk at Madame de Staël's table, tried to teach Emma and Fanny the art of conversation, 'learned', as Jessie wrote to their mother, 'by foreigners from the moment they speak'. But the two Staffordshire girls looked on through their spectacles and tended to give way to 'a disposition of silence that casts almost imperceptibly a gloom around them'. Though their fresh complexions were much admired, they could never learn to be coquettes. Jessie confessed that she loved them for their 'quiet qualities', though Sismondi 'wishes exceedingly to inspire them with some more showy ones'. Nevertheless, she told Bessy, there was 'a pretty gaiety about Emma, always ready to answer to any liveliness and sometimes to throw it out herself, that will cheer everybody that lives with her or approaches her'. Certainly Emma could not have had a better tutor than Sismondi, whose knowledge of European history and politics was unrivalled. Under his tuition Emma may not have learned to converse as fluently as he wished, but she gained a deeper understanding of the continent's intellectual and political affairs which lasted all her life.

The gay existence with Aunt Jessie was not burdened with cultural visits, so Emma's diary was neglected throughout March. She was 'sorry to be so idle about my journal', she wrote, and her entries are brief and hurried, as in the following note: 'Monday 19 March; romping party, danced and sang . . . many young men singing and dancing . . . Edward dreadful company since his love affair.' If the aunts had hoped that Edward Drewe would be captured by Emma or Fanny, they were disappointed. He fell in love with a Swiss girl, Adèle Provost, whom he later married. Emma seems not the least jealous, concerned only that Edward was no longer their useful escort. For the first time Emma's journal shows an interest in young men. 'Monday 26 March: concert – disorderly game of cards . . . very well amused'; '29 March: fine party of young men at home.' The ever-present Fanny, however, must have put off any serious pursuit.

But it was not all pleasure; their education was not neglected. Emma took piano lessons from a German who

despises every music but German very much. I think he is a very good master, for he makes me learn the same piece of music for an immense time, and talks continually of my learning to play things without missing a note. He takes great pains about playing with expression, but I think he plays with so much expression himself that it is as if he was mad. Fanny has enquired about a drawing-master but the Marcets, who are great con-noisseurs, tell her they are all very bad. When first we came here we were troubled with not being able to find time to do anything, but now we find a little more, not that we get up early.

In May they left Geneva for the summer at Sismondi's villa at Chêne. The departure was painful: there were farewell soirées, a last piano lesson, and then it was goodbye to the 'fine party of young men'. Chêne was quieter, and though there were pleasant drives and walks, Emma sometimes now 'took a violent longing to go home, but it goes off in five minutes'; she even wrote to her mother suggesting that she should ask that they should come home, so that Aunt Jessie's feelings should not be hurt – Emma, like her mother, was always very sensitive to the feelings of others. Nevertheless, on their return Emma wrote to 'that naughty woman' Aunt Jessie, telling her that it had been 'the happiest time of my life and that is saying a good deal', and Aunt Jessie replied that she desperately missed her 'dearest toad'.

In the event, Jos decided to go to Switzerland himself and bring his daughters home; and he took with him Charles Darwin and his sister

Caroline, neither of whom had been abroad before. During a short stay in Paris, 'so gay and pretty after London', the Darwins learned greatly to admire their Uncle Jos. As Caroline wrote to Emma and Fanny, 'It was very good natured of Uncle Jos to think of me, but there never was a kinder person and the pleasantest travelling companion. I am quite losing all my former fear . . . and Charles joins me in a chorus of admiration whenever he leaves the room.' Caroline wrote to both Emma and Fanny to prepare them for their arrival, knowing that 'I know you like being classed together . . . Charlotte and Eliza to this day speak as if you were but one.'

Jos in turn was glad that he had persuaded Caroline to come with them. 'I need not tell you', he wrote to Bessy, 'how agreeable a companion she is and she has so much taste for beauty that it is a pleasure to travel with her.' Tall and strikingly good-looking, Caroline was said to carry herself like a duchess; she was serious and rather overwhelmed by the responsibility of bringing up the younger children. She reminded Jos of her mother, his much-loved sister Sukey, and he and Bessy had already decided that she would make an admirable wife for their quiet son, Joe – though it would be ten years before he plucked up the courage to ask her.

The young Darwins – the lively Susan and Catherine, and Erasmus, whom Bessy called 'an inoffensive youth', as well as Caroline and Charles – were frequent visitors at Maer Hall, finding it positively gay after the constraints of their home in Shrewsbury. Since his wife's death Dr Robert had become moody and withdrawn, working even harder than he had done in the old days when Sukey had written that he was sorely 'harassed'. He was often away, and when at home needed quiet and order, so that the children – who had been, according to the Allen aunts, spoiled by Sukey – were rocked between freedom and discipline. Robert had been so stricken by Sukey's death that he could not bear to speak of her, and Caroline, who of all the children had been closest to her mother, wept at the mention of her name. So she was rarely mentioned, and Charles grew up remembering only the waxen figure in the black velvet dress in a coffin in a darkened room, and a 'curious work box' that had belonged to her. Thus, tragically, the vital, intelligent Sukey was blanked out of his memory; while Robert, with his huge bulk, his high piping voice, his bursts of rapid speaking, his sudden black moods, must have been an alarming father. Yet his children loved him, and the visiting Wedgwoods, awed by him though they were, recognized his kindness.

Emma had known Charles since childhood, and they had spent at least one seaside holiday together with their mothers, Bessy and Sukey. There are, however, few references to him in the family's early letters. Emma was away from Maer for long periods in her girlhood, first for summer holidays at Cresselly, then for several months in Paris in 1818, at school in London in 1822, on the Grand Tour in 1825 and in Switzerland again in 1826–7.

Though Charles Darwin had always been regarded with affection at Maer he had shown little sign of intellectual brilliance, and on his visits there he was usually out from dawn to dusk with the gamekeepers, tramping, as he later wrote, 'through thick heath and young Scotch firs . . . and . . . totally devoted to shooting . . . My zeal was so great, that I used to place my shooting-boots open by my bedside when I went to bed, so as not to lose half a minute in putting them on in the morning.' Indeed, his father once exploded with words that burned in his memory: 'You care for nothing but shooting, dogs and rat-catching and you will be a disgrace to yourself and all your family.' Curiously, like his Uncle Tom Wedgwood, Charles combined a hatred of cruelty to animals with an intense delight in shooting wild birds – a passion of which his father strongly and vociferously disapproved.

Did Jos see something of his brother Tom in Charles? Certainly this shared journey gave him the chance to understand the young man better. Was Charles even then over-concerned about his health? According to Jos, he had been 'not quite well on the crossing but made a very hearty dinner of roast beef'. Charles left Jos and Caroline in Paris and returned to England; he was obviously much more interested in the opening of the grouse season at Maer than in bringing Emma home – and besides, he was bewitched at this time by a neighbouring beauty, the flirtatious Miss Fanny Owen. He never set foot on the continent again.

Jos and Caroline rested for two or three weeks at Chêne, much to the delight of Sismondi, who had the greatest admiration for his brother-in-law. On Wednesday 27 June the party said goodbye to a tearful Jessie, then set off for the return journey that would take them through Switzerland, Germany and Holland to Ostend. Jos must have been curious to see again the countries he had visited as his father's young representative taking the famous Wedgwood copy of the Portland Vase to the courts of

Holland and Germany – and gratified that this time he travelled as a country gentleman of some standing, one who had been Sheriff of Dorset.

They travelled by steamboat to Ouchy, then drove to Thun, where they took a boat to Interlaken. There were pleasant halts on their way, including an hour in a chalet near the Jungfrau, where they had the excitement of watching 'two or three avalanches' and Emma happily picked Alpine flowers. At Grindelwald she and Fanny 'went to see a glacier'. This was Emma's kind of country – bracing, green and flowery. Her journal reflects her delight: '5th July. Got into boat, cloudy but beautiful rich banks, Hangstedt, Kirsnacht cheerful and pretty. Walked to William Tell's chapel; lovely view of Lucerne Lake. Beautiful row to Brun. Pappa, Fanny and I walked up a hill to have a view of the lake of Lucerne.' There were bad patches – 'frightful country full of beggars' – but a lovely lake view of Wallensted, and stretches of beautiful 'richly clothed country'. They went by steamer down the Rhine to Rotterdam, but 'were tired of the boat before we left it'. By 8 July they had reached Zurich – 'Papa, Fanny and I walked about the town.' On 13 July they were at Baden, where Caroline Darwin was 'very unwell'; she had found it difficult to keep up with the sturdy Wedgwoods. Karlsruhe was 'smart'; Heidelberg 'a striking place' where Emma and Jos walked on the hill; Darmstadt a 'handsome town'. By now Emma's brief journal entries reflect even their fatigue. '16 July. Ugly country to Bingen . . . castles!!!' 8 July, 'fog at Ems'; 20 July, 'odious windy drive to Cologne'. Antwerp saw 'Rubens' Descent from the Cross – portraits of two wives and his mistress in it!!!' Fanny's journal takes them on to Ostend: 'Saturday 29, landed 2 a.m., slept at ship near Custom House.' They stayed two days in London at the Wedgwoods' apartment at York Street, and on Sunday 29 July they took the 7 a.m. mail coach for Chester. Fanny's journal ends, 'came to Maer. Very happy to be home again. We found a very large party of all the uncles'.

Indeed, the returning travellers found Maer Hall overflowing with relations. Bessy's three sisters, Kitty Mackintosh (with her daughter Fanny) and the widowed Caroline Drewe and Harriet Surtees, were there; but the party was dominated by Sir James Mackintosh. Disappointed that he had not been offered a place in Canning's Whig–Tory Cabinet of 1827, he had withdrawn with his family to Maer, where he hoped to spend a quiet six months working on his interminable *History of the World*. Emma found him very pleasant and talkative and, fresh from the tuition of that other historian, Sismondi, she was able to face him with equanimity, helping to arrange his books in his study. Kitty spent most of her time in her room working on the various humanitarian causes she had taken up, in particular writing letters to *The Times* on the reform of the Smithfield cattle market. In later years Emma, possibly influenced by her Aunt Kitty, would wage a similar campaign against cruelty to animals.

Pamphleteering was in the Wedgwood blood. When Emma paid a visit to her Aunt Sarah Wedgwood – since the death of her sister Kitty, living on her own at Camphill, a house she had built on the Maer estate – she found her also deep in tracts and pamphlets. Her passion was the anti-slavery campaign which had long ago so concerned her father, old Josiah. 'Her mind', Bessy wrote, 'now is absorbed very much by her interest in favour of the Blacks. She spends a great deal in the circulation of anti-slavery publications, and she has herself written or compiled a little pamphlet for the benefit of those who are not sufficiently interested in the subject to seek for information among the many books that are written.'

Jos shared his sister's concern. After their return from the Grand Tour he had, as Bessy told Jessie,

> exerted himself wonderfully for a man of his retired habits in getting up a County Petition for the abolition of slavery and has succeeded and it has been presented. We have also got up a local one from the four neighbouring parishes hereabouts; and I hope shall never let the matter rest. There is certainly a great stir in England at this moment. The Clergy and the Methodists have taken it up very warmly, and now that England is awakened I trust in God this enormity will cease.

Bessy herself was not a natural campaigner, but nevertheless two years later she and her daughters set up a Ladies' Society at Newcastle – 'but we don't meet with much success among the higher gentry. The set below them . . . is much more impressible.'

The Mackintoshes were at Maer for six months, so that there was much interesting talk round the library fire. Mackintosh was not well at this time, and, as Bessy wrote, 'his fits of giddiness . . . [have] very much interrupted the history which goes on so slowly that I am quite in despair about it . . . His spirits are cheerful enough, but the mortification has sank deep.' However, he was soothed by the affectionate sensitivity of his sister-in-law and now understood why her sisters so adored her. And Bessy played 'a rubber with him every night, which he enjoys very much, and considering he is a genius, he plays very decently.' Emma seems to have made little impression on the great historian, and she recorded only her surprise that he shook hands with her on their first meeting. Nevertheless it was impossible for anyone to be in the company of Mackintosh for six months without being intellectually stimulated.

One visitor to Maer in 1827 was particularly deeply impressed by the great historian. Charles Darwin, then eighteen, had come to Maer as he usually did for the autumn opening of the shooting season. Watching the muddy and exhausted young man plodding home, Jos must have remembered his own shooting expeditions with his brother Tom, and admired the methodical way Charles kept a record of every bird he shot throughout the whole season. James Mackintosh, however, saw something more than the huntsman in Charles. After his visit to Maer that year, Charles heard 'with a glow of pride' that Mackintosh had said of him, 'There is something in that man that interests me.' Charles, like Emma, had been fascinated by Sir James, and listened 'with much interest to everything which he said, for I was as ignorant as a pig about his subjects of history, politics and moral philosophy'. And Sir James was at his best when awakening the minds of the young. Was it from him, perhaps, that Charles first heard the theories of Malthus, Sir James's fellow lecturer, that would later influence him? Did he talk to Charles about intelligence in the higher animals – the subject of his thesis when a student?

Charles's pleasure in being at Maer was not confined to hunting and the art of intellectual conversation. In his autobiography he wrote, 'Life there was perfectly free; the country was very pleasant for walking or riding; and in the evening there was much very agreeable conversation, not so personal as it generally is in large family parties, together with music.' At this time Charles scarcely mentions the pretty, suntanned Emma who accompanied her sisters so brilliantly; it was Charlotte's exquisite voice that he would always remember. 'In the summer,' he recalled, 'the whole family used often to sit on the steps of the old portico, with the flower garden in front, and with the steep wooded bank opposite the house, reflected in the lake, with here and there a fish rising or a water bird paddling about. Nothing has left a more vivid picture in my mind than those evenings.'

Charles had been rather afraid of his Uncle Jos. As he wrote, 'he was silent and reserved so as to be a rather awful man,' but during their trip to France he had learned to love and admire his uncle, almost as a surrogate father, so that his family was surprised at their ease together. Jos was, Charles considered, 'the very type of an upright man with the clearest judgment. I do not believe that any power on earth could have made him swerve from what he considered the right course.' Charles's own father was also a remarkable man, sensitive and kind by nature, but the tragedies in his life had left him scarred. Above all, he was acutely conscious that he, the acclaimed physician, had not been able to save his own wife any more than his father, the great Erasmus, had been able to save his beloved Polly.

In the years after Sukey's death, Charles grew close to his elder brother, Erasmus, who in his early letters called him 'Bobby'. Perhaps this had been their mother's nickname for him. When he was eight, he was sent for a year to Shrewsbury Day School, where he was now 'Charles Darwin', and thence to Shrewsbury Grammar School, which, he claimed in his autobiography, 'as a means of education was simply a blank'. He modestly admitted that when he left school he was, for his age, 'neither high nor low in it; and I believe I was considered by all my masters and my family as a very ordinary boy, rather below the common standard in intellect.' He remembered enjoying Shakespeare and Byron, though Emma later frequently expressed surprise that he had read so little, and he never acquired her ability to learn foreign languages.

The young Charles was often uneasy in the presence of his enormous father – at six feet two he was, wrote Charles, 'the largest man whom I ever saw. When he last weighed himself he was 24 stone but afterwards increased much in weight.' Nevertheless Charles admired his 'powers of observation and his sympathy, neither of which I had ever seen exceeded or even equalled'. There is no doubt of the deep love and admiration he felt for his father, and the desire to gain his respect was one of the great motivating powers in Charles's life. Dr Robert certainly understood his sons. Seeing that Charles appeared to be making little progress at Shrewsbury, he sent him at sixteen to join his brother Erasmus studying medicine at Edinburgh University. However, Erasmus was delicate, and

Charles found the lectures tedious and the sight of operations sickening; so Robert, remembering that his own father had pushed him on to an uncomfortable path, did not insist that either become a doctor.

After two years of medical studies, Charles decided that it would be pleasant to be a country clergyman, and with his father's agreement he spent three years at Cambridge, attaining in 1831 an undistinguished BA in classics. Yet during those years of apparent mediocrity he was developing a passion for natural history and a talent for careful observation that was to be the main ingredient of his particular genius. Like Emma's sister Fanny, he kept meticulous records and memoranda – as when he carefully listed the numbers of birds he shot at Maer. At home he learned chemistry, a subject that interested him more than Latin. As boys, he and Erasmus had their own laboratory in a toolshed in the garden where they conducted experiments, and this continued even when Erasmus went to study at Edinburgh. Dr Robert, no doubt remembering his own interest in chemistry when he had shared science lessons with Jos at Etruria Hall, did not discourage his son.

Emma had the deepest respect for the doctor's judgements, but though he was 'kind, you couldn't go on with your own conversation when he was there'. The Allen sisters were never comfortable at Shrewsbury; even the bright Fanny found a seat in which she could hide behind the drawing-room pillar, afraid that the doctor might single her out. But Jos, to whom he was still the Robert he had known in his youth, always enjoyed his visits, and Bessy found the well-run house exquisitely comfortable. Sukey had been well trained in household management at Etruria Hall by old Sally Wedgwood, Charles's grandmother, who had long outlived her husband, Josiah, and until her death in 1815 had been a frequent visitor at Robert's house. No doubt the outspoken old lady had kept them all up to scratch. Her priorities were passed on down the Darwin female line: Charles's sister Susan, in particular, was excessively houseproud, unlike the Wedgwoods, who took life easily at Maer. Susan Darwin claimed that 'she could put [Charlotte Allen] to rights in a week.' Perhaps this is why Susan's family nickname was 'Granny'.

After the excitement of her travelling years, Emma now settled down to an easygoing country life. She was an attractive young woman with clear grey-green eyes, a firm but humorous mouth and hair 'long, silky and thick, the colour of dried tobacco leaves'. Her daughter Etty was to remember it like this even in old age. She enjoyed the pleasures that Midlands society had to offer at this period – the balls in neighbouring towns, especially when the judges came for the Assizes; long visits to friends and relations in country towns or London; and entertaining them in turn at Maer Hall. There were parties on the lawns, and archery competitions at which Fanny and Emma 'were dragonesses', Bessy told her sisters, embarrassed because they always won the prizes. With her sisters, she attended musical events in neighbouring towns. Birmingham in particular hosted excellent concerts which gave Emma the deepest pleasure. Even Charles Darwin, who claimed to be tone-deaf, was greatly stirred by the 'Hallelujah Chorus', on a rare occasion when he was persuaded to attend. But Emma and Fanny must have found the local balls dull after the whirling waltzes in Geneva.

Like all the Wedgwoods, they supported good causes – both local and distant – with energy and enthusiasm. Even Harry took part, in May 1827 helping Charlotte to run a bazaar on behalf of Greek refugees at which Charlotte's paintings were a great success. In April 1828 Emma told Aunt Jessie of their bazaar for fever wards at the local infirmary.

Our table looked very nice with some pink calico on the wall behind us, pinned all over with skreens [sic] and bags. On Wednesday morning Aunt Sarah took two of us in her carriage, very smart in those white hats you are acquainted with, which were of great use. All the world was there, smart people and common people . . . Charlotte's drawings came to great honour. A gentleman paid two pounds for them. Our great difficulty was not having enough cheap things for the shopkeepers and young girls who had not much money to spend . . . We were very much amused with making raffles for some of our cheaper bags, and we sold off every rag on our table getting cheaper and cheaper as it got later in the day. The proceeds of the first day was £700 . . . the second day must have got £3000 . . . our table got £59 of which £34 was of our own making . . . And now we don't mean to mention the name of a bazaar for the next three years.

In fact there *were* more bazaars – for foreign concerns, for Greek and Italian refugees, and for the campaign to abolish slavery.

It was a busy life. As Bessy grew weaker, her daughters took over the running of the house; the garden was the responsibility of Elizabeth and Emma, for whom it became a lifelong passion, encouraged and advised by Uncle John and his Royal Horticultural Society. Then there was service to the local community, visits to sick cottagers, treating their minor and sometimes major ailments. Kindly Elizabeth was pestered by beggars; Emma was brisk with them. Elizabeth's great interest was in the school she established and the Sunday school she ran in the laundry room. Emma helped – she had a genuine love of children and wrote a little reading book with simple stories which kept the rumbustious children quiet. It was later printed and her own children learned to read from it. Elizabeth, for whom teaching was a real vocation, in later life founded schools for the cottagers in Ashdown Forest and even in Wales on Caldey Island. Uncle Tom would have been delighted that the little girl he had watched in the nursery should have taken education so seriously. But Elizabeth's methods were quite different from his.

So the months passed. Though, as Bessy said, Emma was more popular than her other girls, she showed no interest in getting married. It seemed that she would join the ranks of the Victorian supernumeraries, the spinsters, the universal aunts. Here it should be explained that the most popular Christian name in this extended family was Frances – which became Fanny, so to avoid confusion surnames were added. Emma's sister was Fanny Wedgwood, her cousin was Fanny Mackintosh as a girl and Fanny Hensleigh when she married Emma's brother. Her other brother Frank's wife became Fanny Frank. Emma's aunt was either Fanny Allen or Aunt Fanny.

CHAPTER SIX

The Crucial Years

T HE YEARS 1830–2 MARKED A TURNING POINT IN THE LIVES OF CHARLES Darwin, Emma Wedgwood and their families. There were merry weddings, tragic deaths – and fond farewells as Charles left in December 1831 for his epic voyage round the world. The domestic events of these years were set within a scene of political turmoil and near-revolution as the battle for the reform of Parliament raged throughout the country – a scene in which Emma's family was closely involved, her father Jos, her Uncle John Allen and her mother's brother-in-law Sir James Mackintosh all standing as Whig candidates for Parliament in the elections of 1831 and 1832.

During these eventful years Emma and her sisters spent many months in London, staying with relatives. Bessy's widowed sister Caroline Drewe lived in a handsome house at Roehampton with her daughter Harriet, whose husband Lord Gifford had died leaving her comfortably established. Caroline's other daughter, Georgiana, married to Judge Alderson, also welcomed Emma at their stylish house in London. Emma came to town for the christening of their daughter Georgiana, who in future years was to become the Marchioness of Salisbury, wife of the Prime Minister. Dr Peter Holland, a distant Wedgwood cousin who was now a successful doctor, lived in similar style in Park Lane. Jos himself had a small apartment in Palace Yard, Westminister, and there were other friends who were always ready to offer hospitality for weeks at a time.

The most interesting of these homes from home was that of Sir James Mackintosh. Sadly, his friendship with Lady Holland and Mme de Staël –

'those two Jezebels' – had detached him from his wife, Bessy's sister Kitty. She had left him in 1829 and died at Jessie's home in Geneva on 6 May 1830 – an event described by Jessie as 'a most merciful dispensation', for 'she could neither make herself nor others happy.' At the end of her life she was paralysed, 'unable to speak', and her sisters feared a complete mental breakdown. Since her departure his daughter by his first marriage, Mary Rich, and Kitty's daughter Fanny, had run his household at Clapham, and later at Great Cumberland Street – the centre of great excitement during the debates over the Reform Bill. Here he held court for many of the most distinguished men of letters of the period. Fanny, a charming and intelligent hostess, was Emma's favourite cousin, sharing her interest in music and encouraging Emma's interest in politics; she and Emma's brother Hensleigh had long been in love, though Sir James was unwilling to encourage thoughts of marriage. Bessy had noticed that Fanny, even as a young girl, was 'a furious politician', and 'drove the opposition coach' with enthusiasm. She took an active part in the anti-slavery campaign, and was on the committee of Mazzini's Young Italy – much to the alarm of Aunt Jessie in Geneva, who feared that Mazzini, whom the Sismondis mistrusted, would claim that he had the support of the great manufacturer Wedgwood. Mazzini was a friend of Erasmus Darwin and Jane and Thomas Carlyle, and had sat with Jane and Erasmus with their 'toes in the fender' discussing politics. Fanny, in our day, would undoubtedly have become a Member of Parliament herself.

Emma's relish for long political speeches had its limits. Her mother reported her arrival at Clapham for a visit, 'seeing the dining room all lighted up as she drove into the court, and the historian himself (as she saw through the window) with a party of gentlemen'. Emma, no doubt tired from the long journey, 'desired to be shown up to Mrs Rich's room where she had a very comfortable cup of tea and dish of chat with her'. Fanny came up to invite her to join the party and meet 'Mr Wilberforce, Mr Wishaw and Mr R Grant, all of which she declined and I dare say M thought her a great fool for doing so'. Neither then nor at any time did Emma pretend enthusiasm for politicians' long 'harangues'.

Bessy herself would not have missed the chance. As she grew older she hungered for new experiences and in her sixties still enjoyed the excitement of new places, wanting, as she said, 'to refresh my oldness'. But her visit to London in the summer of 1829 proved too much. She was staying at

Lady Gifford's grand house in Roehampton when she had a serious breakdown, succumbing to the first of a series of epileptic fits which almost proved fatal. Her indisposition was described in the family as 'a mysterious illness', which 'it was supposed at the time to have been from an overdose of poppies'. Perhaps only Jos would have remembered Dr Erasmus's fatal prescription of large doses of opium, and, mindful of what happened to Tom, would have refused this treatment. But he was busy with committees and pottery business, and may not have been there to advise. From now on Bessy would suffer repeated attacks, though she kept her sweet and charming character throughout.

Social life may have been too much for Bessy, but her daughters revelled in their visits to London for the season. As they had done in Italy, they took every opportunity to broaden their minds. In 1830 Fanny and Emma were in London for three months. On 11 and 22 April they visited the watercolour exhibition of Copley Fielding, and Fanny had painting lessons from the artist himself. They saw the pictures at Somerset House and the Elgin Marbles – 'too much mutilated', honest Fanny thought, 'for me to take much pleasure'. Both Emma and Fanny snapped up their opportunities to hear good music, attending at least five operas during their stay, including *Tancred* and *Otello* with Malibran as Desdemona, and Lablache whom they had heard in Naples and whose voice was 'more wonderful' than ever. Fanny was so excited she couldn't sleep afterwards.

There were some frivolities; Emma attended a ball, and with Fanny visited the hothouses at Kew and Epsom races. But on the whole they were serious young women, taking equal pleasure in Faraday's Friday lecture at the Royal Institution on 'some new musical instruments'. Did Jos go with them to renew his friendship with Michael Faraday, whom he and Tom had known well as a young man? Even if Jos was not there he would have heard his daughters' reports with great interest; the silent one of the family, he talked little about Tom and their past friends.

Visits to the House of Commons were almost as good as the theatre – depending on the topic under consideration: there could not have been much interest in the debate they heard on forgery. In the years before the great fire of 1834 which destroyed the House of Commons, there was a ladies' gallery which they called 'the Ventilator' immediately above the Chamber. It was a room with seats around an opening in the roof –

originally designed to ventilate the overheated House of Commons below. Here ladies sat looking down through the grille, opposition wives on one side and government wives on the other. It was amicable enough; husbands came up and were surprisingly courteous after bellowing below, although Fanny Allen was once infuriated when Tory ladies left as soon as Whig Members got up to speak. Of all Emma's aunts she was the most politically minded, and fiercely left wing in her opinions. She had almost screamed with excitement when Brougham had demolished his Tory opponents, 'tossing them like a cat with a mouse'. For the next two years, while the House was battling through the stages of the Reform Bill, the Allen and Wedgwood women, along with the great political hostesses, Tory and Whig alike, crowded round their hole in the roof and swore they could hear better than on the floor of the Chamber itself.

On 7 June 1830 they were back at Maer. It had been an exciting season. Nineteen days later, on 26 June, King George IV died. The sick and sad old man who had brought the monarchy into disrepute was succeeded by his brother, William IV, the bluff, eccentric 'sailor King'. On 23 July Parliament was prorogued and the Tory Prime Minister, the Duke of Wellington, faced an election. The country seethed with excitement. Years of distress and unemployment, along with anger at the corruption and injustice of an unrepresentative Parliament, fuelled riots, arson and mob violence. There were 'pocket' boroughs and 'rotten' boroughs in the gift of the great landowners, and while in the south tiny hamlets sent Members to Parliament, the flourishing industrial Midlands and the Potteries were largely unrepresented. Newcastle-under-Lyme was a pocket borough; Stoke-on-Trent, capital of the pottery industry, returned no Members. Birmingham was the centre of the ferment, where skilful organizers like the radical Tom Attwood plotted with the Birmingham Political Union to push reform through, by force if necessary. The Duke's soldiers sharpened their sabres.

During the election campaign news from across the Channel increased the excitement. King Charles X of France was overthrown and fled to England, to be replaced by the citizen King, Louis Philippe, who walked among his subjects, a huge tricolour on his hat, an umbrella in his left hand and his right outstretched to shake the hands of passing citizens – just like William IV. This French Revolution had been comparatively bloodless and was over in a few days. English extreme radicals took

A painting of Emma Darwin by George Richmond commissioned by her father, Josiah Wedgwood II (Jos), in 1840

Josiah Wedgwood I, grandfather of Charles and Emma, captured in oil by Sir Joshua Reynolds. It was probably painted in a single session in Reynolds' studio in London

Josiah Wedgwood I's wife Sarah (Sally), whose abundant hair has been elaborately dressed

Charles Darwin's grandfather, Erasmus Darwin, distinguished physician, poet and inventor. Portrait in oils by his friend, Joseph Wright of Derby

Josiah's dear friend and partner, Thomas Bentley, painted in the year of his death. He was responsible for the decorative art in the business, hence the classic plaque

Emma's mother Bessy Wedgwood née Allen, painted by George Romney, in the year after her marriage to Josiah II

Dr Robert Darwin's wife, Susannah (Sukey), the daughter of Josiah Wedgwood I and mother of Charles Darwin

Emma's father Josiah Wedgwood II, painted by George Romney in 1793

Charles's father Dr Robert Darwin, of whom Charles wrote: 'The largest man I ever knew'

Maer Hall was Josiah Wedgwood II's Staffordshire home, a large Elizabethan country house, seven miles from Stoke-on-Trent, to which he moved in 1807

An earthenware
serving dish decorated
with a painting of Etruria Hall, from the most superb pottery
service of almost a thousand pieces commissioned in 1773 by
Catherine II Empress of Russia. La Grenouillère, the 'frog
marsh', was the site of her Chesmenski Palace and each piece was
crested with a green frog emblem

The Portland Vase. Wedgwood's copy of the famous Portland Vase,
which was made of deep blue glass, overlaid with white. It is believed to have been made in Rome
or Alexandria about 27BC–AD14. It was bought in 1784 by Sir William Hamilton for £1,000 who sold
it to the Duchess of Portland whose son bought it in an auction. In 1786 he lent it to Wedgwood who, in
1789, after much difficulty, copied it in jasper ware to match the original colour

The Wedgwood Family in the grounds of Etruria Hall, by George Stubbs, 1780. Right to left: Josiah Wedgwood I, his wife Sarah and their children, John, Josiah II, Susannah (Sukey), Catherine (Kitty), Thomas, Sarah and Mary Ann (who died aged eight). Josiah's verdict: 'My wife I think very deficient ... Mary Ann more so, and Susan is not hit off well at all ... There is much to praise and a little to blame.'

Charles Darwin painted by
George Richmond in 1840

Emma's uncle, John Wedgwood, who founded the Royal Horticultural Society

John Wedgwood's wife, Jane Wedgwood née Allen, painted by Sir Thomas Lawrence in 1794 as a wedding gift for her husband. She was the beauty of the Allen family

Emma's brother, Josiah Wedgwood III of Leith Hill Place

Charles's sister, Caroline Wedgwood, who was said to resemble her mother, Sukey, in appearance and character. She and Josiah III were the great grandparents of Ralph Vaughan Williams

Cresselly House, near Tenby in
Pembrokeshire, home of the Allen family

John Bartlett Allen, Emma's Allen
grandfather, a bad-tempered retired army
captain, much feared by Emma's mother
and her eight sisters

Sir James Mackintosh, painted before he left to take up an appointment as Recorder of Bombay

Fanny, the cleverest of Emma's Allen aunts, secretly devoted to her brother-in-law, Sir James Mackintosh

Jean-Charles Simon de Sismondi, a distinguished historian of Italian origin. Generous and kindly but ugly, he and Jessie Allen were known in the family as 'Beauty and the Beast'

Jessie Sismondi née Allen. After marriage to Jean-Charles she lived in Geneva where Emma and her sister, Fanny, spent many months with them heart. The monarchy had been debased in the reign of George IV; now England could surely follow the French example.

After the July election Wellington still held a majority of seats, though Lord Grey had increased the Whig opposition by fifty. But the Duke's government would last only three months. The old soldier, skilled as he had been at guessing what lay beyond the next hill, as a politician was surprisingly blind, completely failing to understand the mood of the country and the intensity of the desire for reform. His speech at the opening of the new session of Parliament on 30 October 1830 was monumentally crass. 'The system of representation', he declared, possessed the 'full and entire confidence of the country'. 'Indeed,' he continued, if he 'were asked to form a legislature his great endeavour would be to form one which would produce the same results. Finally he would always feel it his duty to resist measures like this.' Outside the House someone asked the Foreign Secretary what the Duke had said. Grimly he replied, 'He said that we were going out.'

The country raged. The King's proposed visit to the City on Lord Mayor's Day was cancelled for fear of revolution. The Iron Duke at least knew when to make a tactical retreat. On 15 November the Tories were defeated by twenty-nine votes in a minor debate on the Civil List; Wellington's own right-wing supporters had deserted him. The King accepted his resignation with tears: Lord Grey became Prime Minister, with Lord John Russell leading the Whigs in the House of Commons.

Bessy and her sisters were primed with news from Mackintosh hot from the front. Restless, as she often was these days, Bessy had taken Elizabeth and Charlotte with her and travelled 'three days with our own horses' from Maer to her sister Jenny's home at that time, The Hill, near Abergavenny in Wales, to join her other sisters Caroline Drewe and Fanny Allen. 'We are all agog', she wrote to Jessie Sismondi in Geneva, 'about the late extraordinary change of Ministry, it was such a surprise that I don't think anyone on either side expected it.' Mackintosh had written to Fanny Allen on the 'singular overthrow . . . It is likely that he [the Duke] and his accomplices were wearied into submission.' Some of his followers were 'so stupid as not to be aware of the consequences of their votes.' He sent Fanny a list of the new ministers. 'Brougham is Chancellor!!!!', Lady Holland had exclaimed in a late-night note to him. Mackintosh thought the maverick but brilliant radical 'brings with him rashness and odium but without him in either House there could not have been a fortnight's administration'. Fanny Allen's hero had won his place.

As for Mackintosh himself, the hoped-for Cabinet seat still eluded him; he was given a seat on the Board of Control of the East India Company. Bessy consoled her irate sisters, who bitterly complained that he deserved better – a place in the Cabinet at least. At least the salary of £1,500 a year would enable the Mackintosh family to move to a better house, more conveniently situated for the Commons, and they found one at 14 Great Cumberland Street.

The House was now adjourned until February 1831. Harriet Martineau, Erasmus Darwin's friend, said 1830 was 'the year of the People's Cause'.

If 1830 had been full of excitement for Emma, 1831 was even more so, with the same mingling of culture and politics. Once again she spent the season from April to July with cousins in London, staying some of the time with Fanny Mackintosh at 14 Great Cumberland Street, where her sister Elizabeth had been staying in February and March. Elizabeth had reported back to Maer and to her Aunt Jessie in Geneva all the excitement of those months. Like her cousin Fanny Mackintosh, Elizabeth was 'a furious politician', and was enthralled by the weeks she had spent 'at headquarters', Mackintosh's house. For once, she allowed herself some weeks of respite from domestic cares, and was in the thick of the struggle over the early stages of the Reform Bill. On 31 March 1831 Lord John Russell presented his Reform Bill for its second reading in the House of Commons. Then as now, in order to become law, a bill had to pass four stages in the Commons – the first, a formal presentation; then the second reading; then the committee stage, where it is examined in detail; then the third reading, after which it goes to the Lords. If it wins a majority there, it proceeds to the monarch for the Royal Assent. Nowadays the Lords can send a bill back to the Commons only twice if they do not approve it; but at that time, if the Lords rejected a measure that was the end of it.

The bill Russell presented went much further than his supporters had dared to hope. MPs were to be reduced in number from 658 to 596, and forty-two seats were to be allocated to large towns, of which one was to be Stoke-on-Trent. Sixty seats – the infamous 'rotten' and 'pocket' boroughs – were to be abolished. Elizabeth was at Mackintosh's house during the second reading and wrote to Aunt Jessie:

Sir James, in spite of being up almost every night till near four o'clock looks quite a different man . . . he says he has not felt so well for six years. The two nights of the struggle on the second reading of the Reform Bill, Fanny (Mack) went down to Mrs Robert Grant's which is in George Street, just by the House of Commons, and to receive bulletins from the Thorntons in the Ventilator. It was amusing to see how interested even Mrs R.G.'s servants were – the housemaid coming in 'if you please ma'am, John has just been over, and Lord Mahon was speaking *against*'. I sat up for them at home as long as I could, but could not last till four in the morning; but even at that hour there was a crowd about the House of Comons who cheered reform members as they came out. The members in the House were so vehement that Miss Thornton in the chimney [i.e. the Ventilator] expected them to come to blows.

The debate had raged until early morning, outside and inside the Chamber. When at last the Speaker announced the result, 'there was dead silence, then a storm of shouts, cheers and even weeping'. The Whig government had won by a majority of one.

On 26 March Mackintosh held a great celebratory dinner party with Fanny as his hostess. Elizabeth described the evening – an occasion on which not only politicians but men of letters and bishops were present, and marked by Mackintosh's success in bringing about a *rapprochement* between Wordsworth and his fierce critic Francis Jeffrey, the founder of the *Edinburgh Review*. Wordsworth at first refused to meet Jeffrey, saying, 'We are fire and water; if we meet we shall only hiss,' but Mackintosh 'took Mr Wordsworth by the shoulders and turned him round to Jeffrey and left them together'. They were reconciled, and talked long into the night.

The bill should now have gone forward to the committee stage; but, rather than risk defeat at this juncture, Grey persuaded the King to call a new election with the aim of strengthening the government's position, convincing him that the country was on the verge of revolution, as indeed it was. There were riots throughout Britain. Mobs roared through Piccadilly, breaking the windows of Apsley House, Wellington's home, while inside his wife Kitty lay dead.

Mackintosh, who had sat since 1819 as MP for Knaresborough, now persuaded Emma's father, Jos Wedgwood, to stand in the April election against the Duke of Sutherland's Tory nominee, Edmund Peel, for the pocket borough of Newcastle-under-Lyme. The quiet and unassuming Jos was reluctant to enter the fray; on the other hand, as an MP he could fight directly for the abolition of slavery, a cause even dearer to his heart than parliamentary reform. It was a difficult decision. Bessy's health might not take the strain of London, and Dr Robert had prescribed a period of peace; but both men agreed that it would depress Bessy more if she felt she was holding Jos back. Bessy herself rather guiltily confessed that as an MP Jos would lift his family up in the social scale – and she knew that this would be important to him, finally erasing the 'trade' label. Eventually, prompted less by social ambition than by his Wedgwood sense of duty, he agreed to stand. Bessy's brother John Allen was also induced to stand as the Whig candidate for Pembroke in Wales; as a devoted follower of Mackintosh, he needed little persuasion.

Emma's brothers canvassed with enthusiasm. Frank, in particular, was highly praised. As a master potter and the heir to the Wedgwood business, Frank understood the strength of the workers' frustration. Indeed, he was such a persuasive canvasser that it was said that had he himself stood he might have been elected. As it was, Jos was defeated; but his supporters hoped that when the Reform Bill was finally passed a new and more easily winnable seat would be made at Stoke.

Bessy wrote to console her sisters for John Allen's similar defeat at Pembroke, explaining that 'Jos is very little disappointed . . . it was so much on public grounds that he stood . . . I fully expect that we shall be member for Stoke-upon-Trent, i.e. the Potteries, as if we are it will be a much pleasanter seat.' Jos was much touched by the support of his workers at the Etruria factory, who had given him a contribution towards his election expenses. In his address of thanks he acknowledged that sometimes in taking care of 'my own interests, I have not been sufficiently regardful of yours. Now your unexpected and free gift' was a proof that he had won their 'esteem and regard', which he prized 'among the most valuable of my possessions'.

Although neither John Allen nor Jos won his seat, the Whigs swept to victory with a majority of 150. Now Bessy looked forward with pleasure at the thought that when the Reform Bill was passed, Jos would be elected for Stoke-on-Trent and she would be 'obliged to spend part of every year in London'. However, she 'had great misgivings that she would not live so long'. Bessy was now sixty-eight and felt she was nearing 'the confines'. She was still subject to epileptic fits which caused her family and Robert Darwin grave concern, and she worried that she was losing her grasp on life.

When Elizabeth returned home in March 1832, Emma and Fanny were free to spend their usual months in London. Jos was also there for committee meetings and was able to join his daughters on their cultural expeditions. They divided their time among the home of their cousin Dr Holland in New Norfolk Street, their Aunt Caroline's handsome house in Roehampton, and the Mackintoshes' establishment in Great Cumberland Street. So there were great family gatherings of Allens, Wedgwoods and Darwins, all enjoying the excitement of London in turmoil, as Lord Grey and his ministers prepared for the battle that loomed when the bill should come before the House of Lords in October.

On 25 April Fanny recorded in her diary their visit to a great meeting organized by the anti-slavery campaign. Three thousand crowded into Exeter Hall, among them Emma and Fanny Wedgwood, presumably Jos and Fanny Mackintosh, and possibly also Erasmus Darwin, who was unusually energetic these days. Fanny noted, 'Fowel Buxton very good speech, Sir J. Mackintosh very good . . . O'Connell acted very well, voice very good, very changeable countenance which he made diabolical at times.'

Meanwhile, in spite of demonstrations and rioting, the London season went on its way, and preparations were made for the coronation of William IV in October. Once again Emma and Fanny revelled in the theatre, concerts, opera and exhibitions. Emma not only listened to concerts; on 11 April she took piano lessons from the distinguished Czech pianist Moscheles, and later much enjoyed his performance in the overture to *The Marriage of Figaro*. They saw French plays; Fanny Kemble as Lady Teazle; William Macready in *William Tell*; and a number of operas, including Rossini's *La Donna del Lago*.

These were heady days; but there was one visitor to the capital who was completely unmoved by it all. On 15 April 1831 Charles Darwin was staying with his brother Erasmus, who bored him to death with his talk of reform. Nor, at that time, did opera, the theatre or art galleries interest him. He could think only of the expedition he was planning, to make a scientific study of Tenerife in the Azores. His father had backed him, and now he was busy making preparations; science was his only interest, and he had ears for nothing else. When he returned to Cambridge to receive his degree he was annoyed to find his tutor also absorbed in politics, campaigning for Palmerston, who was standing for one of the Cambridge seats.

On 17 April Fanny noted, 'Erasmus and Charles Darwin came to dinner, pleasant evening.' Charles's matchmaking sisters had singled Fanny out as a possible partner for him, and certainly they had much in common: both had a passion for making lists and keeping careful records, and devout little Fanny, they thought, would make an excellent wife for the country parson Charles expected to be. But Charles at this time was head over heels in love with a neighbour, the pretty, flirtatious Fanny Owen, who, he wrote to his cousin William Fox, 'as all the world knows is the prettiest, plumpest most charming personage that Shropshire posseses [*sic*], aye and Birmingham too'. Charles's sisters never let him forget the day they found him 'lying full length' with Fanny, gorging themselves in the strawberry beds. If he thought of his cousins at Maer, it was not Emma he remembered but the 'incomparable Charlotte', whose beautiful voice had once enchanted Charles's mother at a family party in Bath. Sukey had persuaded Charlotte to remain with her there after the others had left, to take singing lessons. Charles paid no particular attention to Emma before he left on the voyage on the *Beagle*, though he noted that she and Fanny looked well after their Geneva visit.

As for Emma, she had much more in common with Erasmus than Charles, sharing his love of music. Paganini was his idol, and it was Erasmus who joined the great family party on 10 July, when Jos took Fanny Mackintosh, Fanny Wedgwood and Emma, Erasmus and Hensleigh Wedgwood to a Paganini concert. Fanny noted in her journal that they had 'a most excellent box' and Paganini's playing 'was more wonderful than I expected and I enjoyed it most exceedingly. LaBlache accompanied him on a silver bell.' It was a 'lovely concert – Mozart's symphony. Paganini has a fine forehead and eyes but he looks wretchedly ill. He has long hair over his shoulders.' The evening finished, wrote Fanny, with 'a ball at the Hollands – came away at 3 dreadfully tired'.

In July Jos took his daughters home; as Bessy wrote, 'They have had their fill of amusements and going about and to crown all are very glad to come home.' However, their rackety year was not over yet. In October Hensleigh accompanied Bessy, Fanny and Emma on a driving tour in north Wales. 'Good weather, good eating,' wrote Bessy, 'and a lovely country put us all in excellent humour. Hensleigh, who drove one in his gig, was a treasure to us, so cheerful and obliging.'

Charles Darwin had also spent the summer in north Wales – on a crash course in geology with Professor Adam Sedgwick in preparation for the expedition to Tenerife. Then his fellow adventurer, Ramsay, suddenly died and the expedition was called off. However, as one door shut, another opened. Impressed by Charles's ability, his tutor Henslow recommended him to Captain Fitzroy of HMS *Beagle*, who was looking for a naturalist to accompany him on a five-year voyage. His mission was to survey the coasts of Patagonia, Tierra del Fuego, Chile and Peru, to visit Pacific islands and to circumnavigate the globe, making a series of chronometrical measurements.

It was at Maer, on 1 September 1831, that the momentous decision was taken that would send Charles round the world. Dr Robert had strongly objected, but had written to Jos, 'If you think differently from me I shall wish him to follow your advice.' Jos did think differently, and so did the family at Maer. Having discussed the matter with Charles, Jos offered to go with him the thirty miles to Shrewsbury and persuade Dr Robert that Charles should not miss this opportunity. Charles was eternally grateful to his 'uncle-father' for this crucial intervention. It was typical of Jos that at a time when he was himself feeling ill, when he was worried about his wife's health and undecided about his new political life, he should have taken time both to guide his nephew in the right direction and to go with him to Shrewsbury to win over his father. But Charles was his beloved sister's son, and he felt his responsibility. Maybe he saw something of his brother Tom in Charles, and hoped that a voyage would do him good. In any event, impressed by Jos's arguments, Dr Robert gave the enterprise his blessing. The crucial decision was no accident: it had stemmed from the mutual respect and affection of two men who had been friends since childhood.

Charles rushed to Cambridge to give the good news to Henslow – only to discover that Captain Fitzroy had made the offer to someone else. A visit to Fitzroy in London followed. It took the captain some days to decide whether this young man would be a suitable companion, and while he waited Charles took a seat to watch William IV's coronation procession. Eventually, having journeyed with Fitzroy to Portsmouth to see the *Beagle*, Charles was accepted. On 27 December 1831, he set off on a voyage that would change not only his life but the history of his time – out of spirits 'at the thought of leaving all my family and friends . . . I was also troubled with palpitation and pain about the heart . . . and was convinced that I had heart disease. I did not consult any doctor . . . I was resolved to go at all hazards.'

While Charles Darwin was preparing for the journey that would change his life, the Prime Minister, Lord Grey, and the Leader of the House of Commons, Lord John Russell, were preparing a bill that would change the country. Throughout the summer of 1831 Grey's government worked to get the 'Bill, the whole Bill and nothing but the Bill' through Parliament. After the King's coronation, on 8 October Grey presented the bill in the House of Lords. It was defeated by forty-one votes. Now the country was a tinder-box: Bristol was in flames; Nottingham Castle was burned down; there were riots in Derby, and especially in Birmingham, where the brilliant radical Francis Place marshalled his men and prepared his plans for revolution. On 12 December Russell presented a modified Third Reform Bill in the House of Commons. It was passed by 116 votes. Now the King reluctantly agreed that if the Lords rejected it again he would create more peers to enable its passage. The second reading in the Commons, and the crucial subsequent presentation to House of Lords, would not be taken until April 1832. There was an uneasy winter ahead.

In the first half of 1832 there were three weddings to cheer Bessy, who had begun to think her children would never marry. Emma's brothers Hensleigh and Frank, and her sister Charlotte, all married in the first half of the year. In January the scholarly Hensleigh married his cousin and Emma's close friend, Fanny, daughter of Sir James Mackintosh. 'How nice it is my dear dear old wife,' Emma wrote when she heard of their engagement, 'now don't be long a marrying.' The wedding in London, at which Fanny and Emma were bridesmaids along with the daughter of Mackintosh's colleague Malthus, was chaotic. There were moments of panic, of high farce and of merriment, ending with a riotous family party in Uncle Baugh's rooms in Dulwich College.

Once again it is Fanny Wedgwood's straightforward, astringent letter that not only sets the scene but sharply brings the characters to life. Fanny Mack had wanted to be married in the smart All Souls' Church in Langham Place, but Hensleigh had not been in the area long enough to qualify and they had to settle for St Andrew's in a poor area of Holborn. In spite of her liberal ideas, Fanny Mack at first refused to be married at Holborn, 'thinking', Fanny wrote, 'I suppose that it would not look well in the newspapers . . . However that was all talk and she bore her fate pretty well.' Hensleigh, who could have lied to claim residence in Langham Place, 'chose to have a conscience', as Fanny Wedgwood wrote to her brother Frank. Hensleigh's conscience was a constant cause of trouble in the family. He gave up his fellowship at Cambridge because he could not subscribe to the Thirty-nine Articles of the Church of England, and later wanted to resign his well-paid position as a Police Magistrate because as a Unitarian he did not believe in taking oaths.

While Emma and her sisters worked for the bride, 'shopping and making favours', Hensleigh was – wrote Fanny Wedgwood – 'lying in bed thinking himself very unwell'. Like his cousin Charles Darwin, Hensleigh tended to take to his bed at times of trial. However, the doctor told him briskly to 'eat a chop and drink some wine'. Even then Hensleigh could not bring himself to go out and buy the ring, so he wrote a note to his bride-to-be and begged her to 'buy a ring which', Fanny thought, 'certainly was not very decorous'. When he did rouse himself to come to the pre-wedding dinner he 'looked very thin and unbridal'.

On the morning of the wedding, Fanny and Emma were preparing to put on their bridesmaids' lilac silk when they were offered a friend's white silk wedding dress. Emma would not put it on, so, typically, 'they made me,' wrote Fanny, 'and by intense squeezing I got into it.' The bride had still not appeared, 'for why her gown was not come which was a white poplin presented by Lady Holland' – Fanny's father being a respected member of the Holland House circle. Typically, the *grande dame* had not sent it in time; so 'they took me,' wrote Fanny, 'as it was getting late and stripped me of my fine gown and Fanny (Mac) put it on with a white bonnet and lace veil which was given her by Miss Fox.' (When Lady Holland's dress did come, that evening, they found she had not bothered to take the bride's measurements and it was too short.)

They reached the church to find no bridegroom. However, he finally turned up and both bride and groom 'behaved with great decorum and they neither of them had their spectacles on. There were a good number of very dirty people in the church who kept pressing on our children and spoiling the beauty of our appearances.' There was no crying at the wedding, wrote Fanny with approval; and certainly none at the 'very elegant breakfast', where Hensleigh made a nice speech. That night the dinner party at the social Uncle Baugh's residence at Dulwich College was hilarious: 'The jokes were all about matrimony and everybody behaved in the most improper manner . . . people betting which side of the table would marry first and Mr Pugh, the attorney telling Charlotte that "all his hopes rested on her" . . . which was as good as a proposal.'

Mr Pugh was right, though it was not he who caught the charming Charlotte, at that time in full beauty; another guest, the Reverend Charles Langton, fell immediately in love, and two weeks later Fanny wrote: 'The happiest day of my life. Mr Langton proposed to Charlotte and we were all in perfect ecstasy.' They were married on 22 March 1832 at a simpler ceremony in Maer church. Charlotte's husband came to be loved by her family; sensitive and understanding, he seemed to see through the increasingly confused Bessy to the charming and intelligent lady she once had been. Charlotte and Charles finally settled at a parsonage at Onibury, near Ludlow, but Charles was never happy as a parson and later, as one by one the birds left the family nest at Maer, he and Charlotte would return to help Elizabeth take care of her frail parents. During Charlotte's wedding festivities her brother Frank, who was now helping to run the pottery, caught the marriage fever in his turn, falling in love with the blonde Frances Mosely. To distinguish her from the rest of the Fannys she was known in the family as Fanny Frank. They too were married in that same spring. As the prospective heir to the factory, Frank now moved into Etruria Hall. It was just as well that Fanny Frank was, according to Susan Darwin, 'a famous scrattler', even if she was (again according to Susan) too fat. The cellars at Etruria Hall were stacked with old documents, and doubtless Frank's new wife encouraged him to turn out the precious Wedgwood archives. Neither she nor the prosaic Frank had any interest in the family history.

There was yet another wedding this year, one which gave Charles Darwin sharp heartache. When the *Beagle* docked at Rio on 8 April, there were letters from Shrewsbury waiting for him. There he learned of the loss of his first love, the delectable Fanny Owen. His sisters wrote to console him. Fanny Wedgwood, they suggested, would make an ideal parson's wife. They could see the devout, practical Fanny running a quiet country parsonage for the Reverend Charles Darwin. How different the history of the nineteenth century might have been!

After all the celebrations, later that spring a cloud darkened the skies of Allens, Wedgwoods and Darwins with the death on 30 May of Sir James Mackintosh. Bessy in particular had become fond of him during the six months he and Kitty had spent at Maer. There was bathos in his end: a chicken bone lodged in his throat, which became infected; and the voice that had held many a grand dinner party enthralled was silenced. Emma's Aunt Fanny Allen was heartbroken; she had been secretly and hopelessly in love with him ever since her girlhood. At Cresselly, as she remembered in the memoir she wrote after his death, 'he made the joy and delight of our circle, his spirits were gay, no care oppressed him and his anticipation of the future, had all the brightness of early life.' When she stayed with him and her sister Kitty in London, she could not 'conceive any society superior to that which I partook while under his roof', where she met distinguished poets, artists and politicians. The Revd Sydney Smith thought his conversation 'was more brilliant than that of any human being' he had ever known. He was responsible for introducing some of the most intellectually distinguished men and women of the period to the Wedgwood family. He was also a born teacher. As Fanny Allen remembered, 'he was ever ready to lend his understanding . . . if he saw you struggling with a thought you could not manage to give clearly, he would instantly disentangle it for you.' Emma could not have been for six months in his company without absorbing something of his intellect. But his political life was a disappointment. Although he became an MP, first for Nairn and then Knaresborough, and a Privy Counsellor, Mackintosh's exclusion from the Cabinet left him frustrated and disheartened. The Whigs never forgave his acceptance of the India post from the Tories, and Thomas Moore maliciously caricatured him in the *New Whig Guide*:

He frequents the assembly, the supper, the ball,
The *philosophe beau* of unlovable Staël.
Affects to talk French in his hoarse Highland note,
And gurgles Italian half down his throat.
His gait is a shuffle, his smile is a leer,
His converse is quaint, his civility queer.
In short, to all grace and deportment a rebel
At best he is but a half polished Scotch pebble.

In his last months, all his former political passion was spent. 'He spoke', wrote his son, 'like one who had no more interest in the changes than that springing from the love of order, justice and the well-being of his country.' While outside his old colleagues battled through the critical May days, he lay quietly waiting for death.

The Bill which had passed its second reading in the Commons in April was thrown out by the Lords in committee on 7 May. Grey demanded the creation of fifty peers. The King refused; Grey resigned; Wellington could not form a government; Grey returned and, faced with near-revolution in the country, the King finally gave in. Wellington accepted the inevitable and promised to abstain with enough of his colleagues to allow the bill through. Mackintosh's son, Robert, brought him the news. It was the eve of the barricades – revolution had never been nearer. On 30 May Mackintosh died; on 4 June the Bill was passed in the Lords. Wellington and one hundred Tories had abstained. Three days later William IV reluctantly gave his assent by commission, refusing to give it in person.

So Mackintosh never saw the successful end of the campaign in which he had fought for so long; nor did he see his protégé, Jos Wedgwood, stand successfully for the new seat of Stoke-on-Trent and John Allen, Bessy's brother, come into Parliament in the election of 1832 as the MP for Pembroke. Throughout the country there were wild celebrations; but for Fanny Allen a bright light had gone out.

In August Emma Wedgwood, too, had to face the first great tragedy of her life.

In the summer of 1832 Elizabeth, Emma and Fanny Wedgwood were living in the rambling old house at Maer with Hensleigh and his new wife, Fanny Mack (henceforward to be known as Fanny Hensleigh). Jos and Bessy may have been away, for they are not mentioned in the reports of the tragic days that lay ahead; Charlotte and her brothers were definitely absent. The eldest and the youngest sisters faced this great crisis of their life aided only by their faithful maid, Mary, and the apothecary.

It must be remembered that at the time, like most women in country houses, Emma and her sisters would not expect to pursue a career but would consider themselves responsible for the health, welfare and education of the poor in their area, and were accustomed to dealing with births, deaths and sudden emergencies. At thirty-one Elizabeth was an experienced, if untrained, nurse and Emma at twenty-four was her competent assistant. They took seriously their duty to the villagers and for many years had doctored their neighbours, almost like district health visitors, or nurses in a modern clinic. This Wedgwood sense of duty to the community was an important part of Elizabeth and Emma's Wedgwood inheritance.

Elizabeth in particular spent considerable amounts of time and money visiting cottages, advising, helping and prescribing medicines, and had for years doctored her patients with astonishing self-confidence. No doubt she and Emma were schooled by Dr Robert Darwin, from whom Emma inherited, via Charles, his large leather-bound book of prescriptions. In 1824 Charlotte had written to Elizabeth asking which bottle of physick was to be sent to 'Lewis's child': 'there is a bottle come from Mr Turner's which as nobody owns, I conclude it to be the one, and I shall venture to send it if I hear from Mr Turner that it is made from a prescription in your drawer.' Three years later Elizabeth wrote to her sister Fanny, 'Little George Phillips has been ill, but with the help of three bleedings, a blister and three doses of calomel, I think I have made a care of him, as it was high time, you will think, I should.'

So when Fanny fell sick in August 1832, Elizabeth and Emma nursed her. Emma wrote her own private account of the agonizing days that followed, as carefully and honestly as Fanny would have done; it is only here that she shows the depth of her grief.

On Monday 13th August 1832, my dear Fanny complained of uneasiness in the bowels. Eliz gave her calomel and jalap but she would come and sit at the dinner table to save appearances as she said. The pain continued all night. Mary [the maid] and

Eliz fomented her and tried to give an injection but without effect. Mr Broomhall was sent for and ordered fomentation with poppy heads, the pain gradually went off. I put on 20 leeches. On Wednesday morning he came and thought her much better but it was of great consequence to move the bowels and ordered 2 draughts which would not stay on the stomach. She had bilious vomittings all day and the next day Thursday, Mr B came and stayed all night. Her bowels did not move till 12 at night when she was much relieved. Eliz then went to bed and I sat up with her. Her bowels were much swelled and we rubbed her. On Friday she had a tolerable day but the medicine worked her too much. Saturday Dr Northen came again. She had a peaceful day and slept a good deal. She asked to have Charlotte's letter read to her. I slept in the room with her and only had to help her up once or twice. Early on Sunday morning she was low and Eliz gave her some hot drink. She revived during the day and nothing was to be done for her but to make herself comfortable. At 8 in the evening she took an injection which gave her violent pain and after that she was restless and uneasy; told Eliz to sponge her face twice and her back and chest. At 4 o'clock sent for Mr B. He found her sinking when he came and gave her brandy and she was thoroughly warmed. At 9 came on the fatal attack and in 5 minutes we lost our gentle sweet Fanny, the most without selfishness of any body I ever saw and left a blank which will never be filled up. Oh Lord, help me to become more like her and grant that I may join her with thee never to part again. Teach me to keep in mind the solemn wishes I now feel to love thee and put my whole trust in thy mercy. Her last words were 'Ring the bell I must have Mary to raise me but do not speak—'

At this time a cholera epidemic was sweeping the country, and it is sometimes believed that it was cholera that caused Fanny's death. Certainly this must have been the fear in the sisters' minds, although the dread word was never spoken. Almost the last entry in Fanny's diary refers to cholera at Bilston. As Emma wrote to her worried Aunt Jessie, 'Cholera has been dreadfully bad at Bilston, an iron place not much larger than Newcastle and hundreds have died in a month.' She, Elizabeth and Fanny were all accustomed to going about among the cottages, and it is possible that Fanny could have caught the infection there. Does this perhaps explain Fanny's odd last words,' . . . but do not speak'? The last thing Fanny would have wanted was to start a panic at Maer. So in the family Fanny's death was said to have been caused by 'some kind of inflammation'.

The loss of Fanny changed Emma. She became more serious, more devout. To her account of Fanny's death she added:

> I wish heartily to profit by this affliction. Let me not have to look back some years hence and find that those wishes to become from this time more sincere and earnest in loving God have all past away. Oh God grant me the help of thy Holy Spirit let me not grow cold hearted and indifferent to thee. Give me a real faith and trust in thee. I trust that my Fanny's sweet image will never pass from my mind. Let me always keep it in my mind as a motive for holiness what exquisite happiness it will be to be with her again to tell her how I loved her and missed her who has been joined with me in almost every enjoyment of my life. I feel afraid of the pleasures and anxieties of the world getting too great an influence over me and drying up these feelings. I am afraid I never valued her enough but let me keep it as a reality before my mind that I may yet make amends to her for any neglect or forgetfulness I may have shown her. God will help me I know if I pray sincerely. Oh God help me pray to thee in spirit and in truth.

Perhaps for the first time, Emma now found real comfort in the Unitarian faith she had absorbed almost without thought. This was not the ritual gabble of creeds learned by rote, but the intense experience of direct communication with a loving God. The firm belief in an afterlife in a 'better land' in which a place could be earned and in the power of prayer were to be the twin bedrocks of Emma's faith. Jos, like Dr Robert Darwin, was something of an eighteenth-century free-thinker, and Bessy took more interest in the mind than in the spirit, but Emma was a child of her age and influenced by the evangelical fervour of the time. Jos watched the growing religious fanaticism and hoped that the 'Maerites' would be too sensible to be in danger of catching the infection. But Emma, though she never indulged in extreme enthusiasm – unlike one of her friends, who took to speaking in tongues ('Poor thing,' wrote Emma, 'I should think she would become quite mad soon') – began to develop that profound and unshakeable faith that sustained her for the rest of her life.

The Darwins had not heard of Fanny's illness until they got the letter telling them of her death. On 12 September 1832 Caroline Darwin sent Charles her own account of the tragedy, knowing 'how you did poor Fanny justice in liking her and valuing her goodness and excellent qualities'.

> About three weeks ago poor Fanny was taken ill with what they thought a sort of bilious fever. She seemed very ill for two days with vomitings and pain and then appeared to get better, so much so that not one of the family had an idea she was in danger. Seven days after she became unwell, Elizabeth sat up with her at night as she (Fanny) was too restless to sleep; towards morning she seemed cold and more uncomfortable and they sent for the apothecary, from some misunderstanding none of the family had an idea her danger was so immediate. Uncle Jos was terribly overcome and Aunt Bessy it was some time before Elizabeth could make her understand what had happened. My father says mortification must have taken place in her bowels at the time, the pain ceasing they all thought she was getting well . . . Mr and Mrs Hensleigh were staying at Maer during the time which was fortunate as they have been a great comfort to them all. Uncle Jos came over yesterday for a day to see Papa, he was cheerful and apparently much as usual, he says they are all better and cheerful at Maer except Aunt Bessy who they cannot make go on with her usual little occupations, she sits by herself and looks very sad and dejected.

Deep though Emma's grief was at the loss of Fanny, she did not brood. As she wrote to Aunt Jessie: 'I do not like that you should be thinking of us as more unhappy than we are. I think we all feel cheerful and susceptible of happiness. I do not expect or wish to miss our Fanny less than we do now. The remembrance of her is so sweet and so unmixed with any bitter feeling that it is a pleasure to be put in mind of her in every way. I feel as if it was a very long time ago since we had lost her tho' it is only a month next Monday.' She took comfort in reading Fanny's journals, though 'sometimes I feel a sad blank at the thoughts of having lost my sweet gentle companion who has been so closely joined with me ever since I was born, but I try to keep my mind fixed upon the hope of being with her again, never to part again.'

Fanny's death also left a 'sad blank' in the life of her father. Emma was always close to her mother, though she respected her father; but Fanny had much of Jos Wedgwood's character. It was she who, on their Italian tour, had taken long quiet walks with him. Patient, competent and orderly, in recent years she had been useful to him. He would miss Fanny, 'his little secretary', Emma wrote, especially in the year ahead when he took his seat as Member of Parliament for Stoke-on-Trent. As for Bessy, her brother, Baugh Allen, and Elizabeth took her on a tour of Wales; Bessy loved travelling and they hoped the jaunt would lift her spirits. Baugh, the chattering and resolutely cheerful Master of Dulwich College, bored the Darwin sisters and the Wedgwoods to death, but Bessy had always responded to him, remembering their childhood at Cresselly, and singing with him snatches of the old Welsh songs. If anyone could cheer her up, Baugh would do it. But she never recovered from Fanny's death. She had not been there when Fanny needed her, and for Bessy, the heart of the family, this was the ultimate agony.

This bereavement was the first real trial in Emma's hitherto protected life. Fanny's methodical, ordered habits had always balanced Emma's cheerful untidiness. Charlotte remembered Fanny as 'so gentle that a harsh word could hardly ever have been addressed to her, and her wishes and expectations for herself were so unpretending that it made her life one of much calm happiness.' But, as her letters and journals show, she was also a sharp and astringent observer, perfectly aware that Emma was the favoured one: in one New Year prayer she had asked to be forgiven her sin of jealousy. The family took her for granted, laughed kindly at Miss Pedigree and her methodical lists and records; but her organized life had provided a firm framework for that of the lively and outgoing 'Miss Slip-

Slop'. It would be some years before anyone would come to fill that 'sad blank' in Emma's existence.

––––––––––

The excitement of the election campaign in the autumn of 1832 helped to raise the spirits of the family at Maer after the summer's grief. Emma's father was upright and honourable, and in the opinion of his brother-in-law Dr Robert Darwin 'the wisest man I know'; but he was not a natural politician. Jos was no orator and disliked the hubbub of the hustings. Like his father, he was a humanitarian and an idealist, but he did not have his father's drive or his inventive mind. Nevertheless, he considered it to be his duty to serve. The two most important planks in his political platform were parliamentary reform and the abolition of slavery. When the election came at the end of 1832 he won the seat (much to his own surprise), becoming the first Member for Stoke-on-Trent in the reformed Parliament.

The family – especially Emma – had campaigned with gusto. She wrote triumphantly to Aunt Jessie: 'Papa was elected with a handsome majority. Papa and all of us were very much pleased at his coming in so grandly, especially as he is become too Tory for these radical times.' She and her cousin, Uncle John's daughter Jessie Wedgwood, went to see him nominated. 'Papa went first with his sons and some more gentlemen, his proposer and seconder in the carriage open with four horses, a few carriages followed and then the rag-tag and bobtail in gigs, carts and phaetons.' Emma was depressed when his nomination speech 'was received with silence' whereas that of the radical Mr Mason was greeted 'with rapture'; so they were surprised when her father was elected 'Wedgwood 822' and the tub-thumping Mr Mason only '240'. Emma maintained this interest in politics all her life.

Even Charles in South America longed to hear the result of the election. 'Hurrah for the Whigs!' he wrote on receiving the news – and wondered whether there would still be a king when he returned. Throughout Charles's five-year absence his sisters sent him affectionate, gossipy letters every month, keeping him in touch with both his own home and the fortunes of the Wedgwood family.

Back across the oceans came his own long, thrilling letters, which were read with excitement and pride at Shrewsbury and recounted to the Wedgwoods at Maer. The man whom they remembered poring over minute beetles now wrote of dense tropical forests, vast mountains, wretched slaves and naked cannibals. Other recipients were equally appreciative. Charles's letters to his tutor at Cambridge so impressed Henslow that he read them to the Philosophical Society of Cambridge, and Professor Sedgwick was inspired to call upon Dr Robert to tell him that his son 'deserved a place among the leading men of science'. Charles, hearing this, had wielded his geological hammer with renewed enthusiasm, delighted that his father at last no longer thought him a mere rat-catcher.

Though Charles sent greetings to all at Maer, there were no specific references to Emma; but he wrote a long letter to Charlotte 'the incomparable', over whom he and his cousin William Fox had sighed with calf love. It was Charlotte who wrote to him from Maer of Fanny's death: 'So good and innocent and unselfish as she was I can only feel that she is very happy to be taken out of the world before any distress or unhappiness came near her. Her life was a very happy one and closed without knowing her danger.'

While his sisters wrote faithfully to Charles, his beloved but languid brother Erasmus could not be persuaded to pick up his pen, though he arranged the transport of parcels of books to the traveller. However, his sisters passed on the Erasmus gossip with relish. He was paying too much attention to Fanny Hensleigh, Catherine reported after a visit to him in London in 1833. 'Papa has long been alarmed for the consequences and expects to see an action in the papers.' In fact, Erasmus delighted in his role as *cavaliere servente*. His Italian tour must have introduced him to the pleasure of being the accepted companion of married ladies, with all the delight of feminine company and none of the responsibilities of husband or lover. So he drove Carlyle's wife Jane, Harriet Martineau and Fanny Hensleigh around London in his stylish carriage, escorting them to dinners, plays or the opera. (He said he considered Harriet as a man, so she was as safe as a wife.) After spending a week with him in London that year, Catherine considered that 'the real danger is with Emma Wedgwood, who I suspect Mr Erasmus to be more in love with than appears or than perhaps he knows himself.' Caroline joined the gossip. When in May 1833 Emma went to London to be a bridesmaid at Charlotte Holland's wedding, she wrote: 'I expect Erasmus will be a very attentive cavalier to her and nobody knows what will be the end of the drives in his cab, he will take her to and fro Clapham where the Hensleigh Wedgwoods live.'

To which Charles replied in May 1834, 'Will Erasmus be married? All these gay doings with cab and horses portend something eventful.' It is quite clear that at this time Charles considered Emma as out of reach – or out of bounds – and, remembering the evenings they had all spent in London, when Emma and Erasmus obviously had so much in common, he must have thought their marriage a certainty.

'Do you remember your prophecy you made to Erasmus? That you should find him tied neck and heels to E [Emma Wedgwood] an[d] heartily sick of her,' Catherine wrote to him, 'and I think it may possibly have a good effect and prevent is own fulfilment.' Charles's sisters had always preferred Fanny to Emma – she presented no competition. But Erasmus, gentle, scholarly and languid, while obviously attracted to Emma, never found the energy to propose; as the poet Alice Meynell said of him, 'He never grasped at happiness.'

While Erasmus was trotting around London in his elegant cab behind the beautiful grey horse his father had sent him, Charles was galloping with gauchos in the interior of South America, or watching with fascinated horror the 'naked savages' of Tierra del Fuego. And while Charles was seeing at first hand the cruel treatment of slaves, Jos was working away on the committee for the Anti-Slavery Bill. Jos was a conscientous constituency Member and took part in the work of several committees, particularly those concerned with canals and the abolition of slavery, but he never spoke in Parliament. The great fire in the House of Commons in 1834 destroyed the old chamber and the Ventilator, and much of Jos's political interest went up in the smoke. He saw the passage of the Anti-Slavery Bill, but he did not stand again in the election of 1835.

Bessy's health caused Jos much concern throughout 1833, and she herself saw the shadow of mental breakdown approaching. In the spring she had joined her husband in London, visited Hensleigh and Fanny at their home in Clapham, and enjoyed the social life at her niece Lady Gifford's house at Roehampton. But once more, as in 1829, the excitement and the effort of keeping up appearances were too much. She fell, presumably during another of her epileptic fits, and broke some bones; she never walked again. Emma stayed in London to take care of her mother. As she wrote to Aunt Jessie in August, 'We feel impatient to . . . see the time when we can return home, but we must not think of it yet and it is very lucky Mamma does not feel at all impatient to move . . .

Papa is not able to come as often as he wishes, as he is on a Liverpool Committee and the Slavery Bill in the evenings; so he is only able to come on Saturdays and stay till Monday.'

At least Emma was able to make what was probably her last visit to the Ventilator. She went with Harriet Gifford to hear the Irish firebrand Daniel O'Connell attacking 'the Reporters, whom he accuses of reporting his speeches falsely, whereupon they say now they will not repeat a word more of his; so now he declares they shall not report at all and he had the gallery cleared of all the strangers and the reporters among them. It was a most foolish passionate thing to do as the Reporters are sure to gain the day in the end.'

Eventually Emma could take Bessy home to Maer – a painful seven-day journey – and from now on she and Elizabeth shared the care of an increasingly ailing and immobile mother. A room upstairs at Maer Hall was made into a comfortable sitting room for her, where she could rest and watch her birds outside her window. Although she had periods of normal awareness, she was gradually slipping into senility. Caroline warned Charles that when he returned he would find Aunt Bessy 'sadly changed since you saw her, her intellect much weakened and from a pain in her leg unable to stand or to move herself in the least. She sits or rather lies down in the big room upstairs which is now fitted up as a sitting room and makes a tolerable comfortable one . . . dear old Maer is not what it used to be and never will be again.' By November 1833 Catherine thought her fits 'more frequent than they used to be and she is excessively altered since her dangerous illness last summer . . . one would not suppose she could last much longer.' She too warned Charles that they would find Maer 'sadly changed . . . as poor Aunt Bessy's health is in a very precarious state, she had three fits in one day lately which Papa thinks exceedingly dangerous. They do not seem to be aware at Maer of the danger of these fits.'

Charles was deeply upset when he heard how much Jos, too, had aged. He never forgot his debt to his 'uncle-father', without whose intervention he might never have made the all-important voyage in which he was now engaged. Jos was by now finding it difficult to control his shaking hands (possibly the onset of what is now called Parkinson's disease); but when Jessie pitied his 'lot in life' he wrote in surprise that he always 'thought myself a fortunate man in spite of . . . some misfortunes: the chief of which my dear Bessy's state is lightened and almost removed by the gentleness, sweetness and cheerfulness with which she bears her lot and with which her delightful nature shines out to the last.' As for his family, 'if they have all taken the quiet path of life they have none of them made us ashamed or sorry.'

From now until her marriage Emma, along with Elizabeth, would nurse Bessy devotedly, taking their breaks in turn. This was a new phase in Emma's life; and as a dutiful and caring daughter she might well have thought her chances of marriage were over, her role in life set. Yet she had plenty of suitors. Bessy had thought her 'more popular than any of my girls. Her manners to men are very much to my taste, for they are easy, undesigning without coquetry. Charlotte is too distant and Fanny a little stiff. Elizabeth is very agreeable in my eyes but she wants personal attraction.' Perhaps because after Fanny's death she became more approachable, Emma suddenly had four or five proposals of marriage; but she laughed at her friends' matchmaking efforts. There were young men who hoped to win her with music: one such claimed to be an expert flautist, but when he did not come up to her standards he and his 'tootlings' were dismissed. At a party at the Tollets' house 'two singing sisters and their brother, a perfect seraph by their account,' were much admired; but Emma, with mock regret, pronounced the seraph too young for her. Once, Bessy found a young curate walking round the lake, weeping with disappointment at his rejection.

Emma was certainly a devoted aunt, and became particularly attached to Fanny and Hensleigh's children, as well as John Allen's at Cresselly. She especially enjoyed visits to Fanny and Hensleigh at Clapham; since her sister's death she had grown very close to Fanny, sharing her love of music, and taking an affectionate interest in her daughter, Snow (Julia). This continued all her life, and when Snow became a serious author it was Emma who encouraged her to write the life of her grandfather, Josiah Wedgwood I.

In these years Emma grew closer to her Allen aunts, who reminded her so much of her fading mother. She had owed much in her own childhood to the encouragement of her Aunt Emma Allen, and now could repay her. On her visit to Clapham in July 1834 she 'heard a good deal of beautiful music and corrupted Aunt Emma so far as to go to three operas with me. She stayed a fortnight with us, which I enjoyed very much as she is a person one always loves the better for being with.' As she grew older, music became more and more important to Emma. She visited music festivals at Worcester and Manchester, from where she wrote to Fanny: 'Last night we had Mozart's symphony in E Flat and the *Midsummer Night's Dream*, and the night before Beethoven in C Minor which I had only heard once before ages ago and I like it better than anything I have ever heard.' She never forgot hearing the great Malibran at Manchester and Clara Novello at Worcester.

She wrote long letters to Aunt Jessie in Geneva, and found much in common with her intelligent Aunt Fanny Allen. She remembered her childhood delight in Tenby and Cresselly, and in the autumn of 1835 she took a long break from Maer and spent seven weeks at the Allen home. Uncle John Allen's wife, Gertrude, had died and his sisters, Fanny, Emma and Harriet, were now living there and enjoying taking care of his children. From here Emma wrote to Aunt Jessie, 'Uncle John makes all the meals and occasions when all the family assembles so cheerful and pleasant. He was in constant gay spirits and most agreeable.' Now that he was MP for Pembroke he could share political gossip with Emma. Since Mackintosh's death he could no longer dine out on the stories of Holland House, so instead he had attached himself to Lord John Russell's circle. Mackintosh's son, Robert, was also there, so Aunt Fanny could relive her memories of her idol. She was, wrote Emma, 'in charming spirits and conversation which was a fresh pleasure to me every day especially in our walks, and [her aunts] used to curl their hair with me'. Nothing gave her greater delight than battling with the wind on Tenby's shore.

I liked renewing my recollections of Tenby and it looked as bright and pretty as it used to when I was a child. The rocks and the Wash I had never seen before and I think it was the grandest thing I ever saw. We had a fine bright day with a very high wind which dashed up the sea most beautifully. We were all great figures with the wind blowing our hair and petticoats no how, and had the good luck just to escape falling in with a large party of Stackpole (Earl Cawdor's place) grandees who arrived just after we set off home.

Aunt Jessie replied that she was delighted to 'read your rapture with Cresselly. You know it is my Paradiso.'

Uncle John's children never forgot their Aunt Emma's paper 'beasts'. Pigs and lions were her speciality, cut out with skilful hands. 'I wish you would do me a bear and a lion good sized,' said Aunt Fanny. Seeing that Emma was so good with children, the Allen aunts longed to see her happily married with her own, but time was passing; Emma was now nearing the end of her twenties, and they were afraid Erasmus would capture her. They could not imagine him as a father.

However, on 6 October 1836 Jos Wedgwood received a letter from Charles Darwin at Shrewsbury which would transform Emma's life. 'The *Beagle* arrived on Sunday evening and I reached home late last night,' he wrote; 'my head is quite confused with so much delight.' He hoped that after his final visit to the *Beagle* he could come to Maer. 'I hope in person to thank you as being my First Lord of the Admiralty. I am so very happy I hardly know what I am writing.'

CHAPTER SEVEN

'Better than a Dog'

CHARLES'S VISIT WAS AWAITED EAGERLY BY ALL AT MAER, AND WITH impatience mingled with apprehension by Emma, who had, she confessed, not read up as much as she should have done for him, having got no further than Sir Francis Head's *Rapid Journies across the Pampas*, published in 1828: 'We all ought to get up a little knowledge for him,' she wrote to Fanny Hensleigh. 'I have taken to no deeper study than Capt. Head's Gallop which I have never read before.' She need not have worried. Her account of the occasion to Fanny was enthusiastic:

> We enjoyed Charles's visit uncommonly. We had been very handsome in inviting the outlyers of the family to meet him and the last morning the chaise from Tern Hill did not come and we persuaded them to stay and had just made ourselves comfortable and planned a walk when the chaise arrived. However we got them to let us send it off though Caroline felt it to be rather naughty and we had a very nice snug day of them to ourselves. Charles talked away most pleasantly all the time we plied him with questions without any mercy. Harry and Frank made the most of him and enjoyed him thoroughly. Caroline looks so happy and proud of him it is delightful to see her.

In the comfort of Maer Hall Emma listened enthralled while Charles told them of his five-year journey. She commiserated over his constant seasickness, marvelled at his courage as he rode hundreds of miles with the gauchos over the pampas, shared his wonder at 'the unforgettable sight of a naked savage in his native land', and was much moved as he told of the 'sense of sublimity which the great deserts of Patagonia and the forest clad mountains of Tierra del Fuego excited in me'.

In his autobiography Charles claimed that this voyage determined his whole career; that he owed to it the first real education of his mind; and in particular that in those years he learned a 'habit of energetic industry and concentrated attention' which he always insisted was the secret of his scientific success. He was especially proud of his 'solution of the problem of the Coral Islands' and his geological studies, but most of all of his discovery of what he called 'the singular relations of animals and plants inhabiting the several islands of the Galapagos Archipelago, and all of them to the inhabitants of S. America'. It was his observation of the similarities and differences in plants and animals in neighbouring islands that sowed the seeds of theories that more than twenty-five years later would blossom in the *Origin of Species*.

This was a different man from the young student with a passion for beetle-hunting, the carefree young sportsman who had revelled in the shooting at Maer; Emma listened with a new respect and interest. There was even an unusual touch of jealousy in her comment when Charles, dismayed at Charlotte's portrait, said, 'I hope to fate she is not like that picture.' 'I suppose,' she wrote to her sister-in-law, Fanny Hensleigh, 'he has rather a poetical idea of her for the picture is certainly very like.' Charles had hoped that Charlotte would be there – 'Maer would not be the same without her.' In fact, the idol of his boyhood was now a matron – happy, but more interested in her music and painting than in her appearance.

After that happy visit Emma saw very little more of Charles in his first months at home. He was busy in Cambridge sorting out his notes and his geological specimens, and she spent most of the winter of 1836 with one of her Allen cousins, Lady Gifford, in Edinburgh. Harriet Gifford's 'handsome' house in Atholl Crescent was 'blazing with gas [only recently introduced for domestic use] and she gave us a very pleasant cordial reception. We are quite surprised at the wonderful civility of all Harriet's friends, calling up on us and inviting us out just as if we were somebody.' Caroline Allen's daughter had moved up several notches in the social world.

On this visit Emma met many distinguished Scottish lawyers and Francis Jeffrey, editor of the *Edinburgh Review*. Yet, hospitable though the Scots were, inviting them to balls and dances, the season was too frivolous for her new, serious tastes: she would have preferred, she told her sister Charlotte, 'the learned season to the gay one'. When Susan Darwin heard this, she was surprised; she had not understood the serious side of Emma – though Charlotte had done so. She still loved dancing and enjoyed the Edinburgh balls, but at twenty-eight no longer waltzed with the same enthusiasm as in her Geneva days. She felt more at home back in London at her brother Hensleigh's house; here she often met Erasmus, who though he lived some distance from Clapham, in Great Marlborough Street, spent much of his time with Hensleigh and Fanny. In March 1837 Charles took rooms near his brother and worked on the reports of his voyage, and when Emma visited London she was increasingly drawn to this new, studious Charles Darwin. As she listened with Fanny and Hensleigh to the talk at Erasmus's dinner table, the impression she had formed on Charles's visit to Maer was confirmed: this was no longer the diffident young sportsman she had known before 1831. The intervening years had changed him fundamentally. He no longer looked forward to a quiet life in a country vicarage; he was now to be a dedicated scientist.

On the voyage Charles had seen huge ancient rocks and fossils that belied the biblical account of Creation. The Earth was more ancient, and its flora and fauna more curious and fascinating, than he had imagined. In the autumn of 1835 the *Beagle* had landed on the Galapagos Islands in the Pacific Ocean, and he had climbed ashore over the bare volcanic rocks into a magical world where giant tortoises and iguana crawled up to the human visitors, unafraid. Here he could swim with tame sea lions among brilliant flamingos, and watch hammer-headed sharks at play; later in the voyage he remembered his observations and, questioning, would be jolted into a new pattern of thought. These were empty volcanic islands that had risen from the sea millions of years before, so where did the plants and animals come from? How could they survive in this harsh environment? Did they change and evolve? If so, the belief that God had created immutable species must be wrong.

It was these memories that persuaded Charles that species were not created in permanent, unchanging form – that they could evolve. But it would take him twenty-four years of patient and painful research to get to the point of publishing the *Origin of Species*, the work that, according to Julian Huxley, 'effected the greatest of all revolutions in human thought, greater than Einstein's or Freud's or even Newton's. It established that Evolution is a fact.'

It is difficult today to realize just how disturbing these ideas were to Charles Darwin's contemporaries. They were not new – other scientists had advanced the idea of evolution, among them Charles's own grandfather, Erasmus. But Charles's contribution to the debate was crucial because his theories were based not on academic studies by armchair scientists, or on unsubstantiated poetic imaginings, but on the personal observations and careful researches carried out with infinite patience over many years and tested repeatedly.

Because he was not a recognised man of science, Charles had to establish his reputation. So on his return to England he had a double mission. Publicly, he worked on his report on the voyage of the *Beagle* and wrote articles for scientific journals; then began eight years' research into *Cirripedia* (barnacles), on which he published a treatise; later he published a highly successful study of the fertilization of orchids. Privately, meanwhile, he set about collecting his ideas relating to his work on evolution in a series of notebooks, the first opened in 1837, supplementing his own researches with replies to his queries addressed not only to distinguished scientists but to farmers and even pigeon fanciers.

The Charles Emma was getting to know was a young man of infinite curiosity about every aspect of life and thought, and dedicated to the pursuit of truth as he saw it. And for the first time, Emma fell in love.

In May 1838 Emma joined the Sismondis, Darwin's sister Catherine, Harry Wedgwood and his wife, and John Allen from Cresselly for a great family party in Paris, a city she had known and loved years before, and was delighted when Aunt Jessie prolonged the party. Sunday, however, was a lost day. According to Emma, 'Aunt Jessie went in the morning to Notre Dame' where 'the music was very beautiful but the mummery quite wonderfully foolish. The Archbishop performed and drank off two such large goblets of wine that she expected him to be tipsey [*sic*].' Emma herself went to 'a most tiresome service' in the little American chapel, where she heard 'an extempore sermon which we thought would never end'. On Monday they braved the rain and sailed 'at the tail of a shower' to St Cloud. The sun came out, the gardens at St Cloud were very pretty, the view of Paris from the top of the park was quite beautiful, they dined in 'a little room looking over the river and to complete our good luck got on board the steamer again just before a thunderstorm that came down like a shower bath'. She enjoyed a ride to St Germain: 'The railroad goes just the same pace as ours, 14 miles in half an hour. It is a very pretty drive,' she told Fanny Hensleigh, 'as you cross the Seine three times.' They visited friends there, took a two-mile ride on donkeys and 'a very indifferent horse', and came back through the woods listening to the nightingales. Emma was less enchanted with a visit to Franconi's circus: 'Tricks by horses are disagreeable when you think how much they have to be teased to perform.' If Aunt Jessie took them shopping in Paris Emma did not think it worth mentioning to her correspondent.

On Emma's return from Paris she spent some time with Fanny and Hensleigh in London and was obviously disappointed that Charles, who was a frequent visitor, appeared uninterested in her. But she hid her feelings – even from Aunt Jessie, to whom she confessed only later, four days after her engagement, that

> When you asked me about Charles Darwin, I did not tell you half the good I thought of him for fear you should suspect something, and though I knew how much I liked him, I was not the least sure of his feelings, as he is so affectionate, and so fond of Maer and all of us, and demonstrative in his manners, that I did not think it meant anything, and the week I spent in London on my return from Paris, I felt sure he did not care about me, only that he was very unwell at the time.

In fact, what Emma took for indifference may have been no more than a self-deprecating reticence. 'Emma chats well and is very pretty,' Susan Darwin noticed; and Charles, watching her with Erasmus, whose interests she so obviously shared, may well have thought her even more beyond his reach.

In July 1837 Emma's eldest brother, the silent Joe, had married Charles's sister Caroline. Perhaps it was the jolt of this unexpected union – after all, Caroline was thirty-seven and Jos forty-two – that prompted Charles to consider marriage seriously; and there was also Hensleigh, who was happily combining scholarship with wedded life. 'Charles', Emma reported to Fanny Hensleigh, 'seems to have been much struck with the sight of Hensleigh walking up the street with a bandbox in one hand and a child in the other.' If scholarly Hensleigh could enjoy fatherhood, Charles might have thought, than perhaps he could too. His own rooms in Great Marlborough Street were uncomfortable and noisy, and the London streets were filthy: he was beginning to realize that he needed a wife.

Methodical as always, he set down on paper two columns of arguments, pro and con, headed 'MARRY' and 'NOT MARRY':

This is the question:

Marry	Not Marry
children – (if it Please God) – Constant companion, (& friend in old age) who will feel interested in one, – object to be beloved & played with. – better than a dog anyhow. – Home, & someone to take care of house – Charms of music & female chit-chat. – These things good for one's health. – *but terrible loss of time.* – My god, it is intolerable to think of spending one's whole life, like a neuter bee, working, working, & nothing after all. – No, no won't do. – Imagine living all one's day solitarily in smoky dirty London House. – Only picture to yourself a nice soft wife on a sofa with good fire, & books & music perhaps – Compare this vision with the dingy reality of Grt. Marlbro' St.	Freedom to go where one liked – choice of Society & *little of it.* – Conversation of clever men at clubs – Not forced to visit relatives, & to bend in every trifle. – to have the expense & anxiety of children – perhaps quarrelling – Loss of time. – cannot read in the Evenings – fatness & idleness – Anxiety & responsibility – less money for books & c – if many children forced to gain one's bread. – (But then it is very bad for one's health to work too much) Perhaps my wife won't like London; then the sentence is banishment & degradation into indolent, idle fool.

Marry – Marry – Marry Q.E.D.

On the reverse side of the page he sums up in his usual orderly manner:

It being proved necessary to marry – When? Soon or Late. The Governor says soon for otherwise bad if one has children – one's character is more flexible – one's feelings more lively, and if one does not marry soon, one misses so much good pure happiness. –

But then if I married tomorrow: there would be an infinity of trouble and expense in getting and furnishing a house, – fighting about no Society – morning calls – awkwardness – loss of time every day – (without one's wife was an angel and made one keep industrious) – Then how should I manage all my business if I were obliged to go every day walking with my wife. – Eheu!! I never should know French, – or see the Continent, – or go to America, or go up in a Balloon, or take solitary trip in Wales – poor slave, you will be worse than a negro – And then horrid poverty (without one's wife was better than an angel and had money) – Never mind my boy – Cheer up – One cannot live this solitary life, with groggy old age, friendless and cold and childless staring one in one's face, already beginning to wrinkle. Never mind, trust to chance – keep a sharp look out. – There is many a happy slave –

The notes may have been haphazard, but the conclusion was clear.

Charles was obviously considering the principle of marriage; there is no hint here that he had anyone particular in mind. Though the Darwin and Wedgwood families had now also decided that Charles needed a wife, and that Emma was the obvious choice, he himself was only just beginning to consider this a possibility. He was perhaps not a little unnerved by Emma's apparent detachment; he was quite convinced that after the lively minds at Maer Hall she would find him boring, and he thought himself unattractive. Emma had crisply rejected a number of other suitors, as his sisters would have told him; she might mock his presumption. Just back from three weeks in Paris, pretty, lively and unusually smart in her new French gown, Emma must have seemed even more unattainable to the modest Charles. At the end of his life he told his sons that he was amazed that Emma, so much his superior in every respect, had consented to be his wife.

She certainly was an exceptionally accomplished young woman, though she was then and always completely unaffected. Not only did she dance gracefully, she spoke French, German and Italian well, and played the piano brilliantly, having been taught by distinguished pianists. She had read widely; she was said to have read *Paradise Lost* at the age of five. Surrounded as she had been by politicians and kept up-to-date on French and Swiss affairs by Aunt Jessie and Sismondi, she could talk intelligently on current events in England and Europe. Prominent political and literary figures were not just names in a history book to her: they were family friends. Aunt Fanny Allen was a lifelong friend of the Revd Sydney Smith, and had known Florence Nightingale as 'little Flo' and then as 'a brave girl' travelling on the continent. Uncle Mackintosh knew not only leading politicians but Wordsworth, Coleridge, Byron and Carlyle, and Aunt Caroline's daughters were married to successful lawyers.

Charles worried. Emma's world was filled with brilliant relations; would she not find his scientific friends a bore? For his own part, he could see how much time would be wasted in paying visits to this immense family. The Allens alone were alarmingly numerous and voluble. Emma would be completely 'becousined', as Aunt Jessie had written after her visit to Cresselly. One of his arguments against marriage had been 'forced to visit relatives'. It is not surprising that, faced with such a momentous decision, Charles, like his cousin Hensleigh on a similar occasion, became unwell. Erasmus, too, must be considered. Was he, as his sisters thought, really in love with Emma? There is no doubt that before proposing Charles would have talked to Erasmus, and perhaps realized that the love of his brother's life was in fact Hensleigh's wife, Fanny.

But Emma had lost her heart. 'He is the most open, transparent man I ever saw,' she later told Aunt Jessie, 'and every word expresses his real thoughts. He is particularly affectionate and very nice to his father and sisters, and perfectly sweet tempered, and possesses some minor qualities that add particularly to one's happiness, such as not being fastidious, and being humane to animals.'

In November 1838 Charles at last plucked up enough courage. On the comfortable sofa by the library fire at Maer Hall he asked Emma to marry him, and was astonished at her immediate acceptance. Sobered by the sudden decision, they sat in unaccustomed silence through the family dinner; after the meal, a worried Fanny and Hensleigh called them into their room to know what the matter was. The excited talk went on until early morning, when Emma, typically unsentimental and 'seized with hunger', sent Hensleigh down 'to forage in the kitchen', as she wrote to Aunt Jessie. There he 'found a loaf and 2lb butter and a carving knife, which made us an elegant refection'. The match that the family had wanted for so long had been at last arranged.

No one could have been more delighted by the engagement than the two old friends Dr Robert Darwin and Jos Wedgwood. 'My father echoes and re-echoes Uncle Jos's words "you have drawn a prize",' Charles told her. Dr Robert wrote to Emma's father: 'Emma having accepted Charles gives me as great happiness as Jos having married Caroline and I cannot say more. On that marriage Bessy said she should not have had more pleasure if it had been Victoria and you may assure her that I feel as grateful to her for Emma as if it had been Martineau herself that Charles had obtained.' This was a family joke – Dr Robert detested the unconventional Harriet Martineau. 'Pray give my love to Elizabeth, I fear I ought to condole with her, for her loss will be very great,' he continued, and signed himself, 'Ever dear Wedgwood, your affectionate brother, R W Darwin.'

Jos replied with equal happiness.

A good chearful and affectionate daughter is the greatest blessing a man can have after a good wife. – if I could have given such a wife to Charles without parting with a daughter there would be no drawback from my entire satisfaction in bestowing Emma upon him – You lately gave up a daughter – it is my turn now – At our time of life our happiness must be in a great measure reflected from our families, and I think there are few fathers who have on the whole more cause to be satisfied with the conduct & present circumstances & future prospects of our families. – I could have parted with Emma to no one for whom I could so soon & so entirely feel as a father & I am happy in believing that Charles entertains the kindest feelings for his uncle-father. I propose to do for Emma what I did for Charlotte

& for three of my sons – give a bond for £5000 & to allow her £400 a year as long as my income will supply it which I have no reason for thinking will not be as long as I live. Give my love to your fireside and believe me, Affectionately yours, Josiah Wedgwood.

This generous allowance gave Emma some financial independence, though until married women's financial rights were recognized by law, technically Emma's property belonged to Charles.

Erasmus sent his brother

most hearty & sincere congratulations on your good fortune, & I feel very glad in what I am sure will give you so much & such certain happiness. Not less than to you, do I give my congrats to Emma though in writing to you I ought I suppose to word it somehow differently. It is a marriage which will give almost as much pleasure to the rest of the world as it does to yourselves – the best auspices I should think for any marriage. I received your letter just as I was going out to drive Martineau about, & lost no time in publishing the fact, & we also took the opportunity to look out for houses.

Emma's sister Charlotte, who understood both Charles and Emma well, 'truly and warmly rejoice in this marriage . . . As much as it is possible to rely on the happiness of any two people I feel a reliance on yours and Emma's . . . There is nothing but satisfaction looking on this on every side and I take particular pleasure in thinking of the great regard that has always subsisted between you and my father . . . Emma can be but ill spared there.'

Now that Charles had made up his mind he could allow himself to fall deeply in love: all his hitherto undeveloped emotions were centred on Emma. From Shrewsbury he wrote, exulting in his good fortune,

Like a child that has something it loves beyond measure, I long to dwell on the words, my own dear Emma . . . My life has been very happy and very fortunate and many of the pleasantest remembrances are mingled with scenes at Maer, and now it is crowned. My own dear Emma, I kiss the hands with all humbleness and gratitude which have so filled up for me the cup of happiness. It is my most earnest wish that I may make myself worthy of you.

It took Emma longer to express openly the love concealed beneath her cousinly badinage. He was her 'old curmudgeon', her 'dear Nigger'. This last was a nickname that stuck; her later letters often begin: 'Dear N.'. When she could not make up her mind where they should live, she wrote, 'Here you remark, tiresome toad, why can't she tell me which she would really like.' (Toad in the Wedgwood vocabulary was a term of endearment.) When she was sick it was 'not, I am sorry to say, at grief at parting with you, but all owing to that horrid little bit of stewed beef we had on Thursday and again on Friday and half poisoned two or three of us'.

The marriage was fixed for 29 January 1839. Suddenly Emma was overwhelmed by the realization that this was too immense a change in her life to be taken so quickly. Elizabeth would miss her. For several years now Emma had shared with her the responsibility of the running of Maer Hall, the estate and the gardens, for Bessy had long lost control, and Jos was increasingly frail. His shaking hands and failing memory worried him now that his sons were married and away from home; and the estate workers were beginning to take advantage of his weakness. Elizabeth was highly intelligent, but was no manager, and without Emma's firm handling she would be even more a prey to beggars. Emma began to feel she had been too impetuous, and that Elizabeth would 'be very sorry if it was to happen too soon'. She appealed to Catherine Darwin, 'I hope you will all hold him [Charles] in a little, especially the Dr [Robert]. Tell Charles to be a good boy and do his lessons and take things leisurely, indeed they can't be very fast. How I wish he would and wait till spring and fine weather! F.A. [Aunt Fanny Allen] says it is the happiest time of Emma's life and it is a thousand pities it should be a very short one – do dear Catty clog the wheels a little.' Wise Aunt Fanny had seen so many brides find their lives quickly circumscribed by annual childbearing.

Charles, however, was impatient. Writing from Shrewsbury, he longed to be with Emma at Maer, sitting cosily by the library fire, discussing their future. There was much to be decided. Where should they live – suburbs or central London?

> The Governor gives much good advice to live, wherever it may be, the first year prudently & quietly. My chief fear is, that you will find after living all your life with such large & agreeable parties, as Maer only can boast of, our quiet evenings dull. – You must bear in mind, as some young lady said, 'all men are brutes', and that I take the line of being a solitary brute, so you must listen with much suspicion to all arguments in favour of retired places. I am so selfish, that I feel to have you to myself, is having you so much more completely, that I am not to be trusted.

As for Emma's appeal to Catherine:

> Since writing the former part, the Post has brought in your own dear note to Katty . . . You must be absolute arbitress, but do dear Emma, remember life is short, & two months is the sixth part of the year, & that year, the first, from which for my part, things shall hereafter date. Whatever you do will be right, – but it will be *too* good to be unselfish for me, until I am part of you, dearest Emma.

Charles was inclined to seek their first home in the city rather than the suburbs since his job as Secretary of the Geological Society was in London. 'And now for the great question of houses,' he wrote.

> Erasmus & myself have taken several very long walks; & the difficulties are really frightful. Houses are very scarce & the landlords are all gone mad. They ask such prices. – Erasmus takes it to heart, even more than I do, & declares I ought to end all my letters to you 'Your's inconsolably'. – this day I have given up to deep cogitations regarding the future, in as far as

houses are concerned. I am tied to London, for rather more than that period; & whilst this is the case, I do not doubt it is wisest to reap *all* the advantages of London life: more especially as every reason will urge us to pay frequent visits to *real* country, which the suburbs never afford. After the two or three years are out, we then might decide whether to go on living in the same house or suburbs.

Emma agreed. 'Let us cast off the suburbs and what is more Susan Darwin thinks so too and you know what a wise woman she is . . . Dear good Susan has offered to get all the household linen which will be a great weight off our minds.' Charles obviously thought he had better invite Susan down to deal with setting up their household, 'for she will save us much trouble, and will do it very well'. 'Granny' Susan was later happy to oblige. Nothing pleased her more than arranging her brother's house; 'scrattling' was her delight. Once again the affectionate cousinly banter hides Emma's deeper feelings. 'The kettles & saucepans have been weighing a little upon my soul too though I think a frying pan & tea kettle w^d be enough at first & any thing you buy in that line or any other will be so much gained & I know I shall be satisfied. Elizabeth & Caroline are grown suburban again & it is very puzzling.' If Emma worried about exchanging the rambling Maer Hall and estate for a small London house, she did not show it. Suburbs or London, she did not mind so long as they were together.

The truth is I cannot at present make myself care much about the 2 sides of the question & so if any fresh reasons arise in your mind to make you more decided one way or the other be sure you tell me. The Tollets were shocked to find I had not read Mr Lyells last book in which you are a great person & I really think I will try. Caroline Tollet [who was also engaged to be married] says in her situation she finds she can read nothing but sermons & Nicholas Nickleby. I have unfortunately read Nicholas & don't find I have much capacity for sermons so I am in a bad way.

Hearing that Charles was wandering up and down the streets of London looking for 'To Let' signs, Emma decided she must go to help: 'whether it will be of much use now, I don't know, but I am sure I shall like it of all things so I am a-coming.' Escorted by her brother Harry, she took the train from Birmingham to London with much excitement – the line had only been opened in September. She stayed with Fanny and Hensleigh, and together she and Charles set about finding a home. Charles wanted to be near a park; Emma liked a house near the opera at Covent Garden; but they both liked one in Upper Gower Street, near Euston and the railway that could take Emma quickly back to Maer. It was hideously furnished with bright yellow curtains and azure walls: it reminded Charles of a tropical parrot, and he called it 'Macaw Cottage'. But they did not care; neither then nor at any time did Charles and Emma aspire to elegance. Fanny Hensleigh, a lady of discernment, suggested they should dye the curtains grey; they probably did not bother. Even Emma's heart must have sunk when, remembering the rolling acres at Maer, she had seen the little sooty garden with its black sparrows and a grisly dead dog. But she did not complain; she wrote lightly that they would remove the dog, and that she intended to plant laburnum trees to shelter them from the neighbours.

Emma decided she should buy her trousseau in London. She told Charles:

> I have had a most affectionate letter from A^t Jessie & Sismondi. Her chief anxiety is for fear I should not dress myself smart enough, so that when you reproach me with extravagance I shall have an answer quite ready that it is entirely from a sense of duty. Susan & Jessie are very sorry that they will not be present to egg me on sufficiently in buying my things, but they think Fanny H[ensleigh] will do nearly as well if properly primed. I suppose I am reckoned very meanspirited in the family.

Aunt Jessie had in fact sent firm instructions:

> Now that your person will belong to another as well as yourself I beg you not to go to Cranbourne Alley to cloathe it . . . If you

do pay a little more be always dressed in good taste: do not despise those little cares . . . because you know you have married a man who is above caring for such little things. No man is above caring for them, for they feel the effect imperceptibly to themselves. I have seen it even in my half-blind husband.

Emma obviously needed the reminder. Obediently, she followed Jessie's advice. 'Though I have not bought many things,' she wrote on her return to Maer,

> they are all very dear and the milliner's bill would do your heart good to see. I have bought a sort of greenish-grey rich silk for the wedding, which I expect Papa to approve of entirely and a remarkably lovely white chip bonnet trimmed with blonde and flowers. Harriet [Gifford, her cousin in Edinburgh] has given me a very handsome plaid satin, a dark one, which is very gorgeous, handsomely made up with black lace; and that and my blue Paris gown which I have only worn once, and the other blue and white sort of thing will set me up for the present . . . And a grand velvet shawl too.

Emma returned home feeling 'quite cockneyfied already and think Maer looks wonderfully fresh and quiet'. The railway was a blessing, as she consoled her mother; she would be able to 'steam up' from London so easily. She was now a railway enthusiast. She and her escort Harry 'had a very prosperous journey from London', she told Charles:

> I found Harry's rug the greatest comfort. We got some biscuits when we were ravenous. There was a young gentleman about 18 sitting in the corner who had a bottle of brandy in his pocket with which he consoled himself very often besides having a ring on & a smart chain taking snuff & smelling of cigars, so I thought to my self what an unpleasant boy that must be, but when he spoke he had the meekest civilest manner in the world & called Harry Sir at every word. There was a great bustle at

Birmingham & we had half an hour to spare which we bestowed in a grand refreshment room lit up with gas where there was a very good dinner going on which came in very acceptably.

On Saturday afternoon, 29 December, Charles wrote triumphantly: 'Gower Street is ours, yellow curtains and all. I have today paid some advance money, signed an agreement and had the key given over to me and the old woman informed me I was her master henceforth . . . I long for the day when we shall enter the house together; how glorious it will be to see you seated by the fire of our own house. Oh that it were the 14th instead of the 24th.' (Charles's eagerness was running away with him; in fact the date they had planned was the twenty-ninth.) Emma was delighted. The house, she told Aunt Jessie, had a 'front drawing room with three windows and a back one, rather smaller, with a cheerful look-out on a set of little gardens, which will be of great value to us in summer to take a mouthful of fresh air, and that will be our sitting room for quietness sake.' Charles, as excited as a child with a new toy, moved into Macaw Cottage on Sunday, 30 December 1838. Proudly he addressed his letter '12 Upper Gower Street', explaining that, after a sleepless Saturday night, he had rung for his servant, Covington, who had been with him on the *Beagle*, telling him, 'I am sorry to disturb you but begin packing up I must for I cannot rest.' On Monday he needed two large vans; Erasmus 'was astounded at the bulk of my luggage and the porters were even more so at the weight of those containing my geological specimens'. By Wednesday evening all his 'goods are in their proper places, and one of the front attics [henceforward to be called the museum] is quite filled.' His room downstairs was so quiet that 'the contrast to Marlborough Street is as remarkable as it is delightful.'

London was already becoming bearable; he had been made a member of the Athenaeum (on the same day as Charles Dickens) and wrote, 'here I am sitting very comfortably and feeling just that degree of lassitude which a man enjoys after a day's shooting terminated by an excellent dinner.' Charles's hunting days were almost over; for the present he had to console himself with walking 'half-an-hour in the garden' and much enjoying 'so easily getting a mouthful of air'. One evening Erasmus took him 'to drink with the Carlyles, it was my first visit – one must always like

Thomas, and I felt particularly well toward him as Erasmus told me he had propounded that a certain lady, was one of the nicest girls he had ever seen. Jenny [Carlyle] sent some civil messages to you but which from the effects of an hysterical sort of giggle were not very intelligible. It is high treason but I cannot think that Jenny is quite natural or lady-like.'

Charles knew how much Emma enjoyed the company of Fanny and Hensleigh, and that she would enjoy meeting Erasmus's friends. 'Erasmus dinner yesterday was a very pleasant one: Carlyle was in high force and talked away most steadily; to my mind Carlyle is the best worth listening to of any man I know,' he enthused. 'The Hensleighs were there and were very pleasant also. Such society, I think is worth all other and more brilliant kinds many times over.' He may have been thinking of the dreaded time-wasting family visits to grand lawyers and doctors that loomed: Emma's Allen cousins, Harriet Gifford and Georgina Alderson, were both married to distinguished lawyers, and her Wedgwood relation, the pompous Dr Holland, was a medical adviser to the Queen. He reiterated to Emma the warning that his own happiness rested

> on quietness and a good deal of solitude . . . But I believe the explanation is very simple, and I mention it because it will give you hopes that I shall gradually grow less of a *brute*. It is that during the five years of my voyage (and indeed I may add these two last) which from the active manner in which they have been passed, may be said to be the commencement of my real life, the whole of my pleasure was derived, from what passed in my mind, whilst admiring views by myself, travelling across the wild deserts and glorious forests, or pacing the deck of the poor little *Beagle* at night. Excuse this much egotism. I give it you because I think you will humanise me, and soon teach me there is greater happiness than holding theories and accumulating facts in silence and solitude.

Emma reassured him that she did not want a 'holiday husband'. At this time Charles was more aware of his own needs than of Emma's; and he had not yet fully understdood the strength of her faith.

As the wedding drew near, there was something more important to

Emma than the 'kettles and saucepans' weighing on her soul. She was painfully aware of a gulf between their different attitudes to religion. Emma's faith was founded on the staunch beliefs of generations of Unitarians, whereas Charles's brother, father and grandfather were all agnostics; indeed, it will be recalled that Dr Erasmus Darwin had dismissed Unitarianism as 'a featherbed to catch a falling Christian'. During his early boyhood Charles had attended the Unitarian chapel in Shrewsbury High Street with his mother and sisters, and after Sukey's death was taken to the Anglican church, his religious education falling to the devout Caroline. Despite her teaching, he was more influenced by the attitude of his sceptical brother Erasmus – even though at one stage he had expected to become a country parson. He discussed his concern with his father. Dr Robert advised him to conceal his religious doubts from his wife, since he knew how much distress this could cause in marriage; perhaps he was remembering Sukey's unhappiness at his own lack of faith, for Charles's mother had held firmly to her Unitarian beliefs.

In London Emma attended a Unitarian chapel with Hensleigh and Fanny and, listening to discussions with the sceptical Erasmus, saw that Charles's sympathies lay with his brother, for he was incapable of concealing his doubts and Emma was too shrewd not to understand that there might be a painful gulf between them. Now that she was taking so awful a decision, she wanted them to be honest with each other. Emma always found it easier to write than talk about her beliefs; and so that Charles should understand before their wedding how important her Christian faith was to her, she had written to him from Maer ten days after his proposal:

> When I am with you I think all melancholy thoughts keep out of my head but since you are gone some sad ones have forced themselves in, of fear that our opinions on the most important subject should differ widely. My reason tells me that honest & conscientious doubts cannot be a sin, but I feel it would be a painful void between us. I thank you from my heart for your openness with me & I should dread the feeling that you were concealing your opinions from the fear of giving me pain. It is perhaps foolish of me to say this much but my own dear Charley

we now do belong to each other & I cannot help being open with you. Will you do me a favour? Yes I am sure you will, it is to read our Saviour's farewell discourse to his disciples which begins at the end of the 13th Chap of John. It is so full of love to them & devotion & every beautiful feeling. It is the part of the New Testament I love best. This is a whim of mine it would give me great pleasure, though I can hardly tell why I don't wish you to give me your opinion about it.

Typically, Emma followed these profound thoughts with banter.

The plaid gown arrived from Harriet Gifford safely yesterday and is unanimously pronounced to be very handsome and not at all too dashing so that I could write my thanks and compliments with a very good conscience. It is blue black and green with narrow scarlet cross bar.

You will kindly mention any faults of spelling or style that you perceive as in the wife of a literary man it w^d not do you credit, any how I can spell your name right I wish you c^d say the same for mine.

Since after their marriage Charles and Emma were seldom apart, their letters to each other in this period before the wedding shed a rare light on their mutual feelings. Charles obviously read her favourite passage in St John's Gospel as she had wished. Writing to him as she sat quietly with her mother instead of going to church, she would, she told Charles,

find it much pleasanter to have a little talk with you than to listen to [cousin] Allen's Temperance sermon. Thank you dear Charles for complying with my fancy. To see you in earnest on the subject will be my greatest comfort & that I am sure you are. I believe I agree with every word you say, & it pleased me that you sh^d have felt inclined to enter a little more on the subject. How can you say you old curmudgeon that you don't know whether I shall care to hear such trifles as your last letter.

I felt very deeply for your sufferings at Birmingham though not quite intensely enough to prevent my laughing a little, but you must have had a horrid journey. Do you think I do not ask myself many times a day 'What is he doing now/ I wonder whether he will call today upon &c &c.' There is nothing too small for you to tell me, for I want to know every thing. Having delivered this scolding I will proceed. What an honour for the great Sedgwick to invite me to his house. *Me* only think of it! I feel a greater person already for it & how my head will stand it when I am really Mrs D. (It does look & sound very odd though I think the two names suit each other) I can't tell.

Again this was mere playfulness: Emma was never overwhelmed by the famous.

Emma imagined Charles's pleasure in his new house: 'I can fancy how proud you are in your big house,' she teased, 'ordering breakfast in the front drawing room, dinner in the dining room, tea in the back drawing room and luncheon in the study, and occasionally looking through your window on your estate and plantation.' If she quailed at the thought of a home filled with rocks, skins and bones she did not complain. A scientist's wife, Emma soon learned, may have to house a museum. 'Where', one of the Darwin children later gravely asked a friend, 'does your father do his barnacles?'

Meanwhile at Maer, Emma prepared for the wedding. They had agreed it must be a quiet one. 'Mamma . . . amuses herself a good deal with planning about houses, trousseaux and wedding-cake, which last we were in hopes she would not have thought of, as it is a useless trouble and expense.' But back in Cresselly these things had been considered important, and Bessy had been the champion wedding-cake maker for the extended family. Emma wrote to Charles, 'Don't you wish you could be married like a royal prince without being at your own wedding?' And Charles undoubtedly did; he was already apprehensive. 'I wish', he confessed to her, 'the awful day was over. I am not very tranquil when I think of the procession: it is very awesome.' Emma was distinctly relieved that he resisted his tailor's desire to get him up in a blue coat and white stockings. January was not the month for such wear. 'I am very glad you resisted the blue coat, you would have looked very unnatural in it. The white trousers were no great temptation in this weather. I wonder what extravagrincies (this word will not come right) you have been committing. A diamond pin for your stock or some such thing I should not wonder.'

––––––––––––

The 'awful day' passed quickly and, as the train bearing the new Mr and Mrs Darwin rattled its way towards Euston, Emma reflected with some sense of guilt on their happiness. She was leaving Elizabeth with the great responsibility of her ailing mother, her frail father, and the house and estate at Maer. Charlotte was married and as the wife of a vicar had her own concerns. Her brothers, too, had their own lives. Joe had sold his share in the Wedgwood business to his brother Frank and could now lead the life of a country gentleman; he and Caroline were to settle at Leith Hill Place in Surrey. Frank, as the future heir to the business, was to inherit Etruria Hall, and had more than enough to do to take care of the firm, which was going through a difficult time. Methodical and business-like, if unimaginative, he was highly regarded, and admired for his punctual attendance at the works. Harry was making a precarious living as a barrister. Hensleigh was also away in London with Fanny and his two children. So now, Emma feared, Elizabeth would have to bear the burden of caring for their ageing parents alone. Fortunately, things turned out better than either of them could have foreseen. Charlotte's husband, Charles Langton, decided that the life of a vicar was not for him; so they came to live at Maer Hall to share the responsibility. It was a happy arrangement; Charles understood Bessy and was able to see through her dementia to the charming woman she had once been.

CHAPTER EIGHT

Gower Street

M<small>R AND</small> M<small>RS</small> C<small>HARLES</small> D<small>ARWIN</small> <small>ARRIVED IN</small> L<small>ONDON ON A DARK AND</small> snowy night, having enjoyed a modest picnic on the way. 'We ate our sandwiches', Emma wrote to her mother,

> with grateful hearts for all the care that was taken of us, and the bottle of water was the greatest comfort. The house here was blazing with fires and looked very comfortable and we are getting to think the furniture quite tasteful. Yesterday we went in a fly to buy an armchair, but it was so slippery and snowy we did not do much. We picked up some novels at the library. Today I suspect we shall not go out as it is snowing at a great rate. I have been facing the cook in her own region today and found fault with the boiling of the potatoes, which I thought would make a good beginning and set me up a little . . . I came away full of love and gratitude to all the dear affectionate faces I left behind me . . . Tell my dear Elizabeth I long to hear from her. Nothing can be too minute from dear home. I don't know how to express affection enough to my dear, kind Papa, but he will take it upon trust. Goodbye my dearest Mamma, your affectionate and very happy daughter.

Bessy replied in one of the rare clear spells in her clouded mind, 'A thousand thanks to you, dearest Emma, for your delightful letter which from the cheerful happy tone of it drew tears of pleasure from my old eyes.' She prayed that this was 'the beginning of a life full of peace and tranquillity . . . My affection for Charles is much increased by considering him as the author of all your comfort and I enjoy the thoughts of your tasty curtains and chairs . . . God bless you my ever dear, you will have no difficulty in believing me your affectionate "Mum." ' Only one more letter from Bessy – on the birth of Emma's first child, William – has survived, written in the shakiest of hands; then the clouds closed in again.

Emma's love for Charles, and her happiness in her married life, was undoubted: 'I am spoilt as much as heart can wish,' she told Elizabeth, 'and . . . there is not so affectionate an individual as the one in question to be found anywhere else.' There remained, however, the one 'painful void' – their religious differences. As always, Emma found it difficult to talk about her beliefs. Writing came more easily – as in an important letter from the early days of their marriage:

> The state of mind that I wish to preserve with respect to you, is to feel that while you are acting conscientiously and sincerely wishing and trying to learn the truth, you cannot be wrong, but there are some reasons that force themselves upon me, and prevent myself from being always able to give myself this comfort. I daresay you have often thought of them before, but I will write down what has been in my head, knowing that my own dearest will indulge me.
>
> Your mind and time are full of the most interesting subjects and thoughts of the most absorbing kind, viz. following up your own discoveries – but which make it very difficult for you to avoid casting out as interruptions other sorts of thoughts which have no relation to what you are pursuing, or to be able to give your whole attention to both sides of the question.
>
> There is one reason which would have had a great effect on a woman, but I don't know whether it wd. so much on a man. I mean Erasmus [his brother] whose understanding you have such a very high opinion of and whom you have so much affection for, having gone before you – is it not likely to have made it

easier to you and to have taken off some of that dread fear which the feeling of doubting first gives and which I do not think an unreasonable or superstitious feeling. It seems to me also that the line of your pursuits may have led you to view chiefly the difficulties on one side, and that you have not had time to consider and study the chain of difficulties on the other, but I believe you do not consider your opinion is formed. May not the habit in scientific pursuits of believing nothing till it is proved, influence your mind too much in other things which cannot be proved in the same way, and which if true are likely to be above our comprehension. I should say also there is a danger in giving up revelation which does not exist on the other side, that is the fear of ingratitude in casting off what has been done for your benefit as well as for that of all the world and which ought to make you still more careful, perhaps even fearful lest you should not have taken all the pains you could to judge truly. I do not know whether this is arguing as if one side were true and the other false, which I meant to avoid, but I think not. I do not quite agree with you in what you once said that luckily there were no doubts as to how one ought to act. I think prayer is an instance to the contrary, in one case it is a positive duty and perhaps not in the other. But I daresay you meant in actions which concern others and then I agree with you almost if not quite. I do not wish for any answer to all this — it is a satisfaction to me to write it, and when I talk to you about it I cannot say exactly what I wish to say, and I know you will have patience with your own dear wife. Don't think that it is not my affair and that it does not much signify to me. Everything that concerns you concerns me and I should be most unhappy if I thought we did not belong to each other for ever. I am rather afraid my own dear Nigger will think I have forgotten my promise not to bother him, but I am sure he loves me, and I cannot tell him how happy he makes me and how dearly I love him and thank him for all his affection which makes the happiness of my life more and more every day.

Charles was deeply moved by this sincere if somewhat incoherent letter, and kept it all his life. He carefully folded it and, at some later date, wrote on the outside: 'When I am dead, know that many times, I have kissed and cryed over this. C.D.' The philosophical gulf would always be there, but because it was bridged by a strong and growing love, it never divided them.

In many ways theirs was a unity of opposites. Emma brought with her a stability and sense of security given by two generations of happy Wedgwood marriages and by the adoration of both Allen and Wedgwood aunts. She was always at ease with herself and with others. Charles was self-deprecating and more than a little unsure; behind him were two generations of disturbed and tragic Darwin marriages and the early loss of his mother. Emma had the solid base of Wedgwood faith; Charles the unsettling background of Darwin scepticism. Charles was methodical and orderly – as Emma's sister Fanny had been. Emma needed a framework of order in her life which Fanny had provided; Charles filled the blank which Fanny's death had left. As Emma's daughter Henrietta (Etty) wrote in her memoir of her mother, her childhood nickname, 'Little Miss Slip-Slop', 'is revealing as to her character ... She was never tidy or orderly as to little things. It was the schatten-seite to a delightfully large-minded unfussy way of taking life which is more common among men than amongst women. My father said after he married that he made up his mind to give up all his natural taste for tidiness, and that he would not allow himself to feel annoyed by her calm disregard for such details. He would say, laughing, the only sure place to find a pin or a pair of scissors was his study.' To Charles's relief, his sister Susan came on a visit to bring order to their household; by way of thanks, Charles and Emma took her to one of the Babbages' brilliant soirées. Charles Babbage, the scientist who invented the calculating machine – the forerunner of the modern computer – was a friend who often called on them at Gower Street. How old Dr Erasmus Darwin would have delighted in the company of this ingenious man!

It was some time before Emma adjusted to her new life as head of the domestic establishment. Unaccustomed to having a butler in the house, she was uneasy with the impressive presence of the handsome Edward; at Maer they had a cook, housekeeper and maids, and the men were employed outside. In March Emma plucked up her courage and dismissed the Cockney cook, feeling 'she is too cute [acute] and rather making the most of us.' Susan promised to find her 'a countryfied person', which would have been 'quite refreshing'. 'I have rather a desire to send off the housemaid too, but I have really no fault to find with her,' she wrote to her sister Charlotte, except that she was 'vulgar and plain'. But since she was a very good servant, Emma decided to keep her. Easygoing and unfussed, she would never reach the Darwin standard of domestic perfection; but nevertheless, as she adapted herself to Charles's needs, she created a home which was calm and comfortable. Throughout their married life they earned the devotion of their servants, foremost among whom was Joseph Parslow, their second butler. A countryman from Gloucestershire, he came to them in 1840 at the age of thirty-one and ran their household until the end of his working life. Unfussy, somewhat careless of his appearance, he was much more to Emma's taste than the glittering Edward had been. Aunt Jessie spotted his virtues when she stayed at Gower Street in 1840: 'Be it observed that Parslow is the most amiable, obliging, active, serviceable servant that ever breathed. I hope you will never part with him.' They never did; Parslow remained with them not only as a servant but as a friend and part of the family. At Charles Darwin's funeral, Parslow was with the family in Westminster Abbey – an honoured guest. His importance in their lives cannot be overestimated.

Happy in each other and their own pursuits, neither Charles nor Emma enjoyed the social round. Visiting in Victorian London was time-consuming. Distances were long and so were the dinners, and one did not clatter across London merely to drink a glass of sherry. A dinner party involved one night or even two absent from work. Once Emma began on her long sequence of pregnancies, and Charles became unwell, they were glad of the excuse to decline invitations; but at the beginning of their marriage, surrounded by well-wishers and scientific colleagues, they had little choice but to engage in some social life. Emma learned to entertain, and astonished Hensleigh and Fanny – and herself – by the success of her own first dinner party. To her mother she wrote of this first dinner, and of their other servants:

> Fanny's maids have been very uneasy at the shortness of our housemaid and are afraid that she is not tall enough to tie my gown. She is about the size of Betty Slaney, so I hope Fanny set their minds at ease on that point. Our dinner went off very

well, though Erasmus tells us it was a base imitation of the Marlborough Street dinners, and certainly the likeness was very striking. But when the plum-pudding appeared he knocked under, and confessed himself conquered very humbly. And then Edward is such a perfect Adonis in his best livery that he is quite a sight.

As far as one can judge from Emma's recipe book, she and Charles enjoyed simple fare. Her Irish apple charlotte was 'baked for six hours in a very slow oven'. Her soups were simple and wholesome – a very popular one was made of three cabbage lettuces, three onions, sorrel, spinach, celery and parsley, and 'at the end of a little cream and yolks of two eggs'. She collected recipes from Cresselly and Shrewsbury, where Darwin's sisters made them jam and preserves.

Emma often found Darwin's scientist friends hard going. Later, Darwin recalled with amusement her reply to his apology, 'You must find this all boring.' Emma cheerfully answered, 'Not more than all the rest!' But the scientific evenings could be long. 'Mr Lyell,' she wrote to Elizabeth after one of her early dinner parties,

> is enough to flatten a party as he never speaks above his breath, so that everybody keeps lowering their tone to his. Mr Brown, whom Humboldt called 'the glory of Great Britain', looks so shy, as if he longed to shrink into himself and disappear entirely; however, notwithstanding those two dead weights, viz, the greatest botanist and the greatest geologist in Europe, we did very well and had no pauses. Mrs Henslow had a good, loud, sharp voice which was a great comfort and Mrs Lyell had a very constant supply of talk.

There were some other highly intelligent women among the wives of Charles's friends. The botanist J. D. Hooker's wife was the daughter of Henslow, Darwin's old tutor at Cambridge; she was, Hooker claimed, 'much cleverer than I'. And Emma herself, although she never pretended to be a scientist, usually understood the direction of Charles's thoughts. Before their marriage she had written perceptively:

I believe from your account of your own mind that you will not only consider me as a specimen of the genus (I don't know which, simia I believe). You will be forming theories about me and if I am cross or out of temper you will only consider 'What does that prove'. Which will be a very grand and philosophical way of considering it.

Reporting to Maer on Emma's appearance in London society, Fanny Hensleigh remarked how endearingly unspoiled and unaffected she remained. Thomas Carlyle found her 'the nicest girl he had ever met', and Emma brought out the best in him. 'He was', she wrote, 'very pleasant to talk to . . . so very natural.' She only wished his writing had been equally so. Charles never was at ease with the Carlyles nor they with him; and Jane was, for once, out of her intellectual depth in the world of science. Charles, for his part, found her Scots accent unintelligible, her manner affected and her nervous giggle disconcerting.

Aunt Fanny Allen wrote to a friend in March that she had found Emma 'as happy as possible, as she has always been – there never was a person born under a happier star than she, her feelings are the most healthful possible; joy and sorrow are felt by her in their due proportion, nothing robs her of the enjoyment that happy circumstances would naturally give. Her account of her life with Charles Darwin in her new ménage is very pleasant.' And in June, after Charles and Emma had visited Maer, Elizabeth wrote to Aunt Jessie of her delight to 'see Emma so entirely happy in her lot, with the most affectionate husband possible, upon whom none of her pleasant qualities are thrown away, who delights in her music and admires her dress.' She even inspired Elizabeth: 'I even mean to dress well myself, now the credit of the family rests on me,' she told Aunt Jessie.

In these early months of marriage each adjusted to the other. Emma had been afraid Charles would continue to dislike the theatre, but she took him to see 'the new play – Richelieu – and he was very much interested and clapped and applauded with all his heart.' She hoped Charles might 'get quite fond of the theatre, but as to dinners and parties he gets worse I think, and I don't care how few dinners I go to either. Drinking wine disagrees with him and it is so tiresome not drinking that he can't resist one glass.' Charles's father had always been concerned that he himself might have inherited Charles's grandmother's alcoholism and had strongly discouraged his sons from drinking spirits. Aunt Sarah Wedgwood, too, had been a lifelong campaigner for the teetotal cause.

Emma was afraid that her husband would never share her passion for music; in March they visited her uncle, Baugh Allen, in Dulwich to 'go to Blagrove's concert which I am afraid will be too deep for Charles'. Charles himself always claimed he was tone-deaf, and he obviously had not inherited his mother's ear for music; she had tried – without much success – to teach the unmusical old Dr Erasmus to play the piano. However, listening to Emma's music as she nightly played on the grand piano in the little back room in Gower Street, he was soothed.

As the months went by, Emma saw how much Charles needed soothing. Plunged by his work into mental turbulence and lacking – to her sadness – consolation of religion, he became stressed and was frequently ill. Late in life he remembered of this period that 'I did less scientific work, though I worked as hard as I possibly could, than during any other equal length of time.' In fact, during his three years and eight months in London he achieved a great deal, in spite of poor health which included one serious illness. On 6 May 1842 he managed to complete his work on coral reefs; he wrote papers on boulders, Glen Roy and earthquakes for the Royal Geological Society of London, of which he was secretary; and he had produced the five parts of *The Voyage of the Beagle*. He calculated that of the period in London, he spent twenty months on this work 'and all rest lost by illness' – though in a letter to Emma he added to this 'and visiting!!!'

In 1835 Charles had opened his first notebook for what he described in his autobiography as 'Facts in Relation to Origin of Species about which I had long reflected and never ceased work for the next twenty years'. As he collected these facts, they led him to disturbing conclusions, distancing him even further from the Christianity he had blindly accepted even during the voyage. But now he became convinced that his early belief in immutable created species was mistaken. Remembering the varieties of finches on the Galapagos Islands, he wrote: 'When I see those islands in sight of each other and possessed of but a scanty stock of animals, tenanted by these birds, but slightly differing in structure and filling the same place in nature, I must suspect they are only varieties . . . If there is the slightest foundation for these remarks the zoology of the Archipelago will be worth examining for such facts would undermine the stability of species.' So began his long search for an explanation of the changes in species which led to his belief in evolution. From now on until the publication of the *Origin of Species* in 1859, Charles continued painstakingly to collect facts to prove his shattering conclusions in a series of private notebooks.

For the rest of his life Charles was to be dogged by chronic illness. Many medical experts have made many different diagnoses, but the truth would seem to lie in a combination of many causes, psychological and physical. He was driven by a powerful, obsessive need to search out the truth. But, unlike many other driven men, he possessed a natural sweetness of temperament which did not allow him the relief of bad temper or outbursts of rage with which others released their tension. Also, his will and dogged determination often pushed him beyond his intellectual capacity. Although, as he claimed in his autobiography, he was capable of prolonged reasoning, he did not enjoy abstract thought. He wrote of 'the excessive labour of inventive thought', explaining that 'the whole effort consists in keeping one idea before your mind steadily and not merely thinking intently.' The stress of prolonged mental effort undoubtedly affected his nervous system. As he himself said, his 'noddle' and his stomach were often in conflict. His particular genius was for observing and collating detail; but the facts which he meticulously collected over the years were leading him to conclusions which he knew would be disturbing. To break through old barriers to a new philosophy demanded a power of intellectual concentration which constantly exhausted him. He knew, too, how disturbed Emma would be by his evolutionary ideas.

Charles believed he had inherited his 'wretched stomach', and feared that he had bequeathed this painful legacy of physical weakness to his children. Certainly there are remarkable similarities between Charles and his Uncle Tom Wedgwood, whose troubles were described by Coleridge as 'suppressed gout in the stomach or/and a thickened colon'. As we have seen, Tom's pain was both eased and prolonged by increasingly heavy doses of opium – a remedy that Dr Robert would certainly not have given Charles, remembering only too well the last visit Tom paid him when, drugged by opium, his brother-in-law was on the verge of committing suicide. Robert's mother had died in agonizing stomach pain, eased only by spirits and opium. So Charles's lifelong stomach trouble may have been inherited from both Darwin and Wedgwood lines.

Any stress found out these physical weaknesses. Charles had seemed healthy enough as a boy, especially when he came for the shooting at Maer; but even then he had suffered from eczema of the hands and mouth, which Dr Darwin had treated with arsenic. Before he left Plymouth on the *Beagle* he had been worried by palpitations, and had been afraid he had heart disease. Then, during the voyage, he had been constantly and violently seasick. 'Sea sickness', he wrote, 'is no trifling evil, cured in a week.' Though he was well enough when they reached land to make punishing long journeys on horseback into the interior of South America, he certainly had one long illness serious enough to make his sister Caroline urge him to return. In his *Journal of Researches* Charles refers to the 'great black bug of the Pampas', *Tritoma infestans*, which had bitten him in Argentina in March 1835 and made him seriously ill. Professor Saul Adler, Dr Ralph Colp and others believe that Darwin might by this means have been infected with the so-called Chagas disease, which can affect the heart muscle and destroy the nerves of the intestine – though other medical experts reject the Chagas theory.

In October 1837, before their marriage, Emma had reported that, according to Aunt Sarah, 'Charles Darwin is very unwell. Something is amiss in the circulation and he has palpitations, but Aunt Sarah is always so apprehensive about health that she always sees this in the worst light. She says he does not appear at all invalidish.' Aunt Sarah, like Robert Darwin, knew that there might be cause for worry. She had been devoted to her brother Tom, and had watched him change from a bright young boy to a neurotic wreck. And Charles reminded her of Tom. In December 1838 Emma had noticed herself that he looked overtired and unwell. She had written: 'Tell me how you are, I do not like your looking so unwell and being so over-tired. When I come and look after you, I shall scold you into health like Lady Catherine de Burgh used to do to the poor people.' He was ill again before their wedding, dreading the formalities; and after their marriage his reaction to stress had gradually become worse, until the mere thought of a dinner party brought on 'violent shivers and vomiting attacks'. Only, he wrote, in the 'excitement' of his scientific work did he forget his 'daily discomfort'. Nor was it just a matter of discomfort: noisy, violent and uncontrollable retching made visiting both painful and embarrassing. This gave him a reason – or an excuse – for avoiding the social engagements that increasingly threatened to waste his time. He was frequently afflicted by skin eruptions, caused by mental stress; on one occasion he suffered a 'frightful succession of boils, five at once'. Before his marriage he had severe headaches. In the days before he sailed on the *Beagle* he had flutterings of the heart.

Certainly, as we have already seen, psychological factors contributed to his ill-health. Charles was much influenced by his father. Dr Robert's attack on Charles for his youthful idleness surely gave him a dogged determination to succeed, and directed his drive. But to suggest, as some have done, that Darwin had a suppressed desire to kill his father, together with God, is ridiculous. His respect and love for his father lasted all his life, even if, like everybody else, he regarded him with awe. It is possible that he sometimes exaggerated his illness in order to excite his father's interest and sympathy; if so, he did not always succeed. When he complained to Dr Robert of the dreadful numbness in his fingertips, all the sympathy he could get was 'Yes, exactly, tut tut, neuralgia, exactly, yes, yes.' He trusted implicitly in his father's prescriptions. In April 1840, when on a visit to Shrewsbury, he wrote to Emma, 'My father says I may often take calomel,' as though he needed reassuring that it was safe.

It is possible, too, that he sometimes gave in to illness when he wanted Emma's comfort. For he was always insecure, and his mother's death when he was eight must have been traumatic, though he could remember little of her. Emma gave him back his security. Many years later Mrs Huxley said of her, 'More than any other woman I ever knew, she comforted.' In 1848, when ill in Shrewsbury, Charles wrote to her: 'Without you when sick I feel most desolate. O Mammy I do long to be with you, and under your protection, for then I feel safe.' It was the forgotten cry of a bereaved child, and it needs no psychologist to see the relevance of the nickname 'Titty' that he sometimes gave her. Later she was always 'our dear old Mother who must be obeyed' – just as, before they were married, he looked forward to a 'good strict wife who will send me to my lessons'.

Whatever the causes, Charles's pain was very real. Dr Lane, who treated him in later years and had come across many cases of violent indigestion, said, 'I cannot recall any where the pain was so truly poignant as in his. When the worst attacks were on he seemed almost crushed by agony.' Late in life Parslow recalled that there were times when he thought his master would die in his arms. Yet Charles bore the burden with singular sweetness and patience. 'What a life of suffering his is,' wrote Fanny Allen, 'and how manfully he bears it ... Emma's cheerfulness is equally admirable. I am sure she is a chosen one of Heaven.'

He kept a careful, almost obsessive, record of his symptoms, but to suggest that he was a hypochondriac in the ordinary sense of the word shows a misunderstanding of his character. Emma's shrewd Allen aunts, who had no disposition to love the Darwins and who positively disliked Erasmus, would certainly have noticed any such tendency in Charles; but, on the contrary, Aunt Jessie in particular remarked on his healthiness of mind. Nor would Emma have encouraged morbidity, for she was no frustrated nurse; there was always a sharp edge to her compassion. It is true that she had cared for her dying sister with devotion and had shared with her eldest sister the care of a sick mother, but there is no mistaking the relief with which she left the sickroom on her marriage. Charles was no malingerer but an observant scientist, and he watched himself as patiently and carefully as he watched for forty years the activities of his earthworms. When his friend Hooker was ill in 1854 he advised him, 'Write down your own case ... and then consider your case as a stranger.' And this he did for many years in a detailed diary of his own health.

In June 1839 Charles and Emma went to Maer and Shrewsbury, but their stay, Elizabeth told Aunt Jessie, 'was rather spoilt by Charles being so unwell almost the whole time of his stay in the country, and Emma not very well herself' (she was pregnant). 'Charles got some of his father's good doctoring and is much better again, but I suppose he is feeling the effect of too much exertion in every way during his voyage and must be careful not to work his head too hard now.'

For the first months of their marriage, as Charles later recalled, 'I was strong enough to go into general society, and saw a good deal of several scientific men and other more or less distinguished men.' Among them were his great friends and champions, Lyell, Hooker and Huxley; Carlyle; and other scientists like Babbage and Richard Owen. But as he became increasingly ill the Darwins withdrew from social life. This suited Emma, for not only did London life tend to bring on the migraine from which she had always suffered, but for the rest of their time in Gower Street – indeed, for the next sixteen years – she was continually pregnant.

Emma had ten children, the last when she was forty-eight. William was born on 27 December 1839; Annie on 2 March 1841; and when the Darwins left Gower Street in 1842 she was expecting her third baby in September. Henrietta – the daughter who was to write her mother's life – was born almost exactly a year later on 25 September 1843.

Elizabeth came to London in December to be with Emma for the birth of her first child – though it was Charles who also needed her support. He could not bear Emma's pain in a difficult labour, and was ill before and after William's birth. Emma derived additional support at this time from the presence just four doors away of Fanny and Hensleigh, who had come to live there in June 1839. 'She will find them a great comfort,' Elizabeth wrote to Aunt Jessie, 'for they are neither of them idle people and run into the error of running in and out at all hours.'

It was not until February 1840 that Emma regained her strength and was able 'to enjoy her baby', whom she called 'Doddy', as she told Aunt Jessie. He had, she wrote, 'very dark blue eyes and a pretty, small mouth, his nose I will not boast of but it is very harmless as long as he is a baby.' Jos came down to admire his new grandson and, Emma thought, 'looked very comfortable in his armchair by the fire'. Surprisingly, he found Gower Street the 'quietest place he had ever been'. There had been a 'different sort of bustle at Maer', and Jos was now a tired old man, relieved to have a break from his much-loved but vacant wife.

A year after William's arrival, in December 1840, the novelist Maria Edgeworth, then seventy-two years old, met Emma and wrote: 'She is the youngest daughter of Jos Wedgwood and is worthy of both father and mother.' Maria had known two generations of Darwins and Wedgwoods. Her father was a friend of old Dr Erasmus Darwin and one of the Lunar Society, and she herself had known Charles's mother and Bessy Allen in their young days. She found Emma 'affectionate and unaffected and young as she is, full of old times. She has her mother's radiantly cheerful countenance, even now, debarred from all London gaieties and all gaiety but that of her own mind by close attendance on her sick husband.'

Charles found it increasingly difficult to entertain house guests. Even in April 1839, when they had had Charles's old tutor professor Henslow and his wife to stay, Emma had found them 'easy guests but Charles was rather ashamed to find his dear friends such a burden'. In 1839 they had given a dinner for the Sismondis, and Emma looked forward to her beloved Aunt Jessie and Sismondi coming to stay in June 1840; but Charles was so ill that they lent the visitors their house and removed themselves elsewhere. It was not, perhaps, only Charles's illness that caused such inhospitable behaviour. He was never totally at ease with the extravagantly courteous Sismondi; maybe, like Emma's brothers, he found it hard to keep a straight face when greeted with his flourishing bows. But he may also have felt shut out by the mutual love of Emma and her aunt; hating as he did to share his wife with anyone else, such exclusion would have been hard to bear in his own home. Then, too, he seems to have found the immense Allen family overwhelming. Jessie wrote after their visit that in Wales they were 'terribly becousined, there never was a greater crowd collected together, and we have visits from immediately after breakfast till dinner at 5 o'clock'. For Charles this would have been a nightmare. Quite possibly this is why he never went to Cresselly, even though his great friend Hooker had found Tenby a wonderful place for the study of marine biology and had taken his wife there for her honeymoon. When later Emma took a holiday there, she went alone with her young children.

Aunt Jessie was not offended. She sent 'grateful thanks' to Charles for his 'magnificent reception of us, even when not there to do the honours . . . it was like having entered an enchanted castle, everything was there before it was wanted.'

While Emma had been recovering from the birth of William, Charles had been very ill – in a 'distressing state of languor'. Dr Holland, Emma's accoucheur, did him no good. But Emma was happy that when he 'is most unwell he continues as social as ever, and is not like the rest of the Darwins, who will not say how they really are but he always tells me how he feels and never wants to be alone, but continues just as warmly affectionate as ever, so that I feel I am a comfort to him . . . he is the most affectionate person possible.' Charles obviously recovered, since by June Emma was pregnant again. The arrival of William had encouraged Emma to keep a diary – a small notebook in which she not only recorded his weight during the next months but also marked her periods with an 'X'. When they ceased she was prepared for the arrival of her second child: Anne Elisabeth, who was born on 2 March 1841.

That spring she longed to take the babies out of the smoke of London: it had taken her some time to regain her spirit and it was not until May that she took to 'playing the piano and enjoying the feeling of health and being able to play with the little boy'. During her confinement 'he got not to care a pin for me and it used to make me rather dismal sometimes but he likes nobody so well as Charles and me now, but I think Charles is the prime favourite.'

So with much joy Emma and Charles took the babies to Maer. Here Emma relaxed among the roses while Charles and Doddy went to Shrewsbury for a while. Doddy had been sent ahead with the maid. His 'reception of me', Charles wrote to Emma, 'was quite affecting. He sat on my knee for nearly a quarter of an hour, gave me some sweet kisses and sniggered and pointing told everyone I was Pappa.' But, he added, he himself was 'very desolate and forlorn without you'. His father and sisters doted on Doddy, but the meticulous Darwins in their apple-pie house made no bones about Emma's housekeeping – or her approach to childcare. Emma laughed when Willy picked up a Cockney accent from the servants, calling himself 'Villie Darvin'; in Shrewsbury they were not amused. Maybe, indeed, Emma chose to remain at Maer when they went north so that Charles and not she should bear the brunt of the carping. Willy, they complained, had a cup of cream before breakfast every morning – the worst thing possible for him. He had no glass of water at his bedside. He was allowed to set off for a journey with wet feet – most dangerous. In July Charles wrote to Emma, 'A thunderstorm is preparing to break on your head, which has already delayed me, about Bessy not having a cap, "looks dirty", "like grocer's maidservant", and my father with much wrath added "the men will take liberties with her if she is dressed differently on that score." I generously took half the blame and never betrayed that I had beseeched you several times on that score.' Knowing that Emma would only laugh he urged her, 'pray do not defend yourself for they are very hot on the subject.'

But while Charles still easily slipped back into his apprehensive boyhood, always metaphorically raising an arm to ward off the criticisms of his adoring but censorious sisters, at heart he had a great deal of sympathy with Emma's more easygoing approach. Years later he told his grandson's nurse that children ought to be allowed to run barefoot and eat green gooseberries. No stern Victorian father, Charles was most demonstrative with his children, kissing and hugging them without embarrassment, and both parents enjoyed playing with the children, just as old Josiah, their grandfather, had done. Still Charles's sisters persisted; and still Emma went her own way. When the Darwin sisters came to stay, Emma noticed with some amusement that they found the disorderliness of the children worrying and were always tidying up after them. Emma, relaxed and serene, preferred to let them play until the chaos became unbearable and then sent for the maid to clear it up.

By February 1842 Emma had regained her liveliness. She went with the Hensleighs to the pantomime, 'for the fun of seeing their children's pleasure. The first thing was the most dreadful blood and murder thing with a gibbet on the stage.' Fanny's children stood it surprisingly well, Emma told her sister Elizabeth. 'Poor Erny put his head down on my lap whenever the chief comic character, with a very red face was on the stage, which he seemed to think quite as alarming as any murderer . . . The first play ended by the military coming over a wall and shooting almost all the characters to our great relief. It was at the Tottenham theatre – very low.' But for all the amusements to be had in the city, Emma knew that London was no place for children. She longed for a proper garden; and when in the spring of 1842 she realized that she was once again pregnant, they decided to look for a house in the country. Eventually they found a house in Kent: on 22 July 1842 Emma wrote briefly in her diary, 'went to Down'. Dr Robert bought Down House for them for £2,200 and Charles took possession on 1 September. Emma followed on 14 September. Charles briefly returned to London, perhaps to supervise the packing of his immense collection of rocks and bones, but he was back at Down on 14 September. Emma had a cold and toothache, and Down House at first seemed bleak and without character. And she was expecting the birth of her third child in three years. Now thirty-four, she had once again to face her 'time of trial', and in a strange place. Even though she now had nurses and maids and above all the indispensable Parslow, it must have been a desperately trying period.

Yet over the years Emma was to make the bleak square house in a bare windswept landscape, beloved by her children and grandchildren, and remembered as filled with flowers, music and sunshine. Old Josiah and Sally would have been at home there. Down House was to be as Maer Hall had been – the hearth to which their extended family would be drawn in joy or sorrow. It was Emma who made it so.

CHAPTER NINE

Down House

Down House, sixteen miles from London, was to be the Darwins' home for the rest of their lives. As Etty recalled, 'the house was square and unpretending, built of shabby bricks which were afterwards stuccoed, and with a slate roof. If faced south-west and stood in about eighteen acres of land. It was of moderate size when bought, but was gradually added to, and became in time capable of holding a large party.' A lane ran past the house to the pleasant little village of Downe with its flint church and shingled spire.

In 1876 Charles recalled their life here in his autobiography:

> Few persons have lived a more retired life than we have done. Besides short visits to the houses of relations and occasionally to the seaside or elsewhere, we have gone nowhere . . . During the first part of my residence [at Down] we went a little into society and received a few friends here; but my health always suffered from the excitement, violent shivery and vomiting attacks being thus brought on, I have therefore been compelled for many years to give up all dinner parties, and such parties always put me into high spirits.

He said that he gradually lost the power of becoming deeply attached to anyone.

As far as I can judge this grievous loss of feeling has gradually crept over me from the expectation of much distress afterwards from exhaustion having been firmly associated in my mind with seeing and talking with anyone for an hour, except my wife and children . . . Nothing to record during the rest of my life, except the publication of my several books.

This sombre account gives the wrong impression. In spite of many worries and tragedies, the letters from the first ten years of marriage reflect a happy and full family life.

In these years Emma's life too was circumscribed, but also was a period of much happiness. They were years of almost continual confinement: her third baby was born on 23 September 1842 and her last on 6 December 1856. Yet, according to her daughter Etty, she did not complain.

My mother had ten children and suffered much from ill health and discomforts during those years. Many of her children were delicate and difficult to rear, and three died. My father was often seriously ill and always suffering, so that her life was full of care, anxiety and hard work. But she was supported by her perfect union with him, and by the sense that she made every minute of every hour more bearable to him. And though her life could not but be anxious and laborious I think it will be seen by her letters that it was happy as well as blessed.

Her patience certainly amazed her less tolerant Allen aunts, who thought her 'surely born of Heaven'. In fact, except for the repeated pain of difficult childbirths, the life at Down suited Emma's easygoing nature – and she loved children. So did Charles. It was sometimes imagined that Charles Darwin wrote his great work, *On the Origin of Species*, while living a quiet hermit's life, retired from the world. Nothing could be further from the truth. For the seventeen years from 1842 until its publication in 1859, he wrote in a house filled with the noise of children – his own, and often the families of friends and cousins. And children were not confined to the nursery; that was the last place to find a child, as it was remembered. So he would wrestle with the problems of evolution with a sick child tucked up on his study sofa, or, in Emma's absence, attempt to relax while little boys 'butted like young bulls' on the drawing-room chairs. No forbidding, authoritarian father, he could write with wry amusement that, when reproved, his son kindly suggested that if their games worried him perhaps he should leave the room. Another once offered him sixpence if he would come and play with them. In his autobiography Charles wrote, 'When you were very young it was my delight to play with you all . . . When all or most of you are at home (as, thank Heavens, happens pretty frequently) no party can be . . . more agreeable, and I wish for no other society.'

Easygoing though Emma was, her patience was sorely tried in the first months at Down House. She moved into a bleak, empty house in the last stages of pregnancy. Nine days later Mary Eleanor was born. Emma was exhausted and the baby did not thrive. On 18 October little Mary died.

'Our sorrow', Emma wrote to Fanny Hensleigh, 'is nothing to what it would have been if she had lived longer and suffered more.' She had consoled herself in the same way after the death of her sister. 'Charles is well today and the funeral over, which he dreaded very much . . . I think I regret her more from the likeness to Mamma which I had often pleased myself with fancying might run through her mind as well as face. I keep very well . . . with our two other dear little things you need not fear that one sorrow will last long, though it will be long indeed before we forget that poor little face.' Less than a year later the empty cradle was filled again: Henrietta (Etty) was born on 25 September 1843.

Emma had hardly recovered from the birth and death of Mary when her brother Hensleigh fell seriously ill and, to relieve Fanny, she took in their three children, Snow aged nine, Bro aged eight, and Erny aged five. Bright little Julia (called Snow because she was born in a snowstorm) was a favourite niece; over the years Emma was to watch her grow into a clever writer and the close platonic friend of Robert Browning. The children were allowed considerable freedom: that autumn the three of them, with Emma's own, William aged three and Annie two, got lost for three hours wandering in the snowy 'Big Woods' at the end of the garden with only their little nursemaid, Bessy. Charles and Parslow found them, eventually, unharmed. 'It was rash of me,' Emma confessed to Fanny, 'and I have forbidden it in future.' What Charles's sisters said is not recorded.

Emma delighted in the gardens at Down House, planting climbing shrubs to mask the walls, setting out the flower beds as she and Elizabeth had done at Maer. 'The flower beds were close under the drawing room window,' Etty remembered. 'They were often untidy but had a particularly gay and varied effect.' Charles, too, enjoyed his new estate. 'The banks are clothed with pale blue violets to an extent I have never seen equalled, and with primroses,' he wrote; 'some of the copses were beautifully enlivened by Rununculus auricomas, wood anenomes, and a white Stellania . . . large areas were brilliantly blue with blue bells . . . Larks abound here and their songs sound most agreeably on all sides; nightingales are common.' But increasingly he observed flowers with the eye of a scientist. Emma was the gardener: it is her handwriting on the seed orders. Her greatest happiness on a brisk autumn day was 'cutting and carving among the shrubs'. She had learned much from Uncle John Wedgwood and had often visited him and Aunt Jenny when they lived near by; the founder of the Royal Horticultural Society was a good tutor. Her Aunt Sukey, Charles's mother, had also been a dedicated gardener and had taken her Wedgwood gardening skills to Shrewsbury. Though Charles had been too young to remember much about her, the famous sea of crocuses she had planted in the grass always gave him much pleasure. 'The crocuses are looking quite brilliant,' he had written to Emma from Shrewsbury in March 1842.

Remembering the sandy walk round the lake at Maer, one of their first improvements at Down was to make a similar sand walk, shady on one side and on the other open to the sun and to the Downs. Here Charles paced every morning with clockwork regularity. His son Frank remembered, 'how unvarying his habits were . . . He walked with a swinging action using a stick heavily shod with iron which he struck loudly against the ground producing a rhythmical click which is with all of us a very distinct recollection.' The sand walk was also the children's playground, and, Frank recalled, Charles 'liked to see what we were doing'. The children were not shut out from his work; even when little they were encouraged to use their eyes, and often their clear sight and fresh vision helped him in his work. Puzzled by the movements of bees along the sand walk, the children watched for him and wondered why they settled from time to time. They delighted in being his assistants, looking out for rare grasses, observing unusual flowers. Along the borders Emma encouraged wild flowers to grow – bluebells, cowslips and anemones – paying a small boy to keep the border weeded. She lost her temper only rarely, but did so once when Charles laughed because she was so upset that the boy had pulled up all the wild flowers and left the weeds and the dog's mercury that she hated.

The regularity of Charles's walk and the luxuriance of Emma's country flowers were symbolic of a marriage in which each complemented the other. When Aunt Jessie came to stay, she found this 'pretty, brilliantly clean quiet house' utterly refreshing. She wrote to Elizabeth: 'The repose and coolness of it is delicious, let alone the sunny faces which met us so lovingly at the door.' All their lives the children and grandchildren would think of Down House with love and nostalgia – still remember the rattle of the flywheel of the old well, the scent of the lime-tree flowers on warm evenings, the murmur of doves and the urgent song of the nightingale. Her granddaughter Gwen Raverat later wrote: 'All the flowers that grew at Down were beautiful; and different from all other flowers.'

Everything there was different. And better. For instance the path in front of the verandah was made of large round water-worn pebbles from some sea beach. They were not loose but stuck down tight in moss and sand and were black and shiny, as if they had been polished. I adored those pebbles. I mean literally adored, worshipped. This passion made me feel quite sick sometimes and it was adoration that I felt for the foxgloves at Down and for the stiff red clay out of the sandwalk claypit and for the beautiful white paint on the nursery floor. This kind of feeling hits you in the stomach and in the ends of your fingers and it is probably the most important thing in life. Long after I have forgotten all my human loves, I shall still remember that smell of a gooseberry leaf or the feel of the wet grass on my feet, or the pebbles in the path. In the long run it is this feeling that makes life worth living, this which is the driving force behind the artist's need to create.

It was Emma who created at Down the environment essential for Charles. Here he could direct the burning 'driving force' which might have destroyed him into the work which changed his world. Darwins, Allens and Wedgwoods all inherited and passed on a remarkable tendency to longevity – Fanny Allen once remarked on her family's 'youthy age'. Nevertheless, while Emma and Charles, Fanny and Hensleigh, Caroline Darwin and Joe were producing families which would continue dynasties of extraordinary talent, the older generation was passing away. Sir James Mackintosh and his wife, Bessy's sister Kitty, had died in 1830 and 1832. Jessie's husband Sismondi died on 25 June 1842 in Geneva. Fanny Allen wrote of him, 'There seems to be a greater destruction of the living principle in Sismondi than in that of any other person I ever knew.' It was an extraordinary epitaph from clever Fanny, who had earlier been so unfair to the courtly historian. Emma, too, when she read his work regretted that she had not valued him more. Her beloved Aunt Jessie now left Geneva and came to live at Tenby with her widowed sister, Harriet Surtees. Vital and affectionate as always in spite of her inherited deafness, Jessie, as her sister Emma Allen said, 'had such a power of loving and of exciting love that . . . I always find it good to be near her.' As Bessy faded, Jessie had taken her place in Emma's affection; to no one except Charles did she write with such unaffected love. Emma longed to visit to her, and to return to the Tenby she had so loved as a child. But she was prevented not only by her own advanced pregnancy but also because of the illness of her father. Jos had grown increasingly frail and in May she had visited Maer to give Elizabeth some support, while Charles had gone on to Shrewsbury and north Wales. The 'terrible shaking and restlessness' had become worse during the last years. His old friend Robert Darwin, though crippled himself, struggled to visit him and was 'quite affected more than once'. Bessy was now beyond the horizon and unaware of Jos's illness – or the death in April 1843 of her much-loved brother, John Allen. He was the same age as Jos, had gone into Parliament at the same time and, like Jos, had left no mark there. He had been a kind and affectionate brother, and since his wife's death, Emma and Fanny Allen had lived happily with him at Cresselly. Now his son Seymour inherited Cresselly and Emma and Fanny moved to Tenby to join their sisters, Jessie Sismondi and Harriet Surtees. Here they lived until their deaths, in a charming long low white house with a neat garden and beyond a distant view of the sea.

Jos struggled on, but in his last ten months he suffered from hallucinations and, like Bessy, became helpless. Elizabeth devotedly took care of them both. Though Emma was expecting her fourth baby in September 1843, she made the difficult journey to Maer that summer and was with her father when, on 12 July, he died peacefully. Jane Carlyle commented spikily that it was extraordinary that Hensleigh and Fanny were pleased they were in London so that they could buy their mourning clothes there. But a Victorian funeral, even one so modest, needed preparation, and there was undoubtedly some relief that his pain was ended. Undoubtedly, too, Jane was a little jealous of Fanny, who was so clearly adored by Erasmus, her own cavalier.

Josiah Wedgwood II had been a conscientious if undistinguished Member of Parliament; he had never spoken in the House, but was a useful member of committees. As an employer he was much respected, though he never enjoyed his work at the Wedgwood factory, and although he was a trained master potter never seemed to take pride in his craft. Perhaps it was not easy to follow in the footsteps of the perfectionist, Josiah I. Above all, he hated the 'trade' stamp with which for years he was marked.

As he had promised his wife on their honeymoon, he was a loyal and devoted husband and a tolerant father, taking infinite pains over the upbringing of his children – boys and girls alike: as a result, Emma had received a remarkably wide education. His lasting legacy was their continuing desire to learn, whether painting, music or literature. Bessy's sisters never forgot Jos's 'incomparable kindness to us all our lives through'; most of all they valued 'the high moral atmosphere into which he introduced us . . . The moral standard of Pembrokeshire was so low how can we suppose we might not have settled under it . . . His was so high, so pure, so true and so engaging by his exquisite modesty.' Knowing that her sister was now beyond understanding and so was spared the pain of Jos's death, Jessie sent her letter of condolence to Elizabeth, but so that Bessy would not feel hurt should she briefly regain awareness, she wrote directly to her beloved sister, recalling how Jos's 'brotherly affection left a warm glow of the heart – his open house to all of us – his ready purse when we wanted help'; he was 'so kind and dear a brother to your sisters and you . . . were always their stay, support and sunshine'.

Jos was so reserved that his family probably never totally understood his quality, although Dr Robert, who knew him best, admired his good sense and balanced judgement. But in future years his granddaughter Snow remembered him with respect and affection. Charles had deep respect and affection for his 'uncle-father'. 'I was greatly attached to and greatly revered my Uncle Jos: he was silent and reserved so as to be a rather awful man; but he sometimes talked openly to me.' His importance to the career of Charles Darwin cannot be overestimated: had it not been for his wise intervention, Charles might never have gone on his world tour, and our history would probably be different.

In 1845 Charles and Emma were much engaged in enlarging Down House and redesigning the garden. 'Our grandest scheme', Charles wrote to his sister Susan on 3 September,

> is the making our schoolroom and one or (as I think it will turn out) two small bedrooms. The servants complained to me what a nuisance it was to them to have the passage for everything only through the kitchen; again Parslow's pantry is too small to be tidy. It seemed so selfish making the house luxurious for ourselves and not comfortable for our servants . . . So I hope the Shrewsbury conclave will not condemn me for extreme extravagance, though now that we are reading along Sir Walter Scott's life, I sometimes think we are following his road to ruin at a snail like pace.

In fact, as his father said, this was 'stuff and nonsense'. At no time were they anything but comfortably off.

That autumn they winkled Erasmus out of London to help with replanning the garden – to the astonishment of Jane and Thomas Carlyle, who knew how the elegant Erasmus hated the country. They were making

> great earth works; making a new walk in the kitchen garden, and removing the mound under the yews on which we found the evergreens did badly and which as Erasmus has always

insisted, was a great blemish in hiding part of the field and the old Scotch firs. We are making a mound, which will be execrated by all the family, viz, in front of the door out of the house. It will make the place much snugger, though a great blemish till the evergreens grow in it.

Erasmus, normally so indolent, was 'of the utmost service in scheming and in actually working, making creases in the turf, striking circles, driving stakes . . . he has tired me out several times.'

In 1846 Bessy followed her husband. In February, knowing that the end was near, Emma had gone to Maer to support Elizabeth and told Jessie, 'Elizabeth is buoyed up by instinctive hopefulness, though if you were to ask her what it was she hoped I don't know what she would say.' Emma, honest as always, could not bear to see her mother so diminished and hoped for a quick and peaceful end; it came on 31 March, and Elizabeth wrote to Emma that she would not have wished the 'half-extinguished life to be prolonged' and was thankful that her death was gentle. 'In the evening I heard her saying as I had done before, "Lord now lettest thou thy servant depart in peace". It was still, however, a happiness to be able to look in that sweet countenance and see a faint gleam now and then of the purest and most benevolent soul that ever shone in any face.'

Years earlier, Mackintosh had thought the sisters' praise of Bessy mere 'hyperbole', but a month spent at Maer convinced him that they did not exaggerate: she was 'a well head of kindness'. Not only her sisters, but her husband and children spoke of her in this way, and her letters reflect a genuinely rare character. Her Allen charm allied to Jos Wedgwood's directness and common sense helped to create Emma's own distinctive character. It was from Bessy that Emma learned her talent as a letter-writer, and it was she who encouraged, by her own example, Emma's love of reading. Above all, she passed on to her daughters a delicate sensitivity to other people's feelings, and a warm loyalty to her extensive family.

After the death of Bessy the family sadly decided to sell Maer Hall. Elizabeth was grateful for Emma's invitation to make her home with them at Down House, but decided to move with Charlotte and Charles Langton to Hartfield on the edge of Ashdown Forest in Kent. She had a house built, called The Ridge, near Charlotte's Hartfield Grove, and Emma helped her design the garden, sending plants and shrubs dug up from Down. Eyebrows were raised at Shrewsbury, where Charles was taking a holiday. 'We all understand', he teased, 'why so many laurels must be dug up, perhaps you would like the Azalea and one of the Deodars for Elizabeth. My dearest I kiss you from my heart. Won't you dig up a few of the apple trees in the orchard? Are they not too thick?'

Elizabeth's house became 'the kindly home for all who are sick and sorry', a welcome refuge for Charles and Emma at difficult times, and remembered by the children with delight. It was twenty miles from Downe, but Emma allowed ten-year-old George to ride there alone on his pony; he stopped for an egg-and-bacon lunch at an inn on the way. Etty recalled the same atmosphere of freedom as there had been at Maer: 'There were streams where we fished for minnows, sand to dig in and wild hearty commons to wander about.' Here Charles was to find sundews, the carnivorous plant that would give him days of fascinated study.

Gradually the family left Staffordshire – all except Frank, who stayed to run the factory and, retaining his old Unitarian loyalty, continued as a faithful member of the chapel there. The others left the pottery without regret; for most of them and their children it was the 'grimy old pot shop' that provided them with diminishing incomes. John Wedgwood had died in 1844. After the death of his wife, the lovely Jenny Allen, in 1836 he had gone to join his family in Tenby, where his son, Tom, who had written so vividly from the battlefield of Waterloo, was now a most respected citizen to whom a monument was erected in the market place. Colonel Tom Wedgwood's fountain remained there until recently.

Now only Aunt Sarah remained of the children of old Josiah. As one by one the family left Staffordshire, perhaps she allowed herself a sigh, remembering Etruria Hall, the music of the old spinet and dancing to the hurdy-gurdy on the green lawns of childhood. A true Wedgwood, however, like her mother she would have felt but not spoken. She now came to live at Petleys, near Down House and Emma, who remained the most loved of all her relations. Aunt Sarah and her household were to remain until her death in 1856 an important part of Darwin family life. Etty remembered her as 'tall, upright and very thin and looked as different from the rest of the world as any old lady in *Cranford*. She used to wear a scanty lilac muslin gown, several little capes or small shawls, and a large Leghorn bonnet. She kept several pairs of gloves by her – loose black ones for "putting on coals and shaking hands with little boys and girls, and others for reading books and cleaner occupations".' How astonished Etty would have been had she known the Sarah who played divinely for an entranced Coleridge. But children find it difficult to see their elders in the round: Etty could not understand how Aunt Jessie could write of 'merry little Emma'.

After her mother's death Emma decided to visit her aunts in Tenby, and in June 1846 she took Willy and Annie with her, travelling by sea from Bristol. Perhaps at this time she wanted to be with the Allens to comfort and be comforted, as only Aunt Jessie could. She found the Allen family sadly diminished: as well as Bessy, Caroline, John and his wife Gertrude, Jenny and John Wedgwood, Baugh and Harriet were all dead. In her absence Charles was supposed to be correcting proofs, but found himself 'so tired and over done' he could not. 'I am an ungracious old dog to howl,' he wrote to her, 'for I have been sitting in the summer house . . . thinking what a fortunate man I am, so well off in worldly circumstances, with such dear little children . . . and far more than all with such a wife. Often have I thought over Elizabeth's words when I married you, that she had never heard a word pass your lips which she had rather not have been uttered, and sure I am that I can now say so and shall say so on my death bed. Bless you my dear wife.' He was delighted with her long letter (as yet unfound) describing the happiness of the children, but he suggested that she should come back by land and not stay more than a fortnight. In fact, his letters reporting his sickness and misery were guaranteed to bring her back. But in that short stay Emma was able to share with her children the pleasures of what she had known as a child and introduce them to their Welsh relations. This was Emma's last visit to Tenby, and a rare outing. Later she would regret that she did not make the effort to return, for this was the last time she would see her beloved Aunt Jessie. Deaf and frail, Jessie remained game and affectionate to the end, dying in 1853. But from now on Emma's main concerns were Charles and their family, Down House and its household, and the village and neighbours at Downe.

There was a sizeable domestic establishment at Down House, but compared with other families of similar income they were not overstaffed. Joseph Parslow, the butler, ran the house with easy competence. Totally devoted to the family and without any of the pretensions common to butlers at that time, he was prepared in an emergency to take on anyone's job. He would buy or sell a horse, help take care of the children or play billiards with the boys as they grew older. He rarely lost his temper with the younger Darwins: Frank remembered with affection that the only time he was 'checked by him was when he wanted to lay the table for luncheon, or being stopped in some game which threatened the polish of the sideboard, of which he spoke as though it was his private property . . . he idealised everything about our modest household, and would draw a glass of beer for the postman with the air of a seneschal bestowing a cup of Malvoisie on a troubadour.'

He was not as careful about his own appearance as the Shrewsbury Darwins would have wished. Dr Robert, affronted by his 'long greasy hair, asked whether he was training to turn into My Lord Judge with a long wig'. But to Charles, Parslow was indispensable, caring for him when he was ill and holding him in his arms during the violent attacks of sickness. More than anyone except Emma, Parslow understood and loved Charles, shielding him from interruptions and disturbances. In due course he married Emma's maid, Eliza, and lived happily with her in the village, where she became the local dressmaker. He became part of village life, singing in the church choir and taking part in local concerts.

Emma's right hand in the household was the children's nurse, Jessie Brodie, remembered with the deepest affection by the children and grandchildren. The daughter of a ship's master who had been captured by the French and lost to his family, she brought to the Darwins all the love of a lonely woman. Tall and red-haired with a pockmarked face, she had given up the chance of a good marriage out of loyalty to her previous employer, the novelist William Thackeray. She would not leave until Thackeray had found a replacement nurse for his wife and children; her well-to-do suitor could not wait and went to Australia. Having lost her chance, Brodie continued to support Thackeray through the desperate times in his life when one of his young daughters died, and when his wife became mad and tried to drown another, aged three. Through the terrible months when daily she listened to the hoarse ravings of Mrs Thackeray, she was a tower of strength. Finally, however, when the Darwins came to Down in 1842, she left the Thackerays and joined their family. Etty remembered her delightful smile: 'I can see her,' she wrote, '. . . sitting in the little summer house at the end of the sand walk, knitting in the Scotch fashion with one of her needles stuck in a bunch of cock's feathers, tied at her waist, to steady it. There she sat, hour after hour patiently and benevolently looking on whilst we rushed about and messed our clothes as much as we liked.'

Once when Brodie was poorly and had difficulty coping with the young maid, Bessy, the girl Emma had brought from Maer, Emma sent her and the other maids to a concert at Bromley, 'and it has done Brodie such a wonderful deal of good, that if she could but get to a play or two, I think it would cure her. There have been many breezes in that department but I have told Brodie that I shall not keep Bessy if she is pert to her, and matters have gone very smooth since . . . I am reserving a sledge hammer for her the next opportunity she gives me by pertness to Brodie.' Easy-going by nature as Emma was, she would stand no nonsense.

The household was a happy and generally harmonious one, but the first years at Down had not been easy. Charles and Emma had lost a baby and suffered the deaths of Emma's father and mother; and Charles had been deeply upset by the loss of his own father in 1848. Dr Darwin died peacefully on 13 November. He had been ill for some time, and in 1843 had only with difficulty been able to visit his old friend Jos Wedgwood in his last illness. Charles visited his father for the last time in May 1848 and was relieved to find him wonderfully well and talking cheerfully. 'He thought with care he might live a good time longer,' Charles told Emma, 'and that when he died it would probably be suddenly.' Catherine wrote to Charles of their father's demeanour in his last days, 'so sweet, so uncomplaining, so full of everybody else, of all the servants, the servants' children . . . He attempted to speak about you this morning, but was so excessively overcome he was utterly unable.' Dr Robert's death was much mourned in Shrewsbury: all the doctors gathered to pay their last respects, and blinds were drawn in the town.

In the autumn of 1848, as Charles remembered in his autobiography, 'my health grew worse and worse, incessant sickness, tremulous hands and swimming head. I thought I was going the way of all flesh.' Having heard of much success in some similar cases from the cold-water cure practised at Malvern, he determined to try it. Encouraged by good reports from his cousin William Fox, and by an old shipmate from the *Beagle*, Bartholomew Sulivan, Charles determined to take his family to Malvern and spend some months taking the treatment. He was not deterred by those who mocked or severely criticized it, although he must have been aware of the furore in that erupted in 1844 after the death of the radical MP Sir Francis Burdett, who had been treated at Malvern. In letters to *The Times*, his daughter, Angela Burdett-Coutts, had claimed that the water cure had destroyed 'the finest constitution known to man'. However, many famous men and women of the time, including Dickens, Macaulay, Jane and Thomas Carlyle, Tennyson and Bulwer Lytton had enjoyed the water cure at Malvern. Princess Victoria had stayed there, and King William IV's wife Adelaide had come a number of times. Later, Florence Nightingale and even Karl Marx joined the list of illustrious patrons.

The water cure as practised at Malvern had been devised by a farmer's son, Vincenz Priessnitz, in Gräfenberg in Austrian Silesia (new Jeseník in the Czech Republic). Born in 1799, as a young man he cured his own broken ribs by keeping cold compresses on his chest for a year and drinking much cold water. Setting up a practice to apply his principles more widely, by 1839 he had hundreds of grateful – and cured – patients, including dukes and duchesses, generals and civil servants, artists and clerics and, it was said, eighty-seven physicians. One of these, an Englishman named Dr James Wilson, later set up an English 'Gräfenberg' in Malvern, a quiet little town in Worcestershire set among lovely hills with ancient springs of pure water and a medieval tradition of therapeutic wet-sheeting. Dr Wilson inspired an old friend, Dr James Gully, to join him. He bought the Crown Hotel and renamed it Gräfenberg House, and Dr Gully established himself at Tudor House, later opening Holyrood House for ladies.

The two doctors were an immediate success, soon made their fortunes and rode around Malvern in stylish carriages. Dr Gully was the more serious and impressive; Dr Wilson was something of a showman, and Charles remarked that he was more interested in his fees than his patients. 'In his ninety foot dining room up to a hundred guests sat at a table glistening with cut-glass decanters of water,' so it was said. Clearly this was not an ideal setting for Charles and Emma, who decided to take a private house with their own staff. From The Lodge he wrote to Henslow on 6 May 1849, 'We all – children, servants and all – have been here for nearly two months.' They intended staying at least until June.

This was a very pleasant holiday for Emma and the children. Etty never forgot her excitement at the prospect, and could remember 'the exact place in the road coming up from the village, by the pond and the tall

Lombardy poplars where I was told'. There was the thrill of the three-hour journey on the London and North Eastern Railway from London to Birmingham – which Emma remembered so well: the refreshments on the bustling station, the change to the train for Worcester and finally the coach ride to Malvern, through farmland and orchards, until in the distance the magical blue line of the Malvern Hills rose over the Worcestershire Plain.

They settled happily at The Lodge, a white-stuccoed house above the Worcester Road, set in pleasant grounds. 'We have got a very comfortable house, with a little field and wood opening on to the mountain, capital for the children to play in,' Charles told William Fox. This was Emma's kind of country. It was a happy interlude, climbing up the hills in the fresh and breezy air with the children to St Anne's Well, listening to the German band playing every morning and watching the patients and visitors who could, according to Dickens, 'slowly imbibe the pure element to an Andante of Haydn's or toss off tumblers from the "sacred hill" to a Pot Pourri of Donizetti, or the measured time of the Presburgh Polka'. There were splendid views from the top, where 'basket women' proffered ginger beer and biscuits to tempt appetites whetted by the invigorating air, and owners of donkeys offered cheap rides back down the hill. Each animal had its name embroidered across the browband, and one remarkably fine and powerful donkey bore on its forehead the name 'Royal Moses' from once having carried the Duchess of Kent (Queen Victoria's mother) to the top of the hill, so the guide book informed visitors. There was even a little cottage near St Anne's Well 'where knives and forks are hired out to tourists, and kidney surreptitiously grilled between meals for hungry patients under water treatment' – probably also for Emma and the children. Such snacks often 'came in acceptably' to her.

Etty remembered how the children enjoyed their holiday in the pleasant little town, running up the lovely hills and doubtless watching with amusement the strangely garbed patients plodding up to St Anne's Well – as did Dickens, who came here in 1851: 'Oh Heaven,' he wrote to John Forster, 'to meet the Cold Waterers (as I did this morning as I went out for a shower bath), dashing down the hills, with severe expressions on their countenances, like men doing marches and not exactly winning! Then, a young lady in a grey polka going up the hills, regardless of legs and meeting a young gentleman (a bad case, I should say) with a light black silk cap under his hat, and the pimples of I don't know how many douches under that.'

Emma relaxed in Malvern, delighting in its musical tradition. Annie was given dancing and music lessons at Pomona House, where tuition was given by 'the most eminent Masters in the country for music, singing and dancing'. At Henry Lamb's Royal Library and Bazaar, as four-year-old George remembered, there were fascinating toys. There was also a music saloon with pianofortes for hire, and a reading room with London and provincial newspapers. Emma almost certainly would have hired a piano.

Meanwhile Charles was undergoing the water treatment, the aim of which was to drive toxic impurities out of the system by sweating. The patient was swaddled in wet sheets held in place by linen bands, with thick quilts piled on top. There he was left to sweat for three or four hours, then briskly rubbed with a dripping sheet. The theory was that 'the blood was repelled from the surface of the body whereon the heart would exert sufficient force to restore circulation.' The expulsion of drugs and poisons from the system produced what the water doctors called 'the crisis' – a much sought-after result when the patient came out in boils.

At this time most diseases were treated with opium and laudanum, quinine or calomel, or laxatives and emetics. The water doctors believed in simplicity and Nature's cures. Almost all diseases, they claimed, could be cured by plain water, applied externally or imbibed in large quantities. Hot and cold fomentations were said to cure constipation and nervous headaches. There were sitz baths (just big enough to sit in) and foot baths and abdominal compresses. The most rigorous of the disciplines was a powerful cold douche. There were ten of these on the hillside, including two for ladies. Fresh air and exercise, too, were deemed essential. 'The hills were alive with scurrying figures making their way up to the Well, mouths wide open to take in the raw air,' wrote Dickens. 'Behind them urchins ran, chanting, "shiver and shake, shiver and shake".'

The treatment does seem to have been effective. Carlyle, who like Dickens was at Malvern in 1851, found relief 'walking on the sunny mountains, drinking of the clear wells not to speak of wet wrappings and solitary sad steepages'. Dickens mocked the cure in 'Mr Nightingale's Diary', but at the same time thought there was a 'great deal in it'. Tennyson, who was here in 1848, was dosed with iron pills and, wrote his biographer, 'altogether this really great man thinks more about his bowels than about the laureate wreath he was born to inherit.' Florence Nightingale, who came in 1857, believed that Malvern saved her life. When asked whether water therapy could cure lung disease, she said 'the patient could hardly fail to benefit from fresh air, ventilated bed-rooms, good diet, mild exercise, mild sponging and wet sheeting.' And, she might have added, in Charles Darwin's case 'the forbidding of all mental exercise'.

Whether it was the pure air and water or Dr Gully's insistence on abstinence from work, Malvern certainly seemed a success. Charles told Henslow that his sickness was 'much checked and considerable strength gained . . . I shall have to go on with the aqueous treatment at home for several more months. One most singular effect of the treatment is that it includes in most people, and eminently in my case, the most complete stagnation of mind. I have ceased to think even of barnacles.'

The Darwins returned to Down refreshed and renewed: Charles believed he had found a cure at last. He had a douche constructed in the garden, in a hut built for him by the local carpenter, John Lewis. Here Parslow acted as Charles's bathman. Gallons of water were pumped up into a steeple in the roof, and when Charles pulled a string the water fell on his back with great force. Etty remembered him running back to the house half frozen. (Charles Dickens built himself a similar contraption, but had a tin hat made at the ironmonger's to protect his head from the weight of the water!)

Fanny Allen met Charles in London at this time looking 'well and stout' and observed 'something uncommonly fresh and pleasant in him'. In fact, Malvern brought only temporary relief, but even this was welcome. Later, Charles wrote to his American friend James Wright Dana, recom-mending that he should try the water cure:

> Most regular medical men sneer at the Water-cure (I do not at all know whether it is adopted in the U. States) but I have tried it repeatedly and *always* with wonderfully good effects, but not permanent in my case. When I first tried it, I could not sleep and whatever I did in the day haunted me at night with vivid and most wearing repetition. The W. cure at once

relieved this. It makes the skin act so vigorously that all other organs get a rest. For years I have been in your state, that an hour's conversation worked me up to that degree that I wished myself dead. But then my head never ultimately suffers; for my peccant part is the stomach and fatigue of any kind always brings on great derangement and ultimately severe vomiting. So that the weak organ seems to save the more important one.

Just as Charles in these years seemed to find some means of relief from his besetting pains, so Emma discovered a way of alleviating the suffering associated with her recurrent ordeal – pregnancy. In January 1850 she was expecting her eighth child. Stoical as always, she was nevertheless apprehensive, for childbirth had become no easier over the years. But now some help was at hand. In November 1847 Dr James Young Simpson of Edinburgh University had published an article describing how chloroform could put to sleep a woman in labour, enabling her to give birth painlessly. Notwithstanding the objections of those who believed that the suffering of women in labour was divinely ordained, chloroform was welcomed not only by women but by many husbands who, like Darwin, suffered with their wives. It could have been given to Emma in August 1848 when her third son, Frank, was born; but Charles, though he made enquiries, dared not take the risk with a treatment still in its experimental stage. (They may have been unaware that many years earlier, Emma's Uncle Tom and her father had helped to finance Dr Beddoes's early experiments with nitrous oxide – laughing gas – in his research centre at Bristol.) However, by 1850 Emma was determined to have the relief of chloroform. Charles described the experiment to his cousin, William Fox.

> The day before yesterday Emma was confined of a little boy [Leonard]. Her pains came on so rapidly and severe that I could not withstand her entreaties for chloroform and administered it myself which was nervous work not knowing anything about it or of midwifery. The Doctor got here only 10 minutes before the birth – I thought at the time I was only soothing the pains

– but it seems, she remembers nothing from the first pain till she heard that the child was born. Is that not grand!

He had in fact administered a stunning dose: Emma was unconscious for an hour and a half!

Charles noted that the chloroform 'was very comforting to oneself as well as to the patient'. It was, he said, 'the greatest and most blessed of discoveries'. Others commented more dismissively. Livingstone wrote from Africa, 'Now all the old ladies will want to be breeding again.' But any criticisms about the new drug were silenced when, in April 1853, Queen Victoria used chloroform for the first time in giving birth to her eighth child, Leopold. She who had complained that giving birth made one feel like an animal welcomed chloroform; it was 'soothing, quieting and delightful beyond measure'. Emma's ninth child, Horace, was born in May 1851 with the help of chloroform and in 1856 Charles Waring certainly was 'produced under blessed chloroform', as Charles told Fox.

Concerned as he always was during Emma's 'time of trial' and knowing as he did the risks, it seems surprising that, as a scientist, Charles had not considered the alternative. It must be remembered that at this time contraception was considered immoral and to promote it was illegal. Nevertheless, Charles was not motivated solely by respect for authority. Like many other progressive and scientific men of his time, he did not agree with family planning. In 1878 he explained in a letter to a correspondent, Jane Hume Clapperton:

> I have lately reflected a little on artificial checks but doubt greatly whether such would be advantageous to the world at large at present, however it may be in the distant future. Suppose that such checks had been in action during the last two centuries or even a shorter time in Britain, what a difference it would have made to the world when we consider America, Australia, New Zealand and South Africa. No words can exaggerate the import-ance in my opinion of our colonisation for the future history of the world. If it were universally known that the birth of children could be prevented and this would not be thought immoral by married persons, would there not be great danger of extreme

profligracy amongst unmarried women and might we not become like the societies in the Pacific. In the course of a century France will tell us the result.

So, year after year, in the cause of national morality and the British Empire, Emma had to bear the pain and discomfort of repeated pregnancies.

As the children arrived, however, they were welcomed into a lively, active and stimulating home. Despite producing nine children in little more than eleven years of marriage, Emma did not allow her mind or her musical talent to atrophy. She played the piano every day, to please herself, to soothe Charles in the evenings and to amuse the children. Etty remembered the old nursery rhymes she sang to them, and the 'galloping' tune she played with the furniture pushed back to the wall and a mob of children dancing round. Aunt Jessie heard with amusement of Emma's party of thirty-five, 'of which half must have been children'. She and Charles had decided at the beginning of their marriage that furniture was not sacred but the happiness of their children was. One of the childhood delights long remembered in the Darwin family was the slide – a specially constructed board on which they were allowed to toboggan down the stairs. It was designed to be adjusted to allow daredevils to shoot down, or the little ones to glide gently. Even Emma and Miss Thorley, Annie's devoted governess, tried it out.

The children were given a great deal of freedom, but they never remembered being disobedient. If necessary Emma resorted cheerfully to bribery, just as her mother had done. When the noise of the children and their cousins at mealtimes was unbearable, she coaxed them into quiet with prizes of pennies for low voices. The children insisted that their parents were also paid to be quiet. Etty and her cousins were allowed to dress up in Emma's silk gowns and, with the bedroom door locked, decked with her jewels, paraded around her bedroom. They caused no damage and were not reproved.

Both parents gave much thought to the education of their children, disliking the idea of boarding schools (perhaps Emma remembered her brother Joe's accounts of life at Eton). Emma taught them herself in their early years, using the little reading book she had written for the children at Maer. Later, Willy was tutored by the Revd J. J. Wharton at Mitcham,

Surrey, then sent to Rugby – where, according to Charles, his mind was closed rather than opened. But he succeeded well in his father's old college at Cambridge. George and Frank also began with tutors, then had a more modern and most successful education in mathematics and chemistry at Clapham Grammar School before also going on to university in Cambridge. Lenny and Horace, both delicate, were mostly educated by tutors at home until they too were sent to Clapham Grammar School.

Etty recalled that she and Bessy had more than one governess but praised them all: 'From our different governesses we learnt nothing that was not good and high minded.' Etty conveniently blacked out of her memory the failures, Miss Pugh who went mad and Mrs Grut who left in high dudgeon; but Miss Thorley, who had arrived to teach the delicate Annie in 1848 (recommended by Emma's friends the Tollets of Betley Hall), and stayed with them until 1856, was certainly competent, if uninspired. Etty's health was so poor that there was never any question of sending her away to school, but Bessy, at her own request, spent some months at a boarding school in Kensington.

There is an unusual hint of criticism in Etty's comment that 'our education, as far as book learning was concerned, was not of an advanced type; my mother apparently did not try to get the best possible teaching for us.' Certainly Etty was a very bright girl and in later times would undoubtedly have profited from a university education; she became an intelligent critic of her father's work. But Emma, like her mother and the Allen aunts, took a relaxed view of formal schooling. Mrs Somerville, who had been maths tutor to Emma's brothers, taught her own children and assured Jessie that 'she never gave lessons longer than ten minutes at a time.' She said longer 'was only pernicious, no child could give undivided attention beyond that period. She then sent them out to amuse themselves as they could, and they always succeeded and were fresh to give her their attention when she called for them.' Aunt Jessie had advised Emma to do without a governess altogether, and while she did not go so far as that, certainly the Allen method of reading aloud good books and encouraging the children to use the library was to prove successful in Etty's case. The evening readings were an important part of family life at Down, as they had been at Maer. Scott, Thackeray, Dickens, Mme de Sévigné (a great favourite with the Allen sisters), light novels (Charles liked a pretty heroine and a happy ending) were all read to them as children. Later in life Etty was renowned among the young for the skill with which she read, smoothly eliminating difficult or unsuitable passages.

The Bible was read at family prayers, and although Emma rarely spoke to the children about religion, according to Etty 'she was not only sincerely religious, this she always was in the true sense of the word – but definite in her beliefs. She went regularly to church and took the sacrament. She read the Bible with us and taught us a simple Unitarian Creed, though we were baptized and confirmed in the Church of England.' Neither she nor Charles thought much of the Revd James Willott, who seems to have resembled a character from the satirical pen of Dickens or Jane Austen, dealing pompously and ineffectually with his parishioners. But he had started the Sunday school and a Coal and Clothing Club, on which Charles served as treasurer. His successor, the Revd John Innes, became a friend of Charles in spite of his High Church background. The two men enjoyed their arguments, and on one occasion when they actually agreed, stopped and burst out laughing: Charles thought one of them must be ill. Together they set up in 1850 the Downe Friendly Society, 'with its clubroom at the George & Dragon Inn'. It would, Charles said, 'teach our clodhoppers . . . encourage them to lay up upon sickness old age and death. A small monthly premium would bring them in a few shillings weekly to live on and £5 to be buried with.' No egalitarian, Charles was benevolently paternal in his dealings with the workmen in the village. Late in life he would reflect guiltily that he had done very little for the improvement of society; but, he said, his work and ill-health had prevented him from doing more – and, he confessed, as he grew older he became less interested in people outside his family.

Emma was too much involved in home affairs to take much part in church activities, and was in any case highly critical of Mr Innes, especially disliking his bigoted attacks on dissenters. She refused to adopt the Anglican practice of turning to the east for the intoning of the creed – much to the embarrassment of the Darwin family, who could not understand why they had to be different; she probably would have also remained silent during the declaration of faith in the Trinity. She envied Fanny and Hensleigh the Unitarian church they attended in London, wishing there had been one at Downe.

Brought up in the good Whig country house tradition, Emma felt responsible for the welfare of the villagers. According to Etty, 'she had a large clientele of the village people from the poorer outlying parishes round Downe.' When she saw the local women hauling their water up to dry, hilltop Downe from Keston, a mile away, she organized a water cart for them three times a week. Her children remembered their mother's 'poories' and the smell of sickness and poverty in their homes with some revulsion; Etty felt that 'it was perhaps doubtful how much good she did in this way as there was not enough enquiry and a good many of her friends were people of bad character.' In fact, Emma had learned from Aunt Jessie a certain tolerance of human frailty. Down House became a kind of welfare centre, as Maer Hall had been. Here bread tickets were given out to beggars, and small pensions to the old. The bread tickets were eventually stopped, however, since there were times when the yard outside the kitchen was filled with rollicking Irish travellers!

Like the Darwin sisters and her own sister Elizabeth, Emma could write prescriptions and make up medicines, and her children recalled the fun of rolling rhubarb pills; Emma held firmly the Victorian faith in 'opening medicines'. Charles, too, remembering his medical training and the times when he had prescribed for his father's patients at Shrewsbury, was occasionally prepared to play doctor to the village. Dr Darwin's book of medicines, labelled on the brown leather cover 'Receipts' and on the back 'Memoranda', was their bible. Many of the additional prescriptions are in Emma's handwriting: 'Citric acid', she confidently asserted, 'alleviates the pain of cancer.' Laudanum (dose one and a half drams) mixed with 'Tinct Benzoin, Tinct Myrrh, Oxymel Squills' made a cough mixture suitable for her son Frank. Laudanum was again used in her remedy for 'Mrs Seymour Hill's bunions'. Mixed with 'goulard', it was 'kept on the joint with lint and oilskin'. Many a woman must have been cheered at the sight of Emma with her bottle of gin cordial made up to Dr Darwin's own prescription and intended for 'poor women weak after lying or with pains in the back'. She also pasted into the book a newspaper clipping on how to trap wasps in a glass inverted over a plate filled with rum, beer and sugar. Emma was obviously concerned about the danger of lead contamination in the water supply at Down, and copied carefully a test recommended by a newspaper. Aware of the danger of 'arsenic in wreaths and dresses', she kept a note on how to detect its presence with a drop of liquid ammonia.

Nor was her philanthropy limited to the practical and medical. Her mother had taught her the value of reading, and throughout her life at Down she took a particular interest in the village library she set up, providing books and personally giving them out every Sunday afternoon, as well as continuing to read newspapers and periodicals avidly to keep herself abreast of current affairs. Even in these years of constant confinements, Jos Wedgwood's daughter was not idle.

CHAPTER TEN

A Flower in the Dust

In the summer of 1850 Emma's bright and lively eldest daughter, Annie, became listless and in October, concerned by her continuing ill-health, Charles and Emma decided to send her with Miss Thorley to Ramsgate to try sea bathing – at that time considered a cure for most complaints, including listlessness and nervous disorders. Emma, remembering her own delight in bathing as a child at Tenby, hoped the brisk air would revive the little girl. (Although Charles would not have known it, his own mother had been dipped in the icy Irish Sea as a little girl to cure her 'pukes and boils'.)

Charles and Emma joined her for a few days. Charles collected sea shells on the sands and relaxed while Emma watched the bathing woman, in her baggy blue costume, encourage Annie into the bathing machine which was then drawn by horses into the sea where, concealed by a canvas awning, the bathing woman would lower her gently into the water. Apparently in Ramsgate they were accustomed to 'encourage unwilling children to enter the sea by singing to them'. However, neither the Ramsgate air nor the brisk sea bathing suited Annie. In the October chill she developed flu and they returned home.

Much as Charles admired Dr Gully, and though he knew he had cured his own little daughter, they were not yet ready to subject their delicate child to the full rigours of the Malvern treatment. So he and Emma decided to administer their own version at home. He had for some time been keeping a methodical 'Journal of Health', recording his own progress and noting by day and night whether he was <u>well</u>, underlining the word once or more according to the degree of health. Now he opened a similar record for Annie. On Dr Gully's advice, Charles used six of the methods designed for very delicate persons. The dripping sheet involved rubbing the trunk and arms with a wet towel and then rubbing the legs in like manner; the spinal wash, rubbing the spine up and down with a wet towel wrung out in cold water; packing, wrapping in wet sheets and covering with blankets – according to Gully 'most soothing'. The shallow bath and footbath were Dr Gully's version of modern reflexology. 'The feet and hands,' he wrote, 'the soles and palms especially contain an accumulation of animal nerves and of blood vessels . . . essential to them, in order to bind them by the closest sympathies and the great centres of thought and volition so that their applications and movements may be accurately directed by the mind.' The most alarming treatment was 'sweating by the lamp', when a lamp containing spirits or wine was lit under a chair on which the patient sat shrouded in a tent of sheets.

Annie apparently was given the dripping sheet and spinal wash every morning; every three or four days she was 'packed', and once a week 'sweated by the lamp and a shallow bath and footbath every morning'. Some treatments left her 'very well', but some made her 'wakeful and uncomfortable', as Charles carefully noted. But her general condition did not improve, and she developed not only a cough but also periods of depression and 'early morning crys'. Perhaps understandably, Annie dreaded wet-sheeting on the cold dark mornings, kindly and gentle though Brodie and Miss Thorley would have been.

When by 21 March Annie had not shaken off her colds and again developed influenza, Charles stopped the water treatment and decided to take her with Etty to Malvern to receive Gully's personal attention. Emma was now seven months pregnant and was not allowed to travel, but she knew she could rely on Brodie to give Annie motherly care. The family party stayed the night with Erasmus at his bachelor house near Hyde Park. Perhaps he took them to Euston Station for their train to Birmingham in the famous 'cab' in which he had squired his lady friends around London; Emma followed them in her mind every inch of the way. In Malvern, Charles settled them comfortably in their lodgings at Montreal House, a white-stuccoed villa on the Worcester Road, opposite the house they had taken in 1849; Miss Thorley would join them there. Then he returned to Erasmus's house in London.

Emma waited impatiently for letters from Miss Thorley and her daughters. If the children took their letters to the Post Office before six-thirty in the evening, Emma would get them at the garden gate at Down House by the following midday. A week after they had arrived Etty wrote to her on a piece of fancy notepaper embossed with floral patterns, 'My dear Mama, we are going to buy the combs this morning. Yesterday I fell down twice. We bought some orangs [*sic*] this morning. Yesterday we bought some canvas, and I and Annie are making a pattern out of our own heds.' One day the postman brought a letter from Etty for six-year-old George. 'My dear Georgy – we went a donkey ride. When Miss Thorley and Annie rode on before, my donkey would not go on, and I was obliged to get off, Brodie and I had to drag it along. I have got some little ladybirds, and I keep them in a little box and I feed them milk, some sugar. There is a shop at St Anne's Well.' Emma remembered it well; 'the thought of it', she replied, 'made me quite thirsty.'

The next letters, however, were worrying. On the following Monday Miss Thorley wrote that Annie had a 'smart bilious gastric fever and Dr Gully was obviously concerned'. On Wednesday an alarming missive arrived from Dr Gully: he thought Charles should come to Malvern immediately. Straight away he left for the train to London and was at Montreal House in Malvern the next afternoon. He found Annie, he wrote, looking 'very ill', though Dr Gully had 'strong hopes'.

Emma's family moved quickly to support her. Elizabeth rushed to Down House from Jersey. Aunt Fanny Allen came too, and was a great comfort through the long hours of suspense. At seventy she was still alert and active, and had ample experience of such trying times: along with her sisters Emma and Jessie she had gone to Caroline's support during their Italian tour, had watched with her as her two daughters slowly faded and died, and had comforted her beside the Italian graves. Astringent but kindly, Aunt Fanny brought strength. Aunt Jessie's demonstrative love would have broken down Emma's guard; but Jessie, deaf and ill, was nearing her end and unable to travel. Fanny Hensleigh travelled to Charles in Malvern. The thought of her gentle care in the sick room was 'an infinite comfort' to Emma, who was reluctant to ask for the help of Susan and Catherine Darwin, knowing how they would have fussed over Charles. Caroline and Joe took charge of Etty and Fanny Hensleigh's children at their home, Leith Hill Place in Surrey. Etty, still uncomprehending, was happy with her cousins, as Caroline wrote to Charles: 'I will take the greatest care of all the dear little set and they shall never be long out of my sight or hearing . . . They are all gone cowslip gathering in the fields.' It was Caroline who would have to comfort Etty and answer the unanswerable questions as, long ago, she had comforted Charles when, as an eight-year-old boy, he too had faced the mystery of death.

Nothing better illustrates the love and understanding between Charles and Emma than their daily letters in that terrible week. Each was concerned for the other: Charles for Emma in the last stages of her pregnancy, and she for him, fearing the strain would make him ill, knowing how he hated seeing pain. From Malvern, Charles wrote hourly reports, rocking between hope and despair. He thought it was best for her 'to know how every hour passes. It is a relief for me to tell you, for whilst writing to you I can cry tranquilly.' He did not spare her the cruel details, the agonizing vomiting, the diarrhoea. 'Poor Annie is in a fearful mess but we keep her sweet with chloride of lime.' They sponged her 'with vinegar and water with excellent effect'. They 'changed the lower sheet and cut off the tail of her chemy and she looks quite nice and got her bed flat and a little pillow between her two bony knees'.

On Good Friday Charles watched in distress as Annie endured three awful fits of retching sickness. 'Her case seems to me an exaggerated one of my Maer illness,' he wrote to Emma. He had written with the same recognition and perhaps hint of guilt to his cousin Fox: 'she inherits I fear with grief, my wretched digestion.' That afternoon Dr Gully gave him some cause for optimism and Charles wrote more cheerfully, 'positively *he has hopes* – Oh my dear be thankful.' Annie had a restful night and Charles, longing to let Emma know, sent an electric telegraph from Worcester to Erasmus, 'Please send man to Sydenham Station thence in fly to Down to say that Annie has rallied – has passed good night – danger much less imminent.' On Easter Saturday Emma received Charles's letters before the telegram came. On reading the cable she hastily added to her own letter, 'I was in the garden looking at my poor darling's little garden to find a flower of hers when John Griffiths drove up . . . we shall hear nothing more until Monday, but I shall wait very well now. I hardly dare think of such happiness. I hope you will sleep tonight, my own.'

Easter Sunday at Down was a day of hope. Emma's sister Elizabeth would have taken the children to church, joining a congregation flowered and gay in its Easter best. Emma, in the last stages of her pregnancy, would probably have prayed at home, alone, desperately seeking consolation and strength from her faith. She took comfort in writing to Fanny Hensleigh: 'I feel very anxious about Charles for fear he should quite break down but your being with him is such a comfort. I don't know what I should have done without Aunt Fanny. By oneself one's thoughts lose all control. The waiting for post time is the worst but one gets used to everything to a degree.' There would be no more post until Monday, and Emma was glad of Aunt Fanny's easy general chat and quiet understanding.

Meanwhile, on Easter Sunday at Malvern Charles wrote almost hourly, still encouraged to hope; but Annie's 'poor hard, sharp pinched features' made her unrecognizable and foretold the passing of her bright spirit. 'There was nothing in common with . . . my own former Annie with her dear affectionate radiant face . . . My dear dear Mammy let us hope and be patient over this dreadful illness.' The surgeon was called to 'draw Annie's water off, this was done well and did not hurt her, but she struggled with surprising strength against being uncovered, etc. She slept tranquilly during the night except for about ten minutes when she wandered in a slightly excited manner.' On Monday morning she asked to have her hands sponged when Brodie had sponged her face, 'and then thanked Brodie and put her arms round her neck, my poor child, and kissed her'. Throughout the day Charles tried not to hope too much: the 'alternatives of no hope and hope sicken one's soul'. A mustard poultice on Annie's stomach 'smarted her a good deal', but in the evening when they bathed her with vinegar and water, 'it was delicious to see how it soothed her'.

On Monday morning at Down the postman brought Emma all Charles's reports of Saturday and Sunday, with their swings from hope to despair and back again. Emma read them over and over. 'Your minute accounts are such a comfort and I enjoyed the sponging of our dear one with vinegar as much as you did.' She was with them in spirit, and began planning meals for Annie's convalescence 'more for the pleasure of fancying I have something to do for her'. She rehearsed her remedies on paper to Charles: 'If the bowles are too loose rice gruel is good innocent and binding flavoured with cinnamon or currant jelly. Whey from milk is very digestible and a spoonful of raw egg beat up in hot water and a little salt.'

But even while she wrote, at Malvern all hope was gone. On Tuesday Charles had seen the change in the little pinched face and could write no more. He let Fanny compose a letter to Emma, warning her that the end was near. That evening she wrote: 'I grieve to tell you a worse report this evening. There has been a change today and signs of sinking. I tell you everything just as it is my dearest Emma, and thankful also for the mercy that is given us of there being not the least appearance of any suffering in your sweet patient darling. We are now giving brandy and ammonia every quarter of an hour.' Fanny promised to write again if there was any improvement. Then quietly she took charge, persuading the exhausted Charles to lie down. All Tuesday night she sat at Annie's bedside, listening as the little voice rambled in delirium. 'I heard her twice trying to sing, so I think her wandering could not have been distressing to her,' she later wrote to her daughter. The next morning the air was heavy with thunder and, as Fanny remembered, 'It was just at twelve o'clock that we heard her breathe for the last time while the peals of thunder were sounding.'

At Down at twelve o'clock on Wednesday, Emma was reading Fanny's warning letter with an aching heart. There was no further message; and, as she wrote to Charles the next day, she knew only too well 'what receiving no message meant'.

> Till four o'clock I sometimes had a thought of hope but when I went to bed I felt as if it had all happened long ago. Don't think it made any difference my being so hopeful the last day. When the blow comes it wipes out all that precedes it and I don't think it made it any worse to bear. I hope you have not burnt your letter I shall like to see it sometime. My feelings of longing after our lost treasure make me feel painfully indifferent to the other children but I shall get right in my feelings to them before long. You must remember that you are my prime treasure (and always have been) my only hope of consolation is to have you safe home and weep together. I feel so full of fears about you, they are not reasonable fears but my power of hoping seems gone. I hope you will let dearest Fanny or Catherine, if she comes, stay with you till the end. I can't bear to think of you by yourself.

Thursday morning brought Charles's heartbroken letter.

My dearest Emma

I pray God Fanny's note may have prepared you. She went to her final sleep most tranquilly, most sweetly at 12 o'clock today. Our poor dear child had had a very short life but I trust happy and God only knows what miseries might have been in store for her. She expired without a sigh. How desolate it makes one to think of her frank cordial manners. I am so thankful for the daguerrotype. I cannot remember ever seeing the dear child naughty, God bless her. We must be more and more to each other my dear wife – Do what you can to bear up and think how invariably kind and tender you have been to her – I am in bed not very well with my stomach. When I shall return I cannot yet say. My own poor dear dear wife.

Emma paused in writing her own letter to read his, then resumed:

Your letter has just come. Do not be in a hurry to set off. You do give me the only comfort I can take in thinking of her happy innocent life. She never concealed a thought and so affectionate so forgiving. What a blank it is. Don't think of coming in one day. We shall be much less miserable together. Poor Willy takes it quietly and sweetly.

Elizabeth, grief-stricken for Emma, the sister she had loved since childhood, wrote to comfort Charles, telling him

how gently and sweetly Emma takes this bitter affliction. She cries at times, but without violence, comes to our meals with the children and is as sweetly ready as ever to tend to all their little requirements. I do not fear, taking it as she does, that she will be made ill. It will be the greatest comfort to her to see you home very soon . . . It is very happy that Willy is here now, and I felt quite glad last night to hear his voice talking to her out of his bed after she was in hers.

Twelve years old, William, home from his prep school, was then and always very close to Emma; his sympathy was a great comfort to her at this time.

Charles, however, was already on his way back to Down. Fanny, sensitive and understanding as always, seeing how broken he was, had persuaded him to leave before the funeral: Hensleigh was to come to Malvern and they would arrange everything. So he left early on Thursday morning, without stopping to pack his clothes, and at half past six he was sobbing in Emma's arms. That evening, as she wrote to Fanny,

> We have done little else but cry together and talk about our darling . . . I think everybody loved her. Hers was such a transparent character, so open to kindness and a little thing made her so happy . . . From her having filled our minds so much for the last nine months it leaves such an emptiness . . . I suppose this painful longing will diminish before long. It seems as if nothing in this life could satisfy it.

At least, as Elizabeth wrote to Fanny and Hensleigh at Malvern, Emma had been spared seeing 'the last impressions of the utter change . . . She is able to read a little too, and goes about as usual amongst the children with even a cheerful smile.'

On Friday Emma and Charles wept through the hour of the funeral. Perhaps they read together the words of the Book of Common Prayer that the vicar would be reciting: 'I am the resurrection and the life, saith the Lord: he that believeth in me, though he were dead, yet shall he live; and whosoever liveth and believeth in me shall never die.' In Malvern, the hearse drawn by black-plumed horses left Montreal House and creaked through the village street to the priory church. Fanny and Hensleigh led the little group of mourners, accompanied by Miss Thorley and Brodie, to the grave under a cedar of Lebanon, and watched in tears as the small coffin was lowered into the earth. 'Man that is born of a woman', the vicar read, 'hath but a short time to live and is full of misery. He cometh up, and is cut down like a flower, he fleeth as it were a shadow . . . In the midst of life we are in death . . . we therefore commit her body to the ground, earth to earth, ashes to ashes, dust to dust, in sure and certain hope of the resurrection to eternal life.' For Emma, that 'certain hope' was the only consolation; for Charles, Annie was a flower cut down into the dust.

At Down the next day Fanny's letter brought Emma some comfort, though they

> feared for Miss Thorley and still more for poor Brodie, and she has suffered, poor thing, most sadly and had to be lifted into the carriage. But since she has been relieved by a long fit of crying, she's lying down now. Miss Thorley was more composed than I expected only now and then bursts of grief – poor thing. There never could have been a child laid in the ground with truer sorrow round her than your sweet and happy Annie.

Fanny and Hensleigh left for London early the next morning; Brodie returned to Down to be consoled by Emma. She retired soon after to Portsoy in Scotland, but kept in touch with the family until her death. Poor Miss Thorley was devastated, and never really recovered from the loss of her beloved pupil. She went to London to stay with her mother, to whom Charles wrote a kind letter, hoping 'that her health may not be injured by her exertions . . . I hope it will not be presumptuous in me to say that her conduct struck me as throughout quite admirable. I never saw her once yield to her feelings as long as self-restraint and exertion were of any use: her judgment and good sense never failed: her kindness, her devotion to our poor child could hardly have been exceeded by that of a mother.'

Some time in the days that followed Emma collected Annie's quills and steel pens, writing paper, sealing wax and seals, and carefully placed them in a small box with other little treasures are mementoes – a small thimble, a silk needlecase, embroidered pen-wipers, a yellow ribbon and pendant, a careful childish letter to the sister of her governess, her pocket book for 1848. With them in the box Emma placed two folds of paper. One still contains the remainder of a withered jonquil flower – maybe picked while there was still hope? – and is inscribed 'gathered Wednesday April 23rd'; in the other a lock of light brown hair, still shining.

'Annie's box' is still prized in the family, with its poignant reminders of a bright little girl and the heartache of that week.

The death of Annie left a deep scar. According to Etty, Emma 'rarely spoke of Annie, but when she did the sense of loss was always there unhealed'. Charles, she wrote, 'could not bear to re-open his sorrow and he never to my knowledge spoke of her.' Emma, who had never fussed over her children, and had let Etty and the boys wander through the woods alone, now became careful of their health. She had good reason. Cholera and scarlet fever epidemics at this time cut great swathes through village and city and, as every reader of the literature of the time is aware, the shadow of consumption spread over rich and poor families alike.

It is probable that Annie herself died of consumption, though the doctor's certificate recorded 'bilious fever with typhoid character'. As Randal Keynes writes, 'in the medical language of the time, typhoid meant "like typhus", a separate and well recognised disease of which delirium was one of the main features.' The medical experts agree 'that Annie probably died of tuberculosis, which was known at the time as consumption, and may have been triggered by her flu in March . . . Tuberculosis may have struck Annie finally in the abdomen causing tuberculosis peritonitis.' Charles himself repeatedly wrote of his fear that Annie had inherited his 'wretched stomach'; and since some medical experts believed that there was an 'undoubted hereditary tendency' to consumption, it may be that Annie had inherited a double weakness, for, as Charles recognized, her sickness was alarmingly like his own. Keynes quotes Dr Thomas Yeoman, writing in 1848, who described tuberculosis as 'the plague spot of our climate, amongst diseases it is the most frequent and most fatal; it is the destroying angel who claims a fourth of all who die.' Once the disease had taken hold there was little hope, as Emma knew only too well from other family losses. Aunt Fanny would remember the deaths not only of Emma's cousins in Italy but of her own sister, Octavia, who had died from consumption as a young woman. The 'destroying angel' had struck down Uncle John Wedgwood's children and Uncle John Allen's wife; she had sought a doctor in Gloucester who claimed to have found a cure, but died there. Before her marriage, Emma and her friends the Tollets had read *Nicholas Nickleby* with its chilling account of 'the dread disease', in which 'the struggle between soul and body is so gradual quiet and solemn, and the result so sure, that day by day and grain by

grain, the mortal part wastes and withers away . . . a disease which
medicine never cured, wealth warded off, or poverty could boast exception
from . . . but slow or quick is ever sure and certain'. The account of
Annie's slow decline was chillingly familiar to Emma, Elizabeth and Aunt
Fanny.

When Dickens killed off his Little Nell in *The Old Curiosity Shop* it was
not mawkish Victorian sentimentality that had the whole nation weeping;
there were too many little coffins in too many darkened rooms. When
Gwen Raverat, in later years, wrote of her great-grandmother Emma's
'dangerous hypochondria', she had not understood the mental climate of
those years. Darwin's colleagues, Hooker and Huxley, lost young children.
Dickens lost a baby in London in the same month that Annie died. To his
wife, Kate, who at this time was also taking treatment in Malvern, Dickens
wrote like a kind father to a child: 'Now observe. You must read this
letter, very slowly and carefully . . . if you have hurried on thus far without
quite understanding, I rely on your turning back and reading again. Little
Dora . . . is suddenly stricken ill . . .' In fact, the baby was already dead,
but Dickens did not dare tell Kate the truth: 'I think her very ill . . . I do
not think her recovery at all likely.' In contrast, confident of Emma's inner
strength, Charles had hidden nothing from her, sharing with her every
moment of the agony of their daughter's last week.

Shortly after Annie's death, Charles wrote a memorial, as a document
of private record for the family, perhaps to give her, if not 'eternal' life, at
least a longer life, and to fix her image so that in future years she would
not be forgotten. He remembered her

buoyant joyousness, tempered by two other characteristics,
namely her sensitiveness, which might easily have been overlooked by a stranger, and her strong affection. Her joyousness
and animal spirits radiated from her whole countenance and
rendered every movement elastic and full of life and vigour. It
was delightful and cheerful to behold her. Her dear face now
rises before me, as she used sometimes to come running down
stairs with a stolen pinch of snuff for me, her whole form radiant
with the pleasure of giving pleasure. Even when playing with
her cousins when her joyousness almost passed into boisterous-

ness, a single glance of my eye, not of displeasure (for I thank God I hardly cast one on her), but of want of sympathy would for some minutes alter her whole countenance. This sensitiveness to the least blame, made her most easy to manage and very good; she hardly ever required to be found fault with, and was never punished in any way whatever. Her sensitiveness appeared extremely early in life, and showed itself in crying bitterly over any story at all melancholy, or on parting with Emma even for the shortest interval. Once when she was very young she exclaimed, 'Oh Mamma, what should we do, if you were to die?'

Then he remembered how affectionate she was.

When quite a Baby, this showed itself in never being easy without touching Emma, when in bed with her, and quite lately she would, when poorly, fondle for any length of time one of Emma's arms. When very unwell, Emma lying down beside her seemed to soothe her in a manner quite different from what it would have done to any of our other children. So again, she would at almost any time spend half-an-hour in arranging my hair, 'making it' as she called it 'beautiful', or in smoothing, the poor dear darling, my collar or cuffs, in short in fondling me. She liked being kissed.

He would never forget the sparkling eyes, the bright smile:

her step was elastic and firm; she held herself upright, and often threw her head a little backwards, as if she defied the world in her joyousness. For her age she was very tall, not thin and strong. Her hair was a nice brown and long; her complexion slightly brown; eyes dark grey; her teeth large and white. The Daguerrotype is very like her, but fails entirely in expression: having been made two years since, her face had become lengthened and better looking. All her movements were vigorous, active and usually graceful; when going round the Sand-walk with me, although I walked fast, yet she often used to go before pirouetting in the most elegant way, her dear face bright all the time, with the sweetest smiles.

She loved dressing up in Emma's clothes: 'One day she dressed herself up in a silk gown, cap, shawl and gloves of Emma, appearing in figure like a little old woman, but with her heightened colour, sparkling eyes, bridled smiles, she looked, as I thought, quite charming.' Like Emma, she was very dextrous, doing everything neatly with her hands: 'she learnt music readily, and I am sure from watching her countenance, when listening to others playing, that she had a strong taste for it. She had some turn for drawing, and could copy faces very nicely. She danced well, and was extremely fond of it.'

He noted one

singular habit, namely a strong pleasure in looking out words or names in dictionaries, directories, gazeteers, and in this latter case finding out the places in the Map: so also she would take a strange interest in comparing word by word two editions of the same book . . . In the last short illness, her conduct in simple truth was angelic; she never once complained; never became fretful; was ever considerate of others; and was thankful in the most gentle, pathetic manner for everything done for her. When so exhausted that she could hardly speak, she praised everything that was given her, and said some tea 'was beautifully good'. When I gave her some water, she said 'I quite thank you', and these, I believe were the last precious words ever addressed by her dear lips to me.

We have lost the joy of the household, and the solace of our old age: she must have known how we loved her, oh that she could now know how deeply, how tenderly we do still and shall ever love her dear joyous face. Blessing on her . . . April 30 1851.

On 13 May 1851, almost three weeks after the death of Annie, Horace was born. At least Emma had the relief of 'the blessed chloroform', but it was some time before she regained her strength and spirits. Elizabeth, who was still at Down during May, was worried. 'We are disappointed at your account of dear Emma,' Fanny Allen wrote to her; 'I looked forward with so much hope to this time for the healing of sorrow.' This bitter blow had rocked even Emma's firm faith. Nearly twenty years earlier, after the death of her sister, Fanny, she had taken consolation in the thought that one day she would join her, 'never to be parted again'. But now, aware of Charles's growing agnosticism and hearing the arguments of Erasmus and his friend Harriet Martineau, there were times in the battle between reason and faith when it needed all the power of prayer to sustain the latter. There was comfort to be found in the thought that those who died young were spared future pain; but heaven, that 'blessed land' on the other side, could no longer be imagined with the innocence of childhood. It took time to accept that now she saw 'through a glass, darkly'; and her pain was doubled by the knowledge that Annie's death had pushed Charles even further away from God, and that he was denied the solace of prayer, although – as if to comfort her – he had three times used the name of God in the last tragic letter from Malvern.

For Charles, the agonized 'Why?' had a clearer answer in 'the survival of the fittest'. The death of Annie confirmed Charles's loss of faith. In his autobiography he claimed that

> disbelief crept over me at a very slow rate, but was at last complete. The rate was so slow that I felt no distress, (and have never since doubted even for a single second that my conclusion was correct. I can indeed hardly see how anyone ought to wish Christianity to be true; for if so the plain language of the text seems to show that the men who do not believe, and this would include my father, brother and almost all my best friends, will be everlastingly punished. And this is a damnable doctrine).

These strong words were written between 1876 and the end of his life, but the passage in brackets was not published during Emma's lifetime. She wrote on Frank's copy of the autobiography, 'I should dislike the passage in brackets to be published. It seems to me raw. Nothing can be said too severe upon the doctrine of everlasting punishment for disbelief – but very few now would call that Christianity (tho' the words are there). The question of verbal inspiration comes in too.' Emma got her way – but only after a considerable argument in the family.

Charles described in his autobiography his attitude to religion in the years when he was working out his ideas on the origin of species:

Another source of conviction in the existence of God, connected with the reason and not with the feelings, impresses me as having much more weight. This follows from the extreme difficulty or rather impossibility of conceiving this immense and wonderful universe, including man and his capacity of looking far backwards and far into futurity, as the result of blind chance or necessity. When thus reflecting I feel compelled to look at a First Cause having an intelligent mind in some degree analogous to that of man; and I deserve to be called a Theist.

This conclusion was strong in my mind about the time, as far as I can remember, when I wrote the *Origin of Species*; and it is since that time that it has very gradually with many fluctuations become weaker. But then arises the doubt – can the mind of man, which has, as I fully believe, been developed from a mind as low as that possessed by the lowest animal, be trusted when it draws such grand conclusions? May not these be the result of the connection between cause and effect which strikes us as a necessary one, but probably depends merely on inherited experience? Nor must we overlook the probability of the constant inculcation in a belief in God on the minds of children producing so strong and perhaps an inherited effect on their brains not yet fully developed, that it would be as difficult for them to throw off their belief in God, as for a monkey to throw off its instinctive fear and hatred of a snake.

I cannot pretend to throw the least light on such abstruse problems. The mystery of the beginning of all things is insoluble by us; and I for one must be content to remain an Agnostic.

In 1885, as will be seen, Emma once more asked Frank to omit a passage: this time the sentence about monkeys, because it would 'give an opening to say, however unjustly, that he considered all spiritual beliefs no higher than hereditary aversions or dislikes. I should wish if possible to avoid giving pain to your father's religious friends who are deeply attached to him and I picture to myself how that sentence would strike them, even those so liberal as Ellen Tollet and Laura, much more Admiral Sullivan, Aunt Caroline etc., and even the old servants.'

After the death of Annie grief bound them closer, but we shall never know if, as they wept together, they talked of an afterlife. Perhaps not: they understood each other too well to need words. Emma accepted that Charles would always need proof and he knew how much Emma was comforted by her faith. But each time Emma had approached childbirth or Charles suffered serious illness, they had faced the possibility of death.

In 1844 Charles had worried that if he died his contribution to science, his theories on evolution, would be lost. In October of that year the publication of an anonymous book, *Vestiges of the Natural History of Creation*, had fuelled his fears. The author, later discovered to be the publisher Richard Chambers, had formulated theories with which Charles disagreed. Not wishing his own ideas to be confused and attacked with *Vestiges*, he wrote a summary of his own theories and entrusted it to Emma, to be published in the event of his death, advising her to ask Hooker to edit and present it. He knew that even though Emma would disagree with it, she would honour his trust and ask Hooker. He knew that as she had once told him she would not wish him to alter his views for fear of giving her pain. Typically, however, Emma disliked the idea of paining their religious friends.

CHAPTER ELEVEN

The Wider World

B Y JULY 1851 CHARLES AND EMMA WERE SUFFICIENTLY RESTORED TO BE able to face the jostling crowds at the Great Exhibition of the Works of Industry of all Nations in the 'Crystal Palace', which had opened on 1 May. As the Queen recorded in her journal, 'This is one of the greatest and most glorious days of our lives, with which to my pride and joy, the name of my dearly beloved Albert is forever associated.' Her pride was justified. The Great Exhibition of 1851 was a triumph for Prince Albert, who had promoted this bold idea in the teeth of strong opposition. Europe was still unsettled after the 1848 wave of revolutions and it was feared that to gather great crowds in London, when the city was full of dangerous revolutionary émigrés, including Karl Marx, was asking for disaster. The Chartist demonstration in England in 1848, it is true, had been a damp squib; but even so it took great courage to build an immense glass palace in the very centre of London. However, on 30 June 1849, at a meeting of the Royal Society of Arts, His Royal Highness communicated his views regarding the formation of a 'Great collection of works of Industry and Art in London in 1851 for the purpose of exhibition and of competition and encouragement'. It was to be international, with exhibits from Great Britain on one side and from foreign countries on the other.

As a consequence of Albert's persistence there arose in Hyde Park what the hitherto sceptical *Times* described as 'an Arabian Nights structure, full of light and with a certain airy unsubstantial character about it which belongs more to an enchanted world than to this gross material world of ours'. In *Punch*, Douglas Jerrold named it aptly 'The Crystal Palace'. The dazzling glass building, covering over eighteen acres of ground, was the brainchild of the remarkable gardener Joseph Paxton, who some years earlier had created a great glass conservatory at Chatsworth for the Duke of Devonshire. By 1851 he had had twenty years of experience of designing glass structures. 'It was at the Midland Station at Derby', he wrote, 'that the first mark on paper was made of the Crystal palace.' His blotting-paper sketch was the basis for the 'rolls of plans' he presented, again at Derby, nine days later 'in company with Mr Robert Stephenson who laid the plans before the Royal Commission the next day'. Thanks to the efficient Mr Cubitt and his army of workmen, the building was finished at phenomenal speed: first iron column was fixed on 26 September 1850, less than nine months before the grand opening by the Queen and Prince Albert on 1 May 1851. Emma's grandparents, Dr Erasmus Darwin of Derby and Josiah Wedgwood, and their friends in the Lunar Society would have been delighted that the Crystal Palace had been born at Derby, and even more so at the exhibits there. Here were machines they had invented, developed and improved; here were the dreams they had had nearly a hundred years earlier made reality – power looms and pressure pumps, carriages and railway trains, vast mowing machines, all as they had envisaged.

Charles's brother Erasmus took Aunt Fanny Allen and Hensleigh and Fanny Wedgwood to the Exhibition in the first week. Fanny Allen thought 'all other exhibitions are killed by this Aaron's Rod . . . it is the most beautiful thing I ever saw. We were two hours there and yet I did not see the 10,000[th] part of what is to be seen, not even the grand avenue entirely. The great Diamond was the only thing that I should have said was a failure . . . I expected to see a diamond 10 times the size.' Indeed, the Koh-in-Noor, the 'mountain of light', disappointed many. 'To ordinary eyes', wrote a French visitor, 'it is nothing more than an egg-shaped lump of glass that refused to sparkle.'

At the end of July, Charles and Emma brought the children to London to see the Exhibition, staying for a week with Erasmus. Charles was 'intensely interested', according to Etty, who was then eight and was taken with six-year-old George, but she 'did not make much of it and remembered deciding not to go again, but stay at home and scrub the back stairs as being better fun'. Fanny Allen reported that Hensleigh's two sons, 'Bro' and Ernie, 'got leave from Rugby for a couple of days' lark! They are all gone to the Hyde Park Exhibition this morning in three cabs . . . every child is gone. I believe it is Erasmus' generosity that treats the children otherwise they never would be so foolish as to take them a second time. All the children I have seen there looked wretched . . . and so it would be with these children except for the sweet cakes and ices.' Messrs Schweppes made a considerable profit of £45,000 from their buffets; their ice creams, costing sixpence and one shilling, were made in the patent freezing machine run by steam on the spot. One suspects that Emma, whose sweet tooth was famous, enjoyed this unfamiliar treat. She must also have been fascinated by the huge grand piano designed to be played by four virtuosi; and no doubt she was intrigued by the 'comfort stations', a welcome novelty in a public building. If she was disappointed that the Queen did not notice the Wedgwood display, she did not say so.

Charles forgot his sickness and revelled in the Exhibition. Richard Owen's concrete replicas of prehistoric animals must have reminded him of the Galapagos Islands, and he was fascinated by the stuffed monkeys in the African section. However, the smoky air of London brought on Emma's migraine, and she spent some of the week lying down in a darkened room in Erasmus's house. She was glad to get back to the clear air of Down; but the Great Exhibition had given Charles intense pleasure, and had refreshed and stimulated his mind. In the next years his health improved, as he noted in his journal: there were many successive days when he was very well and his nights were good. For the next three years he worked patiently on his study of *Cirripedia* (barnacles), carefully dissecting with his home-made equipment, examining and comparing living and extinct specimens. He finally published his findings in 1853–4, in 'two thick volumes describing all the known living species, and two thin quartos of the extinct species'. The task had taken him eight years – although he reckoned that 'about two years out of this time was lost by illness'. Modestly he wondered whether 'the work was worth the consumption of so much time', and was amused to recognize himself as Bulwer-Lytton's 'Professor Long' who had written 'two huge volumes on limpets'. But to his astonishment and delight, in November 1853 the Royal Society awarded him its Royal Medal, not only for his geological studies arising from the *Beagle* voyage, but also because his recent work established him as the world's authority on barnacles.

Indeed, the experience he gained in classifying this difficult group of species was not only useful to him when he came to write the *Origin of Species*, but also served the essential aim of establishing him as a serious scientist who could take his place among qualified academics. But by the time the work was ready for publication he was heartily sick of barnacles and was infinitely relieved when he could pack up his notes and send his specimens back to his correspondents all over the world.

That September, having sent 'ten thousand Barnacles out of the house all over the world', Charles could at last begin to 'look over my old notes on species'. For the next six years he worked steadily on his 'great work', the 'species theory' which was to shake the scientific world.

Although in the early 1850s Charles was 'unusually well', as he told his cousin William Fox, and managed to attend meetings in London, nevertheless 'all excitement and fatigue brings on such dreadful flatulence that in fact I can go nowhere.' He had, he said, three bugbears that haunted him: 'Oh the professions, oh the gold and oh the French' – that is, for their five sons, financial security, and the fear of a French invasion that was widespread following Louis Napoleon's coup of 1851. Even Aunt Jessie had thought, 'Now I think everything may be possible even an invasion.' The discovery of gold in California in 1849 and in Australia in 1851 was creating a mad rush of speculators; Charles feared that the price of gold would soar as a result and their shares plummet. As for his sons, their was much agonizing over their education. Should they go to Eton, like the sons of his neighbour Sir John Lubbock? But Emma's brother Joe had not been happy there, while her younger brothers had enjoyed Rugby. So they settled for Rugby. To these three areas of concern Charles added the fourth persistent anxiety: 'The worst of my bugbears is heredetary [*sic*] weakness.' Then, in the facetious tone he often used to his old friend Fox, he wrote, 'Emma has been very neglectful of late and we have not had a child for more than one whole year.'

In fact, Emma was beginning to hope that at last the burden of childbearing had been lifted, and certainly after the birth of Horace she had a respite for more than four years, though it would seem from her journal that she had two miscarriages during this period. She was even beginning to hope that she could take Charles and the children for a visit to Tenby, where her beloved Aunt Jessie was living with Aunts Emma and Fanny. Jessie was physically ailing, had a weak heart and now was very deaf, but she was as lively as ever in mind. She and Sismondi had known personally many of the characters now shaping the new Europe. She had known Louis Napoleon, had been a friend of his mother, Hortense, and had followed his career from his unimpressive boyhood through his years of exile. She claimed that Louis had been a pupil of Sismondi and that she had once, sat for a whole day with the ageing Queen Hortense and listened, fascinated, to the story of her life as a girl with Napoleon. Now in her widowhood Jessie still followed political events on the continent with a keen interest. She wrote regular reports to Elizabeth and Emma. In 1851 she heard to her amazement of Louis Napoleon's election as Emperor after the *coup d'état* of 1851, and, as she wrote to Emma, considered that 'The Beast has taken the wrong turn' and had become a dictator.

Jessie felt confident that Emma, in whom she had fostered an interest in European politics, held balanced attitudes, but Fanny Hensleigh worried her: she was her sister Kitty's daughter, and Jessie felt responsible. She was more concerned about Fanny's political unconventionality than about her friendship with Erasmus Darwin. In her years in Italy she had been quite accustomed to the role of the *cavaliere servente* – indeed, she had had one herself. Even so, she was concerned that Erasmus was now such an indispensable part of Fanny's life, although Hensleigh did not seem to mind. Hensleigh was passionately interested in etymology and, like Charles, was to work for over twenty years on the great book of his life, *A Dictionary of English Etymology*. He pursued the derivation of words with the same dedication as Charles gave to the origin of species and, like Charles, the intensive study made him ill. Again like Charles, he believed in the continuity of the line from brute to man; he believed that 'language, like writing, is an art handed down from one generation to another,' and tried to trace 'upwards to its origin the pedigree of [the] grand distinction between man and the brute creation'. For years he worked on his great work for six hours a day, leaving Fanny to be entertained and squired by Erasmus Darwin. There is no doubt that she became the love of his life; he became a surrogate father to her six children, especially her two youngest daughters, Effie and Hope, and he affectionately called her 'The Missis'. But it is impossible to believe, as has been suggested, that he was the girls' real father. Undoubtedly Fanny grew to love him deeply, but at first he was simply a useful escort and companion while Hensleigh was locked in his work. While her father lived, Fanny's life had been full of excitement and interest: she had skilfully hosted his dinners for the most distinguished men and women of the day. From early girlhood she had been passionately attached to radical political causes, taking an active part in the campaigns for parliamentary reform and the abolition of slavery. Sir James's death left a huge blank in her life; but with Erasmus to drive her to meetings in his elegant cabriolet she could still take part in the political activity she enjoyed.

Since 1837 Fanny had attracted the admiration and friendship of Harriet Martineau, who wrote to her for many years and welcomed her with Erasmus to her home in the Lake District. This was a friendship Jessie most certainly did not approve; and her alarm increased over the following years, especially when in 1851 Fanny joined the émigré Giuseppe Mazzini's Committee for the Liberation of Italy. Fanny and Hensleigh visited her in Tenby that year, and Jessie wrote to Elizabeth in horror: 'Underneath that refreshing quiet, that delicious calm, Fanny has a lava of living fire that has made her give battle to all the governments in Europe under the banner of Mazzini. She is of his committee in London! How could Hensleigh permit it? It is so contrary to the modesty of her nature to associate her name with such notoriety that I am sure she will suffer.' Jessie and Sismondi had watched Mazzini for years, and did not trust him. She believed he had sent many Italian activists 'to death and dungeon', while keeping himself safe in exile. 'That presumptuous fool . . . will boast he has the daughter of Sir James Mackintosh . . . the greatest of statesmen, and the wife of a Wedgwood, the great representative of the manufacturing interest, on his committee.'

Emma found Fanny the most stimulating companion and shared many of her interests, though she lacked her cousin's drive and fire. But for many years she had also valued Fanny's 'refreshing quiet' and 'delicious calm'. Fanny had been there to comfort her after her sister's tragic death; and she had been an angel of kindness and competence during the agony of Annie's last illness. She was not only a Mackintosh, she was an Allen, and shared their sensitivity and affectionate temperament.

In 1853, a fortnight before her death, Jessie wrote to Emma, 'I am watching France with a sort of personal interest, breathless to see what will come of it.' She was reading an article on Burke in the *Revue des Deux Mondes* and was 'surprised Louis Napoleon allowed it in his Empire'. He was proving to be so 'much more clever' than she had thought him 'that I must ever distrust my judgement or he must have learnt immensely in his prison'.

Jessie loved all her sister Bessy's children as though they were her own, but Emma had a special place in her heart. In 1852 she wrote,

> How I do love you when you talk of your children! You never speak so prettily as then . . . You are poetic without knowing it . . . Blessed mother of happy children you are my Emma . . . Now that I stand at the end of life . . . and commonly called a long one too, the whole appears to me so short, so fleeting as if nothing was worth thinking of but the Eternity in which we recover all our earthly loves.

Jessie's deep love for Emma was returned with an uninhibited warmth unusual in her. Emma, like her Wedgwood grandmother, Sally, felt deeply but usually found it difficult to express emotion, keeping it hidden under a customary serenity. In the months in Geneva that Emma had called the happiest of her life, Jessie had melted the Wedgwood reserve. Sismondi had given Emma a knowledge of French and Italian, and of European affairs; Jessie had given her gaiety and warmth, and a loving and tolerant understanding of people.

Jessie kept her lively mind until the end. On 28 February 1853, she suffered a heart-attack and died three days later. She was quietly giving her sisters, Emma and Fanny, instructions about her last wishes; then, as her doctor told a friend, 'she waited a little, and said quite quietly "I think that is all", and then like a flash "Sismondi I'm coming", and she looked up as if she saw him there before her and died.'

Fanny Allen wrote to her niece Elizabeth, 'I long for her image as I saw it walking round and round the little garden looking so cheerful . . . but it is not grief or melancholy that dwell in it. I feel as if I had been permitted to see something of the rapture of a higher nature, to whose white robe the gleam of bliss was given.' Some years later Fanny Allen sent Emma a photograph of Jessie. She wrote in return that she was 'very glad indeed to have the photograph of my dear Aunt Jessie. It is not a strong likeness, but the look of her sweet eyes is there and the dress looks like her. It is a thing I shall always regret that I did not make an effort to see her once more.' Emma also regretted that Jessie had destroyed Sismondi's journals, since she was sure he had intended that they should be published. Jessie's own journal, likewise destroyed, was an equal loss, since she numbered so many fascinating and influential people of the time among her friends.

———————

In the spring of 1854, Charles was feeling so unusually well that he accepted an invitation to join the Royal Society's Philosophical Club and looked forward to visits to London to attend their meetings. ('Philosophic' was still the term used for 'scientific'.) The success of his monograph on barnacles encouraged him to face society again; as he told Emma, he regretted losing touch with his old acquaintances and 'would endeavour to go oftener to London'. In May he was surprised to find that his London trips 'suit my stomach admirably . . . I begin to think, that dissipating, high living with lots of claret is what I want and what I had during the last visit . . . We are going to act on this same principle and in a very profligate manner have just taken a pair of season tickets to see the Queen open the Crystal Palace.' The Exhibition had been such a resounding success that it was decided not to pull it down but to dismantle it and rebuild it at Sydenham in south London. Charles, Emma and Elizabeth were there for the splendid opening ceremony – and so overwhelmed were they that, to Etty's consternation, 'Aunt Elizabeth fainted dead away', and lay prostrate on the ground. Even more embarrassingly, when Clara Novello sang 'God Save The Queen', Emma broke down and sobbed audibly.

Britain was at war in the Crimea, and the rural calm of Down was shattered by the children's war games. In the nursery, up and down the stairs, along the sand walk, the mock battles raged to the sound of drums and bugles as Frank and Georgy went to war. They learned the parts of guns and Charles, remembering his own passion for firearms in his youth, enjoyed teaching them. They drilled, shouldered their toy rifles and marched along the sand walk to pitch camp, light their camp fire and warm their milk over it. 'Franky stood guard until released by his brother's bugle . . . when Papa came out for his daily stroll and went to kiss the guard, Franky bristled and presented his home made bayonet.' Emma joined in, dressing them up in coats reddened with sealing wax. Charles and Emma's brother Harry Wedgwood even took a party of young ones to see the army manoeuvres and, to their infinite delight, found themselves being charged by the 13th Light Dragoons. For a brief while Charles reverted to his hunting-mad youth at Maer and thoroughly enjoyed the old familiar sounds of gunfire.

But in Tenby the Crimean War was no game. Aunt Fanny was reading Sydney Smith's memoirs; their gaiety, she said, made her forget the miseries of the Crimea and Scutari, where their old friend Florence Nightingale was on the battle front. Fanny Allen remembered her 'a little girl of 3 or 4 years, then a girl of high promise; when I next met her at Geneva and which she has most faithfully kept'. She wrote to Elizabeth, 'Have you heard that the noble Flo Nightingale astonishes all the surgeons by her skill and presence of mind. After amputating a limb, they pass on to another leaving her to take up the artery and do all that is necessary. A high mission has been given her which has cost her life to fulfil.' Looking back, she recalled that 'every time I saw her after her sixteenth year, I saw that she was ripening constantly for her work and that her mind was dwelling on the painful difference of man and man in this life and the trap that a luxurious life laid for the affluent.'

In 1847 Aunt Fanny had stayed at Embley, Florence Nightingale's home, while 'Flo' was travelling in France, and enjoyed her letters describing her journeys by *diligence* (stage-coach). 'This new mode of travelling amuses Flo and she rather likes difficulties too . . . What a wife she would make for a man worthy of her, but I am not sure I yet know the mate fit for her.' In 1856 she wrote: 'There is a more enduring stamp on Flo and her work that no time will change . . . Sidney Herbert's speech pleased me most. Those three touching anecdotes of her influence over the minds of soldiers are beautiful, particularly the one of the soldiers kissing her shadow as it passed over their beds.'

In Tenby in the winter of 1854–5 Aunt Fanny and Aunt Emma were busy packing 'clothing and necessaries' to be sent out to the Crimea and Scutari. Fanny's parcels were for Florence at Scutari, Emma's for 'the fighting part'. In a freezing January the news from the Crimea was as bleak as the midwinter. The list of casualties grew – half of them due to cold and disease. The reports from the Crimea of government incompetence brought down Lord Aberdeen's ministry, and Palmerston took his place.

Charles and Emma were in London at this time with the children for a month's holiday, but the house they took in Upper Baker Street was freezing cold and, as Etty remembered, 'neither my father nor my mother were well, and they did not much enjoy their stay.' Emma was still plagued by migraine, which was always worse in London. They returned with relief to a Down House sparkling in the deep snow, where the children could walk on the tops of the railings and the 'wreaths of snowdrifts were a wonderful and beautiful sight'.

Despite the tribulations of the wider world, the 1850s brought welcome spells of calm and good health to Emma and Charles. In September 1855 Emma went with her husband to the meeting of the British Association at Glasgow, still revelling in the freedom of four years without the agony of childbearing. Etty, aged twelve, was allowed to 'trim her a cap for the occasion, and I snipped up lace and ribbon with immense satisfaction. What it was like, Heaven knows, but I believe it was worn.' The indulgent Emma would certainly let her think so. Etty remembered this time with pleasure, particularly listening to her father's reading of *Guy Mannering*. Emma had brought from Maer the tradition of reading aloud in the evenings, and these occasions 'were a happy part of the family life. Whatever my father did with us had a glamour of delight over it unlike anything else.'

The children were not shut out from Charles's work, and as they grew older they were even encouraged to help. As he beavered away collecting facts and testing theories for his 'big book', he often made use of the children's keen eyes and minds uncluttered with academic theories. Caroline's daughter, Sophy, was sent to look for worm casts – damp evenings were best, he told her. His friend Henslow obliged him by paying schoolgirls sixpence a time to collect seeds for his experiments; William Fox put up notices to encourage boys to find lizard and snake eggs for him. His own children enthusiastically helped in his experiments and were delighted when they bore fruit.

Early in 1856 Emma hoped to take Charles and the children to Tenby – to the great excitement of the local doctor, who had met Charles somewhere and was 'enchanted with him'. This time Charles had not the excuse of pressure of work – his 'confounded barnacles' were finished – nor of ill-health: Fanny Allen met him in 1856 at his sister Caroline's house, Leith Hill Place, and found him 'uncommonly agreeable, fresh and sparkling as the purest water'. However, the plan did not come to fruition. Charles's fear of being 'becousined' by the prolific and exuberant Allen family may have had something to do with this, as his Uncle John

Wedgwood's family were at Tenby at the time; but there was another reason too. In the spring of 1856 Emma realized to her disappointment that she was expecting another child. She was now forty-eight, and this was to be a most difficult pregnancy. Etty, then thirteen years old, 'remembered very well the weary months she had passed and reading aloud to her sometimes helped her to bear her discomforts'.

When Emma was eight months pregnant she had to entertain a houseful of relatives who had come for the funeral of Aunt Sarah Wedgwood. The last of the children of Josiah I and Sally had died at Petleys, her house at Downe. Charles described the funeral without undue emotion to his sons Willy and George, then away at school.

> Aunt Elizabeth and Uncles Jos, Harry, Frank, Hensleigh and Allen all attended, so that the house was quite full. We walked to Petleys and there put on black cloaks and crape to our hats, and followed the [coffin] which was carried by six men, another six men changing half way. At the church door Mr Innes came out to meet the coffin. Then it was carried into the church and a short service was read. Then we all went out and stood uncovered round the grave whilst the coffin was lowered, and then Mr Innes finished the service but he did not read this very impressive service well. Hemmings, Mrs Morrey and Marsha [Sarah's servants] attended and seemed to cry a good deal. Then we all marched back to the house, Mr Lewis and his two sons carrying a sort of black standard before us, and we went into the house and read Aunt Sarah's will aloud. She desired her funeral to be as quiet and possible and that no tablet should be erected to her. She has left a good deal of money to very many charities.

The matter-of-fact tone does not conceal Charles's hatred of funerals, and the shadow of Emma's imminent and possibly dangerous confinement must have darkened the family gathering.

Sarah was the last of the children of Josiah I and Sally, and at eighty-eight, as Etty remembered, was a formidable old lady. In her youth she had had her suitors, among them Basil Montague, the son of King William IV and Mrs Jordan; and, as her sister-in-law Bessy had once said, she was proof that a woman could administer a great fortune as well as a man. In the best Wedgwood tradition, she had a strong social conscience, had campaigned for the abolition of slavery and against alcoholism, and had contributed large sums for the relief of poverty among the hill farmers of Wales.

Like her mother, Sally, she found it difficult to express her feelings, but she had never concealed her special love of Emma from her earliest childhood, recognizing that they had something in common.

CHAPTER TWELVE

The Origin:
Conception to Birth

Having finished with barnacles, Charles could turn his full attention to his book on the origin of species. It had been a long twenty years in gestation, and at times almost as painful as Emma's periods of confinement; the water cure had been his chloroform. But in the 1850s for a brief period he had been well, enjoying his trips to London, especially visits to the Great Exhibition, now in its new home at Sydenham, and to the meetings of the Philosophical Society. A more curious outing which gave him enormous pleasure was to the Columbarian Society: a group of pigeon fanciers who met near London Bridge. As he wrote to William, this was 'a strange set of odd men. Mr Brent was a very queer little fish; but I suppose Mamma has told you about him: after dinner he handed me a clay pipe, saying "here is your pipe," as if it was a matter of course that I should smoke.' It was equally odd that Charles seems to have no recollection of his mother's famous doves, her interest in breeding them and the special cages she created for them. Nor did Emma remember the doves Sukey brought to Maer and their cage built to her prescription – even though she and Fanny may have earned their childhood nickname of 'the Dovelies' from the pleasure the birds had given them as little girls.

Charles told William that pigeon fancying was 'a noble and majestic pursuit and beats moths and butterflies'. It was also part of his research into the mysteries of cross-breeding. Sitting in a smoke-filled room 'in a gin palace in the Borough amongst a set of pigeon fanciers', as he later told Huxley, he listened as a certain Mr Bull was condemned for crossing his 'pouters with runts to gain size and if you had seen the solemn and awful shakes of the head . . . at this scandalous behaviour . . .' Breeding, variations within species, artificial selection, patiently he observed and sought the origins of change. As he did so, he worried that the inbreeding in his own family had caused a 'decrease in general vigour and an increased infirmity among the offspring'. Again and again in his letters he asserted that his 'confounded' illnesses had been inherited and voiced his fear that the risk to his children had been increased by his marrying his first cousin. Was it true, he asked an American friend, that marriage of first cousins was illegal in the United States?

Certainly there was a black bar through the health of their children. Annie's illness had reminded him of his own; three of his children had palpitations of the heart, as he had had; Bessy (in her early years known as Lizzy) was a strange and rather dim little girl, given to talking to herself, and she had a nervous habit of twisting her fingers as he had done as a boy. As for Etty, her health was to give her parents grave concern for many years; remembering Annie, Emma now would take the greatest care of her eldest surviving daughter. Etty wrote of this devoted care: 'The entries in my mother's diary show what years of anxiety she suffered first with one child and then another. Sometimes it is my health which is chronicled day by day, sometimes one of the boys.' There are no complaints, however, in Emma's journals, no outpourings of grief or joy. The entries in the little notebooks, in her neat handwriting, are brief. The simple '12 o'clock' for the death of Annie is characteristic. 'Both parents', Etty continued, 'were unwearied in their efforts to soothe and amuse whichever of us was ill; my father played backgammon with me every day and my mother would read aloud to me.' Charles had played backgammon every night with Emma, counting the score carefully and shouting, 'Bang your bones!' when she won. Now that Etty was a bright little fourteen-year-old, Emma was probably happy to hand over this duty to her daughter; she preferred reading aloud, as the Wedgwoods had done all through her childhood at Maer. All her life Emma had been honest in her judgements of the great and their works; often, one suspects, her most trenchant comments were designed to deflate the overenthusiastic. So she had claimed to dislike poetry, especially Shakespeare. But she had her favourites, in literature as in music; Etty particularly remembered her mother's love of Cowper – both his poetry, particularly his 'Winter Walk at Noon', and his letters.

Emma's patience with her family was phenomenal – especially as she was not patient by nature. Her days and nights were disturbed by Charles's sickness – and while the indispensable Parslow could clear away the vomit, he could not hide from her the sound of the loud retching that filled the house day and night. Then there were the nauseating smells from his experiments: plants rotting in green slime, skinned birds and animals. No wonder her devoted Allen aunts thought her 'born of Heaven'. Fortunately, she had never been houseproud, but the stench that filled the house during the 'skeletonizing' of animal or bird carcasses, or the boiling of rancid ducks, must have been hard to bear during the months of her difficult pregnancies. Surprisingly, Charles bore the smells stoically, anaesthetized presumably by the intense concentration on his work. So he welcomed the smelly parcels of skins sent by his fellow scientist Alfred Wallace from the Far East, the dead half-bred cat from his cousin William Fox, and bird droppings to be searched for seeds. Most welcome was the bird's leg sent by a friend – the foot clutched round a clod of earth. The problems of the dispersal of seeds could only be solved to his satisfaction by practical experiment. So the seeds in this precious clod were soaked in salt water for the time it would take them to cross oceans – and to his delight they grew. The theories which would shake the world of academic scientists were developed not in the cloistered calm of university libraries but in his own house and garden, albeit with the indispensable expert advice he constantly sought from established scientists such as Lyell, Hooker, Owen, Henslow and Sedgwick.

Emma tolerantly accepted the experiments even in the drawing room. Later she was to play the piano with a jar of worms on the lid so that Charles could observe their reactions to music. She was fortunate that her staff were sufficiently devoted to them both to accept with good grace the brunt of clearing up. Emma believed that children's play was important but that tidiness was not. She could not understand wasting so much time in polishing the stairs or the legs of chairs. Similarly, Charles's messy experiments were tolerated with good humour. Yet dearly as she loved her husband and children, after the birth of Charles Waring Emma desperately needed a break from them, and in March 1857 she took Etty for a month to Hastings, where she hoped the sea air would revive them both – though, typically, it was Etty's constant ill-health that worried her rather than her own.

That spring, without Emma, Charles sank under the weight of the worry of his 'everlasting species book'. His friends were beginning to nag him to publish; there was so much speculation on the theme of evolution in the air at this time that he was in danger of being forestalled. In 1844 he was concerned that if he died his contribution to science would be lost, but he still was not ready to face the furore that he knew his book would create. It was not so much Emma's reaction that caused him to delay publication; he knew that she had long ago steeled herself. Caroline, Elizabeth and other religious friends would certainly be disturbed by the book, but after so long period of gestation, he realised that publication was as inevitable as birth. It was essential that his facts should be correct and his arguments unassailable.

As he struggled with chapter six on 'Natural Selection', he worried about the ruthlessness of Nature. 'The good', he wrote, 'will be preserved and the bad rigidly destroyed.' By whom? Did he mean Nature or God? He was not sure. But Annie had been destroyed and Etty was weakening; he was anxious about the health of Lenny, Bessy and Horace; and he watched the baby with a mixture of scientific detachment and an aching heart. Little Charles Waring was so clearly backward; he made strange grimaces and shivered when excited, as Bessy had done. Both he and Emma were too experienced as parents not to notice even in these early months that, as Etty later wrote, 'The poor little baby was born without its full share of intelligence.' In fact, Charles Waring had what would now be called Down's syndrome.

Once more Charles fell prey to sickness and he again took refuge in hydrotherapy treatment. He had tried it at home, with shower baths in the garden, as well as the full Malvern treatment. He even had tried, in vain, electrified chains made of brass and zinc round his waist. Perhaps he remembered reading of the experiments with electric treatments undertaken by his grandfather, Erasmus Darwin. But he needed expert help, and this time Malvern was out of the question; the shade of Annie would meet him at every turn. So he tried a clinic at Moor Park in Surrey, only forty miles from home. Run by an intelligent young doctor, Edward Lane, the comfortable mansion was set in lovely countryside among sandy heaths and woods of silver pines, a gentler and more luxurious establishment than Dr Gully's. Charles quickly responded to Lane's sympathetic treatment; the astute doctor had soon realized that he was not dealing with one of his overfed, self-indulgent patients. 'I cannot recall any [case]', he wrote, 'where the pain was so truly poignant as his. When the worst attacks were on he seemed almost crushed with agony. But they were so stoically borne.' Like Emma, who often saw him like this, Dr Lane was 'touched by the sweetness and gentleness with which Charles endured the pain'.

Whether it was Dr Lane's hydrotherapy, the serenity of the gentle walks among the pines, or absence from the worry of Emma and the children, Charles slowly revived. In May he returned home, glad to be under Emma's wing again; but neither she nor Etty had completely recovered. The birth of Charles Waring had completely exhausted Emma, and her persistent migraines remained troublesome. Yet Horace's sixth birthday on 13 May was celebrated with the usual Darwin exuberance. A week later the house was filled with relations and their children for the christening of Charles Waring. Charles's sisters, Susan and Catherine, came – no doubt longing to 'scrattle' the house into order – and were full of good advice. Charles was worried about Etty and, as he said, always hated visitors when there was sickness in the house. As a result he had a renewed 'fit of vomiting and all Dr Lane's good work was undone'. So, with herself, Charles and Etty all in need of rest and therapeutic attention, Emma decided that she would take Etty for treatment at Moor Park; after a fortnight, she would come home and Charles could take her place. Thus a pattern emerged: during 1857 there were a number of retreats to Moor Park. Sometimes Emma accompanied Charles; sometimes they took it in turns to stay with the children and went separately, often taking Etty, who was still not strong.

It was easier for Emma to get away now that William was at Rugby, whence he went up to Cambridge in 1857. While at school he developed a passion for the new art of photography. Charles must have remembered his craze for chemistry at that age, when he and Erasmus set up their own laboratory, so he willingly paid for his equipment and Emma set aside a workroom for him at Down. Did Charles tell him that Uncle Tom Wedgwood had been considered to be the 'father of photography'? Possibly not: both Charles and Emma still knew little about the history of their Wedgwood ancestors.

———————

'The summer of 1857', Fanny Allen wrote, 'has been perfect and will long be remembered by the young as if it were the customary summer, and not a stray beauty.' In spite of her fragile health, Etty remembered it as

> full of sunshine and happiness, the sounds of summer, the rattle of the fly wheel of the well . . . the lawn burnt brown, the garden a blaze of colour, the six oblong beds in front of the drawing room windows, with phloxes, lilies and larkspur in the middle and portulacas, verbenas and other low-growing plants in front; the row of lime trees humming with bees, my father lying on the grass under them; the children playing about with probably a kitten and a dog, and my mother dressed in lilac muslin wondering why the blackcaps did not sing the same song here as they did at Maer.

Doubtless the inconsistent birds intrigued Charles's ever-curious mind too.

It is remarkable that the Darwin children should remember so sunlit a childhood; for the years leading up to the publication of the *Origin of Species* in 1859 were shadowed by domestic tragedy and academic disappointment. The 1850s had begun with the death of one child and would end with the death of another; and during the intervening years one after another of the seven children became seriously ill. Emma had suffered pain and heartbreak; yet her children all remember the happiest of childhoods. Rarely can a major scientific work have been completed against such a disturbed background. In May 1856 Lyell had persuaded Charles to begin his 'big book', in which he would crystallize the labours of nearly twenty years. By December 1857 the manuscript was half finished, and in September of that year he sent an abstract to his American friend, Asa Gray, asking him to keep it secret.

In the autumn and winter of 1857, as Charles struggled with his great work, there was chaos at Down House. They had enlarged the house twice before – in 1843, when extra bedrooms and a schoolroom had been built on, and bow windows added to the drawing room and the master bedroom above; and in 1846, when further improvements had been made. But they had had five more children since then; and with the children, plus nurses, governesses and servants, they needed more space. They planned to add a large dining room for them all, and for the large number of relations and friends who came with their children to the family headquarters that Down House had become.

So while Charles painfully worked on his theories on the 'struggle for existence', labourers hammered and heavily laden carts rumbled around, filling the house with noise and dust. At the same time, as if to remind him that it was the fittest who would survive, seven-year-old Lenny collapsed with the same kind of palpitations that Charles himself had suffered. Bessy, too, had 'failed, with irregular pulse', though he hoped she had now got over it, 'only having one attack these nine months. What a strange form of inherited constitution this is – my accursed constitution showing itself in a new form.' Christmas 1857 was not a comfortable time. 'My wife', Charles wrote to Hooker on 15 January 1858, 'often ails and Lenny has very frequent bad days with badly intermittent pulse – we escaped a considerable anxiety in George having apparently a regular low fever but it died away and only spoilt a fortnight of the holidays. Oh health, health you are my daily and nightly bugbear and stops all enjoyment in life. Etty keeps very weak.' Charles's mood was not improved by a house full of visitors. Caroline and Joe were there with their children when he wrote this letter. At least Caroline was more understanding than his two other sisters, who as spinsters found the noise and worry of children disturbing. Charles found any visitors distracting at the best of times, but, as he often said, they worried him more 'when there was sickness in the house'.

Once the enlargement of the house was complete, Emma and Charles decided to get rid of some of their Wedgwood possessions in order to buy new watercolours for the drawing room. Neither of them had ever taken an interest in their grandfather's pottery. They had allowed the children to play with beautiful cameos – and 'drat them', Charles cheerfully told Hooker, they were all lost or destroyed. Hooker, who collected Wedgwood, was horrified, but Charles was equally astonished that the great botanist should be interested in dead pots. Unmoved, in February 1858 he asked Harry, Emma's brother, to take his copy of the Barberini Vase to London to be valued. This was one of two owned by Charles, possibly left to them by Emma's father. It was sold for £75 on 3 April 1858. The other, which came from Charles's father was later given to the Museum of Practical

Geology, whose curator, Trenham Reeks, had advised Harry on the sale of the first one. Encouraged by this sale, Charles asked Reeks's advice on some '30 slabs of slate with figures in wax. A knowing clergyman', wrote Charles lightly, 'said they were executed by some "celebrated artist" whose name I have forgotten.' They were probably reliefs by the sculptor John Flaxman, used to decorate Wedgwood jasper ware – some of them exquisite, according to Hooker, who was appalled at his friend's philistinism.

Emma's interest had always been in music rather than the visual arts, and though she had dutifully done the rounds of the art galleries on her Grand Tour, and enjoyed many of the paintings she had seen, her patience was limited and her criticisms trenchant. Looking at paintings in London, she once said, was 'horrid staring work', and she was said to have declared that she could see any church in an hour; but she loved Charlotte's watercolours, and looked forward to spending the Wedgwood money on new works to adorn the drawing room. As for interior decoration, perhaps, as Charles and Emma had themselves feared at the time, her taste in furnishings had been spoiled for ever by the gaudy 'Macaw Cottage'; certainly when she came back from a trip to London with patterns for the new drawing-room wallpaper, the family cried out in horror. 'Mamma went up yesterday and brought down two such patterns of the exact colour of mud, streaked with rancid oil,' Charles wrote to William, 'that we have all exclaimed against them, and I have agreed to take anything in preference and we have settled on a crimson flock-paper with golden stars, though unseen by me.'

The spring and early summer of 1858 were once more glorious; but in the Darwins' private world at Down the shadows were gathering, and in the wider world the horrific news of the Indian Mutiny did nothing to lift the spirits. Even the huge comet that swept 'half across the sky', according to Aunt Fanny, would have presaged doom had they held to the old superstitions. One after another of the children was ill, and Emma for once found it difficult to shake off her own migraine and lassitude. Moor Park was their favourite refuge, and in April Charles wrote from there encouraging her to take a fortnight's hydrotherapy. 'Do you not think it might do you real good? I could get on perfectly with the children. You might bring Etty with you. Think of this my dearest wife. I wish you knew how I value you, and what an inexpressible blessing it is to have one whom one can always trust, one always the same, always ready to give comfort, sympathy and best advice. God bless you my dear, you are too good for me.'

Charles, relaxed there, loitered 'for hours in the Park' and amused himself by watching the ants: 'I have great hopes I have found the rare slave-making species, and have sent a specimen to the British Museum.' He found Dr Lane a most sympathetic young man, and had great confidence in him. In the April tranquillity of Surrey Charles revived, and in the 'delicious' weather he wrote happily to Emma, 'Yesterday I strolled a little beyond the glade for an hour and a half. At last I fell fast asleep on the grass, and woke with a chorus of birds singing around me, and squirrels running up the trees and some woodpeckers laughing, and it was as pleasant and rural a scene as ever I saw, and I did not care one penny how any of the birds had been formed.'

He returned home to his interminable work, trying now to make it less 'tough and obscure'. At Down, too, he watched their little backward baby with his careful scientist's eye, just as he had watched the slave-making ants. Charles Waring was now a year and a half old; as Charles later wrote,

> he was small for his age and backward in walking and talking, but intelligent and observant. When crawling naked on the floor he looked very elegant. He had never been ill, and cried less than any of our babies. He was of a remarkably sweet, placid and joyful disposition; but had not high spirits, and did not laugh much. He often made strange grimaces and shivered, when excited; but did so, also, for a joke and his little eyes used to glisten, after pouting out or stretching widely his little lips. He used sometimes to move his mouth as if talking loudly, but making no noise, and this he did when very happy.

Though a punctilious observer, Charles was far from cold or detached; both he and Emma felt real affection for the baby and played with him as they had with their other children.

He was particularly fond of standing on one of my hands, and being tossed in the air: and then he always smiled and made a little pleased noise. I had just taught him to kiss me with open mouth, when I told him. He would lie for a long time placidly on my lap looking with a steady and pleased expression at my face; sometimes trying to poke his poor little fingers into my mouth, or making nice little bubbling noises as I moved his chin. I had taught him not to scratch, but when I said 'Giddlums never scratches now' he could not always resist a little grab, and then he would look at me with a wicked little smile. He would play for any length of time on the sofa, letting himself fall suddenly, and looking over his shoulder to see that I was ready.

Not many Victorian fathers would have played with a backward baby with such love and tenderness; and, like other parents of Down's syndrome babies, Charles saw intelligence there and that it could be encouraged. Their servants, too, were patient and kind with the affectionate little baby. 'He had a passion for Parslow; and it was very pretty to see his extreme eagerness, with outstretched arms, to get to him.' But the loving parents both worried about their son's future.

Gradually, through the month of May, Emma regained her spirits. Charles delighted to see her 'just starting with the three little boys [for Bromley] as jolly as little dogs'. It was just as well, for she would need all her new resilience for the days ahead.

As so often, Etty was their chief concern, and worry about her made Charles ill again. He had reported Etty's 'bad sore throat' to Hooker, fearing that it was quinsy. In fact, it was a newly identified disease, diphtheria, 'a most suffering illness with dreadful inflammation of the whole throat – there was no actual choking, but immense discharge and much pain and inability to speak or swallow and a very weak and rapid pulse with a fearful tongue.' In the hot bright June Charles wrote miserably to his friend Roderick Murchison that he was confined to his sofa with a boil and that he had 'one child ill with diphtheria and another sickening'.

Then a new horror compounded the anxiety: an epidemic of scarlet fever had broken out in Downe village. 'What has frightened us so much', he later told Lyell, 'is that three children have died in the village from scarlet fever and others have been at death's door with terrible suffering.' On 18 June, Etty had diphtheria, Lenny and Horace were delicate, and now the baby was feverish: Charles and Emma were terrified that scarlet fever had reached Down House.

In the midst of this family distress a bolt from the Far East struck – the famous letter from Darwin's fellow scientist Alfred Russel Wallace. This time the package from the Spice Islands contained not the birds' skins or specimens that Wallace had sent before, but a twenty-page abstract of Wallace's own theory of natural selection – remarkably similar to Charles's own. Numbed, he wrote immediately to Lyell:

> Some year or so ago, you recommended me to read a paper by Wallace in the Annals, which had interested you and as I was writing to him, I knew this would please him much, so I told him. He has to day sent me the enclosed and asked me to forward it to you. It seems to me well worth reading. Your words have come true with a vengeance that I should be forestalled. You said this when I explained to you here very briefly my views of 'Natural Selection' depending on the struggle for existence. I never saw a more striking coincidence. If Wallace had my M.S. sketch written out in 1842 he could not have made a better short abstract!

'All my originality, whatever it may amount to, will be smashed,' Charles wrote, and the word exactly expressed his feelings: his world was shattered. Generously, as he told Lyell, he would offer to send Wallace's manuscript 'to any journal'. He consoled himself that 'my book . . . will not be deteriorated as all the labour consists in the application of the theory.'

But he had no time to dwell on his desperate disappointment. The baby's high fever did indeed mark the onset of scarlet fever, and Emma needed his support. She and the young nurse cared for him devotedly, and on 26 June they were still hoping he would survive; but after three days the struggle was over. Charles had watched him through the last agony and the next day wrote brokenly to Hooker.

You will, and so will Mrs Hooker, be most sorry for us when you hear that poor Baby died yesterday evening. I hope to God he did not suffer so much as he appeared. He became quite suddenly worse. It was Scarlet-Fever. It was the most blessed relief to see his poor little innocent face resume its sweet expression in the sleep of death. Thank God he will never suffer more in this world . . . Poor Emma behaved nobly and how she stood it all I cannot conceive. It was wonderful relief, when she could let her feelings break forth, God Bless you. You shall hear soon as I can think.

Charles could scarcely bring himself to think about his work, or Wallace; but he was determined to act honourably and not stand in the way of the publication of his rival's abstract. Lyell and Hooker now took charge. They knew the 1844 essay had summarized Charles's theories; if it was published as a paper now, with Wallace's abstract, it would be clear that Charles had reached his conclusions earlier and independently. Accordingly they arranged that the two papers should be read together at the Linnean Society's rooms in Piccadilly. Charles agreed – though he could scarcely bear to look at the paper. He need not have worried. When the two papers were read on 1 July no one in the audience, except Hooker and Lyell, appeared to see the significance of them. 'This year has not been marked by any of those striking discoveries which . . . revolutionize . . . [our] department of science,' remarked the President later. Charles was not there; he was attending the funeral of his youngest son in the churchyard at Downe.

For a while he and Emma were desperately concerned to protect their other children during the scarlet fever epidemic. Emma's devoted sister Elizabeth had rushed to her side as soon as the disease was diagnosed, and took Bessy and the younger boys to her home at Hartfield, near Ashdown Forest. Emma and Charles stayed at Down to take care of Etty, who still had not completely recovered. Having sent the children away, Charles told Hooker, 'We are more happy and less panic struck.' But they still had their household staff to worry about: their first nurse had an ulcerated throat and quinsy and left, and the second caught scarlet fever; it was not until 6 July that Charles could report her crisis was over. At the same time they 'had a fear' about their governess, Miss Pugh, 'but she is out of the house and we are getting less frightened and in every way, more composed.' Miss Pugh, who had succeeded Miss Thorley in April 1857, was said to have been of a melancholic disposition, and this crisis appears to have been the last straw. Emma's diary briefly records for 4 July: 'Miss Pugh went.' She came back, however, and stayed until January 1859.

The last years had been a great strain for Emma. She had been ill during much of her last pregnancy, the birth had been difficult and dangerous for a woman of forty-eight, and throughout Charles Waring's brief life she had been often ill and worried about him, as well as Etty. Her love for her last child is clearly shown in the photograph William took of her as she tenderly bent over the little drooping head. She still had severe attacks of migraine, and there had been so many disturbed nights during the last years when Charles in his pain had needed her comfort. She worried constantly about him, too, knowing how stress always affected his health. Charles, at least, had the refuge of his work: within a few days of the baby's death he was writing to his American friend Asa Gray, describing in meticulous detail bees sucking honey from the flowers of *Dicentra*. Emma had no such relief.

They all needed a holiday, and considered going to the Isle of Wight, where William Fox lived. Charles asked his advice:

> I have been much knocked up and so has my poor dear wife but we are now much better. Etty is too weak to move yet: she has not even put on her clothes, but our Dr is strong for her moving as soon as ever she can. We go first to Elizabeth Wedgwoods and thence to the sea, but there is our puzzle. We should much like S. side of the Isle of Wight; but it is indispensable on account of Etty that the House should be very near the sea, and I fear such does not occur on account of cliffs. Should you know anything on this head, will you let me have a line.

In July, Charles, Emma and Etty joined the family at Hartfield, and Charles found relief in idly observing slave-making ants migrating, and watching the pistil of the larkspur bending to direct the bee to the line of the honey. But once again his meticulous observations of the world of insects and plants led him to deeper and disturbing conclusions. It was during this holiday at Hartfield that he watched, fascinated, the carnivorous sundew opening to catch the fly, closing over it and destroying it. Emma understood him and saw where such observations would lead. 'Charles', she wrote, 'is trying to prove that *Drosera* [sundew] is an animal.'

The serenity of Elizabeth's home revived Charles and he could once more face his 'abominable volume' which, he would later say, 'cost me so much labour that I almost hate it'. The threat of being forestalled now spurred him back to work, and at the King's Head Hotel at Sandown on the Isle of Wight he began what he called 'an abstract of natural selection'. Here, in sight of the sea she loved, Emma could at last relax; and they returned to Down House on 13 August both much improved in health. Charles was writing furiously, realizing now that this would be more than an abstract: this would be his 'big book', though, as if to pre-empt criticism, he continued to call it 'an abstract' or 'my rag of a book'. Through the autumn he laboured on, sending chapters to Hooker and Lyell for their criticism, aiming to finish in the spring.

The weeks in the sea air had revived Emma. Though she had been upset at the baby's death, there had also been considerable relief. She had consoled herself after the deaths of her sister and Annie with the thought that now they were spared possible future pain; for Charles Waring, whose future had looked painfully bleak, this was an even greater consolation. Emma had spent several years as a young woman caring for her mother through her mental breakdown: she knew what would lie ahead with a mentally handicapped child.

In October she enjoyed her new freedom, delighted when Charles bought a second horse so that she could take jaunts with the little boys. Like her mother, Emma had always enjoyed expeditions with the pony and trap. 'Mamma has got much more larky since we ran two horses,' Charles told William, now at Christ's College, Cambridge. During the winter and spring he too sought relief from 'the horrid species' by slipping away to the quiet of Moor Park, or by playing a daily game of billiards on the new table he had set up next to his study. He took as much pleasure in potting the balls as he had in potting the pheasants with his gun in the old days.

During this period he was often dragged away from the study of animal behaviour to solve the problems of human behaviour. On 26 January

1859 the melancholic Miss Pugh resigned in order to take up another employment, and they needed a new governess. Bessy was now twelve, not very bright and a little difficult. Etty was sixteen, highly intelligent and, like Emma, possessed of very definite opinions; she and Miss Thorley had often crossed swords. Etty had been exceptionally well educated by her own parents. Emma had always supplemented the governesses' tuition with her own wide knowledge of history, politics and literature; she had read with her daughter good novels and letters, and had given her French lessons herself. In the winter of 1858 Emma had been looking for a Swiss girl who would come 'for six months or so to set you all taking French and German'. In the event she appointed a German, Mrs Grut. Temperamental and obviously unsure of herself, Mrs Grut often had arguments with Miss Know-All Etty. Emma herself found her new employee 'volatile and insolent'. In March Charles was brought in to sort out a blazing row. Etty described the event to William with obvious relish.

Solemn events have happened. Mrs Grut is gone for ever. This is how it came about. On Monday at breakfast Mama said very civilly that she wanted some alteration in Horace's lessons. Mrs Grut was evidently miffed at that, and then I said I thought s'eloigner wasn't 'to ramble' very mildly and that miffed her again and she made some rude speech or other. 'Oh very well if I knew better than the dictionary' . . . Nothing more came of it then, and all went smooth till I went up to my German lesson in the evening. When I came in I saw there was the devil in her face, well she scolded the children a bit and then sat down by me, when I showed her my lesson (a bit of very bad french) she said, if I knew better than she did it was no use her teaching me and so and so on, till it came to a crisis, and she worked herself into a regular rage . . . I left the room then, and went down stairs to tell my injuries. When Papa and Mama heard all about it they settled she should go at once, so Papa wrote a letter telling her she would have her 33£ and nothing more, . . . then Papa was to go upstairs and deliver the letter . . . Papa got *such* a torrent, telling him he was no gentleman, and white with passion all the time, wanting to know what she had done, what he had to accuse her of – telling him he

The Mount, Shrewsbury, the home of Charles' parents. It was impeccably run and immaculate in contrast to Down House

Watercolour of Down House, Kent, where the Darwins lived until Emma's death

Emma, relaxed at the open window at Down House reading aloud to the family in typical Wedgwood-Allen fashion. Bessy is seated and Etty is standing with the sunshade

Some of the Darwin children...

Francis (Frank)

William

George

Annie in 1849,
two years before her death

Charles Darwin with William in 1842. At this period little boys wore feminine dresses until they were four or even later

Etty with her dog at the open window at Down

Etty, Frank, Leonard, Horace and Bessy (Elizabeth) at a lovely house at Caerdeon, near Barmouth, in North Wales which Emma and Charles and the family rented for some months in the summer of 1869

Emma with Leonard

Edna Healey (right) with Randal Keynes, biographer and great-great-grandson of Charles and Emma and Sarah Darwin, also a Darwin descendant, who laid a bunch of jonquils at Annie's grave in Malvern after a memorial service to mark the 150th anniversary of her death

Brantwood, Ruskin's house on Coniston Water to which Charles and Emma were rowed from their hotel opposite

The garden at Down House seen from the veranda. Emma planned and planted these flowerbeds

Wells House in Ilkley, Yorkshire, to which Charles came in the autumn of 1859 for hydropathic treatment while waiting for the publication of *Origin of Species*. Because he was ill and miserable, Emma came up and rented Wells Terrace (below) where he stayed with her and the family until after publication day when he returned to Wells House

Charles and Emma's uncle, Tom Wedgwood, who is credited with discovering photography, although he never found the technique for fixing the negatives

A cameo made by Wedgwood in 1787 in black jasper on a white ground from the seal of the Society for the Abolition of Slavery. Wedgwood distributed it free to supporters

John Wedgwood bought Cote House, a magnificent mansion near Bristol, after the death of his father, Josiah Wedgwood I. In the glasshouses he grew exotic fruits and there became inspired to found the Royal Horticultural Society

Etty (Henrietta) – at this time Mrs Richard Litchfield – reading to Professor Richard Keynes, FRS, then aged three, in the garden of Etty's house at Gomshall

Ursula Mommens, aged ninety-three, still a skilled and successful working potter. The daughter of Bernard Darwin, she is the great granddaughter of Charles and Emma, but also the great-great-great-granddaughter of Josiah Wedgwood I

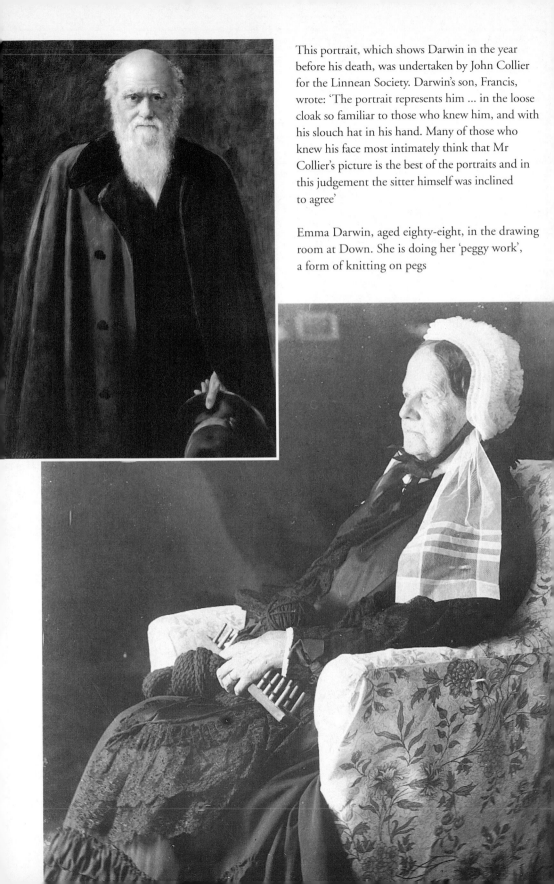

This portrait, which shows Darwin in the year before his death, was undertaken by John Collier for the Linnean Society. Darwin's son, Francis, wrote: 'The portrait represents him ... in the loose cloak so familiar to those who knew him, and with his slouch hat in his hand. Many of those who knew his face most intimately think that Mr Collier's picture is the best of the portraits and in this judgement the sitter himself was inclined to agree'

Emma Darwin, aged eighty-eight, in the drawing room at Down. She is doing her 'peggy work', a form of knitting on pegs was in a passion – she would give him time to think . . . We had a very flustered tea, and all evening we sat preparing for the worst, what we should do if she refused to go out of the house etc. However she did turn out much milder and sent us a letter to say she would go on Wednesday.

Charles did not often lose his temper, and it is more than likely that he watched Mrs Grut's face with a scientist's detachment, observing the effects of rage on muscles and skin, and filing them away for his later book *Expressions of the Emotions of Men and Animals.*

For now, his main preoccupation was with the book about to go to press – and in March 1859, when it was almost ready, Charles was once more reminded that children could be 'the greatest worry'. This time it was not his own. He had sent the loyal Hooker another bundle of manuscript for his criticisms. Hooker told Huxley:

> By some screaming accident the whole bundle, which weighed over 1lb when it came . . . got transferred to a drawer where my wife keeps paper for the children to draw upon and they have of course had a drawing fit ever since – I feel brutified if not brutalized for poor D is so bad that he could hardly get steam up to finish what he did – How I wish he could stamp and fume at me – instead of taking it so good naturedly as he will.

Fortunately Charles had another copy.

Finally, in April, after ruthlessly wielding the knife and reducing the manuscript to 155,000 words, Charles declared the book finished. By this time he was so shattered by the labour that he was incapable of organizing its publication; that was left to Lyell to arrange with John Murray, who bravely agreed to print 500 copies, without even having seen the manuscript. He planned to publish *On the Origin of Species* in November. (Charles had wanted to call it 'An Abstract of an Essay on the Origin of Species and Varieties Through Natural Selection'; Murray persuaded him to shorten the title.) After another week at Moor Park, Charles was able to face proofreading, with Emma's help, making so many changes that he offered to stand the expense himself. It was probably Emma who advised him also to have the proofs sent to her friend Georgina Tollet at Betley Hall, near Maer. She was a novelist and could be relied upon to check Charles's style and correct his notoriously bad spelling.

Knowing what a furore the book would create, Charles had deliberately not included theories about the origin of man, thinking that would be moving too fast and would frighten off the half-converted. But Huxley, who delighted in conflict, was already raising the temperature of the debate and introducing the idea of evolution of man from ape. Charles once more was crippled by attacks of vomiting and giddiness: he could not face the battle, and looked for a place to hide away. Malvern, with its painful memories, was out of the question, and Moor Park was too near. He asked William to look out for a place in the Lake District, but finally chose a new hydrotherapy establishment in Yorkshire, on the edge of the moors at Ilkley. Emma knew the area; she had had a very pleasant excursion with her mother and sisters to Wharfedale and Bolton Abbey and the moors around Ilkley in 1827. Charles set off on 2 October, planning to stay at Ilkley for two months, and hoped to be hidden there when his book was published. The first weeks were miserable. To Hooker, Charles allowed himself a long wail. 'I have been very bad lately; having had an awful "crisis", one leg swelled with elephantiasis – eyes almost closed up – covered with a rash and fiery boils: but they tell me it will surely do me much good – it was like living in Hell.' In his letter to William at Cambridge, however, he made the best of it.

> The House is at the foot of a rocky, turfy rather steep half mountain. It would be nice with fine weather; but now looks dismal. There are nice excursions and fine walks for those that can walk. The Water Cure has done me much good; but I fell down on Sunday morning and sprained my ancle, and have not been able to walk since and this has greatly interfered with the treatment.
>
> It is a curious life here: we sit down 60 or 70 to our meals, and in the evening there is either singing, or acting (which they do capitally) or proverbs & c. I have got amongst a nice set, and get on very comfortably and idly. The newspaper, a little novel-reading and Baths and loitering kills the day in a very wholesome

manner. Did you ever hear of the American game of Billiards
. . . there are some splendid players here who often make breaks
of 20, 30 and 40. These good players never play anything but
the American game. I shall miss the Billiard Table when I leave
here.

Emma must have heard of these letters and shuddered. The physical
tortures were bad enough, but for Charles to suffer meals 'with 60 or 70'
and jolly evenings with games! She hastened up, with the family, to a
rented house near by where she could be with him and protect him. Wells
Terrace was a large, comfortable house, facing south-west, with a wide
view of the moors – but they all hated it. The moors were bleak, the stone
walls hard and grey, the wind wuthering. Still, Emma was there to share
his delight when the first copy of the clothbound book came in its smart
green cover. 'Infinitely pleased and proud at the appearance of my child,'
Charles happily told John Murray. The child that had been gestating for
more than twenty years had made a successful entrance. *On the Origin of*
Species went on sale to the trade on 22 November, and was launched on
24 November. It was an immediate success, the first printing selling out
before publication. John Murray wanted an immediate reprint of 3,000
copies with corrections. Emma was delighted, and wrote to William: 'It is
a wonderful thing the whole edition selling off at once and Mudie taking
300 copies. Your father says he shall never think small beer of himself
again and that candidly he does think it well written.'

Now Charles could face the treatment at Wells House again – and
Emma sent him back for two weeks with an easy heart, while on 24
November she returned to Down.

CHAPTER THIRTEEN

Into the Limelight

THE SUSPENSE WAS OVER. THE CLOUDS HAVING LIFTED, IN HIS LAST TEN days at the hydro Charles responded well to the treatment and could return to Down ready to work on the reprint.

The reactions to his book had been more favourable than he had dared to hope for, most of all from his family. Emma had read the book carefully in proof, and had made some corrections and comments – for example, she had criticized his suggestion that the eye could have evolved as too bold a hypothesis; but he had deliberately not dealt with the origin of man, where he knew she would disagree with him. She would probably have agreed with Lyell, who wrote that he 'never could accept that man could have descended from an ape-like progenitor!' Charles had not explicitly discussed the link between man and ape because he had not wanted to push the argument too far too fast, but he had made it clear that he believed in a continual evolution, stating briefly that 'all organic forms had probably descended from one primordial form into which life was first breathed.' Most of all Emma would have been glad that Charles had not publicly rejected the idea of a Creator. She would have welcomed the enthusiastic letter from the Revd Charles Kingsley: 'It is just as noble a conception of the Deity to believe that he created primal forms capable of self-development into all forms *pro tempere* and *pro loco*, as to believe that he required a fresh act of intervention to provide the lacunas which he himself had made.' This letter, Charles considered, was important enough to be included in the second edition. (Kingsley wrote a fable which he sent to Huxley, in which two priests argued as to which of their

Gods was the most powerful. The winner was the one whose God encouraged man to make himself anew.)

Erasmus's reaction was not only favourable – as Charles expected – but uncharacteristically enthusiastic. 'I really think it is the most interesting book I ever read and can only compare to the first knowledge of chemistry getting into a new world or behind the scenes.' Charles would have appreciated the comparison, remembering their youthful excitement in their chemistry laboratory in the toolhouse in the Shrewsbury garden. Harriet Martineau trumpeted to Erasmus her praise for 'the quality and conduct of your brother's mind ... its earnestness and simplicity, its sagacity, its industry and the patient power by w^h it has collected such a mass of facts, to transmute them by such sagacious treatment into such portentious knowledge.' But what surprised and gratified him most was Caroline's enthusiasm. He waited apprehensively for her rebukes, as he had done as a little boy in the past – but none came. Taken aback, he wrote to her, 'I was astounded that you seem to care as much for my book as you seemed to do.' Perhaps he had not realized how much Caroline had been influenced by their mother's Unitarian faith. Sukey had taken her as a child to the Shrewsbury chapel and brought her up with a tolerance of new ideas and a readiness to look critically at the old ones.

There were, of course, critical letters; some were discounted, some expected. Their Wedgwood relation Dr Holland had been critical of Charles's work on *The Voyage of the Beagle*, which had annoyed Emma. Now they dismissed him: 'He knows nothing,' wrote Charles. More troubling was the reaction of his 'dear old master', Adam Sedgwick, who wrote more in sorrow than anger. He had read the book 'with more pain than pleasure', but sent his letter 'in a spirit of brotherly love'. Charles had 'fully expected' his disapproval, but assured him that he had 'worked like a slave on the subject for twenty years'; and though it grieved him 'to shock a man whom I sincerely honour', he had worked according to his 'best ability'. He concluded, 'Your kind and noble heart shows itself throughout your letter.' Emma must have approved his comment: 'There is a moral ... part of nature as well as physical.'

Henslow, like others of the older generation, found it difficult to accept the new ideas, but thought the work a 'stumble in the right direction'. By contrast, the young Turks, led by Huxley, were delighted and sharpened their swords for the fray which they saw as inevitable. 'No work on natural history science I have met with', wrote Huxley, 'has made so great an impression on me . . . you have earned the gratitude of all thoughtful men.' Friedrich Engels read the *Origin* as soon as it came out and enthusiastically wrote to Karl Marx: 'Never before has so grandiose an attempt been made to demonstrate historical evolution in Nature, and certainly never to such good effect. One does, of course, have to put up with the crude English method.' Marx, reading the *Origin* a year later, was so impressed that when in 1873 the second edition of *Das Kapital* was published, he sent Charles an autographed copy. Charles thanked him, but the pages remained uncut.

At the end of the year Charles could write to Lyell, 'I never even built a castle-in-the-air of such success as it has met with; I do not mean the sale but the impression it has made on you (whom I have always looked on as chief judge) and Hooker and Huxley. The whole has infinitely exceeded my wildest hopes.' But it was the wholehearted approval of his closest friend that he valued most. *Origin* was simply, wrote Hooker, 'your glorious book'.

Back at Down, the euphoria began to fade as the temperature of the debate rose. Huxley was charging ahead, deliberately inviting conflict, determinedly linking ape and man. A stinging review of *Origin* in the *Athenaeum* was countered by an enthusiastic one in *The Times* – written by Huxley himself. Spite and jealousy now coloured comment. Charles told Lyell that the zoologist Richard Owen, 'under garb of great civility was inclined to be most bitter and sneering against me'. He had criticized an extraordinary passage Charles had written about the North American bear swimming open-mouthed to feed on insects. 'I can see no difficulty in a race of bears being rendered, by natural selection, more and more aquatic in their structure and habits, with larger and larger mouths, till a creature was produced as monstrous as a whale.' Emma had copied this sentence out and she may have suggested that it should be omitted on the grounds that it would seem so preposterous to the ordinary reader that it might invalidate the rest of the book. Charles, thanking Owen for his criticism, told him he had struck the passage out (though it remained in the American edition).

'Oh, have you,' replied Owen, 'well I was more struck with this than any other passage; you little know of the remarkable and essential relationship between bears and whales.'

It is difficult for the modern reader to understand fully the uproar that Charles's theories caused at the time. Most Christian believers accepted in blind faith the literal truth of Genesis: at the Creation, God made each species distinct and immutable; two by two, the animals marched into the Ark, and centuries later were still unchanged. The idea that species would evolve led to the uncomfortable conclusion that man was an animal improved, not uniquely made in the image of God. Even more alarming was the notion that evolution was caused by 'natural' selection. If it were so, blind chance, not God, ruled the world. 'We are apes of a cold God,' Karl Marx wrote. Charles had been careful to omit human origins from his detailed speculations; but he had not wished to appear cowardly, and at the end of the book wrote a passage implying that man was descended from the animal world.

For simple churchgoers in 1859 these ideas were as earth-shaking as the earlier theories of Copernicus and Galileo, as a result of which the Earth lost its place as the centre of the universe. Now, it was being claimed, man was no longer the unique work of God. It was not that Charles's ideas were new: in the free-thinking eighteenth century, other scientists had questioned the truth of the Bible, and at the beginning of the *Origin of Species* Charles listed his predecessors. Even his own grandfather, Erasmus Darwin, had suggested in *The Temple of Nature* that:

> Organic life beneath the shoreless waves
> Was born, and nurs'd in ocean's pearly caves,
> First forms minute, unseen by spheric glass
> Move on the mud, or pierce the watery mass;
> These, as successive generations bloom,
> New powers acquire, and larger limbs assume;
> Whence countless groups of vegetations spring,
> And breathing realms of fin, and feet, and wing.

These sentiments had shocked the churchgoers of the 1800s; but half a century later, though many of the devout were hard to persuade, the intellectual climate was receptive to such ideas. Scientists and mathematicians were already casting doubt on the 'truths' of the Old Testament. Improved microscopes and telescopes were transforming what had originally been called 'natural philosophy' into a science, based on careful observation. Even the new railways helped, for as cuttings were dug they revealed the Earth's different strata, encouraging a positive mania for geology and much speculation about the antiquity of the Earth and the time-scale for the appearance of man.

Even so, the *Origin of Species* was accepted only with difficulty, for it shattered accepted patterns of thought. So the battle raged through the spring of 1860; and Charles, worn down once more under the stress, withdrew again to Dr Lane at his new hydropathic establishment in Sudbrook Park, Richmond. Here he sheltered during the famous confrontation at the Oxford meeting of the British Association for the Advancement of Science on 30 June 1860, when his champion, Huxley, routed Bishop Samuel Wilberforce (nicknamed 'Soapy Sam' on account of his unctuous manner). In the shelter of Sudbrook Park, Charles read Hooker's letter describing the Oxford battle, and was glad he had not been there.

> The meeting was so large that they had adjourned to the Library which was crammed with between 700 and 1000 people, for all the world was there to hear Sam Oxon. Well Sam Oxon got up & spouted for half an hour with inimitable spirit[,] uglyness & emptyness & unfairness, I saw he was coached up by Owen & knew nothing & he said not a syllable but what was in the Review [Wilberforce's *Quarterly Review* diatribe on the *Origin*, just out] – he ridiculed you badly & Huxley savagely.

During the debate Wilberforce flippantly asked Huxley whether it was on his grandfather's or grandmother's side that he was descended from an ape. Huxley's fierce reply shamed the bishop,

> If the question was put to me would I rather have a miserable ape for a grandfather or a man highly endowed by nature and possessed of great means & influence & yet who employs these faculties & that influence for the mere purpose of introducing ridicule into a grave scientific discussion I unhesitatingly affirm my preference for the ape.

But it was the gentle Hooker, who had come in to the meeting by chance, who was now so incensed that

> my blood boiled, I felt myself a dastard; now I saw my advantage
> – I swore to myself I would smite that Amalekite Sam hip &
> thigh if my heart jumped out of my mouth & I handed my name
> up to the President (Henslow) as ready to throw down the
> gauntlet. I must tell you that Henslow as president would have
> none speak but those who had *arguments* to use, & 4 persons had
> been burked [silenced] by the audience & President for mere
> declamation: it moreover became necessary for each speaker to
> mount the platform & so there I was cocked up with Sam at my
> right elbow, & there & then I smacked him amid rounds of
> applause – I hit him in the wind at the first shot in 10 words
> taken from his own ugly mouth – & then proceeded to demon-
> strate in as few more 1 that he could never have read your book &
> 2 that he was absolutely ignorant of the rudiments of Bot[anical]
> Science. I said a few more on the subject of my own experience,
> & conversion, & wound up with a very few observations on the
> relative positions of the old & new hypotheses, & with some
> words of caution to the audience Sam was shut up – had not one
> word to say in reply & the *meeting was dissolved forthwith* leaving
> you master of the field after 4 hours battle.

Charles was infinitely relieved to have such doughty generals on the battlefield, but shuddered at the thought of lifting the sword himself. Now, however, he was well and truly caught in the fierce white light of fame, from which for the rest of his life he would try to hide.

In the summer of 1860 Etty became ill again, so at the end of September Emma rented a pleasant, three-storey house on the seafront at Eastbourne, one of a group called 'Seahouses'. From its bow window Emma could look over the Channel and sigh for the France that she would never visit again – though she never gave up hope. Eastbourne was a clean, quiet, growing resort, and Emma enjoyed taking the younger children on expeditions along the coast to the famous white cliffs, the Seven Sisters, or over the rolling Downs to the 'blue goodness of the Weald'.

Here Charles continued to work, firing off almost daily letters to friends and fellow scientists, wondering whether it was true that cats with blue eyes were deaf, and discussing the origin of the dog in connection with the origin of man. He was already rethinking the terminology of the *Origin*, and wrote to Lyell regretting his use of the term 'natural selection'; he would now prefer to call the process 'natural preservation', for 'selection' suggested a selector. And he was still obsessively studying *Drosera*, the carnivorous sundew, observing the red fluid it secreted, noting its antiseptic effect on meat. Emma remarked once again with amusement that *Drosera* was becoming an animal.

Eastbourne's clean sea air failed to cure Etty, and they were still at Seahouses on 2 November when Charles wrote in panic that their daughter was 'at point of death'. She did recover, but it was not until 10 November that they were back at Down.

The strain of the past years was now telling on Emma; but she continued to provide solace to others. At Hartfield, she said, they had had 'the bad luck to fall in with a desponding doctor', and only her natural optimism saved her from acute depression. The visit of Mrs Huxley and her children to Down in March 1861 could not have raised her spirits. The Huxleys were still stricken after the loss of their three-year-old son, and their grief must have opened her own barely healed wounds. After Emma's death Mrs Huxley wrote to Etty, remembering how kind she had been at this time.

> In early days of our acquaintance, just after we had lost our boy, she begged me to come to her and bring the three children and nurse, and that we should have the old nurseries at Down. I first wrote that I was too weak and ill to be out of my home, that I could not get downstairs until 1 o'clock. Her reply was that was the usual state of the family at Down and I should just be following suit. More than any woman I ever knew, she comforted.

In the early 1860s Emma realised how important it was to get Charles away from the close work at his microscope, and she too needed to restore her health. Visits to the seaside always renewed her and the doctors recommended sea air for the delicate Etty. Knowing that Charles always needed seclusion but that she herself wanted the support and company of the family, she rented houses during the summers large enough to take them all, with Erasmus, Fanny and Hensleigh and their children, cook and maids and manservants. As Etty and the boys grew older, they were sometimes sent to reconnoitre.

In the summer of 1861, she took a house in Torquay for two months. The town was full of interesting men and women at the time, but Charles met few of the scientists there, nor did he go into society. Emma and the children always remembered the holiday with delight. Torquay, once a little fishing village, had grown in recent years into a fashionable health resort where the dazzling white houses and elegant architecture recalled Bath, though here the air was fresher and the life simpler. The air itself was said to have curative properties, each level up the hills suitable for different patients. They took a house in Hesketh Crescent – a replica of the Royal Crescent at Bath. Below them the blue sea beat on the rugged cliffs; behind them were the welcome spaces of bare hills and wide open skies. Charles was happy here and better in health, working quietly on the book he was writing on orchids, and Emma relaxed in the bright air, enjoying a much-needed rest. A stormy sea reminded her of her childhood in Tenby.

There was much to interest Charles here if he wished to venture out into the town. There was an excellent little museum where lectures were given by a brilliant geologist, William Pengelly, a friend of Babbage and a man, one would have thought, after Charles's own heart. He had once held a gang of road menders enthralled as he explained to them the history of the fossils among their broken stones and encouraged them to visit his own famous collection of fossils in the museum. Pengelly sent Charles a report of an intelligent dog that could open doors; Charles replied that nothing concerning the intelligence of dogs would surprise him. Many years later, Charles remembered meeting him and contributed to a memorial raised for him.

Many other scientists and geologists were in Torquay, drawn to the area by the excavations at Wookey Hole in Somerset which provided evidence of the antiquity of the world. Later there were to be other distinguished visitors, including Queen Sophia of the Netherlands, the Empress of Russia and Louis Napoleon. In 1861 the great philanthropist Angela Burdett-Coutts had just left No. 1 Hesketh Crescent and leased Ehrenberg Hall, where she wintered for many years. If she was in residence at the time she certainly would have invited the Darwins to her interesting dinners, for there were family links: Dr Erasmus Darwin had been her grandfather's family doctor in Derbyshire, and had treated her aunt and mother; and Emma certainly knew her father, the radical MP Sir Francis Burdett. Miss Burdett-Coutts was greatly interested in the new scientific developments. But Charles, always reluctant to be winkled out of his study, agreed to accompany the family on holidays on condition that he was not expected to go into society. So although there was much in Torquay that might have interested him, he preferred to lead a quiet life with Emma and the family. Whether or not Charles and Emma made anything of the social opportunities the town offered, nevertheless, the local scientists were delighted to have him in Torquay. 'The great Darwin is here,' Pengelly reported.

Hesketh Crescent was a little out of the centre, and this no doubt helped Charles to lead the quiet, retired life he sought. In the calm of Torquay he made progress with his orchid book, although it was not published until 15 May 1862. Methodical as always, he counted the days of labour: 'This book has cost me nine months if I do not count Torquay.' With his usual self-deprecation he had written to William in February that it had been a pleasure to write 'but whether worth writing I know not more than the man in the moon'. In fact, it linked into his major work, since it showed how nearly all the parts of the orchid flower were 'adapted for fertilisation by insects', and therefore 'the result of natural selection'. Charles had found the work soothing; concentrating on flowers was a relaxation after dealing with great philosophical problems. For Emma, too, this was one of the happiest periods in these often difficult times: her family were with her, Erasmus, Hensleigh and Fanny and their children came to stay, and for the first time for many years she was able to leave Charles and take Etty and Fanny Hensleigh's daughter Hope on a little tour of the area. Like her mother, she was always refreshed by such journeys, and now that the burden of childbearing was lifted Emma regained her liveliness. The holiday at Torquay revived them all; but Charles and Emma would need all their strength in the coming years.

In the summer of 1861, Emma's sister Charlotte had fallen ill. Slowly declining through the autumn, she was taken to St Leonard's, a favourite refuge for the convalescent and terminally ill; here she died in January 1862. It was yet another blow for Emma – and also for Charles, who had, of course, been captivated by her beauty in his youth. She was also a talented artist; her watercolours had hung in their sitting room at Gower Street and in Emma's bedroom at Down, and were much admired by both Charles and Emma. Elizabeth had cared for Charlotte in her last illness, and Fanny Allen remembered 'the precious time' she had spent with them both at Hartfield during the summer, recalling Charlotte's 'patient, calm and thoughtful look as I saw her on your [Elizabeth's] terrace while we sat round her chair . . . it was the same countenance . . . that has gone with her from her childhood, and has the stamp of an heavenly birth on it.' Emma was able to visit her at the end at St Leonard's and could console Elizabeth, who had been as close to Charlotte as Emma had been to her late sister Fanny. Charlotte's widower, Charles Langton, now left their house in Hartfield, while Elizabeth moved first to a house in London and in 1868 to a house in the village of Downe to be near Emma, who, wrote Fanny Allen, 'would be her best solace for Emma of all others blends cheerfulness and consolation'. To the astonishment of Charles, in October 1863 his younger sister Catherine, aged fifty-three, married Charles Langton. Perhaps he was glad to have the efficient Catherine 'scrattling' his house in the approved Darwin manner; poor Charlotte had not been a good housekeeper at the best of times.

Emma's greatest trials, though, were within her own home. Only she knew how ill Charles was in the years after the publication of the *Origin of Species*. She cared for him during nights of hysterical weeping and violent retching, days of giddiness and fainting when he desperately needed her and she could not leave him. There were brief periods, as at Torquay, when, as his family remembered, he was the most kindly and charming of companions; then 'the children were their greatest blessing'. But there were years when they were ill, and then they were his 'greatest misery'. Each episode struck Charles deeply. 'It sickens me when I cannot help remembering some of the many illnesses our children have endured.' What especially, and constantly, 'sickened' him was the fear, which he often repeated, that the children had inherited his 'wretched' constitution and that therefore he was at least partly to blame for their suffering.

Work, for so long his refuge from anxiety, was now a source of it. Although the *Origin* was selling well – the German translation had nearly sold out, as had the French – and complimentary letters poured into Down House, lifting his spirits, there was also wounding criticism

battering him into illness again. He could take with good humour the
reservations of the older generation, such as Henslow and Adam Sedgwick,
accepting their difficulties in coming to terms with the new ideas, but
Lyell's reluctance to come out openly on the question of the link between
man and animal certainly rankled; and the sharp arrows dipped in venom
stung. He hated the arguments and public quarrels over his work – 'It is
wretched seeing men fighting for so little fame,' he wrote in 1863. He
knew they would be intensified if he moved on to discuss the origin of
man. Modest, he did not feel himself qualified and a perfectionist, he was
overwhelmed by the prospect of the work ahead. Perhaps, he thought, he
should give his notes for the book that was to become *The Descent of Man*
to Wallace and let him carry on where he had left off.

In the spring of 1863 worry over his work, combined with constant
fear for the children's health, drove Charles to the edge of nervous collapse.
Deeply concerned, some time after 1861 Emma quietly wrote him a letter,
finding it easier to write than to speak.

I cannot tell you the compassion I have felt for all your suffering
for these weeks past that you have had so many drawbacks. Nor
the gratitude I have felt for the cheerful and affectionate looks
you have given me when I know you have been miserably
uncomfortable.

My heart has often been too full to speak or take any notice.
I am sure you know I love you well enough to believe that I
mind your suffering nearly as much as I should my own and I
find the only relief to my own mind is to take it as from God's
hand, and to try to believe that all suffering and illness is meant
to help us to exalt our minds and to look forward with hope to
a future state. When I see your patience, deep compassion for
others, self command and above all gratitude for the smallest
thing done to help you I cannot help longing that these precious
feelings should be offered to Heaven for the sake of your daily
happiness. But I find it difficult enough in my own case. I often
think of the words, 'Thou shalt keep him in perfect peace whose
mind is stayed on thee'. It is feeling and not reasoning that
drives one to prayer.

I feel presumptuous in writing this to you. I feel in my inmost heart your admirable qualities and feelings and all I would hope is that you would direct them upwards, as well as to one who values them above everything in the world. I shall keep this by me till I feel cheerful and comfortable again about you but it has passed through my mind often lately so I thought I would write it partly to relieve my own mind.

Profoundly moved, Charles wrote in a shaky hard at the bottom of this letter, 'God bless you.' Was there still a God in his universe?

Emma wanted to take Charles to Malvern once again for the water treatment, but it was not until September that he was well enough to travel. Meanwhile he found botanical research a therapy and writing to his dear friend Hooker a relief. Their affectionate, easy relationship reminds one of the friendship of old Josiah Wedgwood and Thomas Bentley. Indeed, although Charles had not the physical strength and energy of his grandfather, in temperament they had much in common, though Charles was unaware of it. There was a similar generosity and charm, the same relaxed, friendly relationship of each man with his children; the same affectionate family voice resonates in Charles's letters to his children and those of his mother to her father.

Charles once wondered where his boyhood passion for collecting came from, not realizing that his grandfather had prized his own collection of shells. When Hooker defended stamp collecting, he replied, '6/7ths of my children collect, and I collected seals, franks, coins, minerals, shells, insects and God knows what else. But by Jove I can hardly stomach a grown man collecting stamps. Who would ever have thought of your collecting Wedgwood ware! but that is wholly different to little engravings or pictures. We are degenerate descendants of old Josiah for we have not a bit of the pretty ware in the house.'

Hearing that Charles was selling some of his Wedgwood ware, Hooker hoped he might buy some small items:

I am quite aware of your insensibility to Wedgwood ware, were it otherwise I do not think I could have gone into the foible, for I should have bored you out of your life to beg, borrow and steal for me . . . As it is I do not go further [than] little medallions and such matters – such gorgeous things [as] you had on slates are not for the like of me; and as to the chimney pots on your chimney piece in the dining room, they are not worth carriage.

Charles replied,

I had a whole box of small Wedgwood medallions; but drat the children everything in this house gets lost or wasted; I can only find about a dozen little things as big as shillings and I presume worth nothing; and you shall look at them when here and take them if worth pocketing . . . You sent a gratuitous insult about the 'chimney pots' in the dining room, for you shan't have them, nor are they Wedgwood ware.

To Hooker's delight, among the medallions Charles gave him he found 'some excellent pickings out of the Wedgwood medallions, some of the seals are the most beautiful things'. Charles was amused and astonished to hear that his friend had 'haunted shops in Paris and London' seeking Wedgwood medallions.

Without joking [Hooker told him], Wedgwoods are an unspeakable relief to me. I look over them every Sunday morning and poke into all the little 2nd hand shops I pass in London seeking medallions. The prices of vases are quite incredible. I saw a lovely butter boat and was quite determined to go up to 30/ for it at the dirtiest little pig stye of a subterranean hole . . . in the wall of a shop . . . the price was £25. All this amuses me vastly – and it is an enjoyable contrast to grim sciences. No Lady enjoys *bonnets* more heartily.

Encouraged by Charles's generosity, Hooker also asked to borrow the medallion of Dr Darwin, from which he wanted to make a cast. In return, in February, Hooker sent Charles a cartload of plants from the hothouses at Kew for Charles's new greenhouse at Down. 'You cannot imagine what pleasure your plants give me (far more than your dead Wedgwood ware can give you). Henrietta and I go and gloat over them.' To Charles, living plants were immeasurably more rewarding than dead clay; but he was glad to be able to give pleasure to his friend. Later that year he was to send Hooker a vase, 'black and brown, given [to Robert Darwin] by Jos Wedgwood and which my father valued much. I of course, do not know whether they are really good but I have begged one from my sister Susan and she will send it in about a week's time to Kew.'

At last, stimulated by Hooker's enthusiasm, Charles began to show some interest in old Josiah, and looked out some old letters to send to Miss Meteyard for the biography she was writing. Neither he nor Emma, however, was sufficiently interested to go to Staffordshire for the laying of the foundation stone of the Wedgwood Institute at Burslem in October 1863, when Gladstone spoke, praising Josiah Wedgwood and the 'beauty and quality of the ware'. In his speech at the Town Hall luncheon Gladstone declared, 'If the day shall ever come when she [England] shall be as eminent in taste as she is now in economy of production, my belief is that that result will probably be due to no other single man in so great a degree as to Wedgwood.' ('I wish Gladstone would hold his tongue,' Hooker complained, 'and not raise the price of them with his nonsense.') To Miss Meteyard's anger, of the Wedgwood family only Emma's brother Frank and his son Godfrey (who took over as head of the pottery in 1862 on Frank's retirement) were present on this occasion; indeed, until Miss Meteyard's two-volume life appeared in 1865 none of the Darwins appeared to realize the historic importance of Josiah Wedgwood I nor the exceptional quality of his enquiring mind.

In any case, in 1863 Emma had much more to worry about than Wedgwood ware. Throughout the spring and summer Charles was seriously ill, assailed by violent and almost continual sickness, once again reducing him to hysterical weeping. Emma insisted that he should try the Malvern treatment once more, but Dr Gully was now so busy that he was unable to take Charles and recommended his colleague, Dr Ayerst at Malvern Wells, two or three miles from Malvern itself. On 1 September 1863, Emma went ahead with Horace to find a suitable house to rent; Charles would follow later.

It was fourteen years since Emma's first visit to the spa town with the children; this time it was from the comfort of a railway carriage that she

saw the blue remembered Malvern Hills rising sharply from the wide
Severn Plain. The railway had reached Malvern in 1861 and the town
now boasted an elegant little station, where slender iron pillars capped
with brightly painted wreaths of fruit and flowers greeted the distinguished
patients who flocked to the hydros. Malvern had become smart, and so
popular that Emma could not find a suitable house in the town itself and
had to settle for Malvern Wells. It was a dull little hamlet, but at least it
was near Dr Ayerst's hydro. She took the Villa Nuova, a roomy establishment but conveniently near the road and under the shadow of the
overhanging bluff. Dr Ayerst's establishment was above them, reached by
a steep path. Here Horace apparently had some successful treatment, but
Charles, when he arrived, was too weak to climb the hill and Dr Ayerst
came down to treat him. It was not a cheerful beginning.

It had taken much courage to face Malvern again, but Emma had long
wanted to see the place where her beloved Annie was buried. Four years
earlier, when William Fox had gone to Malvern for treatment, he and his
wife had visited the church and had told the Darwins how they had stood
sadly by Annie's grave. But, as Charles now wrote to Fox,

> Emma went yesterday to the churchyard and found the grave-
> stone of our poor child gone. The Sexton said he remembered
> it, and searched well for it and came to the conclusion that it
> had disappeared. He says the churchyard a few years ago was
> much altered and we suppose that the stone was stolen. Will
> you tell us what you can remember about the stone and where
> it stood. I think you said there was a little tree planted. We
> want, of course, to put another stone.

It was some days before Fox's reply came:

> What you mention about your poor child's gravestone is to me
> almost incredible. Is it possible you have overlooked it in
> consequence of it being buried up by surrounding trees and
> shrubs. Either I or my wife could go to the spot almost blindfold.
> A line drawn with east end of church to the road would nearly
> cut it I think ... Entering the yard from the lower gate and

following the path to the main entrance to the church it is almost
1 third of the way . . . among several tombs which have shrubs
and trees thickly planted round them and even when I last saw
it a good deal covering up the stone. I'm sure it was there in
June 1859. It was a good strong upright stone . . . To a good and
dear child.

Emma asked Eliza Partington, the owner of Montreal House where
Annie had died, to help her find the grave. Did she call on Eliza and
climb the stairs to see the four-roomed apartment where Charles had
spent the agonizing last hours with the dying child? Two little dark
rooms facing the road and two looking out over the breathtaking
landscape, green to the distant Cotswolds: here Charles had written the
last heartbroken letters. For Emma, the serenity of that incomparable
view would have eased the pain.

Following Eliza Partington's advice and Fox's instructions, Emma once
again returned to the graveyard of the ancient church and searched through
the tangled shrubs. At last she found it, greened over with lichen and
hidden in the undergrowth. Emma had not expected the stone to look so
old; in her mind the death was only yesterday, and Annie eternally fresh
and young. It was hard to realize that her eldest daughter would now be a
woman of twenty-two.

Emma wrote to Fox,

I am writing instead of Charles to thank you for your precise
answer to his enquiry. I am glad to say that by the help of your
directions & the lady at whose house our poor Annie lodged we
have found the tomb stone. It is very much covered with trees
& looks so green & old I am sure I looked at it many times
thinking it quite out of the question that should be it. Also the
iron palisades are gone, at least both the sexton & lady thought
there had been rails round it, but that does not signify. This has
been a great relief.

Emma, the gardener, must certainly have wished to clear away the weeds
herself from the grave of her 'good and dear child'.

This time the water cure did not help Charles, though Dr Gully visited once or twice and approved the treatment prescribed by his colleague. Emma put a brave face on it, though she thought that Dr Ayerst had not the 'influence' of Dr Gully. 'Charles has been quite ill last week but for the last five days, he has decidedly improved, but I expect his recovery to be very slow,' she told Fox. Perhaps the successful doctor did not want to be responsible for so obviously a hopeless patient. Emma noted in her diary that Charles was sick every day from 20 to 23 September.

In October, as the days drew in, a heartbreaking letter came to Charles from Hooker: 'My darling little second girl died here an hour ago, and I think of you more in my grief than of any other friend.' Six-year-old Maria, he later wrote, had been 'the companion of my walks, the first of my children who has shown any love for music and flowers . . . It will be long before I cease to hear her voice in my ears or feel her little hand stealing into mine by the fireside and in the garden. Wherever I go she is there.' How well Charles and Emma understood those last words. Malvern was haunted by memories of Annie; there could be no cure here for Charles. He wrote shakily to Hooker, his letter of condolence finished, 'I am very weak and can write little . . . my head swims badly, so no more.' It was clear that Dr Gully and his partner could do no more for Charles, so they returned to Down, where he broke down completely. He could not think or work, and only with the greatest difficulty penned a few broken words to Hooker: 'My dear old friend, I must just have the pleasure of saying this, Yours affectionately.' It was a long time before he could write again. He hoped he might be able to work a little: 'Unless I can . . . I hope my life will be short, for to lie on the sofa and do nothing but to give trouble to the best and kindest of wives and dear good children is dreadful.'

On 8 December 1863, Emma wrote to William Fox from Down.

I can give rather a better account of Charles this week, but he is never long without attacks of sickness. The water cure seemed to do him harm and Dr Gully quite owned that he was not strong enough to bear it. Since we came home he has consulted Dr Brinton of Guy's Hospital and I hope mineral acid is doing him some good. He is wonderfully cheerful when not positively uncomfortable. He does not feel the least temptation to disobey orders about working for he feels quite incapable of doing anything. His good symptoms are losing no flesh and having a good appetite so that I am full of hope that in time he will regain his usual standard of health which is not saying much for him.

Throughout 1863, and for months at a time until 1865, Charles was seriously ill. Much of the time he lay upon his sofa, unable to work. Yet even then his mind was not at rest. Watching the climbing plants in his study with his usual care, he noted how they moved; they almost seemed to see. Should he look beyond the animal kingdom for the origins of human life? There was no end to his obsessive questioning. Again and again Emma wished he would 'smoke a pipe or ruminate like a cow'.

Now more than ever he needed Emma, his 'cheerful comforter and wise adviser'. And in the ensuing years, as Charles grew weaker, Emma grew stronger. She was able to deal with many of the letters that flooded in from all over the world, translating them for him from French, Italian and German, and answering them on his behalf. She protected him from visitors, nursed him and hardly ever left him. At the same time her old liveliness and energy returned; and her old interests were revived.

She began a campaign against cruelty to animals, often writing in Charles's name. As his children always remembered, he rarely lost his temper but any cruelty to animals roused him to real anger. On one occasion he reported a neighbouring farmer to the RSPCA for working horses with sore necks. One of the reasons why Emma had loved him in the beginning was that he was 'kind to animals'. But this was Emma's own campaign, her first independent contribution to a family tradition; as a girl she had watched her Aunt Kitty Mackintosh writing letters on similar subjects to *The Times*, and Aunt Sarah Wedgwood had also encouraged her support of the RSPCA.

Emma's letter to William Thackeray's daughter Anne explains the cause to which she gave much time and energy. Their old nurse, Brodie, it will be remembered, had been governess to the Thackeray family.

My dear Mrs Thackeray,
I enclose a paper which Mr Darwin and I concocted together in the hope of exciting some interest in what I think must be

allowed to be the greatest cruelty of modern times. Dear old Brodie told me a certain story of your taking in a wretched lost cur which makes me sure that you are very compassionate to animals so I venture to sent it you in the hope that you will feel some interest or even I am ambitious enough to ask you to get Mr Thackeray to look at it. If you would write something on the subject nobody would do it so well. I have distributed nearly 1000 of the little paper and I find *all* women interested and horrified and a great many men, MPs and Landowners, so that I really do hope that some impression might be made. A good many papers and periodicals have admitted it but I tried the *Times* in vain which would have done the most good.

Henrietta desires to be very kindly remembered to you and your sister, I am,

My dear Mrs Thackeray

yours very truly

Emma Darwin

I copy a striking passage. It is an account of what Mr Frank Buckland calls a 'gamekeepers' museum'. The first article is 53 cats' heads. Speaking of one of them he says 'This one had died fighting bravely to the last, inch by inch had it yielded up its 9 lives. Caught possibly in a trap in the *early part* of the evening by one of its legs it had lingered thro' the night in agony, the pain of its entrapped limb causing it to make furious efforts to escape, and those very efforts adding additional torments to the wound. In the morning the keeper had come with his gun and his dogs; putting his foot on the spring of the trap, he had let out the wounded and exhausted animal to the mercy of his terriers, what little life was left in it the dogs worried out. It had died a martyr to its natural instincts. Do you doubt this? Look at the head now dried by the heat of two summers, the wrinkled forehead, the expanded eyelids, the glaring eyeballs, the whiskers extended to their full stretch, the spiteful lips exposing the double row of tiger-like teeth envenomed by agony, tell us all this. The hand of death has not been powerful enough to relax the muscles racked for so many hours with terror and pain'. The next item is 130 hedgehogs – it is horrid to think of . . .

Emma's aim was to foster the development of a humane trap. She fought with energy, enlisting the support of friends. She wrote to William Fox on 8 December 1863:

> Dear Mr Fox,
> Thank you very much for your letter. I must own it has discouraged me a good deal as to the necessity of steel traps. I believe you are the only person in England who has energy & humanity to visit the traps at midnight & Charles tells me you once carried a toad over the Menai Bridge for fear he should come to a bad end – I want to ask you to do me a favour. My game keeper friend here who is so smooth spoken I suspect he chiefly tells me what he thinks I want to hear, tells me that the animals almost always break the leg in their first frantic efforts to escape – is this true according to your experience? But I want you to be so kind as to have a trap wound round with cloth or flannel over the iron teeth so as to see whether it will save much suffering to have the leg only pinched instead of torn with the teeth. I thought if it is true that the leg is broken the animal would suffer nearly as much in whatever way it is held fast.

Emma's campaign had been partly inspired by a letter about steel traps sent by the writer William Howitt to the *Morning Star*, and aroused much interest. 'I have met with a good deal of encouragement and I see it today in the Worcester paper endorsed by the member of parliament.' As a result it was suggested that a prize might be offered by the RSPCA for a humane trap. Emma took up the project with vigour, as her letter to William Fox shows:

> I am going to send out papers for subscriptions & when I have got as many names as I can I must put it into the hands of the

Soc. in Pall Mall, as awarding the prize will be a difficult matter. I sent you a paper to shew what sort of a beginning we have made & I am more grateful for two 5s/subscriptions than one at £1, for I think the number of names who take an interest in the attempt is what chiefly signifies.

During the early 1870s the RSPCA continued to campaign against steel traps through the columns of its monthly paper *Animal World*, and prominently linked Charles Darwin's name to the offer of a prize for a humane trap. *Animal World* of 1 January 1870 reported Emma's involvement:

The RSPCA Annual Report for 1864 records that 'a benevolent lady, intensely interested in the matter, induced several noblemen and country gentlemen to subscribe an amount, which she kindly placed at the disposal of your Committee'. Such funds were raised to fund a £50 prize for the design of a trap serving the purposes of game preservers 'without inflicting torture'. The scheme received the support of 'many of the leading sportsmen of the country, and Francis Trevelyan Buckland, well known to sportsmen through his regular columns in the *Field* newspaper, was a prominent supporter of the campaign.' An exhibition of more than 100 humane traps, submitted in competition for the prize was held at the Royal Horticultural Gardens, South Kensington, in June 1864 . . . However, despite an optimistic start, the competition failed to produce a design that was portable, cheap and effective. The judges appointed by the RSPCA awarded three competitors a total of £10 in recognition of the merit of their designs, but the remaining £40 was reserved in the hope of finding a better design in the future.

For all the efforts of Emma and other like-minded campaigners, however, steel traps continued to be used; it was not only in weighty matters of science and religion that Victorian attitudes were hard to change.

CHAPTER FOURTEEN

An Exception to Every Wife

FOR MOST OF THE YEARS 1864 AND 1865 CHARLES WAS A COMPLETE INVALID and entirely housebound, his sickness growing worse as the battle over his work raged. Huxley and Hooker and other young like-minded friends had formed a Darwinian club – the X Club – to defend Darwinism from the slings and arrows of the aroused church militant. At the sound of battle Charles retreated even further into his shell, protected by Emma and the family. During these months of complete collapse Emma was indispensable. She eased his headaches, massaged his temples, soothed him with music and read light novels to him. Most worrying was Charles's loss of control and his hysterical crying, which must have reminded them both of Annie in the months before her death. At least Etty and Bessy, now twenty-one and seventeen, could lighten the burden; but for months Emma could leave Charles only for short periods, and never at night. In November 1864 Emma wrote to Aunt Fanny, pleased that she was coming to visit, 'as I do not feel easy to leave Charles for a night, he is so subject to distressing fainting feelings, and one never knows when an attack may come on.'

Charles was desperate; he had tried everything, even sent bottles of his vomit and urine to be analysed by specialists. In the summer of 1864 he decided to try Dr Chapman's ice cure, which was recommended for those patients 'whose minds are highly cultivated and developed, and often complicated, modified and dominated by subtle physical influences whose intensity and bearing on the physical malady it is difficult to apprehend'. He sent the doctor a summary of his case.

Age 56–57. For 25 years extreme spasmodic daily and nightly flatulence: occasional vomiting, on two occasions prolonged during months. Vomiting preceded by shivering, hysterical crying[,] dying sensations or half faint, and copious very pallid urine. Now vomiting and every passage of flatulence preceded by ringing of ears, treading on air and vision focus and black dots. Air fatigues, specially risky, brings on the head symptoms. Nervousness when Emma leaves me.

Dr Chapman came to Down and fitted Charles with a spinal bag – freezing him three times a day for ninety minutes. For a while the treatment revived him; but before long he was as weak as ever, and in July sank back into the cocoon of his room for the rest of the year. Eczema made shaving difficult, so he grew the beard that transformed him. Now he not only felt old, he looked an aged patriarch.

A year later, in the summer of 1865, he was little better. 'What a life of suffering his is,' Aunt Fanny wrote, 'and how manfully he bears it! . . . Emma, dear Emma's cheerfulness is equally admirable. O that a pure sunshine would rise for them all.' In July she reported that Emma 'had waited for a good moment . . . Charles' *four* days of tolerable wellness had given her spirits to give me the treat of a letter, and that with all her boys about her! I am sure she is a chosen one of Heaven.' Aunt Fanny had watched Emma's devoted care of Charles during those grim months just as she had seen her bearing grief with fortitude during the period of Annie's death. She spoke of a friend, Etty recalled, 'as the most devoted wife she ever knew, except Emma and she is an exception to every wife'.

There were times when even Emma's spirits sank. She was concerned about her own health; but it is Charles's symptoms that are recorded in her journal rather than her own severe and recurring headaches. Gardening always restored her. In May 1866 she wrote, 'I have often been surprised when I was feeling sad how cheering a little exertion of that sort is. I also like cutting and carving among the shrubs, but as my opinion is diametrically opposite to the rest of my family, I don't have my own way entirely in that matter.' Emma was often consoled by the thought that God, like a good gardener, knew that there was a time for the knife – just as she regretfully but firmly had a hamper of kittens destroyed, 'and am not sorry to be free of their meals poor little ducks. They would all sleep in the mowing machine and did not look clean.' But now that Charles was famous she had to be prepared to entertain his distinguished visitors, so regretfully she could not always wear her faded old gardening clothes. When she took the distinguished botanist George Bentham through the garden, she was glad she was not in her 'rags', which 'do not look well in the sunshine. My new gown is respectable and handsome,' she told Etty.

More grief was in store. The year 1866 began badly with the death of Charles's youngest sister Catherine: her unexpected late marriage to Charlotte's widower, Charles Langton, had not lasted long. Dominated by her stronger sister Susan, according to Fanny Allen, she had 'somehow failed to work to her capabilities either for her own happiness or that of others'. She died at Shrewsbury where she had come to take care of the ailing Susan, who, in the autumn, would follow her. Susan had been the controller of the household, the keeper of the accounts, the 'granny' who criticized Charles's spelling and Emma's housekeeping – but also the generous aunt who had brought up their sister Marianne's four sons and daughter after her death in 1858. Now it was 'sad sad Shrewsbury which used to look so bright and sunny', Aunt Fanny wrote, 'though I did dread the Dr a good deal, and yet I saw his kindness – but my nature was and is fearful.' The memory of Fanny's own fierce father, Captain Allen, had left its scar. Now the Shrewsbury doors were closed, the house and Dr Robert's greenhouse sold and only the memories remained.

In 1869 Charles and Emma called in to see the new owners of his old home in Shrewsbury, and Charles was sad that he was not able to wander alone among his ghosts, to remember the past, the exquisite order of the rooms, and the neat garden. Had he done so, he wrote, he was sure his father would have reappeared in his wheelchair among the flowers. In 1880 Etty visited Shrewsbury, wandered round the garden and was saddened to see it so overgrown and neglected. 'All the pretty walks in the bank have been let to grow up so that you don't see the river and are stuffy and dank. The little summerhouse where all the children used to play, is in ruin. Poor old house.'

But in other ways 1866 was a better year. Charles's health was so improved under the care of Dr Bence Jones, his physician for many years, that they were able to visit London again. In April Emma wrote happily to Aunt Fanny of their pleasant and successful days. 'Charles went last night to the soirée at the Royal Society where assemble all the scientific men in London. He saw every one of his old friends, and had such a cordial reception from them all as made it very pleasant. He was obliged to name himself to almost all of them as his beard alters him so much. The President presented him to the Prince of Wales. There were only three presented, and he was the first. The Prince looked a nice good natured youth and very gentleman-like. He said something Charles could not hear, so he made the profoundest bow he could and went on.' Probably neither Charles nor the Prince was aware that Charles's grandfather, Josiah Wedgwood, had been an honoured visitor at Court in the days of the Prince's grandparents, George III and Queen Charlotte. Indeed, the Royal Family hardly loomed large in the Darwins' lives: Court affairs are scarcely ever mentioned in the extensive Darwin correspondence.

Emma's event was 'nearly as wonderful':, an outing to see *Hamlet* with the great actor Charles Fechter. 'The acting was beautiful, but I should prefer anything to Shakespeare, I am ashamed to say.' This brisk honesty was typical of Emma, but Fanny Allen was doubtless shocked to read it, for she worshipped Shakespeare. On the same London visit, Emma took Elizabeth to see 'poor mad Miss P[ugh]', who had been with them at the time of little Charles Waring's death. Like her mother, Emma never forgot old friends and had kept in touch with Miss Pugh, sending her a generous pension and a regular donation to provide her with holidays from her nursing home. For once concerned about her own health – never good since the birth of her last child – while they were in London she also consulted Dr Bence Jones, who told her, 'I am to drive every day, and Charles ride!'

They were again in London in May, staying with Erasmus. 'Monday I drove about and did one set of pictures, which is staring unwholesome work, and did not suit either of our heads and a little shopping.' 'The real treat for Emma this time was the concert at the Philharmonic to which she was taken by Elizabeth, who at this time was living in London, in Chester Place. 'It was our dear old G Minor Mozart, and very charming, we used to play it quite fast enough (and very well) and gave it quite the right air. A Mlle Mehlig played the P in Arabella [Goddard's] style but more beautifully, and I enjoyed it much. Singing hideous, Mlle Finico sang Vedrai Carino as slow as a Psalm tune and as loud as she could.' On these visits Emma was young again, enjoying the theatre and concerts as she had done in the years before her marriage. But, she told Henrietta, 'Papa was pretty well done up.'

In 1866 Etty was twenty-three, lively, intelligent and somewhat bored by the constricted life at Down. Uninvited visitors were not encouraged, for Charles had to be protected; so unexpected arrivals were greeted with alarm. They had a mirror fitted at the front door so that they could have advance warning of any unwanted callers. Etty vividly sets the scene of one such occasion in a letter to her brother George.

> I had got the drawing [room] full of pots – the furniture in confusion – Anne & self with muddy hands, gowns tucked up & sans crinoline when a ring at the door made our hearts sink within us – but after a hasty rush to Mama to see whether they might go into the dining room I sent Thos to the door when Mama started up galopped [*sic*] to the top of the stairs & began yelling loudly 'Stop a bit, stop a bit.' I had to flee into the drawing room & cdnt stop & this was the way the curate of Cudham was received in his first call & so Mama made abject apologies saying it was the state of the drawing room caused her agony & then to verify her words brought them in upon poor me to my horror. He is not a high toned gentleman but a very good man & Irish to the backbone. It must be something in the air of Cudham produces them Irish.

In the same letter she gives a summary of a typical Darwin menu:

> Boys have just gone after a hearty dinner at 5¼ – lunch at one – two helps beef rice pudding – parmesan & hunches of bread – dinner soup chicken two helps pudding – two helps welsh rabbit – pretty well isn't it?

Seclusion was not easy to preserve, for now that Charles was famous visitors came from all over the world – some expecting to see a hermit at the end of a mule track. They were surprised to find the great man and his wife so simple and unaffected in the midst of a lively family. Etty enjoyed the excitement of visitors from the outside world. In the spring of 1866 she described the arrival of the German professor Dr Haeckel.

> On Sunday we had a gt visitation. One of Papa's most thorough going disciples, a Jena professor, came to England on his way to Madeira and asked to come down & see Papa. We didn't know whether he cd speak [English] & our spirits was naturally rather low. He came quite early on Sunday & when first he entered he was so agitated he forgot all the little English he knew & he & Papa shook hands repeatedly, Papa reiteratedly remarking that he was very glad to see him & Haeckel receiving it in dead silence. However afterwards it turned out that he could stumble on very decently – some of his sentences were very fine. Talking of dining in London – 'I like a good bit of flesh at a restoration'. Of the war in Germany he remarked as an advantage the Russians had from their good education, 'Zat ven ze officers are deeded ze commons take ze cheap,' i.e. when the officers are killed the privates take the chief command. He told us that there are more than 200 medallions of Papa made by a man from Wm's photo in circulation amongst the students in Jena. Papa has just begun his gt Pangenesis chapter.

It is obvious that Etty was now taking an intelligent interest in her father's work, and when Charles was well enough to receive guests, Etty longed to stay behind with the men after dinner to 'listen to the talk'. It was bliss when Uncle Hensleigh and Fanny came, as in July 1867, when she wrote to George that

> I was busyer than can be told whilst the Hensleighs were here – wanting to talk 6 hours a day & croquet 7 left not much time for anything else. We had a most heavenly little visit – fine weather all the time & we sat out & worshipped on the lawn all day long & they were all partic. nice. I find their company like dram drinking – the taste for it insidiously creeps on & on & I do sometimes feel what my life would be like without them. A

wicked feeling of delight comes over me when I hear Uncle H. [Hensleigh] say that they won't be rich enough to go abroad next winter.

Down House was now the family hearth at which young and old gathered, as Maer had been – especially as Charles's health improved. In the spring of 1867 Emma offered to look after Mrs Huxley's seven children so that she could attend the Liverpool meeting of the British Association of which her husband was president. After Emma's death Mrs Huxley told Etty, 'Towards your mother I always had a sort of nestling feeling . . . Few, if any, would have housed a friend's seven children and two nurses for a fortnight . . . what wonder that I had for her always the most grateful affection.'

In 1868 Charles again seemed in better health, and again they took a month in London – this time in March, staying first with Erasmus in Queen Anne Street and then at Elizabeth's house, 4 Chester Place. Once more Emma and Elizabeth enjoyed concerts and plays together. Their childhood friendship had been renewed and strengthened after Charlotte's death, and now Elizabeth was planning to move to a house in Downe; here, Etty remembered, she would spend the last twelve years of her life, happy with her garden, her little dog Tony and her devoted servants, helping her village neighbours and sheltered by Emma's constant love and care.

In the summer, Emma persuaded Charles that they all needed sea air once more. In his autobiography, as was mentioned earlier, Charles maintained that after their move to Down they went nowhere except to visit family and occasionally to the seaside. In fact, for many years they spent many weeks at a time with relations or at one seaside resort or another. In his book on *Down: The Home of the Darwins*, Hedley Atkins lists these periods away from home in the early years of their marriage:

1843 July	Week at Maer and Shrewsbury	
" October	Twelve days at Shrewsbury	
1844 April	Week at Maer and Shrewsbury	
" July	Twelve days at Shrewsbury	

1845 September 15	Six weeks, Shrewsbury, Lincolnshire, York, the Dean of Manchester, Waterton, Chatsworth
1846 February	Eleven days at Shrewsbury
" July	Ten days at Shrewsbury
" September	Ten days at Southampton, etc., for the British Association

And so it continued later. They were at the King's Head Hotel in Shanklin on the Isle of Wight for ten days in 1858; at Moor Park in the summer; in Ilkley that autumn. In 1860 Charles visited Dr Lane at Sudbrook Park and Elizabeth at Hartfield. September to November was spent in a rented house on the Marine Parade, Eastbourne. In 1861 he paid a rare visit to London, and the whole family, with the Hensleighs and Erasmus and their children, spent July and August in Torquay. In 1862, after Emma and Lenny contracted scarlet fever they convalesced at Bournemouth. In April 1863 they visited Hartfield, and from September to October they were at Malvern. Then there was a long spell at home: except for short visits to London in 1866 and 1867, Charles did not leave Down again until their month in London in March 1868. Because Charles carried the protection of Emma, family and servants with him, and moved in society very little, he scarcely knew he was away from home. His perpetual retirement, even on holiday, provoked a wit to call him the 'missing link'.

In spite of her persistent attacks of migraine, Emma entered her sixties with much of her old liveliness. When Fanny Allen praised her for being 'a wise woman settled on a rock', Emma assured her that Charles considered she had a good deal of 'gadabout' in her. In fact, from now on Emma organized summer holidays – usually for a month and generally by the sea – when a house would be rented large enough to take all the family, often including Erasmus as well as various cousins and their children, and a complete staff – maids, nurses and governesses and 'Evvy', Mrs Evans, their devoted cook, who had to deal with a succession of difficult kitchens.

In 1868 their destination was to be Freshwater on the Isle of Wight. Their first days on the island were deeply disappointing, as Etty's lively letter in the family shorthand to George shows:

To G.H.D. Dumbola Lodge, Freshwater, I of W (Summer '68)
Dear George. Here we are . . . We had a carriage to our selves &
Papa really did not mind [the journey] at all. I am quite sure if
he was not nervous he cd get to the Lakes quite well & I hope
next year we shall make a longer move. He saw Dr B. Jones who
said that he must take a rest much oftener than he usually did –
every 3 months he said. Well, just after Yarmouth we thght it
very pretty – but afterwards as we got towards Freshw as Anne
said it got 'huglier and huglier' till it reached its climax in the
mean little valley with half a dozen sordid red brick houses in
which we are placed. I won't seek to denige [homage to Dickens's
Mrs Gamp] that we are low at our prospects. There are the
Downs 'tis true & if you can walk 5 or 6 miles they may be nice
(You can walk 15 miles on 'em) but two miles which seems
awfully hard work on my legs doesn't seem to get you any way
at all . . . There is no beach – gt big chalk cliffs if you like 'em.
I don't – chalk is chalk all the world over & I feel as if I knew a
deal too much about it for any romance to be left. We are ¼
mile from the sea – we do see it out of our croquet ground –
and drawing room window. The croquet ground is good & will
be a resource to Lizzie [Bessy] & me.

They had taken a house belonging to the famous photographer Julia
Cameron:

Today has been amusing as regards people. At 10 o clk Papa
Mama & I went to call on Longfellow who is here meeting
Tennyson & Tom Appleton who is their Barnum as he says, was
most amusing. He says he has had 'Spirits on the brain, but he
has got thro now & is waiting for something more wonderful to
believe'. And oh my goodness the stories he told. He dined last
night with Tennyson & then took him into a wood with a candle
& said he told him such things as he'd never heard before – wh.
we cd well believe – but it is his funny Yankee turns of expression
that are so amusing . . . Then our landlady Mrs Cameron who
was quite as queer in her way as Tom Appleton. Just now she

has sent in her maid with her love & she was feeling so depressed without a photograph of her son Henry, wd we sent it over. She'll do my Pa of course.

Mrs Cameron duly took the celebrated photographs of Charles, though she refused to take Emma, maintaining that no woman between the ages of eighteen and seventy should be photographed. But she kindly accompanied Emma and Bessy to call on the Tennysons. 'It was pouring with rain, and the more it rained the slower we walked, so when we got there we left our dripping cloaks in the hall,' Emma recorded. Tennyson brought them 'a bottle of white wine and gave us each a glass to correct the wet'. Mrs Tennyson, Emma told Aunt Fanny, 'is an invalid and very pleasing and gracious', and she liked Tennyson even if 'his absurd talk is a sort of flirtation with Mrs Cameron'. Charles had spent an hour pleasantly with the great poet. 'We ended in a transport of affection with Mrs Cameron, Eras calling over the stairs to her, "you have left 8 persons deeply in love with you".' Mrs Cameron had taken a fancy to the delicate young Horace; 'the Madonna' (her maid, and the model for many of her photographs) was often coming over – 'Mrs Cameron's love and would Horace come over . . . she wanted to pack photos etc.'

Aunt Fanny read Emma's account with amusement. Emma was no admirer of Tennyson but Etty and Emma's brother Harry tried in vain to make Fanny a convert. The poet offended her by his patronizing criticisms of 'bland and mild' Shakespeare. 'It grated like gravel in my teeth – one who could so measure such a genius has no wings to soar into the higher regions of poetry.' At eighty-eight, Aunt Fanny was still reading widely and deeply, and expressing herself as trenchantly as ever.

At the end of the holiday Etty conceded that Freshwater had not been such a disappointment.

To G.H.D. Dumbola Lodge, Freshwater. Tuesday (Summer '68)
We are in m. better humour with this place & Mrs Cameron keeps us nice & lively. Yesterday the little Abyssinian Prince & his Capt. Speedy came to be phoed – they dressed up in Abyssinian dress & we went over to see them.

Charles's health was much improved in the last years of the 1860s, but overwork and anxiety still set him back. In the winter of 1868 he was working on the final stages of *The Descent of Man* and anticipating the disapproval of friends and relatives – especially Emma – and the sharp attacks of his critics. He ended his two-volume work with the statement that man with all his noble qualities . . . with his god-like intellect . . . with all these exalted powers – still bears in his bodily frame the indelible stamp of his lowly origin. Emma had read the early draft with misgivings. 'I think it will be very interesting but that I shall dislike it very much as again putting God further off,' she wrote to Etty, who was on holiday at Cannes. Charles sent the proof sheets out to her there, and 'Miss Rhadamanthus' made corrections and suggestions, many of which Charles adopted with gratitude. The ever-watchful Emma now saw the dangerous signs of stress again, and with the enthusiastic support of Leonard and Horace, who were 'very crazy on the scheme', she planned a summer holiday in Wales, where there was a house 'to be had'. Perhaps surprisingly, there seems to have been no plan to visit Tenby, although Emma's beloved Aunt Fanny still lived there, as vital and fond as ever, and there were still many Allen relations in the area – maybe it was the fear that they would be 'becousined' that decided Emma against such a visit. In Charles's present delicate state of health, the exuberant Welsh relations would certainly have given him a relapse. However, Etty spent some time that December with her great aunt – her first and last visit to the low white villa on Heywood Lane. She never forgot the 'little old lady, upright and so strong that she would stand for an hour before the fire reading the newspaper in the sunny drawing room'. She remembered, too, the 'sleek black spaniel Crab, and the well cared for garden with a wealth of summer shrubs, and peeps of the blue sea beyond'.

In April 1869 Charles's quiet old horse, Tommy, 'stumbled and fell rolling on him and bruising him seriously'. As Etty reported to George,

We've had a very unpleasant event this week. The immaculate Tommy has thrown Father. They were cantering over Keston Common when Tommy tripped & fell bang down – so completely head over heels that his ears & the pommel of his saddle were the two parts muddied. Father of course imitated Tommy's movements & wd not have been hurt at all if Tommy had not hit him a fearful blow in the back. This numbed his back & prevented his getting up – but as it was a frequented place someone soon came to his help & he was taken into a house & lay down on a sofa for a bit. After ½ an hour Tommy was caught & as the fly Father ordered was very long in coming he got on Tommy & was led home. He came in, exhausted & in considerable pain – but Spingle [their doctor] is sure no bones were broken . . . It is very bad that all confidence in Tommy is gone. It isn't only once or even twice he has badly stumbled in a canter & it seems that it must be something in his way of going wh. is downright unsafe. I fear another Tommy will never be found & I fear Father's nerve will be considerably shaken so it is altogether a bad job.

No other horse ever suited him so well. Charles was now more than ever in need of a break. Fear of the storm that would follow the publication of *The Descent of Man* made him ill.

The family rented a lovely house with a pleasant terraced garden in Caerdeon, on the north shore of the Barmouth Estuary in north Wales. They were there from 19 June to 29 July, but Etty seems to have recorded little of the visit, although she did remember that they called in at Charles's old home at Shrewsbury. Sadly, Charles was so ill most of the time they were at Caerdeon that he hardly went further than a few paces from the house. He was depressed by his weakness, remembering the vigorous young man he once had been, when he had visited Barmouth and climbed the Welsh hills on his geological expeditions. However, he still worked, revising and preparing a French translation of his book on orchids, and his restless mind still probed: he made notes on 'Expression in Insane People'; worked out the proportion of sexes in lambs; and recorded with some pride that his son George had established the rate of increase of elephants by the rule he invented for 'calculating the product for any number of generations'.

As always on these family holidays, Charles liked to remain incognito, but Barmouth at this time attracted lively visitors who were delighted to find 'the great Darwin' among them. Emma usually contrived to protect him, but on one occasion the fearsome Miss Cobbe, bluestocking and feminist campaigner, waylaid him, confident that he would like to hear her views on Mr Mill and the subjection of women, with her reflections on the philosophy of Kant. Charles retreated to his sickbed.

Emma, however, found Miss Cobbe interesting and amusing, and, unlike many intellectual women, capable of laughing at herself. After the publication of *The Descent of Man* she wrote to her, commenting that the newspapers had been 'quite mild and civil' but that 'Charles knew so well how much you and many others will disapprove of the moral sense part that he will not be surprised at any degree of vigour in your attack . . . It appears to him that as long as hatred is felt against any one, the social instincts are overmastered and there is no room for repentance . . . However,' she continued, 'speaking in my private capacity I quite agree with you. I think the course of all modern thought is desolating as removing God further off. But I do not know whether his views on the moral sense would *exclude* spiritual influence though not included in his theory – so you see I am a traitor in the camp.' Emma obviously still hoped that there was a chink in her husband's intellectual fortress through which she could let in the light. But Charles was immensely relieved that 'everybody was talking about [the *Descent*] without being shocked'. Public opinion had moved on since the *Origin*.

Children, Charles had said, were 'the greatest misery and the greatest happiness'. In the 1870s the Darwin children brought both their parents a great deal of happiness.

In his autobiography, Charles claimed that as he grew older he became less interested in people and that the only company he really enjoyed was that of his own family. During the following years he took pride in hearing of their successes. As for Emma, she claimed that she had 'little ambition in me'. When Caroline Wedgwood was concerned that Horace had not a more interesting job, she replied that she only wanted them to be happy in their work. Charles, by precept and example, encouraged them to 'follow the bent of their talents and work as hard as their health would permit'. When Horace passed the 'Little Go', the examination enabling him to go to Cambridge, he wrote reflecting on 'what makes a man a discoverer of undiscovered things . . . many men who are very clever . . . never originate anything. As far as I can conjecture the art consists in habitually searching for the causes and meaning of everything which occurs. This implies sharp observation and requires as much knowledge as possible of the subject investigated.' Horace, as he accepted, was not clever; but, by following his father's counsel, he became very successful as the head of the Cambridge Scientific Instrument Company. The youngest and least talented of the family, he was, as his nephew Bernard Darwin declared, 'the most conscientious'. All the brothers were 'almost painfully honest, but none quite so honest as he . . . he had the sweetest and gentlest smile, but could be ferocious at the thought of dishonesty or cruelty. It must have been pure goodness that made him become Mayor of Cambridge for I do not think he can possibly have liked it.' He is remembered even today in the family for the party trick which delighted the young: standing on a chair, he delighted in dropping a stream of treacle from a spoon with perfect accuracy on to a saucer on the floor.

William was now a banker in Southampton and George was thriving in his academic career at Cambridge. Charles had been particularly close to William ever since 'dear old Doddy' had sat on his knees, with the 'sweetest and most affectionate disposition in the world'. With the same affection and pride he had watched his eldest son's progress from his schooldays at Rugby, when he was 'dear old Gulielmans', to his years at Cambridge, where to his great pleasure the 'dear old man' had occupied his old rooms. They had settled for him to be a barrister, but when Emma's brother Harry asked, 'Has he the gift of the gab?' they decided he had not. Charles, advised by their banker neighbour, John Lubbock, had bought him a partnership in a bank in Southampton where, steady and respected, he worked until retirement.

For their other sons they wanted a more modern education, and at Clapham Grammar School all four did well. George's master there gave him a lifelong interest in astronomy. George was always close to Emma: when he was seven, she had thought him 'a remarkable child, a promising genius, the nicest little fellow'. In spite of ill-health, his success at Cambridge in 1868 in becoming Second Wrangler delighted them all. 'I always said,' wrote Charles, 'from your early days such energy perseverance and talent as yours would be sure to succeed, but I never expected such brilliant success as this . . . that you have made my hand tremble so I can hardly write. God bless you my dear old fellow, may your life so continue.'

Etty was delirious with excitement.

Dear good old Gingo [she wrote], We've all been bursting over the telegram. It is splendid – too too splendid. I'm too mad & too glad & too everything to write coherent – I can only cry. Avast ahoy. My head is in a whirl – Captain he *is* Loblolli boy & I'm Loblolly girl! You shammed v. badly in pretending you were going to be low – you didn't take us in but we pretended that we didn't know you were pretending. In my privatest corner of my heart I settled you to be third – second I never dared count on even in that corner where one stows away one's wildest dreams. Oh my good gracious me I can only return to my original vent – You are Loblolli boy! Write me a linekin to C. Place to say how you feel – whether you are got on your feet. I am still on my head & I mean to stay there a good bit – one doesn't often get such a chance for a good stay in that position. Good-bye my dear G. Your affec. & distracted, H.E.D.

Leonard and Horace and the boys at Clapham Grammar School were 'given a half holiday to celebrate George's success'. According to Emma, the headmaster, Dr Wrigley, 'gave the fact out as if he was going to cry . . . When the boys heard about G in the 1st class room they had a regular saturnalia and played at football for some time to the great danger of the windows and pictures.'

George's success continued. In 1878, by which time he was Professor of Astronomy at Cambridge, Charles congratulated him on his 'discovery' of the moon's period and the internal heat of the Earth. 'Hurrah for the bowels of the Earth and their viscosity and for the moon and for the Heavenly bodies and for my son George (F.R.S. very soon).'

Frank, steady and reliable, intended to become a doctor, but instead studied botany at Cambridge, then worked at Down as his father's assistant and would later write his *Life*. In 1868 Leonard had come second in the entrance examination for Woolwich Academy. Charles 'burst with pleasure' and wrote to Horace, 'By Jove, how well his perseverance and energy have been rewarded.' In 1874 Leonard, now a major in the Royal Engineers, went to New Zealand to observe the transit of Venus; later he became an instructor in chemistry at Chatham. In 1876, after congratulating George on his presentation of papers to the Royal Society,

Charles wrote with pride, 'Horace goes on Monday to lecture on his dynamo at Birmingham. Frank is getting on very well with Dipsacus and has now made experiments which convince me that the matter which comes out of the glands is real live proto plasma about which I was beginning to have horrid doubts. Leonard going to build forts. Oh Lord, what a set of sons I have, all doing wonders!'

When Miss Meteyard's two-volume *Life* of Josiah Wedgwood came out in 1865 it caused no offence to the Darwin family: indeed, Emma thought there was much of interest there, especially in the early years. But in 1871 Charles and Emma received the proofs of Miss Meteyard's new book, *A Group of Englishmen*, which dealt with the lives of the younger generation of Wedgwoods. Emma was angered by some of what she read. Among others the book dealt with Sir James Mackintosh, Fanny Hensleigh's father, and Emma's Uncle John Wedgwood, the gardening expert and father of her friend and cousin Eliza. Emma had been particularly fond of her Uncle John and his radiant wife, Jenny Allen, and, like her mother, always sensitive to the feelings of others, she was afraid that Miss Meteyard would have deeply offended the Mackintoshes and the John Wedgwoods by suggesting – quite accurately – that they and others were in debt to her father, Jos. So she wrote sharply to Miss Meteyard: 'The recording of the fact that these persons received help from the Wds [Wedgwoods] would be no doubt painful to their families, but the imputation of being unreasonable in their demands is almost disgraceful to them, & whether just or not, every member of our family would think it a breach of confidence to consent to the publication of such a statement.'

Perhaps she felt guilty that she and the Darwins had so ignored their distinguished ancestors. In any event, Miss Meteyard replied to the criticism with justice and some acrimony:

> The majority of the papers used in the biography – as also in this more miscellaneous account of his descendants and friends – were thrust ignominiously forth from Etruria as rubbish and waste. After multitudes of them had been dispensed for use in a low neighbourhood, Mr Mayer, a most worthy gentleman and

who honoured Wedgwood in a day when no one cared for his name and few for his works, came upon them by mere chance – and from that day they thus became his property through purchase.

She went on to say that in deference to the Darwins' feelings she would make a few alterations, but that she would not change the whole book in order to fit one point of view. 'I have a duty to perform to Mr Mayer, to my publishers, to myself and what is of still more account – my duty to posterity – who will receive these truths of good – many of them great – men – however chequered by the good and ill of human character – with an interest which *we* cannot conceive.' In fact, when the book was published little offence was taken by Hensleigh and Fanny or the rest of the family.

While the sons flourished in their different careers, Etty and Bessy, now in their twenties, lifted much of the responsibility of running a home from Emma's shoulders. Bessy, who had seemed so backward as a child, was helpful, if slow. Her nephew Bernard, who knew her better than most of the family, considered that though so much Etty's inferior in intellect she was

> more sensitive . . . and I think I would rather have had her judgment of character, which was instinctive but wonderfully sound. She was a little helpless in managing certain things and never could be quite sure what five per cent meant . . . She always liked a good play (even tackled Hugo's Hernani in French) and a good novel. If she had not the wits of the rest of the family . . . she had better health and was certainly free from their tendency to cosset themselves.

Emma's sensitive and loving treatment of Bessy had brought out the best in a child who might otherwise have been difficult. Given confidence by her mother, she had gamely chosen to go as a boarder to a school in Kensington to continue her education, and struggled to learn French.

It had seemed that Etty and Bessy would remain good Victorian spinsters, helping their mother, caring for their invalid father. But to the

family's astonishment – and even to her own – in June 1871 Etty
announced her engagement to Richard Litchfield, a member of the
Ecclesiastical Commission responsible for the management of Church of
England property. He was also a friend of John Ruskin, and his real interest
was the Working Men's College in London, which he had helped to found
and where he taught music. There had been no talk of love affairs involving
Etty, although there were mentions of young men at balls held by their
neighbours, the Lubbocks. Yet, tiny, vivacious and intelligent, Etty was
attractive enough to sweep Litchfield off his feet in a fortnight. Richard
was small and no Adonis, but Etty loved him and his huge brown beard,
and he opened up a new world for her.

Nothing better illustrates Etty's real character and the warmth of her
affection than her letters at this time to George, the sibling nearest in age
to her and the closest.

Please prepare your mind for the most tremendous piece of news
concerning myself I could tell you. *The* supreme crisis of my
life. I am going to be married to Mr Litchfield. You will say that
I don't know him, – that was true a fortnight ago when he asked
me, but since then I do, & he has made me believe that he does
care for me, as I have dreamt of being loved, but never expected
that supreme happiness to fall to my lot.

I am sure he is no relation to the pastry cook, however like
their beards are. His father was a retired Indian Officer. He is a
Cambridge man – 2nd class Classics & just escaped being a high
enough wrangler to get a Trinity Fellowship – which enraged
his Father – but as he was even then profoundly unorthodox
was a relief to him. He is clerk of the Ecclesiastical Commission
where he says his work is amusing eno & varied which is not
generally the case in a government office. He enraged his Father
also by giving up law for which he was educated, but he felt no
desire for either nothing or too much to do & has never repented
his unambitious choice, especially as he has enough money – I
think he said abt £1000 a year. His only near relations are
Sister, married a solicitor, living near Cheltenham poorish & 9
children. Four nephews & nieces – Steele by name, children of

a dead sister, the father Capt. Steele just coming home from India so that he will be relieved of his guardianship. Uncle, General Litchfield, living in London and Aunt at Mortlake & clergyman uncle in Dorsetshire. He seems to be friendly with all our sort of people – Spottiswoodes, Vincent Thompsons, Lushingtons etc. The only other fact is that he is 39 years old.

I write this letter to Frank as well as to you. Tell him not to hate the 'cool beast' if he can help it. We all like that name and Uncle Ras especially. By the way, it is to be announced to you boys only just for a day or two – to get our courage up to tell the world. Sympathise with me in my happiness, my own dear boys. You must try to like him for my sake for I couldn't bear anything to come between our most precious friendship. There are very few sisters in the world who have received more happiness than I have from all of you.

Just before her wedding day she wrote again to George.

Dear George
I guess this will be my last letter as H.E.D. The marriage has advanced day by day – until it now stands for Aug 31st – think of me then.

I haven't anything to say to you. I know you & Frank wish me every possible good wish. My dear boys – you have been such a happiness to me both of you. It feels rather like dying – so I like to say this to you. I do care for you so much. I've got a heap of faults but I can care for people & if I married a 100 times over you will always have my truest love thro all your lives. Goodbye dear George & dear Frank – forgive me all the times I've been cross & selfish & bothering.
Your ever loving
H.E.D.

Etty and Richard were married in the church at Downe on 31 August 1871. Charles braced himself to do his duty as the father of the bride and doubtless Emma, remembering Aunt Jessie's advice on her own wedding, for once dressed in style. Richard was surprised and touched by the appearance in the congregation of a party of his students from the Working Men's College, who had walked the four miles from the station to wish them well. The College, whose members obviously regarded him with much affection, gave the couple a party on their return from their honeymoon and presented them with a picture; the founder and principal, F. D. Maurice, made an enthusiastic speech.

Charles and Emma may well have been somewhat saddened initially by the loss of Etty, but when they heard her account of the praise of Richard at the College reception, they were impressed. 'What a grand career he has run,' Charles wrote to her; 'I congratulate you with all my heart at having so noble a husband. What an admirable address and well written. Even you Miss Rhadamanthus could not have improved a word.'

Etty's marriage to Richard Litchfield was supremely happy. He was forty and Etty was twenty-eight, but they suited each other admirably. Some time after her wedding Etty wrote to Emma,

> To Emma Darwin.
> . . . Good-bye dear Mother, we have both enjoyed our stay so much at Down – & it is such a delight to me that you like R & made him so tame there. It is such a happiness to me to have two homes & I feel as long I have Father & you it does instead of our having children & makes our lives quite full – for you are the dearest Father & Mother that ever anyone had. Your H.E.L.

Richard has been immortalized in Gwen Raverat's *Period Piece* as a docile little man, happy to be cosseted by Etty, wrapped in shawls and covered with dust sheets when the room was aired. Gwen was fond of her great-aunt and -uncle, but her brilliantly wicked little cartoons diminish them both. Richard was highly respected in the family and had been considered a possible suitor for Fanny Hensleigh's daughter Snow (Julia), who wrote to a friend, 'There was a very nice letter from Florence Nightingale about the marriage in which she says the bridegroom is the one man she would like to know.'

Richard brought a new dimension into the Darwin lives. Emma in particular welcomed him as a musician. She, Richard and Frank were to have many enjoyable evenings playing Mozart and Beethoven together. She was also intrigued and enlightened by his friends at the Working Men's College. She had inherited from her father a sense of her family's place in the social hierarchy. She was no snob, and had a strong commitment to improving the lot of the poor; she was no sentimental do-gooder. But she had also little knowledge, until Richard's arrival in her circle, of the intelligent urban working class with their passionate determination to improve themselves. Later she was to describe with wonder to Aunt Fanny Etty's adventure at the working men's ball, where her daughter had 'danced with a grocer and shoemaker, who looked and behaved exactly like everybody else and were quite as well dressed. The ladies were nicely dressed but not expensively, and much more decently than their betters are in a ball room now-a-days.'

Etty would be missed at Down, as Charles wrote sadly to her. 'But', he went on,

> I have had my day and a happy life notwithstanding my stomach: and this I owe almost entirely to our dear old mother, who, as you know well is as good as twice refined gold. Keep her as an example before your eyes and then Litchfield will in future years worship and not only love you as I worship our dear old mother. I shall not look at you as a really married woman until you are in your own house. It's the furniture which does the job.

Richard and Etty duly set themselves up in a house in London; Emma kept closely in touch, writing to her daughter almost every day, and the couple were often at Down, spending long holidays there.

Emma was particularly glad of Etty's presence when confronted by some of Charles's odder visitors – none stranger than the Russian who came in September 1875, as Etty reported to her brother George:

> To G.H.D.   Down Wednesday (Sept. 15. 1875)
> . . . Father has borne up very well against an invasion of a Russian ornithologist which took place on Monday. Father let himself in for it by writing very civilly to say how grieved he was to miss him. – Understanding that he would be on his way

back to Russia & so the wretched man put off his journey for a day. He was quite the most awful foreigner that has ever set foot in the house – very big & very dirty & hideously ugly. They say scratch a Russian & you find a savage – but you hadn't got to do that with this man & yet he was we believe a man of good position – had estate and serfs at any rate. He had been travelling in Kashgar and Kokhand & all those places & if he hadn't spoken with a voice uglier even than his face, & been also as unintelligent as he was repulsive, he might have had interesting adventures to tell. He had had his head almost cut off & the great gashes & scars made him uglier than nature did. He was brought down by a Mr Dresser . . . who has now taken to ornithology. He was the best satisfied man I ever came across. Even his dogs die for love of him & he can fire a gun quicker with his left hand than anybody else can with their right.

We had a farewell call from Carlyle on Sunday . . . He harangued us for an hour or more.

Etty entered her new life with zest, joining Richard and members of the Working Men's College on their Sunday walking parties, travelling by rail 'to some place near London' and walking a few miles to a spot suitable for luncheon and a tea picnic. 'Singing, gathering flowers, games and tea filled up the day and we used to come home, well tired out, by an evening train.' This was not the hypochondriac Etty of family legend.

In the summer of 1873 they brought the walkers to Down House for the first of many picnics. In this unaccustomed company, Emma was not entirely at ease; despite all Aunt Jessie's efforts, she had never learned the art of conversing easily with strangers. But she did her best, and Etty happily reported, 'My father and mother's gracious welcome, an excellent tea on the lawn, wandering in the garden and singing under the lime trees, made a delightful day, ending with a drive home to Orpington Station for the ladies of the party.'

CHAPTER FIFTEEN

Silk Gowns and Galantine

As the century moved towards its last quarter, there was an increasing interest – perhaps fostered by the intellectual and scientific ferment of the mid-century – in the occult, in 'animal magnetism' and spiritualism, and in all those forces which could be called upon to prove that there are more things in Heaven and Earth than were dreamed of by the scientists. Séances were organized and paid mediums were hired to produce in comfortable drawing rooms the manifestations which would prove the existence of an afterlife. As the old vision of the Pearly Gates of Heaven and its jasper floor faded, it was replaced for many by the image of 'the other side', from whose misty shores the dear departed were able to send messages. Clever mediums, like the American Daniel Douglas Home, produced astonishing effects, with voices and music. Even coolly rational scientists like the Scottish publisher Robert Chambers, author of *The Vestiges of the Natural History of Creation*, were persuaded that spiritualism should be investigated. After carefully noting the manifestations at a number of séances, Chambers decided that they 'compelled a reasonable man to believe in a spiritual agency, immortality and the hereafter'. When, at a séance in 1860, he called for his father's favourite tunes and 'Ye Banks And Braes Of Bonny Doon' and the 'Last Rose Of Summer' were played, he was convinced – and was even more firmly persuaded when Home repeated correctly the last words of Chambers's dead daughter.

Many of Charles's scientific friends, like Dr Gully, were believers, and – most surprisingly of all – some scientists, like Alfred Russel Wallace, openly supported spiritualism. Even Charles's brother, the sceptical

Erasmus Darwin, in 1874 arranged for a séance with a paid medium to be held in his drawing room, presumably as a form of light entertainment. Hensleigh and Fanny were to become involved in psychical research.

Emma and Etty brought a reluctant Charles to the party, at which George Eliot and her partner, George Henry Lewes, were also present. According to Etty, 'we were a largish party sitting around a dining table . . . Mr Lewes I remember was troublesome and inclined to make jokes and not play the game fairly and sit in the dark in silence. The usual manifestations occurred: sparks, wind blowing and some rappings and moving of furniture. Spiritualism made little effect on my mother's mind and she maintained an attitude of neither belief nor unbelief.' Charles, however, was irritated, and left the stifling room, as he told Hooker, 'before all these astounding miracles, or jugglery took place . . . the Lord have mercy on us all if we have to believe in such rubbish.' But Emma, who believed in an afterlife, did not dismiss spiritualism so completely. As she sat in the dark room, maybe she half hoped, half feared, to hear her sister Fanny's quiet voice – 'It's all a hum, Em' – or the thin cry of a child long dead. Aunt Fanny Allen read Emma's account with amusement and wrote briskly, 'Spirits do not meddle with matter and when heavy bodies are moved, it is matter that moves them.'

Snow Wedgwood wrote to a friend that year describing her 'interesting conversation about spiritualism' with her Aunt Emma. Her aunt's feeling for Charles, she said, was 'almost the most remarkable I know in a wife, the union of absorbing devotion and perfect impartiality is so striking. I don't know any wife quite so absorbed in a husband – of course there is not often so much to be absorbed in – and her time is quite taken up by ministration to him, and yet there is something peculiar in her clear sightedness to his narrowness of view.' Emma told Snow, 'I think he has quite made up his mind he *won't* believe it, he dislikes the thought of it so very much. Otherwise I'm sure Mr Wallace would be just the sort of man he would have believed.' Snow reported, 'I could not help saying rather spitefully, "I thought he used to look upon it as a great weakness if one allowed wish to influence belief." "Yes, but he does not act up to his principles." I said, "Well that seems to me what one means by bigotry." "Oh yes, he is a regular bigot." '

Emma was perfectly aware of Charles's faults and accepted them, just as he had accepted that she was still something of a 'little Miss Slip-Slop'.

But her patience was not unlimited, as their friend Laura Forster once saw and related in a letter to Etty. Emma, trying to find a moment's peace to write a letter to Leonard, escaped into the study, but she had not sat down two minutes before

> Bessy came in asking about Leo's letter & then your father, saying 'I am the most ill used man in the world. There's been a letter from Leo in the house half an hour & I have not heard a single word of it'. I condoled and said neither Bessy nor I had heard a word either and then I think it was that your mother from the writing table, 'If you go on chattering so I shant get my letter done'. Your father made a face as if of alarm and surprise at so sharp a rebuke from your mother, & we all sat dead silent for at least a minute – the silence was broken by your mother's saying, 'Ring the bell Bessy', on wh. your father added 'Look sharp Bessy. Mother isn't the woman to be trifled with when she speaks in that tone, I can tell you.' Which made your mother laugh so she could hardly begin the letter we were waiting to have read to us.

It was Emma's – and Charles's – sense of humour that saved many a difficult moment in their marriage.

This was on the whole a happier decade, but there were two deaths that deeply grieved them both. On 6 May 1875, at the age of ninety-four, Fanny Allen died in the little house on Heywood Lane, Tenby, where she had lived with Emma's Aunt Jessie and Aunt Emma, and, since their deaths, on her own. In the autumn of 1874 Fanny had paid her final visit to Emma at Down House. In the past years Emma had grown very close to her aunt, enjoying the stimulus of her sharp mind and sharing her unfading enthusiasm for politics. After her visit Etty had been amazed at her vitality, as she wrote to Laura Forster in the family shorthand.

> The little A^t Fanny has left us now & gone home. The more I saw her the more lost in astonishment I felt at her sharpness & freshness of mind & at her vehement prejudices. It is a gt mystery how anybody can have lived 90 years & not have lost

some of these last. She is a gt example of the differences between our way of looking at things & the last generation's – none of that groping into the foundation of all things. I'm afraid none of us doubting questioning 19th centuryers will have the vigour to stand against 90 years of life & show so bold a front. The more I thk of the difference the m profound it seems. I was thinking over Miss Austen's novels if I could remember one single abstract remark upon life or any of its difficulties such as one meets with by the score in the most matter of fact novels nowadays. The nearest to it is Anne Eliot's depression at the aimlessness of her life – but it is only part of her love affair.

A few days before her death, Fanny had written to Emma,

I have been trying my hand in writing with a lithographic pencil but I have not the patience to wait as your pretious [*sic*] letter with its grateful remembrance of the sad April days of 51 makes my heart beat with gratitude to you for its recollection – coupled as it was by the memory of your grief for your darling. It is true gaps can never be filled up, and I do not wish them to be filled other ways than our memory fills them.

Clear-eyed and unsentimental as ever, she had left a firm message: there was to be no emotional deathbed scene. 'My love to all who love me, and I beg them not to be sorry for me. There is nothing in my death that ought to grieve them. For death at my great age is rest. I have earnestly prayed for it. I particularly wish that none of my relations should be summoned to my bedside.' Emma would have understood. But Fanny was the last of her Allen generation, and she would miss her. In that bright mind she had held a lifetime of extraordinary memories which remained sharp and clear to the end and which enriched Emma's life. She had been a friend of politicians, like Sir James Mackintosh and his circle, and of Sydney Smith and Florence Nightingale; she had known Coleridge and Byron, and had heard Wordsworth and Jeffrey make up their ancient quarrel. Emma never forgot Aunt Fanny's account to Elizabeth of an evening at Hensleigh's when Carlyle and Mazzini argued about Beethoven.

'TC could see nothing in Beethoven's sonatas, "it told nothing". It was like a great quantity of stones tumbled down for a building and "it might as well have been left in a quarry". He insisted on Mazzini telling him what he had gained by hearing music, and when Mazzini said inspiration and elevation, Carlyle said something not respectful of Beethoven and Mazzini ended with *Dieu vous pardonne*.' Fanny had seen the great in their mortal dress, and gave Emma a healthy disrespect for the trappings of fame.

The death of Aunt Fanny ended an important part of Emma's life. Her mother's sisters and their husbands had given her a cultural richness and a lifelong interest in politics and world affairs that Charles did not have. As a young man, listening to Sir James Mackintosh, he had felt, he said, 'as ignorant as a pig about politics'. A passionate humanitarian, hating cruelty, Charles had never forgotten the brutal treatment of slaves he had seen in South America, and always keenly supported the abolition of slavery; but as he became older his interests narrowed as he concentrated on science. Emma, however, closely followed British and European politics, to the end of her life reading with interest reports of parliamentary debates in her favourite newspaper, *The Times*. In 1862, she had followed the progress of the American Civil War with great interest, but though, like Charles and all the Wedgwoods, she was passionately concerned to see the abolition of slavery, she thought carefully and independently. Aunt Fanny heard, to her astonishment, that 'Emma D was on the side of the Federals.' In fact, both she and Charles regarded the ending of the brutal war, which had divided so many families, as of paramount importance. They were sickened by the reports of a continent steeped in blood, where families were torn apart by hatred.

In the last years of Aunt Fanny's life, Emma was following the Franco-Prussian War of 1870. 'We talk and read of nothing but the war,' she wrote to Aunt Fanny.

> I think L. Napoleon's fate might make a tragedy if he was not such a prosaic character himself. I can't help hoping that when he is kicked out, which must happen soon, Prussia may be persuaded to make peace. What an enormous collapse it is of a nation tumbling headlong into war, without a notion of what the enemy

was capable of. Leo tells us that almost all the Woolwich young men are 'French', Leo himself is a staunch Prussian.

Meanwhile Emma was reading a life of Napoleon Bonaparte, whom Aunt Fanny had so admired in the old days. After the death of Aunt Fanny, Emma's letters became briefer and less revealing, and she developed a habit of writing in her own shorthand, increasingly concealing her deepest feelings, becoming more Wedgwood than Allen. In her last letter to Fanny, Emma had thanked her for her support and understanding at the time of Annie's death. Her aunt would not be there to console her in the second great tragedy of Emma's life.

―――――――――

In the summer of 1874, the gap in the family circle left by Etty's departure was filled. Frank married and brought his charming young Welsh bride, Amy Ruck, to live in a little house near by, where he continued to work as Charles's secretary. Emma felt an immediate rapport with Amy, whose lilting Welsh voice brought back memories of Cresselly and the Allen aunts. For a brief time she enchanted them all.

Frank and Horace had been schoolfriends of Amy's brothers, and had visited her family at Pantlladw. At that time it appears from her diary that Horace was the attraction. He was seventeen, she twenty, and Horace had from early days been given to intense passions for older women. After her death, Amy's son, Bernard, found her 'heart breaking little diary' in which she described Horace – 'little Horace, simple, kindly and clever'; Leonard was merry and good-natured and bright, but Horace was 'entirely interesting . . . His nature seems a richer one than the others, with more passionate feeling, he is more of a poet in nature,' but she wondered whether he felt 'the beauty of things' as keenly as she did. However, they 'climbed sand hills and rushed down hand-in-hand screaming with laughter and even changed hats on a drive.' Amy brought fun to the good, sober Darwins, though when she visited Down House she was somewhat subdued and rather frightened of Charles, kind though he was, 'making little jokes' and letting her 'clean some manuscript for him'. She and Horace idled together in the Well House, throwing stones into the well and timing the splash; she listened somewhat awed to George and Horace talking about mathematics. But this brief love ended when she returned home and Horace went up to Cambridge. Four years later it was his brother who won the prize.

Much as she loved Frank, Amy's heart was always in Wales. In her letters to him she slips easily into Welsh; Pantlladw was paradise, her home a 'tiny grey house set on a little plateau carved out of a hill side'. Her mother, wrote Bernard, was a 'unique personage', the 'noblest creature that I have ever known'. With her sister and four brothers, Amy had the happiest of childhoods. Once, her diary describes, she had 'climbed the hill at the back of the house and saw simultaneously, sunset, moonlight and a rainbow . . . it was a place where magical things could happen.' Her journal describes 'a mad escapade' when she climbed out of her bedroom window down knotted towels to a stepladder and climbed the hill at the back of the house in pitch blackness. 'I have really at last spent a night in the darkness alone. It has always been my wish . . . Everybody believes I have been in bed all night. I am sitting in a pink and white dress, quite fresh and untired, waiting for breakfast.'

This was the girl who, at twenty-four, captured the heart of serious, studious Frank. Two of her letters, written to him before their marriage, survive. Simple, fresh and affectionate, they explain why to Emma she became a much-loved daughter-in-law.

Thank you my own Frank for your letter. It makes me so glad – the words are full of your love and bring you close to me. I thought of them in church today. It does make me want to come to you Frank, but it is a happy longing. It is not long now to wait only to me the days drag rather. I can't get away to talk to you – you will remember the lines in Browning to show me, my darling – Frank I always wanted to tell you what a great good I feel it to have such love as yours. But I can't tell you. I feel so blessed, it is so wonderful. Your letter makes me more conscious that we have a world to ourselves that outside things do not matter.

I want this letter to go off today, you will be surprised dear and I want to answer things in 'yours' to day how nice I think the table and the jugs . . . I couldn't help laughing when I came to that disconsolate bit of your letter – I'm so glad you bought them my boy, crack and all because of their delightful quaintness, the purple one must be pretty. I think the shapes are very – and no doubt that crack can be done something to. We had a jug in which the bottom came out and after it was cemented it held water . . . Another present came last night from Chls Lloyd, such a dear little jug and basin, blue and white Delft I think with a charming blue scrawling pattern. It belonged to our great great grandmother so it is nice having it, isn't it?

In the autumn of 1876 Amy gave birth to Bernard. In the early morning a week later she died of puerperal fever. Frank, Charles and Emma were with her. To Hooker, who of all his friends would understand, Charles wrote simply, 'At seven o'clock this morning, I watched her die.' Their grief was intensified by anguish for Frank. He was heartbroken, and never quite recovered from his loss. Years later, after Charles's death, Emma wrote to Etty, 'I feel I can bear your father's loss. I felt I could not bear Amy's.' Frank brought Bernard to Down House; once again Emma had a young child to care for, and Bessy had a baby on whom she could lavish all the love of her simple heart. But Amy's death had shaken Emma profoundly, and while Bessy was affectionate and comforting, she was hardly a stimulating companion.

Charles, as so often, could find at least some solace in his work. He had been relieved, when *The Descent of Man* was published in 1871, to find that the hostility he had so fearfully anticipated did not, to any great extent, materialize; and so he could return, with considerable relief, from the great philosophical questions that he had found so taxing to his real love of detailed scientific observation and analysis. Over the ensuing decade he published four more books, returning with particular enthusiasm to his investigation of the world of worms – a subject that had enthralled him for more than forty years. Emma's father had long ago noticed how the action of worms improved the soil, and Charles had begun measuring the amount of soil they could move. In June 1877, feeling in comparatively good health, he decided to go to Stonehenge to find out if and how worms had covered up the ancient stones. With Emma, he set off at 6.45 a.m.

from William's house at Basset on a brilliantly clear day that was soon to become hot, taking the train for Salisbury where George met them with their open carriage and pair. It was a two-hour rail journey and a twenty-four-mile drive, but Charles was determined: worms apart, he had always wanted to see Stonehenge. Emma resisted the temptation to wait at Salisbury and read her book in the cathedral, and went along. She chatted with the old soldier who was caretaker of the site while Charles – or George – dug for worms in the broiling sun. Emma dryly remarked, 'They did not find much good about the worms, who seem to be very idle out there.' She was astonished that 'F[ather] was wonderful, as he did a great deal of waiting out in the sun.' Typically, she regarded the expedition and Charles's obsession with worms with amused tolerance, and was glad to see him improved in health. Charles was now called 'F' in the family.

In the autumn of 1877 the gaps left by Etty's marriage and Amy's death were partly filled when William married. He had met his American bride, Sara Sedgwick, nine years earlier when she was staying with her brother-in-law's family at Keston near the house the Darwins had rented for the summer, but it had taken him a long time to pluck up the courage to propose. Emma was delighted. 'Loveable and transparently honest,' according to his brother Frank, William had the same sweetness of character that she had first loved in Charles. He, too, welcomed Sara with exceptional warmth. 'You will believe me when I say that for many years I have not seen any woman whom I have liked as esteemed so much as you.' He was afraid she might find life as a banker's wife in Southampton dull, and that she might be sacrificing too much in giving up her American home; but, he wrote, 'Judging by my own experience life would be a most dreary blank without a dear wife to love with all one's soul.'

By 1877 Charles had been crowned with honours from all over the world; but the one he most valued was conferred by Cambridge University, when on 16 November 1877 he was made Doctor of Law. Emma sent William an account of the proceedings.

It was a great disappointment your not coming yesterday to witness the honours to F., and so I will tell you all about it.

Bessy and I and the two youngest brothers went first to the Senate House and got in by a side door, and a most striking sight it was. The gallery crammed to overflowing with under-graduates, and the floor crammed too with undergraduates climbing on the statues and standing up in the windows. There seemed to be periodical cheering in answer to jokes which sounded deafening; but when F. came in, in his red cloak, ushered in by some authorities, it was perfectly deafening for some minutes. I thought he would be overcome, but he was quite stout and smiling and sat for a considerable time waiting for the Vice-Chancellor. The time was filled up with shouts and jokes, and groans for an unpopular Proctor, Mr—, which were quite awful, and he looked up at them with a stern angry face, which was very bad policy. We had been watching some cords stretched across from one gallery to another wondering what was to happen, but were not surprised to see a monkey dangling down which caused shouts and jokes about our ancestors, etc. A Proctor was foolish enough to go up to capture it and at last it disappeared I don't know how. Then came a sort of ring tied with ribbons which we conjectured to be the 'Missing Link'. At last the Vice-Chancellor appeared, more bowing and hand-shaking, and then F. was marched down the aisle behind two men with silver maces, and the unfortunate Public orator came and stood by him and got thro' his very tedious harangue as he could, constantly interrupted by the most unmannerly shouts and jeers; and when he had continued what seemed an enormous time, some one called out in a cheerful tone 'Thank you kindly'. At last he got to the end with admirable nerve and temper, and then they all marched back to the Vice-Chancellor . . . in scarlet and white fur and F. joined his hands and did not kneel but the Vice-Chancellor put his hands outside and said a few Latin words, and then it was over and everybody came up and shook hands.

Of all days in the year I had a baddish headache, but managed by dint of opium to go and enjoyed it all. F. has been to Newton's Museum today and seen many people – also a brilliant luncheon at George's. J.W. Clark did me a good turn, as I followed his lead in tasting galantine – which is very superior. I felt very grand walking about with my LL.D. in his silk gown.

The letter is typical of Emma: her relaxed attitude to fame and her humour, the juxtaposition of silk gown and galantine, was characteristic. It was her way of staying sane. Also typical is Etty's omission of 'by dint of opium' from the published letter. Small doses of opium were almost as readily accepted as Valium is today.

In the summer of 1879 Charles was again exhausted, and Emma determined to whisk him away from his desk and microscope for a holiday. 'I have been working pretty hard of late,' he told Hooker, 'so we all go to Coniston for a month. It is an awful journey to me.' He always dreaded a move, as Frank remembered – 'There was always a miserable sinking feeling from which he suffered immediately before the start' – but once embarked he enjoyed even a long journey in 'an almost boyish way and to a curious extent'. They left Euston at 10 a.m. with the Litchfields, Bessy, little Bernard, nurses and maids; Frank was to join them later. They took rooms at the Waterhead, a commodious hotel, built in 1861, at the head of Lake Coniston, with spectacular views of the long, level lake set in green pastures and, beyond, the high fells.

A neighbouring magnate, Victor Marshall, called, offering them the use of his carriage and the freedom to roam around his great estate. 'A little steamer plies on the lake,' Emma wrote appreciatively, 'which will suit Bernard.' Charles was 'in an idiotic state of idleness . . . a golden state of vacuity . . . The place is most beautiful and the inn very comfortable, but there are too many human beings for my taste,' he complained, and the weather was cold and wet.

Emma, despite the weather, was enchanted; like her mother she enjoyed travel. The railway 'across Morecambe Bay is v grand & striking – the immense expanse of sand flanked by such fine mountains. We are v comfortable at this quiet hotel and have 2 sitting rooms. The lake can only be called hideous in this weather, black & stormy & dark green banks – The mts over the immediate bank are grand & the walks up the valleys are endless & beaut.' Unfortunately, as Emma grew older, her journal, as well as her letters, was increasingly written in shorthand. It is tantalizingly elliptical, her delight measured in exclamation marks:

Saturday 2 August set out for Coniston. 3 Cloudy. Marshalls called. 4 do sun in p.m. Walked out. Frank came. Fire. 5 Fire. 7 2 fires. Drove & walked. 9 2 fires. Went in boat. Called on Miss Beavers. Walk. 9 one fire. Fine. Walked up by torrent w. F. 10 Went in boat. One fire. 11 No fire. Drove 2 [to] Ch[arles's] View of Yewdale. George came. 12 No fire. Lunch at Ruskins. 14 Went to Grasmere!!! 15 Went in boat. 16 Fire. Leo came. Drove up to Tilberthwaite farm. 17 Rain. Fine. Beaut row on lake to old Coniston Hall. 18 Drove to Skelwith Bridge. Pretty lights rainy. 19 Drove by Hawkshead road & Marshalls grounds. 21 Went to Furness. Ugly day. 22 Stormy day. 23 Drove to How Tarn!!! & row on Lake. 24 Drove out in p.m. !! 27 Came home.

Charles expanded on Emma's 'Drove 2 Ch view of Yewdale' in a letter to Marshall:

> It is a constant pleasure to me to recall the scenes at Coniston, – the one out of your grounds which is most indelibly impressed on my brain, is on the cross-road from beneath your house, near the Ewedale road, where a fine rugged mountain is seen over a flat field, with an old farm-house with fine sycamores on the left-hand. It seems to me a perfect picture. I heard lately a story of a rough Yankee who was showing the Hudson River to an English Lord who admired the view greatly. The Yankee then said 'yes, Lord, we take a deal of pains with our scenery' & I think that you all at Coniston have taken a deal of pains with your mountains.

Fortunately Etty, like Emma's late sister Fanny, enjoyed writing and gave a fuller account of her father's reactions.

> We had a peculiarly delightful expedition to Grasmere. A perfect day & his state of vivid enjoyment & flow of spirits is a picture in my mind I like to think of. He could hardly sit still in the

carriage for turning round and getting up to admire the view from each fresh point, and coming home even, he was full of the beauty of the bit by Rydal Water. But he wouldn't allow that Grasmere at all equalled his beloved Coniston. He reread most of the Excursion during this visit after an interval of I suppose thirty or more years. I think it was a disappointment. He found parts of it preachy & it did not give him much pleasure. Parts of it he had admired extremely & his old Wordsworth – a funny [?serious] edit in one volume – is marked with his notes as to what to skip & what he cared for.

Emma's relative silence is intriguing. In the old days she would have written long letters to Aunt Jessie or Aunt Fanny, who knew Wordsworth and Coleridge well; but they were gone. Did she and Charles get out of the carriage and walk up to Wordsworth's door as their Uncle Tom had done with Coleridge more than seventy years before? Did Emma know that the postman had walked up this cobbled street bringing letters to Wordsworth from her father, lending him money for his tour of Germany? If they knew the history of their family it would have given an extra dimension to their excursion to Grasmere, which had rated three exclamation marks in Emma's code.

A letter from Emma to Ida Farrer (soon to become her daughter-in-law) merely mentions in passing that Mark Twain was a fellow guest at their hotel. 'Mr Sly [the landlord] told your uncle . . . that "that was Mark Twain" and I suppose had done the same thing with respect to him to M.T. so they had a pleasant talk. His manner is oddly like that of Carlyle.' They must have had an interesting discussion, since Emma and Charles both loved his books; Charles told a visitor in 1872 that he always kept *The Jumping Frog* by his bedside for midnight amusement. Emma's brief 'Lunch at Ruskins' is again tantalizing. They had met Ruskin earlier when they were staying at Keston, not long after Ruskin had wrongly quoted Carlyle as speaking bitterly of Charles and his doctrines; and Richard Litchfield, of course, had known him well through his work at the Working Men's College, though there had been some differences between them. On this visit, Richard noted in his diary, they 'saw a good bit of Ruskin at Brantwood', Ruskin's last home across Lake Coniston, and he seems to have been friendly. Etty fills in the story in the memoir she wrote after Richard's death.

> He was our near neighbour at Brantwood. He had been seriously ill with brain trouble and when he got excited in talking there was a painful look in his wonderful blue eyes; but it was a great delight to Richard to meet him again. One day we rowed across the lake to see him and set off back again at the beginning of a thunderstorm . . . Ruskin was charming . . . though, as is well known, he thought my father's views on evolution pernicious nonsense.

She also remembered that after their visit Ruskin wrote to her:

> It has indeed been a very great pleasure to me to be brought into some nearer and kinder relations with Mr Darwin: but you must not think I did not before recognize in him all that you speak of so affectionately. There is no word in any of my books of disrespect towards him, though I profoundly regret that the very simplicity and humility of his character prevents his separating what of accurately observed truth he has taught us from the wild and impious foolishness of the popular views of our day.

Ruskin had called on them at their hotel, as Etty describes:

> We all thought we could trace a slight embarrassment in his manner during his first call – his manner to my father was rather elaborately courteous & by some odd blunder he knighted him in his imagination & constantly said 'Sir Charles'. It was not very long after Ruskin's great illness [the 'brain trouble' Etty mentioned above] & my father noticed the flush that came over his face when he began to talk abt the clouds & the bad influence that was now at work in the heavens – My father turned the conversation with his usual tact. It was very charming to see his

manner to Ruskin & how these two – so different by nature & with such opposite interests – could find so much in common to discuss. It is needless to say that my father owed Ruskin no grudge for any of the hard things he might have said of him & listened to him with his usual courteous deference. Ruskin had changed in feeling to Richard – why we do not know. But my father knew this & took special pains to tell Ruskin when we were not present how true a follower R [Richard] was, & how he, Father, wd not like to stand in the shoes of any man who spoke disrespectfully of Ruskin 'in Litchfield's presence'. It was so like him to remember to say this. Ruskin sent over some photographs, I forget why. Amongst these there was a Holbein of Erasmus I believe – I remember my Father's saying to Ruskin that he supposed it was very bad taste but he admired it the most of any of the photographs sent – and his being pleased at Ruskin's saying that he considered him perfectly right. I do not think my father got any pleasure out of Ruskin's Turners. He said 'they are beyond me'. I believe he was struck by a little Bewick of some bird I think, in watercolour.

Once again one longs for a glimpse of the scene at Brantwood through Emma's eyes. As it is, we must imagine the meeting of the two white-bearded patriarchs in Ruskin's cool, spacious drawing room, so sadly childless. Did they stand before the wide windows and admire the incomparable view of the still lake among green pastures? Was the weather dull, the lake silver grey and the stone walls iron black? Or was it sparkling blue, the stone walls lit with green? Beside the window stood Ruskin's piano, as it still does. Now it bears a notice: 'Please play if you wish.' If Emma was persuaded to play after lunch, what would she have chosen? A Beethoven slow movement might have been her choice for so historic an occasion. But certainly she would not have gushed over the event. She had been accustomed all her life to meeting great men and women and, like her grandmother, old Sally Wedgwood, remained staunchly unfazed by any of then. She was not, moreover, much in sympathy with Ruskin. When later she read Waldstein's life of him she agreed with the author in criticizing him for obsession with himself, contrasting his style with that of Charles, and attacking Ruskin's 'narrow want of sympathy: e.g. thinking it a real misfortune that railroads should desecrate beautiful places by enabling vulgar people to crowd into them'.

At the end of their visit Charles wrote to thank their host, Mr Marshall:

> I cannot leave tomorrow morning this delightful place without thanking you cordially for all your kindness. Your permission for me to wander over your estate & grounds has made all the difference in my enjoyment, & in the good which the visit has done me. I can call your garden nothing less than Paradise. We have used your carriage several times & your coachman has been most obliging. We went one very long expedition to Grasmere, home by Ambleside. The three miles between these two places is the most splendid drive which I ever took. Nevertheless I am a staunch Conistonite & feel indignant if anyone prefers Grasmere or Ambleside to Coniston. Pray tell Mrs Marshall that we disobeyed orders & went to Furness; & we were punished, for the day was dark & gloomy. On our return we said that a walk along your Terrace was worth half a dozen Furness Abbeys; & in the afternoon I proved the truth of this by taking 2 or 3 turns along the Terrace, & though the afternoon was dull they gave me intense pleasure.

Marshall replied: 'I am very glad that you had a good time here. Next time you come I hope we may be able to get hold of a house for you . . . Ruskin told someone the day after he had heard that you had arrived, that if Mr Darwin would get different kinds of air & bottle them, & examine them when bottled, he would do much more useful work than he does in the contemplation of the hinder parts of monkeys. I communicate this valuable suggestion to you free of all charge.' To which Charles replied with his customary good humour: 'Your letter amused us much. It was very acute of Mr Ruskin to know that I have a deep and tender interest about the brightly coloured hinder half of certain monkeys.'

The break at the Lakes had set Charles up, and 1880 began well with the long-delayed marriage of their youngest son, Horace, to Ida, the daughter of Sir Thomas Henry Farrer by his first wife. In 1873 Farrer married as his second wife Effie (Euphemia), the daughter of Hensleigh and Fanny Wedgwood, and the couple lived at the Farrer family home, Abinger Hall, near Dorking in Surrey, where Charles and Emma often visited them. Ida was herself distantly related to the Allen family; Emma had known her for some time and was fond of her. Farrer was a rather pompous barrister and civil servant who – to Emma's annoyance – initially opposed the marriage of Ida to Horace, whom he considered unworthy of his beloved daughter on grounds of health, temperament and income, calling him in no uncertain terms 'too damned hypochondriac'. Certainly Horace, born in the tragic month after Annie's death, had always been delicate. However, Ida was a determined young lady and loved Horace and, after many anxious interviews with his prospective father-in-law, Horace won the day. They were married on 3 January 1880. Emma was delighted; Ida became a much-loved addition to the family. 'F and I often reflect how well off we are in daughters-in-law,' she told Sara, 'and how easily our sons might have married very nice wives that would not have suited us old folks, and above all that would not really have adopted us so affectionately as you have done. I never think without a pang of the third that is gone.'

It had been a happy start to the year; but in the chill of March, Emma's eldest brother, Josiah Wedgwood III (Joe), died at his home at Leith Hill Place in Surrey. At eighty-five, the quiet old man had been glad to slip away; but although there had been a wide gap in age between them, Emma was saddened by his loss, and Charles grieved for Joe's widow, his own sister Caroline. The marriage had been happy on the whole; Caroline had had a nervous breakdown causing her to withdraw into seclusion at Leith Hill Place for twelve years; but she made a full recovery and by the 1870s was her old self again. Both Joe and Caroline had inherited substantial fortunes, and Leith Hill Place and the beautiful estate (now in the care of the National Trust) reflected his position as a country gentleman of means. Quiet and undemonstrative, he had been an affectionate father to their three daughters, Sophy, Margaret and Lucy, and a loving grand-parent. A charming letter from him to his grandson, Ralph Vaughan Williams, still bears the imprint of the gold coin it enclosed. Emma and Charles had always enjoyed their visits to 'L.H.P.'; although Emma found the house somewhat bleak, with its dark, cold, uncarpeted corridors, they both liked to wander round the estate. Seeing Caroline with her children reminded Charles of his own childhood, and of the days when she had taught him to read; he repaid her as best he could, encouraging her children to enquire and learn. When the girls were young he enrolled them in his army of observers and wrote to them, as he had to his own children, with affection and respect. 'My dear Lieutenant Lucy' was asked to look up plants in a botanical magazine for him: 'Were the flowers of the plant as Erica Massoni, glutinous? How about the Paeony seeds – do the pods open, are they brilliantly coloured? Do birds eat them? Have the seeds a thin fleshy coat? Your affectionate Uncle/Commander.' The little girls were flattered, and worked with a will. Lucy prodded the earth with knitting needles, researching earthworms; Sophy observed their casts; and they delighted in his praise: 'My dear Angels! I can call you nothing else. I never dreamed of your taking so much trouble. The enumeration will be invaluable . . . but I write now to ask whether you will be more angelic than angels and send me in tin, not tightly packed, with little damp (not wet) moss (perhaps tied round stems?) 2 or 3 flowers of both forms of Hollonia; I much wish to measure pollen and compare its grains.'

Now, in helping Caroline through the loneliness of her widowhood, Charles renewed himself. 'Our visit has been well worth while,' Emma wrote to her son. 'It seems to have roused poor Aunt C and done her real good . . . She came down about 11 and sat all day having a great deal of talk with F for the whole day till 9. F exerted himself enormously and with the daughters also.' But Emma's sharp eyes saw in Sophy the shadow of the mental illness that was to come. 'Poor Sophy strikes one anew every time one sees her as utterly dead and quite as much dead to mother and sisters as to the outsiders.' So, when they came to Down, Emma encouraged Sophy's one interest passed on by her mother – music. Thus the musical tradition was handed on. Sukey had taught Caroline to play the piano; Caroline's daughter Margaret, who had married the Revd Arthur Vaughan Williams, and was now widowed, also lived at Leith Hill Place. Sophy taught their son, Ralph Vaughan Williams, to play the piano: he was destined to become one of England's great composers. Emma watched his development with interest. No doubt she played for the six-year-old his first composition, 'The Robin's Nest', and heard of his progress as a schoolboy at Rottingdean near Brighton.

In 1884 she wrote to George's wife, from Brighton, that 'Ralph comes every half holiday for some hours. He got into a scrape the other day for playing his violin after he had gone to bed which set the boys dancing in their shirts and the masters came in.' So from Sukey to Ralph the chain of music linked the generations.

Despite these emotional upheavals, in the spring and summer of 1880 Charles was unusually well and was able to take an interest in the Midlothian election which brought Gladstone to power as Prime Minister. As always, Emma had followed the affair with keen interest, and the Liberal success sent her 'head over heels with excitement'. She was only sorry that Etty did not share her political views. 'Our mental champagne', she wrote to her Liberal son, Leonard, 'has had very little sympathy except from Aunt Elizabeth as Frank hardly cares and George cares a little the wrong way, though he says now that he hopes the Liberals may be as strong as possible so as not to have to truckle.' She and Elizabeth lived again the heady days of the Reform Bill when they had cheered on their father in his election. But Charles's attention soon returned to his scientific preoccupations. Emma wrote to Leonard that Charles, with no proof sheets to worry about, had 'taken to training earthworms, but does not make much progress as they can neither see nor hear. They are, however, amusing and spend hours in seizing hold of the edge of a cabbage leaf and trying in vain to pull it into their holes. They give such tugs they shake the whole leaf.'

In June that year Charles received a present from his family that gave him the deepest pleasure – not only on account of the gift itself but also from the manner of the giving, illustrating the warm affection that surrounded him. Though he always was sensitive to cold, Charles would never have allowed himself the extravagance of a fur coat. Frank arranged the surprise and described it in a letter to Etty.

I think the coat exploded very well. I left it on the study table, furry side out and a letter on top at 3, so that he would find it at 4 when he started his walk. Jackson [the butler who had succeeded Parslow] was 2nd conspirator, with a broad grin and the coat over his arm peeping thro' the green baize door while I saw the coast clear in the study. You will see from Father's

delightful letter to us how much pleased he was . . . I told
Mother just before so that she might come and see the fun.

Charles thanked them with tears in his eyes.

> I have just found on my table your present of the magnificent
> fur coat. If I have to travel in the winter it will be a wonderful
> comfort, for the last time I went to London I did not get over
> the cold for 2 or 3 days. The coat, however, will never warm my
> body so much as your dear affection has warmed my heart, my
> good dear children. Your affectionate Father, Charles Darwin.

Also that summer, Charles and Emma visited Horace and Ida in their new
home in Cambridge, and the trip greatly lifted Charles's spirits. The railway
company offered them a special carriage that took them from Bromley to
Cambridge via London, to Emma's pleased surprise. They were 'shunted
backwards and forwards' till she was quite confused and when she called
out 'why there is St Paul's, F calmly assured me that it must be some small
church as St Paul's was three miles from Victoria.' He worried that they
were giving so much trouble, but, wrote Emma, 'I was hardened and
enjoyed the journey.' A visit to his old college 'set Charles up'; Emma
enjoyed seeing Horace's new house, and was taken to Trinity Chapel to
hear the organ. 'I went to the organ loft and Mr Stanford showed the
effects of stops etc.,' she told Etty, and then in her characteristic way
added '(my bed is quite comfy)' – as Etty wrote, 'what the connection was
between the two no mortal man can tell.'

The autumn brought more sadness when Emma's sister Elizabeth died
on 7 November at her house near by. She was eighty-seven and for the last
ten years had been gradually going blind; although, as Emma told Aunt
Fanny, she could at least see enough to do some gardening, 'the beauty of
the flowers is very much lost to her.' Emma felt for her sister, who had
been so active all her life – teaching in her little school, caring for her
parents, doctoring the villagers, always besieged by beggars; even after
leaving Maer Hall, her house at Hartfield was always a welcoming home
for the family especially when 'sick or sorry'. She had cared for Emma in
childhood like a mother and had always been there to give support at the

birth of her babies; and now Emma saw her sitting depressed and idle, with hands folded. So she gave her the old Broadwood piano and taught her to play simple tunes unseen. Elizabeth had been revived, too, by visits to Fanny and her brother Hensleigh in London; but increasingly she had stayed for days and nights at Down with Emma. For more than a year, Etty remembered, her spirits had been 'a little failing and she seems so troubled with the vivid remembrance of old painful things and she said she should like everything past wiped out.' The memory of the sad last years of her parents haunted her, and in the growing darkness she feared for her own mind. When the 'little bent figure' came into the drawing room, leaning on her stick and followed by her dog, Tony, Emma put everything aside to help her. 'She never let sense of hurry appear and was always ready to give her warm and equable welcome.'

Now Emma had the task of clearing Elizabeth's house. 'The most pathetic thing I saw was the old parasol in its own place,' but, unsentimental as always, she was not tempted to take it away – 'it would be little to me anywhere else and the maids might like it. Tony is rather pathetic too, never barking, and wanting notice so much.' As she had always done after the deaths of her loved ones, she took comfort with the thought of 'what her life might have been this winter, even with something like recovery', and felt 'nothing but joy'.

Now only the solid, respectable Frank, the merry, irrepressible Harry, and the erudite Hensleigh remained of Emma's family. To Frank, Emma wrote: 'We shall be most glad to see any of those who loved her for the funeral (on Thursday probably about 2 o'clock) but I very much hope you will not take a long winter journey.' Nevertheless, sweet-natured, unselfish Elizabeth had been much loved, and Frank insisted on making the journey. 'I could not let her be buried and me not there,' he told Emma. Her brothers were now old men: Harry was eighty-one, Frank eighty and Hensleigh seventy-seven; they were joined by Charles's brother, seventy-seven-year-old Erasmus, though he was now very frail. Slowly, the four old men walked behind the coffin into the cold church and felt the chill of approaching winter.

CHAPTER SIXTEEN

Andante Con Amore

İN THE SUMMER OF 1881 EMMA PERSUADED CHARLES TO TAKE ANOTHER holiday in the Lake District, with the excuse that William needed to convalesce after an illness. This time they took a house, at Patterdale, large enough to accommodate most of the family – William, Bessy, Leonard, Bernard and his nurse, and Evvy the cook. George came later, and the Litchfields joined them for part of the time. Etty remembered this second visit as 'nearly full of enjoyment as the first. It was an especial happiness to my mother for the rest of her life to remember her little strolls with my father by the side of the lake. I have a clear picture in my mind of the two setting off alone for a certain favourite walk by the edge of some fine rocks going sheer down into the lake.'

'The House is excellent,' Charles wrote to Frank, 'most comfortable with plenty of large rooms . . . Bernard walked with us into the Marshalls' park carrying all the way the soldiers [presumably a present from Frank] received this morning, which made his little eyes sparkle like diamonds.' Emma encouraged George to join them. 'The place is delightful. We have not yet seen any mts quite so grand as the Old Man etc, but the lake and its close surroundings are infinitely prettier than Coniston and our house is most comfortable and luxurious and a little rocky shore of our own . . . Yesterday we went a sweet little row in the evening . . . There are per contras in kitchen but Evvy makes the best of them.' Mrs Evans had been with them for more than forty years and was used to 'making the best' of strange kitchens in rented holiday houses.

Once more Emma describes their month in her inimitable shorthand.

Thursday 2 June Slept at Penrith. 3 Came on to Glenrid. Fine mg. 5 Fine mg. Walked up the hill. RBL [Litchfield] came. Rain . . . Party steamed to meet. 5 Cold. Went in boat w. Hor.!!! [Horace] 6 V. cold. Drove towards Penrith. Walked in evg by lake. 7 V.cold. Snow on mts. Drove up Kirkstone Pass. Cold pretty storm. 9 Drove up the Grisedale Pass w. F. Cold. Gleams. 9 In bed most of day. 10 Went to see Mrs Ruck. Dull day. 11 Pretty morning. Calm. Went on Lake & after dinner. 12 C & I, B & L!!! crossed over & wandered on the other side. 13 Went in boat w!! – Fasker Glencoin 14 To Gore Barros w F. some pretty sights. 15 Dull day. Drove up Glencoin & seldom seen beaut brook. G. came. 16 Rain most of day. Mrs Ruck came. 17 Hen. went. Rain all day till drove Mrs Ruck home & looked at Mrs Varty's. 18 Wm came. He & Ch. & I drove to 3 lodgings. Walked up Glenridding, rain & gleams. 19!!! Went across in boat. F & I walked up to rocks! 22 Rain mg. Called on Mrs Ruck. Walked w her up brook. 23 Drove to Troutbeck. V. cold. Saw the island & beaut view of Borrowdale. 24 Fine. Tired after Keswick. 25 Rain, rain. W. & Leo went. 26!!! Row on Lake. 28 Mrs Ruck went by boat – picnic. 29 Rain most of day. Bessy & [I] walk. F. & I do Patterdale. 30 Rain! Storm all day. 1!!pm. Went to Howtown in steam boat. 2!! mg. Went w Bessy to Grisedale, she to St Sunday crag. 4 Came to Penrith. 5 Home.

The three exclamation marks accorded to the boat tips on the lake witness Emma's lasting delight at these outings, first experienced on the lake at Maer.

The Mrs Ruck whom Emma visited was Amy's mother, staying near by. She now spent long holidays at Down House and had shared with Emma the delight in their grandson. These two remarkable old ladies, walking beside the brook, could comfort each other as they thought of the lovely, lost Amy.

In spite of the scenery, which he thought 'quite wonderfully beautiful', Charles had periods of black depression. It was 'damnably cold and this precludes enjoyment,' he told George: Charles was always unusually sensitive to cold. To Frank he wailed, 'I have nothing in the world to do which I shd not much care about if the weather was decent but it is cold as winter & the lake is as black as ink with breakers on the shore and the sky like lead. Rain is driving by the north wind against the windows & all is cold and dismal.'

Emma, made of sterner stuff, sent Frank a more cheerful letter.

Sunday . . . actually a bright mg – & we are thinking of climbing up by B's rocks & doing a little trespassing. Yesterday G. & W. & Bessy set off for a Mt walk v soon W. [William] gave up – (it was most soft & muggy). G & B enjoyed it & had a few gleams – Wm loitered all up in those beaut parts – F & I had a rainy turn up Glenridding w. I was surprised to find so pretty. 2.30. The day has turned out even more beaut than the first Sunday – we all but F went in the boat first up & then coasting downwards as far as the How Town landing place – (where you embarked) we got out (B. was with us & dabbling his hand in the water & very quiet & happy). It was charming up among the junipers & rocks – Wm was much delighted but is rather troubled by wishing for Sara. [William had been happily married for four years, and longed for his wife's company.] The 4 young ones are going to have a carriage & go a little way up the Kirkstone Pass & turn off up Dovedale . . . Leo had no luck at Coniston one day he never stirred out. He took 4 photos, but thought they wd not be v good. He went up every evening to the Marshalls for their evening meal at 7.30 . . . F. got up to his beloved rock this morning but just then a fit of his dazzling came on & he came down – I mean to try and get there soon.

Emma never forgot the happiness of the weeks at Patterdale, walking quietly with Charles by the edge of the lake or standing with him at his favourite viewpoint, glad to see his old delight in nature restored once more; or laughing with him as he clambered up the rocks overlooking the lake, calling for her to join him. But she had watched with concern the 'fit of dazzling' which brought him down and sent him back to bed. When they said goodbye to Patterdale they both knew that they would not come again.

Charles, in fact, was slowly descending into the valley of the shadow.

For so long he had been addicted to work, and now that his major tasks were over, he found the withdrawal from his drug painful and depressing. As he told Hooker: 'I am rather despondent about myself . . . idleness is downright misery to me, as I find here, as I cannot forget my discomfort for an hour. I have not the heart or strength at my age to begin any investigation, lasting years . . . This place is magnificently beautiful & I enjoy the scenery, though weary of it; & the weather has been very cold & almost always hazy.'

Writing to his German friend Haeckel, Charles complained: 'I feel very old.'

———————

The relief of returning to Down, however, restored Charles, and he enjoyed the warm July days. Emma's diary for the sixteenth – 'Litches, Lushingtons, Miss North' – reminded Etty of their happiness 'when we could sit out under the limes all day. My father was in his happiest spirits, responding to Mrs Lushington's charming gaiety, and enjoying her grace and beauty and her enchanting music. This is a happy memory of the Down of our youth.'

But autumn came early that year. Ten days after that idyllic day under the scented lime trees, Charles's brother Erasmus died at his home in London. He was seventy-seven and had suffered for many years with acute intestinal pains. Unlike Charles he seems to have eased the agony with opium, and in the last years had hardly left his house.

Their sister, Caroline, herself now crippled with arthritis, was determined to come up to London from Leith Hill Place to see the brother she had brought up after their mother's death. With the help of her daughter, the widowed Margaret Vaughan Williams, she struggled up the three flights of stairs to Erasmus's bedroom and stayed in the room next door all day. Although in acute pain with violent sickness, he was glad she was there, and from time to time was able to smile with her at memories of their Shrewsbury youth.

After Caroline and Margaret had left, the visitor he most longed for came, and remained with him till his quiet end. Fanny Hensleigh, as all the family recognized, was the love of his life. He had been part of their family for years, called her his 'wee wife' and her daughters, Effie and Hope, 'our children'. But this was no scandalous *ménage à trois*; Hensleigh would not have tolerated it, nor would the fastidious Erasmus have so insulted him. He was Fanny's devoted *cavaliere servente* to the end. And Hensleigh, buried in his work, welcomed it, just as Carlyle had been grateful for his attentions to Jane, his wife. Caroline, who had not realized that Fanny had managed to be with Erasmus when he died, wrote to her, 'It is hard on you who have made the happiness of his life.'

Erasmus's body was brought to Downe, and his funeral was conducted by the Revd Allen Wedgwood, the son of Emma's Uncle John Allen. He had married Charles and Emma and officiated at the deaths of most of the family. Always so careful of his own health, now at eighty-five he seemed to be outlasting them all. (He died in the following year at Tenby, where he had gone to be with brother, Robert.) Erasmus was buried in the country churchyard at Downe. His epitaph was taken from Carlyle's memorial: 'One of the sincerest, truest and most honest of men.'

The younger Darwins would miss him. Fanny Hensleigh's daughter Julia (Snow) loved him dearly and wrote a memorial in the *Spectator* which did him more justice than Carlyle's rather patronizing article. She described his 'playfulness, tenderness, humour, lightness of touch . . . his memory retains a youthful fragrance, his influence gave much happiness of a kind usually associated with youth.' Charles was deeply grieved. Frank remembered him standing sadly at the graveside, his long black cloak sprinkled with snow. (Frank probably remembered the snow from Elizabeth's November funeral; or perhaps it was a scattering of summer blossoms.) Since the days when they had been Bobby and Philo (short for 'philosopher') in their laboratory in the Shrewsbury shed, the brothers had remained very close, and the tall, languid figure had been in the background of so much family life. Emma, too, had long admired him, had seen the sadness of his wasted potential.

Now only Charles and Caroline were left of the children of Dr Robert and Sukey, and both of them were aware that the days were drawing in. But the autumn still brought happiness. Emma and the boys were planning a hard tennis court, to be made on a strip of field beyond the orchard. 'We are boiling over with schemes about the tennis-court, and as soon as they are matured they are to be broken to F.' They could well afford this luxury, since apart from their considerable joint income they had inherited half of Erasmus's large fortune. In addition they had the promise of an inheritance from a Mr Anthony Rich which could come to Charles after his and his sister's deaths. He wished to honour a man 'whose abilities . . . had been devoted . . . for the benefit of mankind'. Now that Charles had the additional income from his brother's bequest, he offered to free Mr Rich from his promise. 'But he protested that he should do nothing of the kind and that with so many sons I required much money.' Charles agreed, 'though your mother is quite sorry!'

There was more pleasure that autumn when Charles and Emma spent a week at Cambridge. They went to see Richmond's picture of Charles in the library of the Philosophical Society. Emma 'thought it quite horrid, so fierce and so dirty. However, it is under glass and very high up so nobody can see it. Our chief dissipation was going to Kings, for which the tram was very handy.' Charles's health must indeed have improved if Emma was able to get him on a tram!

In September 1881 Emma found herself playing hostess to two leading atheists, admirers of Darwin. The President of the Congress of the International Federation of Freethinkers, Dr Ludwig Büchner telegraphed to ask for the 'honour of an interview' and wished to bring Dr Aveling. Clever, honey-tongued but sinister, the latter would drive his wife, Marx's daughter Tussy, to her death. He described their visit – Charles's 'serenity and strength', his 'quiet majesty'. At lunch 'Mrs Darwin was at the head, nearest the window that gave on the garden. The Revd Brodie Innes sat between her and Aveling and Charles between him and Büchner. Frank faced the mother and opposite to us were little children'. Charles talked of the effect of education and heredity and afterwards he and Frank took their guests into the study and had a fierce argument. Aveling found it difficult to place this affable country gentleman who was studying worms! Charles explained that he was an agnostic, not an atheist, though he agreed with them that Christianity was not supported by evidence. He explained that he had not given up his faith until he was forty years of age. He was concerned that the uneducated were not ready for free thought and would be dangerously disturbed by it. The two visitors left the unassuming squire in his country retreat. Dr Büchner could not understand the English.

The year drew to a close, however, with an additional delight – the birth of little Erasmus to Horace and Ida. 'In the night,' Emma told them, 'it has been my first and last thought.' She longed to see Ida with her baby 'before it gets the least stale'.

In the cold of February, Charles's health failed him again. There were some good days, when he could walk out a little way into the garden. But in March even gentle exercise brought on a pain in the heart. Emma tried in vain to persuade him to send for Dr Clark, but Charles knew how busy he was and was embarrassed that he always refused to take a fee for his visit. So Emma quietly wrote to him on her own initiative: he 'replied by telegram that he would come on the 10th of March but could spare a half to three-quarters of an hour during which he must have some dinner'. His hurried visit and diagnosis of angina pectoris so depressed Charles that he took to his bed, deciding that he could never work again. This time Emma sent for Dr Moore who made light of the diagnosis and calmed Charles's fears. Greatly cheered, for the rest of the month his health improved: he even walked out into the garden to admire the crocuses.

But on Saturday 15 April the old pain struck again. That night at dinner he became giddy and staggered, fainting, to the sofa where he collapsed, face down. He recovered and seemed somewhat better until at a quarter before midnight on Tuesday 18 April, he woke Emma, saying, 'I have got a pain and I shall feel better, or bear it better, if you are awake.' He asked her to get a capsule of amyl nitrate from his study, but it took her some time to find it and when she returned he had fainted. Brandy revived him and when he recovered, thinking death was near, he murmured to Emma, 'Tell all my children how good they have always been to me', and, as though to comfort her, 'I am not in the least afraid of death'. But dying was agony for him to suffer and for Emma to watch. Later she would tell a friend how impossible it was to erase the memory from her mind. It was not an easy end. Etty and Frank were with him and remembered his anguish: 'All that morning and afternoon the old nausea and retching returned. Again and again he moaned, "if I could but die" and Emma prayed for his release.' Etty gave him his smelling salts, rubbed him and once 'gave him a little pure whisky by his own desire. His hands were deathly cold and clammy and Frank could not feel his pulse at all.' All that afternoon, Etty recalled, 'he kept lifting his hands to hold his rope, and then they dropped off with a feeble quivering motion, and many times he called out, "Oh God, oh Lord God!", but only as exclamations of distress I think.' Etty did not record the death agony but Emma later worte of 'the last few hours of suffering which dwell upon the mind in an unreasonable degree because they are the last and which I would do much to forget'.

At about twenty-five minutes past three, Charles said he felt faint and Emma was sent for. Totally exhausted, she had been given an opium pill and was resting in Etty's room. She came quickly and found Charles grey and cold and breathing heavily. At 3:30 it was all over. The next day Etty wrote to George, a brief, broken letter:

> To G.H.D.   (Ap 20 1882)
> My dearest George
> Father was taken very ill last night with great suffering. They sent Dr Allfrey & he staid the night & was a great support to Mother. She was all alone with Bessy. They sent for Dr Moxon & he came just to see him take his last breath. Mother said he was longing to die and sent us all an affectionate message. He told her he was not the least afraid to die. Mother is very calm but she has cried a little.
> You will come at once.
> Your H.E.L.

Throughout the days that followed Emma remained calm, natural. Etty wrote in amazement on the day of her father's death:

> She came down to the drawing room to tea, and let herself be amused at some little thing, and smiled, almost laughed, for a moment as she would on any other day. To us, who knew how she had lived in his life, how she had shared almost every moment . . . her calmness and possession seemed wonderful then and are wonderful now to look back upon. She lived through her desolation alone and she wished not to be thought about or considered, but to rebuild her life as best she could and to think over her precious past. The wish for obscurity came out in her eager desire to get the first sight of her neighbours over, and then, as she said 'they will not think about me any more'.

She had never in the past made a parade of grief, and though this was the greatest desolation of her life she did not do so now. She had anticipated Charles's death for a long time, and found it bearable in a way that Annie's and Amy's had not been. Bernard remembered how that day she helped him with his French lessons, and never forgot that Wednesday afternoon – Grandmamma so still and grave, comforting Aunt Bessy; his father in tears explaining, as he led him out into the April garden, that Grandpapa would not suffer any more; and how he picked wild flowers, the first lords-and-ladies, to cheer Grandmamma.

On Thursday Leonard arrived, 'in such deep grief', Emma told him, 'I felt you were doing me good and enabling me to cry, and words were not wanted to tell me how you felt for me.' She wrote this to him in a letter the next day, because 'it is always easier to write than to speak, and so though I shall see you so soon, I will tell you that the entire love and veneration of all you dear sons for your father is one of my chief blessings and binds us together more than ever.' A letter from Fanny Hensleigh's daughter, Hope, had also given her great happiness. 'I should not be pitied,' she had written, 'after what I have professed and had been able to be to him.'

The funeral was planned to take place in the following week. Charles was to be buried with Erasmus in the ancient churchyard in the heart of the village. John Lewis, the village carpenter who had worked at Down ever since he was a boy, prepared the coffin – rough and plain, as Charles would have liked it. The Revd Brodie Innes, his old friend, offered to conduct the burial service. The publican at the George & Dragon, opposite the church, prepared to receive the expected crowds. But they were all to be disappointed. Charles's scientific friends and his cousin, Frank Galton, persuaded the President of the Royal Society to telegraph the Darwins to ask their consent to a burial in Westminster Abbey.

A notorious free-thinker honoured in the Abbey? The idea shocked conventional Anglicans – but Darwin's supporters won the day, canvassing support from all sides and arranging an appeal to the Dean of Westminster from the Houses of Parliament. The cause was taken up by the *Evening Standard* on behalf of the public: 'One who has brought such honour to the English name and whose death is lamented throughout the civilised world . . . should not be laid in a comparatively obscure grave . . . if it should not clash with his own expressed wishes, or the pious feelings of the family, we owe it to posterity to place his remains in Westminster Abbey, among the illustrious dead.' Finally, it was settled. Charles Darwin should take his place among the great scientists – many of them friends of both his grandparents, Josiah Wedgwood and Erasmus Darwin. Emma, after agonized discussion with the family, had given her consent. 'You will hear about Westminster Abbey,' she sadly told Fanny and Hensleigh,

> wh.[ich] I look upon as nearly settled. It gave us all a pang not to have him rest quietly by Eras – but William felt strongly, and on reflection I did also, that his gracious and grateful nature wd have wished to accept the acknowledgment of what he had done . . . I am sure dearest Fanny, that you wd have wished to attend if you had been in London, but it will be long and agitating and prob. cold and considerable risk and I am sure this applies to Hensleigh too.

The villagers were disappointed, their moment of fame wrested from them, and the carpenter, Lewis, was deeply hurt. 'I made his coffin just the way he wanted it, all rough, just as it left the bench, no polish, no nothin', but his coffin was not wanted and a smart shiny one sent – you could see your face in it.' Now the fashionable and famous funeral director Mr Banting would be in charge of the occasion.

On Tuesday morning Emma said goodbye with an aching heart as she watched the hearse, drawn by four horses, leave under a grey sky for the sixteen miles between Downe and the chapel of St Faith in Westminster Abbey, where Charles would lie in state. Frank, Leonard and Horace followed; Bessy and Etty would travel up the next day for the funeral. But Emma would not be there. Her grief was deep and must be private. All her married life she had prayed that they would never be parted. Now she watched him go alone to take his place in the Hall of Fame. It was her last sacrifice, and she made it willingly as always, because she loved him.

The next morning Emma sat alone at Down House while in London a vast congregation of mourners filled the Abbey. Later she would read the newspaper reports and her family would tell her all about the service. But now she was glad to follow quietly in mind the coffin, draped in black velvet and decked with her spray of white lilies, as it was lowered into the cold grave. For Emma it would have been a morning of quiet prayer, with a faith beyond reason, to a God of love who would not cast out a good man who had so earnestly searched for truth. As she had done after the death of her sister, she would have prayed that she would meet Charles again, 'never to part'. As she looked out over the rainswept garden, she remembered the happiness of those last July days under the scented lime trees and began holding such memories in her mind, to fix in her journal later.

When the family returned she could listen with quiet pleasure at their account of the day: the scientists and distinguished scholars in the congregation, the politicians who came from Parliament across the road, and the ordinary people who filled the back of the Abbey. Etty, who had sat with Bessy before the altar, had watched William, now head of the family, lead the procession – thirty-three Darwins and Wedgwoods followed the coffin; even Emma's brother Hensleigh, now eighty-two, made the effort. Their devoted butler Parslow and his successor Jackson followed, representing the household. Like Charles, Parslow avoided funerals, but he and Charles had always been comfortable together. Etty, proud of her five brothers, impressive in their funeral black, amused Emma with her description of 'dear old William' sitting through the ceremony with two black gloves protecting his balding head from the Abbey chill. Frank had admired the music – the choristers singing 'I Am The Resurrection' as they led the procession into the Abbey. Emma found this affirmation of faith a consolation, and had approved the music commissioned for the occasion to accompany the words, 'happy is the man that findeth wisdom and getteth understanding.' Etty, seated by the open black-lined grave, was proud that the father she loved was buried among the greatest scientists, below the monument to Newton and beside Sir John Herschel. 'His body is buried in peace,' the choristers had sung, 'but his name liveth evermore.' It was the kind of immortality that would have delighted her father.

In the following days Emma read the eulogies with pride, especially prizing the resolution from the British and Foreign Unitarian Association, which praised Darwin for unravelling 'the immutable laws of Divine Government' and for shedding light on the 'progress of humanity'. Old Josiah Wedgwood would have been delighted that his grandson was honoured by Unitarian friends. But Emma would have been amused at the extravagant language used by John Chadwick, a Unitarian preacher from New York, to describe the Abbey ceremony: 'The nation's grandest temple of religion opened its gates and lifted up its everlasting doors and bade the King of Science come in.' Caroline, now crippled and confined to her home at Leith Hill Place, wished that Charles's father could have shared her pride, and perhaps sighed that their Unitarian mother was not there.

But the structure of Emma's world was shattered. Her whole life had revolved around Charles, and the regular rhythm so essential to him had made the pattern that her own easygoing nature needed. Wisely, she now recreated her own life, gradually reviving interests which she had neglected when her work was Darwin's. Now the family provided the framework of her new life.

Day after day the village postman came laden with letters of condolence from all over the world. Pages were filled in newspapers and magazines in praise of Charles. Seated in his chair in the study, or in the basket chair on the veranda, or walking among the daffodils and bluebells, Emma tried to call up all the happy memories of the past. She kept a little diary, 'putting down some things for fear I should forget if I lived long' – just as, long ago, Charles himself had written down his treasured images of Annie. 'I can call back precious memories by looking only a short while back,' she wrote on 2 May, remembering the visit on Sunday 8 January of the Litchfields, and walking past the 'Sunday Tramps'. Charles was delightful to them and enjoyed their visit heartily. 'March 3. His state was now more languid, walking short distances very slowly.' She remembered that it was a sign that Charles felt well when they were able to go beyond the sand walk through Stonefield to a grassy terrace looking across the quiet green valley on to the woods beyond. 'There were banks of the wild flowers Emma loved, yellow rock rose, milkwort, lady's fingers, harebells, scabious and gentian,' Etty remembered. Sometimes Emma would sit there watching their little dog, Polly, chasing the rabbits and wait for Charles to pull her up the steep bank.

> I remember one walk with him on the Terrace on a beautiful still, bright day, I suppose in February . . . a peaceful time without much suffering, exquisite weather – often loitering out with him: I used to go to bed early when he suffered so much from fatigue, and often read some time. Also got up early and read to him early after my breakfast – generally found him doing nothing, but the two last mornings he occupied himself for a short time and felt more like recovery.

Memories flooded back and she fixed them in her notes: their happy visit to Horace and Ida in their new Cambridge house (66 Hills Road); his affectionate greetings, 'always speaking a gracious and tender word when I came up at night – "it is almost worth while to be sick to be nursed by you". I don't know what he said to which I answered, "You speak as if you had done just the same for me." '

'Oh,' she wrote, 'that I could remember more, but it was the same loving gratitude many times a day . . . His tenderness seemed to increase every day.' She recalled how he had never forgotten his pleasure in the kindness of his sons in giving up their billiard room to make a larger study for him, and how even near the end, on 10 April, he was glad to see George home from the West Indies and hear his news, though he was not able to talk much.

Then, briefly, she noted his last night. Even at this time Charles had carefully recorded his feelings. Painfully, she put down his last words to her. 'After the worst of the distress, he said, "I was so sorry for you, but I could not help you". Then, "I am glad of it" when told I was lying down. "Don't call her; I don't want her".' There were so many things she wished she had told him – especially her deep pleasure that he kept her photograph by his chair in the study.

In May she wrote with gratitude to William and Sara for an affectionate letter, telling them how on one evening, 'they all drew me in the bathchair to see the bluebells, and it was all so pretty and bright it gave me the saddest mixture of feelings and I felt a sort of reproach that I could in a measure enjoy it'. Reading over Charles's old letters – so few because they were so seldom apart, 'never I think for the last 15 or 20 years' – she was consoled by the thought that 'the last 10 or 12 years were the happiest – as I am sure they were the most overflowing in tenderness.'

To Etty she wrote, with the same unaccustomed emotion:

> I am trying to make stages in the day of something special to do. It often comes over me with a wave of desolate feeling that there is nothing I need do, and I think of your true words, 'Poor mother you have time enough now'. The regularity of my life was such an element of happiness, and to be received every time I joined him by some word of welcome and to feel he was happier that very minute for my being with him. Some regrets will come on, but I don't encourage them.

Etty's visits were now most welcome, but even so, 'Last night when I parted with you I had a vivid and painful regret which sometimes returns and sometimes is softened away.' Emma also visited the crippled Caroline and her children at Leith Hill Place, and they comforted each other; but she was glad to be home.

In the summer of 1882 Leonard married Elizabeth Fraser. Now only Bessy and Frank, with young Bernard, were left with Emma at Down House. She therefore decided to buy a house in Cambridge, where she could be near George and Horace and where Frank could work more easily. In the autumn of 1883, Emma moved to 'The Grove', a large pleasant house on the Huntington Road, a mile from the university church of St Mary's, surrounded by fields. Its large garden was the 'very place for an old person, such nooks and corners for shelter and seats'. From now on she spent her winters here, and in the summers returned to Down.

Emma sent instructions to her sons for the painting and improvement of the house, but was more interested in planning her new garden, establishing climbing plants on the old walls and bringing shrubs from Down. She loved her 'dear old Azaleas', she told Etty; 'I know their faces so well.' Sitting under the spreading Wych elms, she took wicked delight in deciding which trees must go. 'I attended the downfall of the great elm over the lodge and it really was a grand sight, especially when it took the matter into its own hands and resolved to crush a good-sized sycamore, instead of going the way they were pulling.' This is a characteristic phrase;

Emma's vision of the world was always anthropomorphic. Flowers had faces, and the elm a will of its own; and she always spoke of her adored little fox terrier, Dickie, as though he were human. He was to be her constant companion for thirteen years. At the end of her life she wrote that Dickie had a strong attachment to the postman and accompanied him on his rounds; when he fell ill, Dickie was sent to visit him, and 'there was a tender meeting on both sides', the postman kissing Dickie.

Emma had comfortably absorbed Charles's view of the relationship of man, plant and animal, and it is reflected in her vivid imagery. One of her joys in Cambridge was feeding Horace's little baby, Erasmus. 'He sits every day in his chair at luncheon and insists upon having a great deal of pudding besides his own broth flapping his fins between each mouthful.' She had been amused at Charles's attempt to prove the sundew an animal, and had written of his climbing plants 'twitching their little ears' when they were 'asleep'; so that a baby should have 'fins' was perfectly acceptable. When 'Erasmus called in his pram, driven by his mother', Ida, she was delighted that he put his arms out to her and trotted about the room 'quite tame'.

CHAPTER SEVENTEEN

The Last Summer

IN THE SPRING OF 1884, GEORGE FINALLY FOUND A WIFE IN THE CHARMING American Maud Dupuy – brought vividly to life by their daughter, Gwen Raverat, in her own 'childhood memoir', *Period Piece*, published in 1952. Emma liked Maud, finding 'something in her (I don't know what), that made me feel sure you would always be sweet and kind to George when he is ill and uncomfortable'. George, like his father, often had unidentified pains in his stomach, and Emma had always cosseted him. He was a favourite of hers: Etty once wrote to him that, more than any of the others, he had shared her love of Down House.

At Cambridge she enjoyed the visits of Charles's old friends, especially Hooker – now Sir Joseph – and listened and remembered as he talked with 'the boys' about Charles and the *Life and Letters* Frank was writing. 'The boys', Hooker thought, 'are not a bit altered – just as nice as they were at Down.' To him, as to Emma, they were still 'boys' – although in 1884 they were all well over thirty.

In the autumn of 1883 Frank had married for the second time; his bride, Ellen Wordsworth Crofts, was a lecturer at Newnham College, Cambridge. Emma was pleased that he had found a wife, but the rather chilly bluestocking Ellen was not Amy, and Emma foresaw some problems ahead. Nevertheless, after Charles's death Emma's greatest consolation was in taking care of Bernard, and in helping Frank, she helped herself. She and Bessy doted on the boy; when he was away she was 'thirsty for his little face', and she played with him as she had done with her own children. 'On a lovely autumn day,' she wrote to Etty, 'every leaf shining, Bernard spent almost all day on his tricycle, going to the end of the kitchen garden and back whilst Frank timed him with his watch. He is gone out alone and I am going to time him presently.' Later, at Cambridge, she would spend an exhilarating day with him flying kites in her field. She taught him to read with the books she had used for her own children, including her own book of moral tales, and later introduced him to French.

Frank was proposing to build a house for himself, Ellen and Bernard next to Emma on part of her Grove field. Tactfully Emma pointed out that it was important that Bernard should consider Frank's house his real home, however pleasant it would be for Emma and Bessy to have the little boy 'running in and out'. Bessy would feel the 'weaning from Bernard much more painfully than she herself would'. Then, in a characteristic postscript, 'I don't in the least mind talking about it, but I can write more clearly than speak.' She invited them all to live at The Grove until Frank had decided on his future: at the moment he was looking no further than the completion and publication of his father's biography.

There was more social life at Cambridge than at Down. Emma noted an elegant dinner party when 'the soup was universally admired after the company left' and a garden party where 'if it were not for the bother of talking and still more of listening, I should like it very well. I pretended to know everyone and only came to dire disgrace on one occasion by rashly mentioning a name.' However, Emma became increasingly deaf – an inheritance from the Allen family – and as the years went by avoided dinner parties, glad to be back at Down for the quiet summers. Increasingly crippled with arthritis, she accepted being taken out in the bath chair, with Dickie snuggled under her rug and a bag of chicken bones to prevent him straying. One day in September 1884 she was 'drawn to the Green hill . . . It looked so pretty and the lane so grown and bowery and put me in mind of the times when I used to sit and watch for him [Charles] while he went further. I shall try to get to the terrace below Stoney field' – here Dickie could chase the rabbits and she could pick wild flowers.

There were wild flowers, too, in the fields and wood around The Grove – 'Oxlips in masses in the wood, and with such variety that they seemed of different species. How F would have liked to see such variation going on' – and 'tipsy' nightingales singing their hearts out and 'a babel of birdsong'; but as the years went by she disliked living on 'such an ugly road'. Taking a walk with her dog one day the 'ugly surroundings made me resolve it was not worth while – Dickie liked it, however, and met some pleasant dogs.'

In June 1885 Emma paid a rare visit to London to see the memorial statue of Charles at the Natural History Museum. She had regretfully refused the invitation to the university for the formal unveiling three weeks earlier, preferring, as she wrote, 'to avoid all greetings and acquaintances'. Parslow, however, now retired, had attended and visited her afterwards to tell her about his tremendous day at the university when he was recognized by Charles's old friend, Admiral Sulivan and when 'the reception at Leonards' down to the port and sherry was all delightful.' She stayed at 31 Queen Anne Street with Fanny and Hensleigh, who took her to see the statue. She found 'the situation unique and I liked the attitude but I do not think it is a strong likeness.' However, she had not expected to be satisfied with the likeness, 'and the general look of dignity and repose is of more consequence.' George had not liked the hands, and had his own cast to indicate their size; but Emma believed that 'if the sculptor, Mr Boehm, attempted to alter them and make them as small as they really were they would look out of proportion with the size of the figure.'

The statue movingly reminded her of Charles, but returning to Down on 'a dismal black day' made her feel his absence more acutely.

That evening in London, Hensleigh and Fanny had taken Emma to a meeting of the Society for Psychical Research, in which Hensleigh had become increasingly involved. They frequently held séances at their home in Queen Anne Street, at which members of the Fabian Society, such as George Bernard Shaw and Beatrice and Sidney Webb, were also present. Emma was interested but, aware of the many imposters in the world of spiritualism, remained cautious – neither believing nor disbelieving, while always prepared to accept that there were more things in Heaven and Earth than she could understand.

That September Emma held a family gathering at Down with Frank, Hensleigh and Fanny, and her two brothers enjoyed fierce arguments over spiritualism and religion. Frank had remained a firm Unitarian, supporting the local chapel in Staffordshire, and respected as a local dignitary. Emma enjoyed his visit, believing his to be 'the happiest old age' she had ever known; he was, she told Etty, 'entirely without the faults of old age and wise and gentler than when he was young'. Harry had been invited as well, but was too ill: he was to die in the following month. Emma was saddened, for she had particularly loved Harry in their youth. Imaginative, merry and kind, he had cheered her by his visits when she was lonely at school in London.

As the years passed, Emma would outlive her generation. On 5 January 1888 Caroline, Charles's sister, died at Leith Hill Place: 'She was the last real link with the old times,' Emma sadly reflected. 'Hers was a very wonderful nature in the power of her affections and interests conquering such discomfort as she constantly had.' Fortunately Charles, before his death, had been able to thank her for all her care of him during his childhood, and Emma was glad that she had written more often than usual in the last years. Frank died in the autumn of the same year. Hensleigh, who, like Charles, had been so careful of his health, lived on until 1 June 1891.

Emma's generation was passing; but her grandchildren were growing up, and gave her the greatest pleasure. Ever since his birth, Bernard had been, after Charles, the centre of her life, and even after Frank's remarriage she watched him and taught him. Horace's son Erasmus brightened her life at Cambridge, and she early spotted the unusual characters of George's children, Gwen and Margaret. Margaret was to become Margaret Keynes, author of *A House by the River*, about her Cambridge childhood; Gwen became the artist and writer Gwen Raverat. Gwen was a favourite, 'a most remarkable and interesting child, so intent, and watching one's face, not like some busy and animated children who are so intent on their own aims they never look at you.' Gwen remembered Emma as a very old lady who always went out in a bath chair and whom she liked 'very much indeed'. Every morning, after breakfast, she would visit Grandmamma, who was having breakfast in bed, and Emma would set out little pots and pans – she called them 'Pottikins and Pannikins' – which she filled with pieces of liquorice kept in her workbasket. Gwen would watch Matheson, Emma's most dignified Highland maid, putting on her caps. She remembered her grandmother's hair, still brown, the colour of tobacco leaves – just like her father's hair. (This distinctive colour was a Wedgwood inheritance from Emma's grandmother, old Sally Wedgwood, and has been passed on through the generations right up to the present.) First Matheson would put on 'a black silk lining cap, then a white lawn cap with beautiful crimped and frilled edges and long lawn strings, and then if she were going out yet another black hood after that'. Emma would tell the girls about her schooldays, and how she had written a little reading book for the Sunday school children at Maer and her brothers had laughed at her because she had written 'plumb pie'. Gwen remembered Emma's 'peggy' work – long strips of knitting in thick wool made by pulling the wool over the pegs of a wooden frame. Gwen did not remember her grandfather, but a 'faint flavour' of Charles 'hung in a friendly way about the house . . . he was obviously in the same category as God and Father Christmas'.

Gwen remembered Down House with intense love: 'at Down there were more things to be worshipped than anywhere else in the world – the cool empty country smell' of the house through which they ran in an ecstasy of joy, the smell of the cupboard under the stairs, the shifting shadows of the mulberry tree outside the window on the white nursery floor, the sound of the squeaking well on hot afternoons. All the flowers at Down were beautiful and different from all other flowers. She even adored the black and shiny pebbles on the path in front of the veranda, the foxgloves, the stiff red clay out of the sand-walk clay pit. 'This kind of feeling hits you in the stomach, and in the ends of your fingers, and it is probably the most important thing in life. Long after I have forgotten all my human loves I shall still remember the smell of a gooseberry leaf or the feel of wet grass on my bare feet . . . it is the feeling that makes life worth living, this which is the driving force behind the artist's need to create.' Emma, watching little Gwen running home in ecstasy clutching one wild strawberry, would have been touched by this eloquent testimony to the enduring power of the home she had created. Gwen's sister Margaret would also feel and pass on to her Keynes family the love of the magic of Down House.

Emma took something of this atmosphere to her home in Cambridge. 'On a nice cool May day in 1887,' she wrote to Etty, 'all the little children assembled on the lawn and Gwen and Nora [Horace and Ida's daughter] tottered about hand in hand, Nora often tumbling over. Gwen was quite tipsy.' If only Emma could have looked into the glass of time and seen the distinguished historian Nora Barlow, the editor of Charles's letters, and Frank and Ellen's daughter Frances, a charming poet herself and mother of the talented poet John Cornford. But now, as she played her old galloping tune for them while they danced around, it was enough to know that they gave her as much delight as she gave them. It was as well that she could not see the tragic end of the little Gwennie who danced so happily. In 1925 she helped her terminally ill husband, Jacques, out of his agony by smothering him with a pillow. In 1957, five years after publishing her immensely successful *Period Piece*, she suffered a stroke and, paralysed, took an overdose of aspirin.

Emma's influence on the young was perhaps greatest on Fanny and Hensleigh's daughter Julia 'Snow' Wedgwood. She and Charles had been interested in her from the days when they had all been neighbours in Gower Street. The Allen sisters had admired precocious little Snow, regaling each other with reports of her poems and clever remarks. But the talented little girl grew up into a withdrawn bluestocking, frustrated in her human relationships by her acute deafness, inherited from her grandmother, Kitty Allen. Her unfulfilled love affair with Robert Browning, after his wife's death, is another story. For a time she became Mrs Gaskell's secretary, and, inspired by her, wrote anonymously a novel entitled *Framleigh Hall*, which in 1856 she brought to Down seeking Emma's advice. Although this was the time of Aunt Sarah's funeral, Emma and Charles took time to encourage her, and she finished it at Down House. Though this attempt at a writing career was not successful (the book was published but did not sell well, and gave her father Hensleigh 'a pain in the stomach'), she went on to work for twenty-two years on a history of human aspirations called *The Moral Ideal*, a philosophical study which attempted to reconcile Darwin's scientific theory with her own religious philosophy. To everyone's surprise, this work was a success, and at fifty-five Snow became famous; her novels were published, her *Life of Wesley* reprinted. Emma read *The Moral Ideal* carefully and was impressed. At the end of her life she would encourage Snow to write the life of Josiah Wedgwood I, although she did not live to see it published.

In her last years Emma became increasingly interested in philosophy. In 1887 she was 'wading through Emerson as I really wanted to know what transcendentalism means and I think it means that intuition is before reason (or facts). It certainly does not suit Wedgwoods, who never have any intuitions.' She felt she would enjoy F. D. Maurice if she did not try to understand him – a typical Emma remark. She asked Richard Litchfield, Etty's husband, to give her advice on Plato and the classics, but she lightened her 'stiff reading' with novels, often keeping two books on the go at the same time. For example, in 1888, she was reading *Paradise*

Regained and Rousseau's *Confessions* and Henry James sandwiched with Leslie Stephen's *Hours in a Library*. Guiltily she confessed that 'I find I use up more than a volume a day of novels,' but later she tackled Milman's *History of the Jews* and recommended to Leonard *The Life of Henrietta Ker – A Nun*. Now that her sight was fading, she employed a prim student teacher to read to her: 'I embarked with her on such a frivolous novel all about flirtations and lovers that I have changed it for Miss Young – all about scarlet fever and drains.'

She continued to search for light on the great philosophical mysteries right up to her death. In 1873 she had spent much time reading the Liberal writer Charles Buxton, whose *Notes and Thoughts* were 'quite my Bible at present. He hits so many small nails on the head that suit my feelings and opinions so exactly, and I think he is so very acute, and sometimes a little cynical to my surprise.' What were these 'small nails'? Was it 'The microscope is almost as humbling as the telescope?' Or 'Are not lessons a mistake? . . . Just put them [children] in the way of reading, give them pleasant books; but leave them to read, play, or wander at their own sweet way. Would they not grow up healthier and happier in body and soul?'? Emma, like her mother and Aunt Jessie before her, certainly believed that. Another of Buxton's comments was certainly true of Charles: 'What man of genius had not a cranky frame? Rude health may bestow good sense, but not originality.'

In July 1895 she wrote to Etty that she partly agreed with Balfour's *Foundation of Belief*. 'The belief in a God who cares, is an immense safeguard for morality,' but only partly agreed that the doctrine of Atonement is any additional safeguard, and found his view that morality is impossible without some religion surprising. 'I quite agree that the remains of Christian feeling makes us unable to judge of the present race of agnostics.' Reading Clough's *Life* to Etty, Emma regretted that his religious feelings had changed. 'It is rather sad to see how age disperses such feelings especially with thoughtful men.' Etty once wrote that Emma's religion, too, had grown less vivid with age; in fact, she had never thought so deeply about her faith than she did in the last ten years of her life. The basis of her thought was still Unitarian; she had attended a Unitarian chapel in London with Fanny and Hensleigh, and still wished there was one at Downe. She had little in common with the Evangelicals, who 'imagine they feel shame for an inherently sinful nature . . . I remember the infants at school at Kingscote shouting out so jollily "There is none that doeth good. *No not one.*" ' She was quite out of temper with the local vicar, now the High Church Revd George Sketchley Ffinden, and in her last years preferred to be taken to the church at neighbouring Cudham. She had conducted a fierce warfare with Ffinden over the school at Downe, which was supposed to be non-denominational, but which he was trying to set in Anglican concrete, insisting that lessons be given on the Thirty-nine Articles. Etty called him 'the enemy'. They had a secret weapon in Etty's husband, Richard, who was a member of the Ecclesiastical Commission with responsibility for church affairs. Emma's continuing interest in the village school went beyond spiritual matters. In 1884 she waged an effective war against Mr Skinner, the sadistic schoolmaster, herself investigating the punishment book – 'a violent flogging for some moral offence, one caning for blotting his copybook!!!! one for talking and another for not doing dictation or sums right'. She reported him repeatedly, and encouraged mothers of pupils to do the same, but feared that 'nothing will cure a man who has a habit of caning for such small offences. It shows that he must rather like it.'

For some years she had been crippled by arthritis, but she still was taken in her bath chair to visit her 'poories' in the village. Never sentimental about them, she often cheerfully wished they would die: 'B has been in bed for a week . . . you know what my feelings must be about the poor old man, but I am afraid he will recover.' She applauded the conversion of a notable old drunkard 'old M', noting that Mrs Evans the cook attended a prayer meeting in which old M 'made as nice a prayer as ever you heard in your life'. Emma had an unusually brisk attitude to death. She had welcomed the death of her father and mother as release from pain, and greeted Elizabeth's 'with joy'. Mrs Evans had been unwilling to tell her about the death of a 'dirty old woman' in case it should upset her. 'She little knew my feelings,' she told Etty; 'I wished I had looked after her sooner, not by way of keeping her alive though.' Once Bernard heard her talking about the Greek play *Electra*, which Bessy had gone to see, and asked, 'Is it nice?' Emma answered, 'Yes, very nice.' 'What is it about?' he asked: 'About a woman murdering her mother.' The account of a 'nice' play was too much for Jackson the butler, and he laughed aloud.

Emma's household underwent some changes in her final years, but remained as happy as ever. Emma had pensioned off Parslow, and firmly and wisely refused to let him come back to supervise Jackson. Mrs Bromwich also replaced the devoted Mrs Evans. Bernard remembered them vividly in his book *The World that Fred Made*. Fred, the groom, made the 'stableyard an alluring place'. But Jackson, the butler in his pantry, was to a little boy's eyes 'a deity in a sacred shrine. He was a little man, with very red cheeks, little loose curly wisps of side whiskers . . . with the aspect of a comic character on the stage.' His masterpiece, a model of Down House made of corks, seemed to Bernard 'the high-water mark of ingenuity'. He was by no means an orthodox butler, 'not very tidy or efficient and in a less quiet or more worldly household he might not have kept his place'. But he could always be persuaded to play cricket with Bernard, and the boy adored him. Then there was John, the quiet coachman, who drove the sleepy old horses, Flyer, Tara and Druid; his kingdom was the harness room and his carriage whips magic wands.

Like all the children Bernard remembered the Well House at Down, the creaking wheel and the 'tremendous moment when the bucket at last reached the surface, breaking through its wooden gates'. He also remembered Evvy the cook, and that unforgettable moment when he had been taken through the maids' bedrooms to see the comet from the roof and had 'seen Mrs Evans in bed and the vision abides'. Most of all he remembered the lovely Harriet, who had come as a young maid and remained with Etty after Emma's death until the 1950s. She was 'sonsy and pink and handsome, with a healthy laugh that no baize doors could stifle'. She played cricket with Bernard on the top floor at Down House with a little red fire engine at one end as the wicket. Even when he was grown up, a great golfer and a successful writer, Bernard remembered with acute nostalgia the 'big, pleasant unpretending house . . . and the really noble row of lime trees, the bright flower beds and the sundial, and the old mulberry tree under my nursery window, everything . . . full of sunlight'.

In November 1887 Frank's *Life and Letters of Charles Darwin* was published and Emma breathed a sigh of relief, as she told him, that 'what I have been rather dreading is over' and that 'I don't believe there is anything disagreeable to go through.' In fact, she was delighted with her son's work: 'The picture is so minute and exact that it is like a written photograph, and so full of tender observation on Frank's part . . . I feel astonished that I can make out a cheerful life after losing him. He filled so much space with his interest, sympathy and graciousness, besides his love underlying and pervading all.' She wrote a note to Frank, afraid she 'might break down in telling him what I felt'. Emma had made sure, in spite of her son's opposition, that sentences which she felt would give unnecessary offence to old friends and family were omitted or toned down; so now she could take unalloyed pleasure in many passages. 'I have been reading the scientific letters and in almost every one there is some characteristic bit which charms one. A little mention of me in a letter of his to Laura sent me to bed with a glow about my heart, coming on it unexpectedly.' This was a reference to an afternoon on the lawn when he had put his arms round Emma and told Laura what she meant to him.

In 1888, Emma was eighty and still full of vitality, reading Carlyle and remembering how angelic he had been when his manuscript of *The French Revolution* had been accidentally burned by a maid and he had had to rewrite the whole book. Politics remained a great interest. At Cambridge she took tickets for the installation of the Duke of Devonshire as Chancellor. 'It would amuse me intensely', she told Etty, 'to see Bright [and] Salisbury.' John Bright had been a hero of Aunt Fanny's, as Emma remembered, and her Aunt Caroline's granddaughter, Georgiana, had married Lord Salisbury. Emma, however, took a seat near the door so that she could slip out before it was over.

In the spring of 1889 Emma was ill, but her mind was as active as ever. Now she was reading the biographies and letters of people she had known, and her judgements were as trenchant as ever. Reading the life of her father's friend Tom Poole, she found that 'every word of Coleridge's letters revolts me, they are a mixture of gush and mawkish egotism and what seems like humbug . . . I can't imagine how my father liked and admired Coleridge. I believe Dr Darwin would have been more acute.' Later she wrote, 'Such a loathsome crawling letter of Coleridge to De Quincey, declining to pay his debt'. She also took great delight in reading parliamentary reports, particularly that of the commission of inquiry into the affairs of the Irish leader Charles Parnell: 'baiting Parnell helps me over the time beautifully.'

When her son Leonard decided to stand as a Liberal Unionist for Lichfield, Erasmus Darwin's old home town, in the general election of July 1892, Emma followed his progress with intense excitement. 'We are living in the election,' she wrote to her niece in New Zealand, lamenting that 'our old men', Parslow and Lettington the gardener, declined to vote at all. 'They had always voted Liberal, and did not care a penny about Home Rule.' But Emma did, and coloured in a map of England with losses and gains as the election results came in – including a win for Leonard. She invited George and Frank, with Leonard and his wife, for a great celebration at Down: 'They will not have a brother elected to Parliament every day. William laments that he cannot come. Also Horace. I always feel how your father would have enjoyed it.' Emma and Charles had been supporters of Gladstone and the Liberals, but Emma lost patience with him over Home Rule for Ireland. In the election of July 1895, Emma hoped for Leonard's re-election: Anne at the village shop supplied materials for celebration flags for free and Emma was halfway through making one when she heard the sad news that her son had been ousted.

In her eighty-eighth year Emma's health improved, and she still wrote letters almost every day to Etty and the boys – as she still called them – and to her grandchildren. Bernard wrote of the quality that is so noticeable even in her early letters. Aunt Jessie had called her 'poetical', especially in her 'Babbiana' (anecdotes about babies). Her humour was unique. 'She had a genius', Bernard wrote, 'for dry and definite statement of her own particular flavour.' The statement 'I dislike all poetry, especially good poetry' is attributed to her, though it certainly did her an injustice. In fact, loathing sentimentality, she delighted in shocking. Crabb Robinson's diary was a favourite, because 'his prosaic moderation does so suit me, and Miss —'s gush does not suit me.' She felt she could 'talk with him for a few minutes any time and feel refreshed'. He even might persuade her to read Wordsworth's 'Excursion'. She kept a notebook in which she wrote out passages from her favourite poems. In February 1893 she copied these lines from Tennyson's 'In Memoriam':

Not all regret: the face will shine
Upon me while I muse alone;
And that dear voice, I once have known,
Still speak to me of me and mine.

Yet less of sorrow lives in me
For days of happy commune dead;

Less yearning for the friendship fled,
Than some strong bond that is to be.

Her wide range of interests and her mental alertness made her the best of
listeners to all ages. Like Fanny Allen, she 'enjoyed a youthy age'.
Something of the gay radiance of her youth had gone – Etty, reading old
letters, was surprised at the young Emma's liveliness, finding it difficult to
imagine her mother waltzing the night away in Geneva – but the
tranquillity which had always been there was now remarked upon by all
who met her.

Emma still quite enjoyed the house at Cambridge, especially in the spring
when the nightingales sang along the Backs. 'The east wind and bright sun
are just what I like,' she wrote to Etty, 'and our old nightingale sang 8 or 9
hours at a stretch yesterday. I wonder whether it is the same – he is louder
and more tipsy than ever.' She noticed how in early spring the elm buds
along the Backs had 'taken a purplish glow', and later in the season she
wrote, 'The day was perfect . . . and it is the first time that the tulips have
really opened their eyes. I am always divided at this time of the year between
the wish to stay on to enjoy the spring and early summer here and the
opposite wish to be at Down before the trees have become dark and summer-
like.' Each summer she looked forward with excitement to the return to
Down, yet on each first day there the sense of blankness depressed her. But
she was resilient, and there were honied summer days with tea on the
veranda, haymaking and tennis to watch. 'Life is not flat to me,' she wrote
to Etty, 'only all at a lower pitch and I do feel it an advantage not to be
grudging the years as they pass and lamenting my age.'

In the last year of her life her health was good, though her eyesight
failed. 'It is a surprising thing,' she wrote, 'that at 87 I should feel stronger
and better in every way than I did at 85.' It was difficult to realize that on
2 May 1896 she would be eighty-eight. Matheson, her devoted maid and
friend, read aloud to her, and took care of her, and all her old attendants
were as faithful as ever. She regarded the new ones with amused tolerance.
'Nurse's manner to me is like one housemaid to another a little beneath
her, but I am not in the least offended.' Old friends still called at Down
and found her as lively and interested as always. Lady Derby, who had
become a warm friend in the last years, enjoyed talking about the Duke of

Wellington, who had come to see her when she was unhappy at the death of her eldest brother; he had said, 'I shall write to you every day,' and did so till his death.

During that last summer of 1896 most of the family came in turn to Down, as Etty and Richard Litchfield were always happy to remember. Emma found Richard stimulating when he roused himself, but how he could sit quietly without reading even a newspaper astonished her. He in turn found Emma the most tranquil person in the world and liked to sit quietly with her on the sunny lawn. Etty's mental energy could be exhausting. Charles's nieces Margaret and Sophy, Caroline's daughters, came too, bringing news of Margaret's son, Ralph Vaughan Williams, now at the Royal College of Music where his best friend was Gustav Holst. That August he was planning to marry the beautiful Adeline Fisher and spend their honeymoon in Germany, where he would continue his musical studies. None of his family, except his mother and Aunt Emma, thought much of his talent. Etty had been annoyed with him when she and Richard had stayed at Leith Hill Place in August 1894. Although he had chatted amiably with Richard about music, he 'wdnt play anything – said he couldn't. Don't you think that hopeless after 4 or 5 hours practice per diem?' Emma, however, understood and sympathized: she too, as a girl, had constantly been called to perform, and Ralph had been the only one impressed that she had taken lessons from Chopin in her youth. (As yet it is not clear when and where those Chopin lessons took place. Paris, London, Geneva?) At this time Ralph was a very poor pianist, as Emma's great-granddaughter Ursula still remembers. Emma was saddened to see that, as she had always foreseen, at fifty-four Caroline's other daughter, Sophy, was becoming increasingly deranged.

Once more Emma played her old galloping tunes for the grandchildren, but now it exhausted her. Sitting quietly in her basket chair on the veranda, she watched them and remembered her own childhood. She must buy brooches for the little girls – what intense pleasure a little amethyst brooch had given her when she was fourteen! A letter from Etty, who had taken the ailing Richard to Dover, brought more painful memories. In her reply she recalled how she used 'to abuse and dislike Dover when I came with William and poor Annie to take you back, and they took to crying and being miserable and the shore there was unwalkable; but I should now like sitting on the shingle with Mildred', the granddaughter of her sister

Charlotte and now a loved companion. After Emma's death she would become Leonard's second wife.

She longed to see the old walks again and took a drive into Holwood, admiring how tall the beech trees had grown. 'The mare is perfect on grass and up the hills, not pulling and straining. I went in and out among the green drives and I shall go again and never drive anywhere else.' In August she sent the children there blackberrying: 'Gwenny brought a tinful, while Boy and Margaret eat [*sic*] most of theirs.' On 5 September, as she wrote to Etty, 'I made John take me a circuit in the chair by Downe Hall. I was glad to see Cudham Place once more. It looked ever so much deeper with high hedges and trees grown. I came back over the big field and through the Smith's yard. I felt a sharp wind over the bare field quite like an old friend.' It was her last ride through the green lanes.

Three weeks later Emma faced a sharper wind. On Sunday, 27 September 1896, she was reading Henry James, Hardy and Shaw at alternating intervals when she was suddenly taken ill. On Monday she revived and even wrote a letter to her daughter, but she was clearly unwell when Etty arrived at Down House on 1 October. On Tuesday evening, Etty came in to say goodnight and watched her mother wind up her watch as usual; then Emma 'fell back on her pillow and never recovered'. That evening Etty 'went in to see the beautiful, solemn, sweet face composed for its last rest'; then she returned to her home to take care of Richard.

It was a quiet funeral; only close friends and family were invited. Emma had outlived her own generation, but five sons followed the flower-filled hearse along with members of the household; the procession was accompanied by the carriages of Lady Derby and other famous friends. Villagers and shopkeepers joined the mourners in the little church. The Revd Allen Wedgwood, Emma's cousin, who had conducted their family christenings, weddings and funerals, had died in 1882, so it was Emma's old sparring partner, the hated George Ffinden, who officiated: it was as well that she was beyond knowing. She was buried in the country churchyard in the family vault, which had been prepared for Charles; but he now lay in Westminster Abbey, and only Charles's brother Erasmus was here. Elizabeth and Aunt Sarah were with other family members in the grave by the church door.

Slowly the flowerless, empty hearse left the churchyard and the cortège wound through the green lanes back to Down House, past the closed shops and houses with drawn blinds. Of late years, Emma had only occasionally been seen in the village, drawn in her bath chair, as the local newspaper remembered in its obituary. 'But her acts of benevolence always performed in the most unostentatious manner, and her constant thoughtfulness for others had endeared her to the hearts of all the inhabitants not only of Downe and Cudham, but of all the neighbouring villages. Though not a member of the established Church, she was a liberal subscriber to the church at Downe, and on a few occasions had worshipped there.' Perhaps it was Mr Ffinden who contributed the significant first phrase in the last sentence.

Blinds drawn, silent, Down House itself was suddenly dead. Quietly Etty and her brothers discussed the future of the house, and poor Bessy feared an empty world ahead. Eight days after Emma's death, Etty wrote to George wishing 'that the country might buy Down, but it doesn't seem to me very likely . . . Now our centre has gone we must write more to each other,' she told him. 'I am so glad the children are old enough to remember her – all but Billy – and he can be told what pleasure he gave her last few months of life. Dear old George your constant faithfulness gave her such pleasure and she was always so glad that you loved Down in a way the others did not. If it is possible I should like to pay my last visit to Down when you are there if I can. The dear chicks wd make it less sad and I should feel Maud's calm presence a help.'

Almost the last essay Emma had read was by Leslie Stephen. It had pleased her. She liked his notion 'that the world does not know a quarter of the goodness and happiness that exists and that every perfect character causes a sort of halo of influence and example around it'. This might well have been her own epitaph. From earliest childhood until old age she had been loved and esteemed not only by her family but by all who knew her, yet she had remained straightforward and unaffected. She brought a sharp mind and an astringent humour to her marriage. Neither fame nor controversy rocked her. She had been the centre of the family and the heart of Charles Darwin's life. In her life with Charles she was totally supportive, yet when he had gone, her mind continued to develop and grow. Married to a man whose life's work had disturbed the world, whose ill-health was a constant strain, she had kept her own personality and her own beliefs. Acutely conscious of their differing religious views, she had accepted that her faith was beyond reasoning: she saw Charles's unbelief as that of a man who was colour blind. The God she believed in would not have rejected a person who was so clearly good, but would have regarded him with the same compassion as she herself did. If there was a gulf between them, it was bridged over and over again by enduring love.

Charles Darwin's debt to Emma can never be fully estimated. Without her he might have been, like his own brother Erasmus, a clever man who yet achieved nothing; or, like his Uncle Tom Wedgwood, a nerve-shattered invalid who despite early brilliance never fulfilled his promise. He might have been a dedicated scientist destroyed by ill-health. Emma kept Charles Darwin alive, and he knew her value. She was his 'pattern wife', 'twice refined gold' whom he 'loved and worshipped'. As he doggedly struggled through the dark in his search for truth it was essential to know that Emma was there at the end of the tunnel, serene in the sunlight. In his autobiography he addressed his sons:

> You all know your mother, and what a good mother she has ever been to all of you. She has been my greatest blessing and I can declare that in my whole life I have never heard her utter one word which I would rather have been unsaid. She has never failed in kindest sympathy towards me, and has borne with the utmost patience my frequent complaints of ill-health and discomfort. I do not believe she has ever missed an opportunity of doing a kind action to anyone near her. I marvel at my good fortune, that she, so infinitely my superior in every single moral quality, consented to be my wife. She has been my wise adviser and cheerful comforter throughout life, which without her would have been during a very long period a miserable one from ill-health. She has earned the love and admiration of every soul near her.

With characteristic modesty Emma had not allowed this paragraph to be published in her lifetime.

CHAPTER EIGHTEEN

The Legacy

E MMA HAD MADE HER WILL SOME YEARS EARLIER, THOUGHTFULLY allocating her treasures to her children and grandchildren, remembering the vicar's wife at a neighbouring church and her devoted staff. She had left Down House to George, and trusted him to carry out her wishes. Etty thanked him for sending

the list of what Mother left me. I am touched at her leaving the two dear ugly blue jars on the mantel piece which I shall love to have. And Aunt Susan's inkstand I think was broken 20 years ago or so. It was the one that the ink dried up in one moment, but I shall like its remains if they exist. I am quite puzzled as to what the black & white vase is. Uncle Rases one is black & red. Also I did not think there was a picture of Maer in her bedroom – the little ghostly one which she was very fond of was in her upstairs sitting room, latterly anyway. The red plate is no doubt the De Morgan which I gave to the Grove. Water colour of Shrewsbury is given back to M.V.W. so do not hunt for that. If no one is left the little water colour by Ellen Tollet, I should have a sentiment about it & I think it is worthless as art. I think she once said she would leave it to me – but I dare say she forgot. It was not very long in her possession, (only after Ellen's death) so it would have no primordial associations for anyone.

Now it was Etty who would become the centre of the family, keeping in touch with all of them and above all making her finest memorial to the mother she loved, her collection of the family letters in her *Emma Darwin: A Century of Family Letters*. Richard was to help her with a work which would take many years to reach fruition (it was privately printed in 1904). In a letter to Horace thanking him for sending Emma's letters, she explained her aims and the problems:

> The object of the book is mainly to leave a record of an exceptionally beautiful character & of course how she affected others and especially Father is a main agent in this. But it remains a matter of feeling & not reason when all is said, only that I think some consideration may somewhat alter the feeling. When one considers what Mother wd have felt one *must* consider her as alive & then of course it is impossible. So that in trying to judge her feelings one is attempting an impossibility. Nothing in these letters could not be read out by any man woman or child before any company. There is nothing in them of such an essentially private nature that there wd be any instinctive shrinking. The feelings revealed are so wholesome as well as deep, & there is a wholesome reticence in expression. I think if Mother knew that it could only ennoble him & show the perfectness of married life she would not shrink. Perhaps the best way to put it is wd she think it out of taste if such letters were printed of Sir Charles to Ly [Lady] Lyell 7 or 8 years after the death of the survivor? I shd not have thought so.

In 1901 she was at the Hôtel St Charles at Cannes, working on the book, when she wrote to Leonard thanking him for the bundle of letters from Emma he had sent her. 'Her letters', she explained to him,

> must be all treated as extracts. No one wd care for the little itinerary of family movements [which] has a quite ephemeral interest. I more & more feel that, & I am afraid it will make it rather snippety. If I was a Leslie Stephen, I might join them together, but I think that on the whole the extracts had better

be left to speak for themselves & not have my heavy hand enforcing their moral. I always have before me a signpost what *not* to do in the editing of André Empère's letters – the most pathetic & charming love letters I know anywhere, & I shd like to paste up all the editor's comments. I remember too how savage they made Mother.

Richard died in 1903; Etty was deeply distressed but, like her mother, she was emotionally resilient; from now on she was the keeper of the family flame, watching over the careers of her brothers, their children and grandchildren as Emma had done.

Life does not start with birth, nor does it end in death. The genius of Charles Darwin did not spring suddenly out of nowhere. He inherited genes and attitudes and traditions from his Darwin and Wedgwood ancestors, although he was never fully aware of his debt to Josiah Wedgwood I. Emma, too, combined the charm, intelligence and good looks of the Allens with the direct honesty and reserve of old Sally Wedgwood – and the distinctive colour of her hair. The partnership of Charles and Emma continued and built on the past, and bequeathed to the future an extraordinary dynasty of talent. Their seven surviving children all fulfilled or even surpassed their promise, and Charles's scientific legacy was prominent: three of his five sons were Fellows of the Royal Society.

William, the least intellectual, was a successful banker, becoming a partner at Grant & Maddison in Southampton. He outlived his kindly but formidable American wife, Sara, whom Bernard had found 'engaging and with an unforgettable slow rather musical voice'. William survived a hunting accident when he rashly 'tried to go through a swinging gate'; as a result he lost a leg but remained one of the healthiest of the family. The little 'Doddy' of childhood had, Bernard recalled, grown into a delightful figure, with 'the sweetest smile, the tidiest clothes, the most exquisite little suggestion of whiskers'. His Uncle Erasmus once said that 'he looked so clean that you could eat a mutton chop off him anywhere.' In 1902, after Sara's death, he moved to London and lived next to Leonard in Egerton Street, in great comfort, 'with a butler almost too perfect to live'. He died there in 1914.

George had been Emma's favourite son from earliest childhood. The little boy who had so excitedly played at soldiers during the Crimean War retained a love of heraldry and uniforms and bows and arrows; he had taken to archery while at Cambridge. Did Emma ever tell him that she and her sister Fanny had once been 'dragonesses at archery', winning all the prizes? Did she try her hand again? One would like to think so. George had been called to the Bar in 1874 but never practised and worked in Cambridge on astronomical problems. He was elected a Fellow of the Royal Society in 1879 and knighted in 1905. Etty was delighted, but disappointed that the 'newspapers had not been full of . . . Sir G.H.D.K.C.B. or is *it* still (whatever *it* is) still to come.' When Sir George died in 1912, Etty grieved but was cheered by his bright daughters, Gwen (Raverat) and Margaret (Keynes). In 1922 she wrote to console Maud who, over the years, had lost her usual spirited good humour, counselling her from her own experience. 'I do wish my dear M. you did not feel so lonely. My only plan was to try & accept it as my lot & to treasure the memories of the past. Also not to attempt to alleviate it by leaning on others, which is of course really included in accepting one's lot. I often think how hard it is for you now, without George, to be away from your own flesh & blood in U.S.A.'

Frank, possibly the cleverest of the sons, had taken a first-class honours in natural science, and qualified as a physician, though he never practised. After Charles's death, he moved to Cambridge, where he became a Fellow of Christ's College and a university lecturer in botany. Made a Fellow of the Royal Society in 1882 and knighted in 1913, he wrote a number of books and articles but is best remembered for his editing of the basic biographies of his father, three volumes of *Life and Letters* and two volumes of *More Letters*. He was the only son to share Emma's talent for music and was remembered by his grandchildren for his skill with many different instruments, including the harp.

Frank never really recovered from the death of Amy, though he outlived two more wives, Ellen Wordsworth Crofts, who died in 1903, and Professor Maitland's beautiful widow, Florence, who died in 1920. Frank's friend, the artist and writer William Rothenstein, who painted him, noted his strong likeness to Charles and said, 'He had much of his father's directness and simplicity. There was never any doubt about what nor whom he liked and disliked. The sweetest and gentlest of men, he was moved to anger by cruelty, cruelty to animals particularly. Nor could he be indifferent to attacks on his father, which he thought unfair.'

After Frank's second marriage, Emma saw less of Bernard, who was sent to a prep school and then to Eton and Cambridge. For a while Bernard practised law, until writing became a full-time career and golf a lifelong passion. His *The World that Fred Made* draws a lively picture of his early life with Emma and Charles at Down House. As he grew older he became more aware of his Welsh background and spent idyllic holidays with his much-loved grandmother 'Nain' Ruck in Wales. He married a clever sculptor, Elinor Mary Monsell; they had three children, Robin, Ursula and Nicola. Robin became a painter who taught art at Eton and was from 1948 to 1967 a very successful principal of the Royal College of Art. He was knighted in 1964 and became a full Academician in 1972, the last year of his life. Bernard's wife encouraged the artistic ability of their children. Ursula remembers Bernard as a wonderful father, reading his magical stories to them and reciting poetry with tears in his eyes. She married Julian Trevelyan and later, as Ursula Mommens, became a well-known potter; still working at the age of ninety-three, she throws a perfect pot. The craft became her passion at the age of ten, when she spent an hour watching a potter on the stand at the Ideal Homes Exhibition. Neither then nor later was she really conscious of being the great-great-great-granddaughter of Josiah Wedgwood I. But she does remember how her grandfather, Frank, encouraged her interest in music and Robin's artistic talent. He lived near them for a time and often sat enthralled as he played his many musical instruments.

Leonard, whom Bernard had idolized in his childhood, was remembered 'playing tennis on the asphalt court at Down, when he wore a flannel coat of narrow red and blue stripes in Sapper colours, and was rather plump. Anyone less like a soldier it would be impossible to imagine.' Bernard considered he had an excellent brain and wonderfully cool, sound judgement, but there was a vital spark lacking. It was probably Leonard's wife, Elizabeth Fraser (Aunt Bee), who persuaded him to stand for Parliament as a Liberal Unionist, and whose elegance and spirited canvassing brought him success by the narrowest of majorities. He was the first to acknowledge that he made little mark in Parliament, but he was a successful Mayor of Cambridge in the Jubilee Year of 1887, bringing better relations to the conflicting sides of town and gown; and from 1908 to 1919 he was President of the Royal Geographic Society.

After Elizabeth died, Uncle Lenny married the charming Mildred Massingberd. Emma would have been delighted. She made Cripps Corner, their home in Sussex, 'a haunt of ancient peace', as Tennyson described her former home in Lincolnshire. After Mildred's death in 1940 Lenny lived on alone in the house, 'utterly solitary, flanked by woodland looking away to a lovely south country blue distance'. Here he could remember happy holidays with his Aunt Elizabeth at her house in nearby Hartfield. Leonard held the Darwin record for longevity: he lived serenely on to the age of ninety-two in 1943, and is still remembered by members of the family.

Even Horace, so frail as a child, lived until 1928, and made a surprising success of a company he established – the Cambridge Scientific Society – though is still remembered among the family today mostly for his party trick with treacle. His wife, the elegant Ida Farrer, created an exquisite home with a secret garden that Gwen Raverat remembered as 'an image of Paradise'. She was much loved by Emma, though they were totally different in character.

Horace's daughters, Ruth and Nora, became highly qualified. Ruth (later Rees Thomas) became Senior Commissioner of the Board of Control; Nora, who married Sir Alan Barlow, is credited with having founded the Darwin industry. She studied Charles's manuscripts in depth, transcribed his *Voyage of the Beagle* and restored the omissions to his autobiography. The present writer remembers her still resembling her grandfather, Charles, and still working in old age until her mind dimmed.

The Darwins were always accused of being hypochondriacs, and Emma was partly blamed for encouraging them. But she might well have retorted that at least she had kept them alive. At a time when the average expectation of life was around forty, Emma's children were exceptional. Except for two who died in infancy, and Annie, the other seven were all long-lived. William died at seventy-five; Frank was seventy-seven; George sixty-seven; Leonard ninety-two; Horace seventy-seven; and Bessy seventy-nine. As for Etty, so often in the past at death's door, she lived until 1927 when she was eighty-four. Ursula, at ninety-three in 2001, is only two handshakes from Charles and Emma.

All the sons learned much from their father, who taught them to observe carefully, to describe accurately and to pursue their theories 'to the death'. They had all inherited something of his sweetness of temperament and the quality which Emma had first loved in Charles, a certain limpidity and innocence. He had been 'the most transparent man' she knew. Bernard's poem on his Uncle Lenny was true of all the brothers, and indeed of Emma herself.

> Serenely kind and humbly wise,
> Whom each may tell the thing that's hidden,
> And always ready to advise,
> And ne'er to give advice unbidden.

Like Gwen Raverat, Emma was very conscious and proud of her Darwin inheritance which Rothenstein describes as 'an aristocracy of virtue, a sort of yeoman integrity and a fastidious sense of conduct'. Frances Cornford saw as what others have done throughout the generations:

> That eager, honouring look
> Through microscope or at a picture-book,
> That quick, responsive, curious delight –
> For half a century I have seen it now
> Under the shaggy or the baby brow,
> And always blessed the sight.

Even Bessy, who might have been dismissed as simple-minded, created a useful life after Emma's death. She bought a large, ugly house in Cambridge, where she lived with a companion, helping old people at the workhouse, even venturing to travel abroad. She lived until 1926, long enough to enjoy Bernard's success as a sportsman and writer – particularly his book for children, *The Tale of Mr Tootleoo*. Twice every year she entertained his children, and Ursula still remembers her large ungainly body, her fluttering hands, her warm embrace. If, with the cruelty of childhood, they laughed at her, it was with affectionate amusement. She knew she could not compete with Etty, who was always her superior and who had created a magical place for children at her home in Surrey. But she won Ursula's heart with a marvellous present – three horse-riding lessons. And Gwen Raverat remembers how she trotted tirelessly on their walks, 'always hoping to find a little secret path', as she called it in her inherited Wedgwood tongue, and how when she took them to the theatre 'she was always glancing at your face to see what you were feeling about it.' She had inherited Emma's gift for loving.

As for Etty, she surpassed expectation. Her life of Emma – *A Century of Family Letters* – is a fascinating survey of the family over a hundred years. After Richard's death she moved from their home at Kensington Square – which was, according to Gwen, a 'William Morris tapestry' worked in bright colours to a complex pattern – to Burrow's Hill, a house near Gornshall in Surrey, where she 'transformed a very ordinary villa into an earthly paradise'. Here she and her smiling maids welcomed her brothers' children and grandchildren. 'There would be Aunt Etty', Gwen remembered, 'on the drawing room sofa, in her red chuddar shawl and her little lace cap, with all her bags and books and papers around her: and I would see again her small downy, soft-skinned face and would know that here . . . I was loved and welcomed by everyone.' Gwen and Margaret were her beloved George's daughters, and were therefore Etty's especial responsibility. She would sharpen their wits and improve their minds by making them 'Churchill . . . or the Pope of Rome', and then would fire devastating questions at them like, 'How on earth did you expect to take the Dardanelles?' Gwen remembered a tiny, frail figure in a red dressing gown and white shawl appearing at the end of her bed saying, 'I could swallow the Pope of Rome, but what I can*not* swallow is the celibacy of the clergy.' If all Etty's bright little girls became successful in later life, it was mainly because of their aunt's guidance and encouragement, for she carried on the family tradition of reading aloud good books, begun by Emma's mother, Bessy, at Maer Hall, and continued by Emma herself. Etty, game and enterprising, endeared herself to the lively Ursula, who wheeled her one night to the wood to hunt and destroy the hated toadstools, slipped, tipped up her heavy bath chair and admired the cool way Etty gave instructions while the girls righted her again.

Etty lived on through the First World War, writing lively letters on world affairs to her nieces, and was still fighting the family battles nearly ten years after it was over, as the following letter of July 1927 makes only too clear. As noted in an earlier chapter, it is curious that neither Charles nor Emma had any recollection of the famous doves Sukey bred; clearly Etty had no inkling of them either. She obviously had not read Eliza Meteyard's life of Josiah Wedgwood I, a book which had so annoyed Emma; nor, it would seem, Julia Wedgwood's life of her great-grandfather. It is probable, indeed, that Emma would not have had Miss Meteyard's book in the house.

Conduit Head

Madingley Road
Cambridge
July 7.27

My dear Leo
. . . As regards what is known of Sukey there is nothing wh I have come cross which in the least confirms the statement that she kept pigeons or was interested in Dr Eras D.'s scientific views. I give in Emma D. what I found about her in the old letters. If I can I'll give you the refs. Then there are the Wedgwood letters printed by K.E.F. & Snow's Life of Josiah 1ˢᵗ. All I can remember is that she was carriage sick & drove up to London in the 'Sulky' alone. In the last Century there was a false life of Josiah published in U.S.A. & of my father, also published in America. They quoted from an imaginary diary of old Josiah & I *think* gave an imaginary letter from Josiah to Sukey. I think also there was an imaginary letter from Father to Annie. Hope did possess these books originally, but I am afraid they are non existent. If those facts as to the pigeons & science were in these two lying biographies, I have forgotten them. I shd v.m. like to read the biographies sometime.

This letter was annotated by Leonard: 'I wrote to H.E.L. about the Evolution of Charles Darwin by Dorsey [Doubleday Page 1927] which contains nonsense about Mrs Robert Darwin. L.D.' The following note was also included with Etty's letter:

Kempf, a German American – a Freudian psychologist, wrote a huge book, name forgotten by Frances, which is chiefly about the insane, but genius thrown in. She had it lent her by a psychologist about 2 years ago. This Kempf wishes to prove that Susannah, Mrs R.W.D., was one of the chief influences in C.D.'s life & states how interested she was in sex development especially in flowers. Frances thinks this man (an oculist) would lend the book to you in all probability if he was well buttered. This Kempf says that C.D.'s remembering so little about his mother, shows how much she impressed him & he was repressing his memory.

In 1917 George's daughter Margaret married Sir Geoffrey Keynes, brother of the distinguished economist John Maynard Keynes, so bringing into the Darwin family the genes of another exceptional family. Etty enjoyed reading to their eldest son, Richard, who grew up to become professor of physiology at Cambridge and FRS in 1959. He shares his grandfather George's particular affection for Down House, and has watched it through its various transformations to its present rehabilitation by English Heritage. His son, Randal, is the author of *Annie's Box*, a scholarly and sensitive study of the childhood of Annie, the daughter of Charles and Emma, and the effect of her death on Charles's philosophy. There are many distinguished academics who bear the genes of these two remarkable families, Darwin and Keynes, among them Dr Milo Keynes. Quentin Keynes is a traveller and lecturer. 'Anyone who married a Darwin,' Sir Geoffrey Keynes wrote,

became allied . . . with a family group comprising three generations, held together by their deep veneration for Charles and Emma Darwin, as the unchallenged patterns of what it meant to be a 'Darwin'. The grandchildren had not known the great scientist . . . he was always referred to as CD and his image was present in their minds . . . through the reminiscences of his sons and daughters. Besides his legendary aura there were the strongly developed mental characteristics inherited through the generations and still to be seen in the generations following our own.

The dominance of the Darwin line is such that it is often forgotten that Charles and Emma were grandchildren of Josiah Wedgwood I. In late life Emma regretted that she knew so little of her Wedgwood forebears. The high-minded integrity, the dogged pursuit of perfection, the generosity of temperament are all qualities that Charles inherited from Josiah. The easy, friendly relations of Charles and Emma with their children, the importance of their family and their education all remind one of the Wedgwood grandfather. Emma, too, owes something to her Wedgwood grandmother, Sally. They had in common a sturdy common sense and an unsentimental but deeply loving nature. From somewhere on the Wedgwood side comes an ear for music, evident in Sukey and carried on through Caroline to Ralph Vaughan Williams, and through Emma to her son Frank and her great-granddaughter Ursula.

Though many of the Wedgwoods preferred, as Emma's father once said, to take the quiet path, there are many of distinction. Emma was particularly proud of Hensleigh's daughter, the writer and philosopher Snow (Julia), whom she persuaded to write the biography of Josiah I, having belatedly recognized his importance. She would have read with pleasure the works of the historian Veronica Wedgwood, DBE, OM, FBA, the great-granddaughter of her brother Frank. And she would have canvassed happily for Josiah Clement Wedgwood as she had for her father in 1832 and her son Leonard in 1892 and 1895 in their campaigns for election as Liberals. Josiah Clement was Liberal MP and later Labour MP for Newcastle-under-Lyme for thirty-five years. 'His deepest faith', according to his biographer, Veronica Wedgwood, was 'neither in a theory nor a cause. He strove to preserve in politics and through politics, a certain quality of the human soul which does not cease to protest . . . friendships and personal memories pass with the passing of time, but the inspiration of a strong personality survives in time and history and can be carried over to fresh causes and younger generations.'

In a broadcast in 1956, Veronica Wedgwood spoke of her great-great-grandfather, Josiah I, who was still 'for his family a lively presence', and Sarah, his wife, 'who made sure that . . . teapots . . . poured without dripping . . . in a very practical sense presided over our teatable.' Belonging to a large family, she said, 'is like being at a large school. There are traditions and relationships that you are expected to know by instinct . . . every time you go back to the Potteries – after two months or after twenty years – you will find this huge, multiple, multiplying family ready to draw you once more into its cosy, cheerful, undemanding warmth.' This Wedgwood tradition Emma notably upheld, and like her grandmother Sally, she is still a living presence in her descendants today.

Envoi

WESTMINSTER, 2001: OUTSIDE THE ABBEY, THE TRAFFIC ROARS unceasingly. Inside, tourists gather with their guides, shuffling round among the statues of the frozen great, peering in the dim light at names on plaques. Around the tombs of the scientists, guides murmur in many languages the names of the distinguished dead: 'Here is Charles Darwin, next to Herschel and near his friend Lyell, beneath the statue of Sir Isaac Newton.' A sudden cascade of music breaks the silence. The organist is practising for the next great state ceremony.

A June morning in the quiet Kentish village of Downe. Across the road from the little flint church, the inn doors are shut. On the silent street two women stand gossiping, frozen in time: a child tugs at a skirt. Through the lich-gate the churchyard grass is rough. Emma's tomb is hard to find. There are no flowers, and the words on the grey headstone are fading. Emma Darwin is buried here with Charles Darwin's brother, Erasmus. Charles's mortal remains are in Westminster Abbey but, high on the tower of the church, a sundial placed there in his memory glints in the sun.

Suddenly from the trees above Emma's quiet grave a blackbird sings and sings, a pure, plangent melody that fills the air. It was a requiem she would have loved.

Appendix

Emma's nephew Godfrey Wedgwood succeeded his father Frank as head of the pottery and he in turn was followed by his son Cecil, who was killed in 1915 in the First World War. His widow Lucie joined the board of directors, his daughter Audrey became the company secretary, and his cousin Frank succeeded him as managing director.

During the late 1920s and early 1930s four great-great-great-grandsons of Josiah I became directors; but mining subsidence under the old workshops at Etruria made a move necessary. A new factory at Barlaston, six miles away, was built in 1940, where new techniques and new equipment increased the profitability of the company. In 1967 Wedgwood changed from a private to a public company, and in 1968 Sir Arthur Bryan became the first chairman who was not a direct descendant of Josiah I.

Etruria Hall is now part of a hotel complex and Josiah's gardens and grounds have been built over.

Bibliography

Allen, Colonel F.S., *Family Records of the Allens of Cresselly*. Privately printed, 1905

Allen *Papers*. Privately owned

Arbuckle, E.S., ed., *Harriet Martineau's Letters to Fanny Wedgwood*. Stanford University Press, 1983

Atkins, Sir Hedley, KBE., *Down – The Home of the Darwins: The Story of a House and the People who Lived There*. Rev. edn, Phillimore for the Royal College of Surgeons of England, 1976

Barker, Juliet, *Wordsworth: A Life*. Viking, 2000

Brent, Peter, *Charles Darwin: 'A Man of Enlarged Curiosity'*. William Heinemann, 1981

Briggs, A. *The Age of Improvement, 1783–1869*. Longman, 1959

Bullock, Alan, *Building Jerusalem: A Portrait of My Father*. Allen Lane, Penguin Press, 2000

Burkhardt, F. and Smith, S., eds, *The Correspondence of Charles Darwin*, 2 vols. Cambridge University Press, 1985–91

Buxton, Charles, *Notes of Thought*. John Murray, 1883

Calder, G.J., *Erasmus A. Darwin, Friend of Thomas and Jane Carlyle. Modern Language Quarterly*, 20 (1959), 36–48

Carlyle, Jane, *Letters and Memorials*. ed. Thomas Carlyle, 2 vols. Lane, 1883

Chadwick, O., *The Victorian Church*, 2 vols. Oxford University Press, 1966–70

Cobbe, F.P., *Life of Frances Power Cobbe as told by Herself, with Additions by the Author*. Sonnenschein, 1904

Coleridge, S., *Unpublished Letters*, ed. Earl Leslie. Griggs Constable, 1932

Coleridge and the Wedgwood Annuity. Review of English Studies, vol. vi, no. 12 (Jan. 1930)

Colp, Ralph, Jr, *To Be an Invalid*. University of Chicago Press, 1977

Cornford, Frances, *Collected Poems*. The Cresset Press, 1954

Correspondence of Charles Darwin 1821–1882, 11 vols. Cambridge University Press, 1994

Cottle, Joseph, *Early Recollections of S. T. Coleridge*, 2 vols. Longman, 1837

Cottle, Joseph, *Reminiscences of Coleridge and Southey*. Houston and Stoneman, 1847

Darwin, Bernard, *John Gully and his Time*. Chatto and Windus, 1955

Darwin, Bernard, *The World that Fred Made*. Chatto and Windus, 1955

Darwin, Charles, *A Calendar of Correspondence of Charles Darwin 1821–1882*. Cambridge University Press, 1994

Darwin, Charles, *The Descent of Man and Selection in Relation to Sex*, 2 vols. Murray, 1871; 2nd rev. edn, 1874

Darwin, Charles, *The Expression of the Emotions in Man and Animals*. Murray, 1872

Darwin, Charles, *The Formation of Vegetable Mould, through the Action of Worms, with Observations on their Habits*. Murray, 1881

Darwin, Charles, *Journal of Researches into the Geology and Natural History of the Various Countries visited by H.M.S. 'Beagle'*. Henry Colburn, 1983; rev. edn (1845–60). War, Lock and Bowden, 1894

Darwin, Charles, *The Life of Erasmus Darwin*. Murray, 1887 (*see also* Darwin Archive, Cambridge University)

Darwin, Charles, *The Movements and Habits of Climbing Plants*. Murray, 1875

Darwin, Charles, *On the Origin of Species by Means of Natural Selection, or the Preservation of Favoured Races in the Struggle for Life*. Murray, 1859

Darwin, Charles, *The Variation of Animals and Plants under Domestication*. 2nd rev. edn, 2 vols, Murray, 1875

Darwin, Charles, *The Various Contrivances by which Orchids are Fertilised by Insects*. 2nd edn, Murray, 1877

Darwin, E., *The Botanic Garden*, Pt I, *The Economy of Vegetation*. J. Johnson, 1792

    Pt II, *The Loves of the Plants*. J. Jackson for J. Johnson, 1789

Darwin, E., *Zoonomia*, Pt I. J. Johnson, 1794
 Pts II and III. J. Johnson, 1796

Darwin, Francis, *The Life and Letters of Charles Darwin, including an Autobiographical Chapter*, 3 vols. Murray, 1881

Darwin, G., *Marriages between First Cousins in England and their Effects. Fortnightly Review*, new ser., 18 (1875), 22–41

Darwin, Leonard, *Memories of Down House. Nineteenth Century*, 106 (1929), 118–23

Darwin, Leonard, *The Need for Eugenic Reform.* The Cresset Press, 1954

Desmond, A. and Moore, J., *Darwin.* Penguin, 1991

Fielding, K.J., *Froud's Second Revenge: The Carlyles and the Wedgwoods. Prose Studies*, 4 (1981), 301.16

Freeman, R.B., *Charles Darwin, a Companion.* Wm Dawson and Sons, 1978

Freeman, R.B., *Darwin Pedigrees.* Privately printed, 1984

Goodwin, H., *Funeral Sermon for Charles Darwin.* 'Walks in the Region of Science and Faith', 297–310. Murray, 1883

Grant, Duff [U.], *The Life-Work of Lord Avebury (Sir John Lubbock), 1834–1913.* Watts, 1924

Hayter, A., *Opium and the Romantic Imagination.* Faber, 1968

Healey, E., *Wives of Fame: Mary Livingstone, Jenny Marx, Emma Darwin.* Sidgwick and Jackson, 1986

Holmes, Richard, *Coleridge: Darker Reflections.* HarperCollins, 1998

Holmes, Richard, *Coleridge: Early Visions.* HarperCollins, 1989

Holt, R.V., *The Unitarian Contribution to Social Progress in England*, 2nd rev. edn, Lindsey Press, 1952

Hooker, J.D., *Reminiscences of Darwin. Nature*, 60 (1899), 187–8

Huxley, L., *The Home Life of Charles Darwin. The RPA Annual for 1921*, 3–9. Watts, 1921

Huxley, L., *Life and Letters of Sir Joseph Dalton Hooker, OM., CGSI., based on materials collected an arranged by Lady Hooker*, 2 vols. Murray, 1918

Inglis-Jones, E., A *Pembrokeshire County Family in the 18th Century* (*the Allens of Cresselly*). *National Library of Wales Journal*, vol. 17 (1971–72)

Irvine, W., *Apes, Angels and Victorians: Darwin, Huxley and Evolution.* McGraw-Hill, 1955

Jones, Major Francis, *Historic Houses of Pembrokeshire.* Brawdy Books, 1996

Keynes, Geoffrey, *The Gates of Memory*, Oxford University Press, 1983

Keynes, M., *Leonard Darwin, 1850–1943*. Cambridge University Press, 1943

Keynes, R.D., ed., *Charles Darwin's 'Beagle' Diary*. Cambridge University Press, 1988

Keynes, Randal, *Annie's Box: Charles Darwin, his Daughter and Human Evolution*, Fourth Estate, 2001

King-Hele, Desmond, *Erasmus Darwin*. Giles de la Mare, 1999

King-Hele, Desmond, *The Letters of Erasmus Darwin*. Cambridge University Press, 1981

Lane, Richard, *Life at the Watercure*. Longman, 1846

Litchfield, Henrietta, *A Century of Family Letters*, 2 vols. Murray, 1915

Litchfield, Henrietta, *Emma Darwin: A Century of Family Letters, 1792–1896*, 2 vols. Murray, 1915; private edn, Cambridge University Press, 1904

Litchfield, Henrietta, *Richard Buckley Litchfield: A Memoir Written for his Friends*. Cambridge University Press, 1910

Litchfield, R.B., *A Memoir*. Privately printed, Cambridge, 1910

Litchfield, R.B., *Tom Wedgwood*. Duckworth, 1903

Longford, Elisabeth, *Victoria R.I.* Weidenfeld and Nicolson, 1964

Lyell, [K.M.], *Life, Letters, and Journals of Sir Charles Lyell, Bart*, 2 vols. Murray, 1881

Mackintosh, Robert James, ed., *Memoirs of the Life of Sir James Mackintosh*, 2 vols. Edward Moxon, 1836

Martineau, Harriet, *Autobiography*, 2 vols. Virago, 1983 [1877]

Martineau, Harriet, *Letters to Fanny Wedgwood*, ed. Elisabeth Arbuckle. Stanford University Press, 1983

Martineau, J., *The Bible: What It Is, and What It Is Not; A Lecture delivered at Paradise Street Chapel, Liverpool, on 19 February 1839*. Willmer & Smith, 1839

Memorable Unitarians: Being a Series of Brief Biographical Sketches. British & Foreign Unitarian Association, 1906

Meteyard, E., *A Group of Englishmen 1795–1815*. Longmans Green, 1871

Meteyard, E., *Life of Wedgwood*, 2 vols. Hurst and Blackett, 1865

Montgomery, H.E.L., *Emma Darwin. The Month*, 29 (1963), 288–94

Moore, J.R., *On the Education of Darwin's Sons: The Correspondence between Charles Darwin and the Reverend G.V. Reed, 1857–1864. NR*, 32 (1977), 41–70

Morris, M.G.R., *Romilly's Visits to Wales, 1827–1854*. Gomer, 1998

O'Leary, Patrick, *Sir James Mackintosh*. Aberdeen University Press, 1989

Paley, W., *The Principles of Moral and Political Philosophy*. 17th edn, 2 vols, printed for J. Faulder, 1810 [1785]

Raverat, Gwen, *Period Piece: A Cambridge Childhood*. Faber & Faber, 1952

Reilly, Robin, *Josiah Wedgwood*. Macmillan, 1992

Roberts, Gaye Blake, *The Genius of Wedgwood*. The London Decorating Studio, Victoria & Albert Museum, 1995

Rothenstein, William, *Men and Memories*. Faber & Faber, 1932

Seward, Anna, *The Letters of Anna Seward*, 6 vols. Constable, 1811

Seward, Anna, *Memoirs of the Life of Dr Darwin*. Johnson, 1804

Shuttleworth's Popular Guide to Ilkley and Vicinity. 8th edn, Shuttleworth, n.d.

Spalding, Frances, *Gwen Raverat*. Harvill Press, 2000

Tipton, John, *Fair and Fashionable Tenby*. Tenby Museum, 1987

Turner, E.S., *Taking the Cure*. Michael Joseph, 1967

Turrill, W.B., *Joseph Dalton Hooker: Botanist, Explorer and Administrator*. Nelson, 1963

Webb, R.K., *The Unitarian Background*. In B. Smith, ed., *Truth, Liberty, Religion: Essays Celebrating Two Hundred Years of Manchester College*, 1–27. Manchester College, Oxford, 1986

Wedgwood, B., and Wedgwood, H., *The Wedgwood Circle: Four Generations of a Family and Their Friends*. Studio Vista, 1980

Wedgwood, C.V., *The Last of the Radicals, the Life of Josiah Clement Wedgwood, MP*. Jonathan Cape, 1951

Wedgwood, E., *My First Reading Book*. Reprinted privately, 1985 [*c.* 1823]

Wedgwood, Julia, *The Personal Life of Josiah Wedgwood*. Macmillan, 1915

Wood, Ursula, *A Biography of Ralph Vaughan Williams*. Oxford University Press, 1964

CATALOGUES

Dawson, Aileen, *Masterpieces of Wedgwood*. British Museum Press, 1995

Victoria and Albert Museum, *The Genius of Wedgwood*. 1995

Index